DATE DUB			
Dec 15 '76			
Dec 4 '77			

THE ARTHUR OF THE ENGLISH POETS

THE ARTHUR OF THE
ENGLISH POETS

BY

HOWARD MAYNADIER

BOSTON AND NEW YORK
HOUGHTON, MIFFLIN AND COMPANY
The Riverside Press, Cambridge
1907

JOHNSON REPRINT CORPORATION   JOHNSON REPRINT COMPANY LTD.
111 Fifth Avenue, New York, N.Y. 10003   Berkeley Square House, London, W. 1

First reprinting, 1969, Johnson Reprint Corporation
Printed in the United States of America

TO

THE MEMORY OF

MY MOTHER

PREFACE

THIS book has grown from a course in English Litera-
ture which I planned for my students at Harvard Uni-
versity and Radcliffe College in the spring of 1900.
I thought that there was enough interest in the Arthu-
rian legends to warrant a course of lectures which
should give an account of their origin, development,
and history in our poetry, to those who, without car-
ing to study mediæval literature extensively, desired
some knowledge of its finest poetic theme. Such
knowledge it was difficult to obtain, for almost the
only book on the subject both accurate and readable
was Mr. M. W. MacCallum's *Tennyson's Idylls and
Arthurian Story*, and that dealt chiefly with the Ar-
thurian legends from Malory to the present time. My
purpose was to tell more fully of the early days of the
legends, their origin and growth, and in discussing
their later history, to keep more closely to English
countries than Mr. MacCallum had done. Of neces-
sity treating much of the material that he had treated,
I have been indebted to his work for many valuable
suggestions in preparing both my lectures and my
book, though in general my methods of approaching
the subject have been different from his.

Because my lectures as first given, and as repeated

two or three times, have had a reasonably favorable reception, I have tried now to make them acceptable to a larger audience than that for which they were first intended. In doing so, I decided, as in the lectures, to discuss no authors who have not written in English except those — like Geoffrey of Monmouth, Chrétien de Troies, and Richard Wagner — who have directly or indirectly influenced the poetry of the English race. I have not sought to advance new theories regarding the origin and the development of the Arthurian legends, though here and there may be found some new suggestion. My purpose has been rather to select what seem to me the sanest of the frequently conflicting opinions on the Round Table stories which students of mediæval literature have held, and to present them clearly. Nor have I sought to mention every Arthurian author in the United Kingdom or America, but only to indicate the general tendencies of Arthurian literature in the English world from its first appearance to the present.

In preparing my book I have been helped by the advice and information of various of my colleagues and other friends, whom I now take pleasure in thanking. Especially are my thanks due, and most heartily I offer them, to Professor Wendell, Professor Kittredge, and Mr. Bentinck-Smith.

H. M.

CAMBRIDGE, MASSACHUSETTS,
November, 1906.

CONTENTS

THE ARTHUR OF THE ENGLISH POETS

I

THE VIGOR OF THE ARTHURIAN LEGENDS

> *   *   *   " No little thing shall be
> *   *   *   *   *   *   *   *
> The gentle music of the bygone years,
> Long past to us with all their hopes and fears."
> WILLIAM MORRIS, *The Earthly Paradise.*[1]

MR. KIPLING'S three-decker has not been the only means of transportation during the last century to the Islands of the Blest, nor Mr. Kipling the only writer who has felt that something else than modern science is necessary to take us thither. His " ram-you-damn-you liner " is highly convenient in getting us to our destination quickly ; and one on its decks is hardly less sensible of the wonders of this world than a mariner sailing into the unknown Atlantic with Columbus, or returning to the shores of Devon with Drake, after the first voyage of an Englishman round the world. Then, too, the scores of travellers comfortably stretched in their steamer-chairs, going thousands of miles merely for pleasure, or because their business interests may lie in what were once provinces of the Roman Empire, as well as in lands undreamt of while that empire still endured, — these travellers are almost as

---

[1] Prologue.

wonderful to contemplate as the daring explorers of
the sixteenth century or the sturdy colonisers of the
seventeenth. But the throb of the friendly, faithful
engines, if it makes you wonder at man's mastery
of various forces of nature, keeps you, nevertheless,
from forgetting the millions of prosy lives spent to
maintain this mastery. For the blackened, sweating
stokers feeding their fires, machinery has no poetic
marvels. Even at sea, where more than anywhere
else you are impressed by the poetry of nature and
the poetry of science, you cannot entirely forget the
" counties overhung with smoke," the " snorting steam
and piston stroke," the " spreading of the hideous
town," from which William Morris yearned to escape.
Now nothing in the last hundred years has been in
stronger contrast to the smug self-satisfaction of the
eighteenth century, or, at all events, the first half of
it, than dissatisfaction with surrounding conditions —
with prosy material prosperity — and the desire to
get away from hurried, noisy, ugly conditions into the
fair calm of an " earthly paradise." Among the ways
of reaching this which have commended themselves to
various men, none has commended itself to a larger
number than seeking the ideals of beauty and repose,
apparently gone from the modern world, in the simpler
life of the Middle Ages. From Chatterton's time to our
own, so many have done so, that mediævalism is likely
to be one of the phenomena of the century just passed
which will most attract the attention of historians and
critics in the centuries to come.

In English literature, the most marked manifesta-
tion of this mediævalism is the interest in the stories
about King Arthur and the knights of his Round

Table. During the last hundred and thirty years, these stories have been one of the chief sources of inspiration for poets, musicians, and painters ; they have engaged the attention of antiquarians ; and (Heaven save the mark !) they have furnished many a plodding student with material for his Doctor's thesis. Everybody of education nowadays knows something about Tristram and Iseult, and the Holy Grail, and the great King Arthur and his fair Queen, Guinevere, who was loved by his bravest knight, Sir Lancelot. Everybody knows something about them, and yet many seem to think that these people of the Round Table stories are not very distantly related to the people of the Nibelungen legends. One reason for this impression, no doubt, is that both have become known to the public in Wagner's operas, whither they seem to have come out of the barbarian dimness of northern antiquity. Another and a more surprising reason is that there exists in English no history of the Arthurian legends at once accurate, well-proportioned, and readable.[1]

That no such book exists is no reason why one should not exist ; the stories about Arthur are worthy of study for various reasons. For one, they were the favorite fiction of our mediæval ancestors, surpassing in popularity the native French hero-tales which clustered round Charlemagne ; the native Germanic hero-tales, of which the most famous are those of Siegfried ; and the literary tales invented in the later Middle Ages about the fictitious Amadis of Gaul, whose

---

[1] The nearest approach to such a history is Mr. W. M. MacCallum's admirable book, *Tennyson's Idylls and Arthurian Story*, Glasgow, 1894. Mr. MacCallum's plan, however, makes it necessary to subordinate the early history of the stories to their later development.

wonderful deeds fired Don Quixote to emulation.
Then again, they are worthy of study because, since
classical antiquity, no stories have enjoyed such con-
tinued popularity. From the early twelfth century
there has not been a time when they have not inter-
ested English-speaking people more or less. Further-
more, thanks to their adaptability, to their frequent
changes to suit contemporary taste, these stories only
of the great mediæval cycles have survived the Renais-
sance. The Amadis romances are dead. The native
French cycle is dead.[1] The old Germanic cycle, at
least in Wagner's Nibelungen tetralogy, has waked
recently to a new but still rather uncertain life. But
the Arthurian cycle, which in the eighteenth century
seemed moribund, has in the nineteenth century come
out with the lusty vigor of renewed youth. In the last
fifty years no English narrative poem has been so much
liked as the *Idylls of the King*. Could box-office re-
ceipts be compared, they would probably show that
in the same time no opera has been more popular than
Lohengrin, the story of the Swan-Knight, sent from
the Grail Castle to aid Elsa of Brabant. *Tristan und
Isolde* is generally counted one of the greatest music
tragedies of the world. The recent discussion of the
propriety of playing *Parsifal* anywhere outside of the
theatre at Bayreuth has shown again the interest in
Wagner's treatment of Arthurian themes. And finally,
the legend of the Holy Grail has of late given Mr.

---

[1] I refer to the French and Germanic cycles as subjects for serious
literature. In a popular way they are more alive than the Arthurian
cycle. Siegfried is still the hero of many a German *Volksbuch*. In
Italian puppet-shows, one may still see Roland's heroic struggles
against the Saracens; and even in America, in the public libraries of
the large cities, Italian urchins still ask for *I Reali di Francia*.

Abbey subjects for pictures which have been widely noticed in two continents.[1]

Thus the Arthurian stories are very much alive to-day, at least for the English race, both in the British Empire and in the American Republic: so much alive, that there is reason for a history of them which shall try to give a reader who is in no sense a mediæval scholar some idea of their sources, and of their literary development both before and after the Renaissance.

[1] The pictures were painted for mural decorations in the Public Library of Boston, Massachusetts.

II

THE HISTORICAL ARTHUR

THE stories of Arthur, as we know them, and of his knights of the Table Round, have two main sources, one of which is easy to discover, the other, difficult; both more or less connected with the history and traditions of the Celts. The source which is easily traced, about which scholars to-day are virtually agreed, is the historical. It carries us far back of the years when the Arthurian romances first took literary shape. The other, which we may call the popular source, is traced less easily. It carries us even farther back into the past; according to some scholars, at times to immemorial Celtic antiquity. No two scholars agree about it exactly, and some eminent German and eminent French scholars have held opinions regarding it in many respects diametrically opposite.

The historical source is found in the English conquest of Britain, a conquest especially remarkable in that it was the beginning of the end for one of the great members of the Indo-European family of nations. With the arrival of the Anglo-Saxons in Britain, the days of the last Celtic independence were numbered.

And yet time was when no Indo-European race was more powerful than the Celts. Spread over Europe in the days of Herodotus,[1] from the upper Danube to the

---

[1] Herodotus is the first Greek to use the noun Celt (Κελτός), though before him Hecataeus of Miletus, a Greek who wrote a geographical work, Γῆς Περίοδος, late in the sixth century B. C., spoke of

Straits of Gibraltar, these Celts, for some reason or other, came to be filled with the same spirit of unrest which later sent the Germanic tribes pouring over the Roman Empire. One result was the Celtic invasion of Italy, with the subsequent capture of Rome in 390 by the Gauls, as the Latins called the Celts. This was the culmination of Celtic power in the Italian peninsula. Had the Gauls continued to occupy Rome, they would have changed the history of the world; but they hurried off to fight the Veneti, selling their victory for Roman gold — a failure to enjoy the fruits of victory characteristic of the Celts in all ages. "Good soldiers," says Mommsen, "but bad citizens," they "have shaken all states and founded none."[1]

Nyrax, a Celtic city (which I believe is unknown to-day) — Νύραξ πόλις Κελτική, — and of Massilia bordering on Celtic territory — Μασσαλία πόλις τῆς Λιγυστικῆς, κατὰ τὴν Κελτικήν. This is the earliest known mention of the Celtic peoples.

Herodotus, as is well known, was born at the time of the Persian Wars, whose historian he became. He introduces the name " Celt " in connection with the Danube, which river he says (in bk. ii, ch. 33, of his history, written about 445 B. C.) rises among the Celts — ἐκ Κελτῶν — and flows across the middle of Europe. He speaks of the Celts as living also outside of the Pillars of Hercules.

After this, Greek references to the Celts become more and more frequent. Why the Greeks gave them the name which has stuck to the race to this day, is not surely known. Probably it was the name of that tribe or branch of the Celtic race with which the Greeks first came in contact, for their first settlement in Celtic territory was at Marseilles, according to Hecatæus, as just noted, near Celtic territory, and the name of the tribe was extended to the whole race. It is certain that it was not the generic name of the Celts themselves. Confirmation of this theory as to the Greek use of " Celt " for the whole race we seem to get from Cæsar in his *Gallic War*, bk. i, ch. 1, who implies that the name Celt belonged only to the people of a definite part of southern Gaul : " qui ipsorum lingua Celtae, nostra Galli appellantur." Livy (v, 34) also speaks of the Celts as a part of the Gauls : " Celtarum quae pars Galliae tertia est . . ." For all the early history of the Celts, cf. H. d'Arbois de Jubainville, *Cours de Littérature Celtique*.

[1] Theodore Mommsen, *History of Rome*, bk. ii, ch. 4.

The Italian movement was only one form of the
Celtic migrations. For some time, in this same fourth
century before Christ, the Celts threatened northwest-
ern Greece. Then, after the division of the Macedo-
nian Empire, which followed the death of Alexander
the Great, the Celts, now called *Galatæ* by the Greeks,
swept down on the Grecian states, pushing thence
across the Ægean Sea to establish themselves perma-
nently in a province of Asia Minor, which from them
received its name, Galatia.[1]

The Celts were now stretched across the world from
Asia Minor to Ireland; but the " bad citizens " could
not hold what the " good soldiers " had won. In the
year 225 B. C., the Gauls, who had been menacing
Rome more or less ever since their capture of the city,
suffered an overwhelming defeat in Etruria. Two
years later the Romans, crossing the Po, for the first
time gained a victory over the Gauls in their own
territory. From then till now the history of the Celtic
nations may be summed up in that quotation from
Ossian which Arnold saw fit to put at the head of his
Essay on the Study of Celtic Literature, — " They
went forth to the war, but they always fell."

The details of this shrinking of Celtic power are
not known. In the East it seems to have waned
gradually, disappearing last in Galatia in the third
or fourth century of the Christian era. Of the con-
quest of the Western Celts we know more, thanks to
the Roman historians; but even of this we have no

---

[1] Neither the origin of the later Greek name, Γαλάται, nor of the
Roman name for the Celts, " Galli," is known. Possibly each is con-
nected with an old Irish word, "Galdae," meaning " brave." In time
both " Gallus " and " Γαλάτης " came to be restricted in use, as are
their derivatives to-day — " Gaul " and " Galatian."

full account prior to Cæsar's *Commentaries on the Gallic War*. Through these, every schoolboy knows something of the conquest of Gaul, and of the first tentative expeditions of the Romans into Britain. Yet they made no permanent settlement there till 43 A. D., in which year, in the reign of Tiberius Claudius, began the Roman occupation, which was to last for three centuries and a half. This we must consider with some care; for in the events of its last years we find the historical root of the Arthurian romances.

It took the Romans long to pacify Britain. There were several revolts — the most famous, that of Queen Boadicea, who, after causing the death of thousands of Romans, was defeated, and took poison rather than fall into the hands of her conquerors. Conditions remained disturbed till the proconsulship of Agricola, from 78 to 85. He carried the Roman armies to the north of Scotland; he built a chain of forts between the Clyde and the Forth; he even stood with his legions at the southwestern extremity of Scotland, looking over to the misty Irish hills and meditating a descent on Ireland, which he never made. But Agricola was more than a good general; he was also a man of tact and kindness — qualities which seem to have accomplished more than his generalship in pacifying the British. Through his efforts, many of the young chieftains of the island lived in companionship with the Romans, learned the Latin language, and put on the Roman toga. Yet the Romans did not remain in secure possession of all the territory which Agricola had conquered. The Wall of Hadrian, built about the year 120, from the Tyne to the Solway, marks the limit of their settlement. North of this, the land up to the Forth, though owing allegiance to Rome, was much overrun by the Picts. South of the Wall, Britain was a fairly peaceful province, as Roman remains in all parts of the country show. Still it was never entirely peaceful; and towards the end of the fourth century, as the disruption of the empire approached, the condition of the province became turbulent.

About 383 the Roman general, Maximus, then commanding in the island, mutinied, and with an army, probably of both Romans and Britons, crossed into Gaul and thence into Italy, where he maintained himself in imperial state till he was put to death in 388 by the Emperor Theodosius, who had come from Constantinople to the rescue of the Western Empire. After this there were more revolts in Britain, which the few Roman legions now left there had difficulty in quelling. Then in 410 came the final separation of Britain from the Empire. In that year the Goths sacked Rome and plundered Gaul. Some historians believe that the Britons took advantage of the weakness of the empire to expel the last remnant of the Roman Legions: others believe that the weak Emperor Honorius recalled the Roman troops from Britain in order to oppose them to the invading Goths. At any rate, there is little doubt that in the year 410 he wrote a letter to the Britons, telling them to be their own guards against their plundering neighbors, the Picts and the Scots. The wording of the letter is such that it may have been either an exhortation to the Britons to hold out till the Romans could help them again, or a warning that henceforth the Britons must protect themselves without help from

Rome.[1] Yet the meaning of it is clear, — that in the year 410 the Roman legions had left Britain.

At the beginning of the fifth century, then, Britain was again free. What is more, it was the only part of the Celtic world, once so extensive and so powerful, to retain its independence or even its own tongue. In Gaul, in the remotest corners, the last vestiges of Celtic language had disappeared in the fourth century. The Celts of Central Europe, along the Danube, had been crushed out between the Germans on the north and the Romans on the south. In the eastern Celtic land of Galatia, assimilation with neighboring people had destroyed all Celtic nationality. And so in Britain only was the Celtic race distinct.

But it was not now as it had been four hundred years earlier; during the Roman occupation the Britons had changed considerably. When Cæsar first saw them, they were, according to his account, savages. He tells us[2] that they raised few crops, and lived almost entirely on milk and flesh; that they clothed themselves in skins and painted themselves horribly; that they shaved all the hair from their bodies except on the upper lip and the head; and that men had wives in common.[3]

The Romans no doubt suppressed the most savage practices of the Britons. They set them the example of city life; they constructed roads and bridges; they introduced villas and baths, so much like those of their own country that, to this day, in Bath, by going down

---

[1] Ὀνωρίου δὲ γράμμασι πρὸς τὰς ἐν βρεττανία χρησαμένου πόλεις φυλάττεσθαι παραγγέλλουσι. . . . Zosimus, bk. vi, 10. 2.

[2] *Gallic War*, bk. v, ch. 14.

[3] Cf. the Pictish custom of matriarchy.

from the Pump Room, dear to Jane Austen, Sheridan, and Smollett, to the Roman bath under it, which still exists almost in its perfection, you may feel yourself suddenly transported from eighteenth-century England to imperial Rome. Moreover, during the Roman occupation, the Britons became converted to Christianity. When the Romans left, therefore, the civilisation of the Britons must have been considerably higher than when the Romans entered the land. Nevertheless, it is a fact that Britain, though somewhat civilised by the Romans, was not Romanised. In France and Spain the Italian conquerors left their language behind them; in Britain scarcely a trace of their language remained. The explanation must be that the occupation of Britain was in the main military. Of the Latin inscriptions on stone which have been discovered in England in late years, a very large number refer to military affairs; and the names of the Roman officers in Britain, so far as we know them, point to a military occupation. In short, the Roman occupation of Britain must have been analogous to the present English occupation of India. There the English have stopped the progress of the Car of Juggernaut; they have suppressed Suttee and other barbarous customs; they have built railroads and great public buildings. Throughout the country, especially in the hill districts, are English villas more or less like English country houses. The English, too, have carried their sports to India, as the Romans carried their baths to Britain. Some of the Indian princes have taken on a certain amount of English civilisation. They go from time to time to Cambridge or Oxford to be educated; they put on flannels to play cricket, frock coats for afternoon func-

tions, and swallow-tails for evening, as some of the Brit-
ish chieftains, at the persuasion of Agricola, donned the
Roman toga. Yet if the English occupation of India
were to cease to-day, or were to last two centuries more
and then cease, at which time it would have endured
as long as the Roman power in Britain, India, though
it would have learned much from the English, would be
by no means Anglicised. And Britain, though owing
much to Rome, was by no means Romanised.

It is probable, though, that at least in the towns
some Latin-speaking population remained after the
legions were withdrawn : the nucleus of a Roman party
in the island, who would grieve to see the imperial
connection severed. Apart from their loyalty, they
had reason to grieve. Directly the protection of Rome
was removed, mere shadow though it had been at the
last, the Britons even more than before were vexed by
the harrying Picts,[1] who came down over Hadrian's
Wall from the north, and by the plundering Scots,
who came across the western seas from Ireland. Mean-
while, with Germanic pirates from time to time rav-
aging the eastern coasts, many of the Britons, like
Tennyson's King Leodogran, must have

> " Groan'd for the Roman legions here again,
> And Cæsar's eagle : " . . .

And so we are not surprised to read in the pages of
Gildas, the earliest British historian whose work is ex-
tant, who in 547 wrote an historical sketch of Britain,
that many of his countrymen besought the help of

[1] In spite of their ravages, " there is no evidence that any . . .
Picts were able to effect a single settlement south of the Clyde or
the Forth." J. Rhys and David Brynmor-Jones, *The Welsh People*,
p. 105, London, 1900.

Rome again in a letter which eloquently and concisely set forth their sad condition.

" Repellunt barbari ad mare, repellit mare ad barbaros; inter haec duo genera funerum aut jugulamur aut mergimur."

"The barbarians drive us into the sea, and the sea drives us back to the barbarians. Between these two kinds of death we are either murdered or drowned." [1]

In spite of this, Rome had to leave the Britons to take care of themselves; and they struggled on, with varying fortunes, against the Picts and the Scots, until a worse scourge came upon them in the shape of the Anglo-Saxons. In just what year these began to settle in. Britain is uncertain, for it is a remarkable fact that scholars have never determined exactly the date of that momentous event which changed Britain into England, and so into the mother of the most wide-ruling race that history has known.

Probably it was in 428, and not in 449, as most historians say, that the English made their first permanent settlement in the island.[2] The history of their arrival, though dressed out with many legendary adornments, seems in the main founded on fact. According to the usual account, one of the British princes, Vortigern, had somehow made himself chief king of Britain. One day he was surprised to hear that three ships, full of tall, light-haired strangers from Germany, had

[1] R. Thurneysen, *Wann sind die Germanen nach England gekommen? Englische Studien*, xxii, p. 177, thinks Gildas was mistaken in saying that these complaints referred to the ravages of the Scots and Picts. It was really in reference to the later ravages of the Saxons. The letter was said to have been written to Aetius, for the third time Consul — " Ter Consuli." The third consulship of Aetius was in 446.

[2] Cf. W. F. Skene, *Four Ancient Books of Wales*, i, p. 36, and R. Thurneysen, *op. cit.*

appeared in the mouth of the Thames. When their leaders, Hengist and Horsa, were brought before Vortigern at Canterbury, he expressed regret that they worshipped heathen gods, but nevertheless received them gladly as possible helpers against the Picts and the Scots and certain disaffected subjects of his own.[1] If the strangers would assist him, Vortigern promised them grants of land; and he gave Hengist permission to build a castle on as much ground as might be included within a bull's hide. Hengist, resorting to the same sort of trick which is related of Dido when she got her land for Carthage, cut up the hide into the smallest possible twine, with which he was able to include ground enough for a strong castle. Meantime, more Saxons came over from Germany, among them Hengist's fair daughter Rowena, with whom Hengist hoped Vortigern would become infatuated. The British king fell into the trap. He asked for the hand of the Lady Rowena, which Hengist granted with seeming reluctance. In return he received Kent as a home for his people.

Though the Saxons,[2] according to their promise, helped Vortigern, they kept coming into the country in such increasing numbers that soon there was friction between them and the Britons, and then open war. For years the Saxons carried everything before them. Then came a brief turn in the tide : the Britons won several victories. According to Gildas, the historian already mentioned, their leader at this time was one Ambrosius Aurelianus, a noble of Roman descent.

[1] Cf. Nennius, *Historia Britonum*, § 31.

[2] The first German settlers in Britain have always been called Jutes. They seem to have differed little from the Saxons who soon followed them.

According to a later British historian, Nennius, who wrote early in the ninth century, the British leader was a certain Vortimer, a Briton with presumably no Roman blood. However this may be, the check of the Saxons was only temporary; they pushed on soon more fiercely than ever. Vortigern and Hengist and Horsa died, and all their generation, and the Lady Rowena and all hers, but the storm of conflict never ceased. Then came a lull, thanks to another and greater success for the British arms. About the year 500 the Britons, under the generalship, tradition has it, of a man named Arthur, won a series of victories — the chief of which seems to have been that of Badon Hill (Mons Badonis, or Mons Badonicus) — that for something like fifty years held the English in check.

Here, then, for the first time appears Arthur, but so dimly that he has often been supposed only a creature of the imagination. Nowadays, however, most scholars think him to have been a man of flesh and blood. What the man was, I shall presently try to show. Beforehand, in order better to understand how he became world-famous, a glance is necessary at the later events of British history while the Anglo-Saxons were establishing themselves in their new dominion.

During the half century following the British victory at Badon Hill, the Germanic invaders did not cease entirely from crossing over to Britain. In 519 the kingdom of the West Saxons was established; and by the middle of the century the English advance began again. In 552 the Britons were defeated in a battle near Salisbury. In 577 a great victory at Deorham made it possible for the Saxons to push on to Bath and Gloucester. They had now reached tidewater on the western coast; they had cut the British lines and divided the British population into two parts.

In the next century the Germanic advance was chiefly in the north, in the districts which the Angles overran. In the year 607 [1] Æthelfrith led his army to Chester, and there made a great slaughter of the Welsh. The neighboring country now lay open to the Angles, who, like the Saxons, had reached tidewater in the West. The British lines were again cut; and the British population was now split into three parts — one in the northwest of the present England and in the southwest of Scotland; another, and the largest, in the present Wales and the land just east of it; and a third in the present counties of Cornwall, Devon, and Somerset. Finally, in the eighth century, the Anglo-Saxons tore away from the Welsh principality of Powis the land between the Severn and the present boundary of Wales. A kind of wall, built from the mouth of the Dee to the mouth of the Wye, and corresponding roughly to the present boundary between England and Wales, marked the division between the two races.

While Celtic supremacy was dying in Britain, a new Celtic land was being born on the Continent. Thither fled certain Britons, who saw in emigration the only escape from their Saxon foes. They did not flee to Ireland, whose nearness seemed to make it their natural refuge, because they were at feud with the Irish. The next nearest foreign country was the Gallic peninsula south of the British Channel, and they

[1] Green, *Short History*, 607; J. Rhys and D. Brynmor-Jones, *The Welsh People*, 616.

took refuge there solely because of its proximity. The Britons could have felt no kinship with the inhabitants of Armorica, as the peninsula was then called, for it was entirely Latin.

The Celtic occupation of Armorica is even more obscure than the Anglo-Saxon occupation of Britain. Gildas tells us that his countrymen began to seek lands beyond the sea — " transmarinas regiones " — before the British victory at Mount Badon. After this victory, it is to be presumed that for a time the British migration ceased. Then, with the renewed Saxon advance against the southwestern Britons, emigration began again. This was probably the time when the Britons left their country in the greatest numbers. So many of them crossed the Channel that by the end of the sixth century the whole Armorican peninsula was Celtic and had received the name of Britannia. The Britons seem to have had an easy conquest of their new land, until, as they pushed east and south, they ran against the Franks, who checked them in the southeast. They still pushed along without much trouble in the northeast, till they were in the region which later became Normandy, where they might have established themselves permanently, had not the Normans arrived in the second half of the ninth century, and forced the Britons back into the present province of Brittany. This event, at the beginning of the tenth century, virtually fixed the divisions of the Celtic peoples as they are to-day. Since then the tendency has been for the French on the Continent, and the English in the British Isles, gradually but resistlessly to crush out Celtic dialects and customs.

These facts of history show that from the early

fifth century, for hundreds of years the bitterest foes of the British branch of the Celtic family had been Germanic — the Anglo-Saxons in Britain, and on the Continent the Franks, whom possibly the Britons recognised as akin to their enemies at home. All this time the greatest success of British arms had been the series of victories about the year 500, which for nearly half a century stayed the Saxon advance. These fifty years, then, were a remarkably bright page in the history of the Britons, in whose traditions, it is not fantastic to surmise, still lingered reminiscences of the tragic downfall of their race from those days of power, when their ancestors may have been among those who made Rome and Greece tremble. If the Britons were going to cling to the memory of any past years, it would be to the memory of these of comparatively recent victory, when for a while the Celtic prowess of centuries past seemed to have come again. If they were going to make any part of their wars with the Saxons the foundation of a hero-story, it would be this part. Now if we find the nature of the British Celts such as to make it likely that they would lengthen this page of their history, on which were inscribed the victories of the general called Arthur, into an epic, then we may say with tolerable certainty that there is historical foundation for the stories of wide British conquest which we read of in so many mediæval chronicles and in the pages of Malory and of Tennyson.

That the British Celts would thus lengthen this page of their history is likely for two reasons. Even more than most primitive peoples, the Celts seem to have been fond of exploiting the feats of their great men ; and they have been inclined, more than any other Indo-

European race, to keep their customs unchanged from generation to generation, from century to century, under varying conditions of success or disaster. The earliest accounts of the Celts show that from Galatia to Ireland they gave official recognition to a literary caste which they held in high esteem. In this caste were the bards,[1] whose duty it was to put into song, or recite, the glories of kings and chieftains, in which hero-tales of ancestors took their place with praise of the living. At the time of Cæsar, and in the half century before him, we first hear of such bards in Gaul, who accompanied their songs of praise with musical instruments, something between harps and lyres. The flag of Erin still testifies that the bard's harp was dear to the later Irish. In the tenth century, in Wales, bards were so important that in the Welsh code of law drawn up by King Howell Dha (Howell the Good), much is said about the bard of the king's household. His place, his privileges, and duties are carefully fixed. Gray's *Bard* bears evidence to the wide currency of the tradition that more than two centuries later, when Edward I conquered Wales, the bards were still influential there. And earlier, in the twelfth century, when the Norman-Welsh writer, Giraldus Cambrensis, was describing Wales, the fondness of the people for their bards and for what they recited or chanted was the same. When guests arrived at a Welsh house, Giraldus tells us, they were entertained throughout the day with music of the harp.

---

[1] Βάρδοι is the name given to them by the earliest Greek geographers and historians, Posidonius and Diodorus Siculus, who mention them. Compare H. d'Arbois de Jubainville, *Cours de Littérature Celtique*, i.

The Welsh esteemed noble birth and generous descent above all things. Even the common people were familiar with their genealogy, and could not only readily recount the names of their grandfathers and great-grandfathers, but refer back to the sixth or seventh generation or beyond. "The Welsh bards and singers, or reciters," he says in another place, "have the genealogies of their princes, not only in their ancient authentic books, but they also retain them in their memory." [1]

It may be seen, therefore, that the Celtic nature from first to last was such as to make probable the growth of a hero-story, if the Welsh obtained any decided success over the English invaders. Moreover, as popular tradition generally exaggerates the importance of small incidents, the story might in time grow into the alleged historical account of Geoffrey of Monmouth, who, composing his work in the early twelfth century, was the first writer to give at length the story of Arthur's conquests. According to Geoffrey, Arthur, having succeeded to the throne of his father, Uther Pendragon, not only defeated the Saxons, but drove them entirely out of his land. Having subdued the rest of the British Isles, Arthur turned his attention to foreign territory, and brought under his sway Iceland, Norway, Denmark, and France. Then, in answer to a demand for tribute from Lucius Hiberius of Rome, Arthur mustered his forces and set out to overthrow the empire. Victory having crowned his arms, he was ready to march upon the imperial city when the news reached him that his nephew Mordred, whom he had left in Britain, had usurped the throne, mar-

[1] Cf. Giraldus, *Description of Wales*, i, chs. 3, 8–17.

ried the Queen, Guinevere, or Guanhumara, as Geof-
frey names her, and called to his aid Arthur's old
enemies, the Saxons. Arthur hastened back to Britain,
and there, in trying to overcome his rebellious nephew,
lost his life.

Such an Arthur as this, it is needless to say, a
figure almost as impressive as the historical Charle-
magne, never lived. It is not improbable, though,
that the British Celts, in magnifying their few actual
victories over the Saxons, proportionately magnified
their leader. The best scholarly opinion nowadays is
that Arthur was an actual man.

To find out if Arthur ever really lived, and if so,
how many of the feats attributed to him he really
performed, we naturally go back to the chroniclers
nearest his time. Of the important ones before Geof-
frey of Monmouth, who tell of what we may call
Arthur's wars, only two were native Britons. The first
was that Gildas previously mentioned, a Welsh monk,
who gives us the earliest extant account of the Saxon
Conquest in his *De Excidio et Conquestu Britan-
niae*, an historical sketch in Latin written shortly
before 547 — that is, a little more than a hundred
years after the beginning of the Saxon invasion. The
work consists of two parts — the first historical; the
second, which is the main part, not a history but a
sort of exhortation and reproof addressed to his coun-
trymen, denouncing their vices and their lack of both
patriotism and religion. Gildas got his historical ma-
terial, which is meagre, either from earlier writers or
from oral tradition. The fact that he makes no men-
tion of Arthur, who, if he lived at all, was at the
height of his fame about 500, — the year in which

Gildas was born, — and might conceivably have been alive when Gildas was writing, has, more than any other circumstance, made people doubt the famous Briton's existence.

For the earliest extant mention of Arthur, we must pass from the historical sketch of Gildas to the ampler *Historia Britonum* of Nennius, another Welsh monk, who is supposed to have written about 800 or somewhat later, more than two hundred and fifty years after Gildas. Nennius's work differs in a few important details from Gildas's. The date for the arrival of the Saxons in Britain Nennius makes twenty-one years earlier, 428, than the Anglo-Saxon historian Bede had understood it in Gildas's account, that is, 449,[1] which, since Bede, most historians have accepted. Nennius hints, moreover, at civil war among the Britons, which Gildas for some reason does not mention. According to Nennius, it was fear not only of the Scots and the Picts, but also of the Romans and of the Briton Ambrosius, — one would judge from his name a Romanised Briton, — that in 428 led the British king Vortigern to receive with joy the three shiploads of Germans arrived in the Thames.[2] In other respects, Nennius's account is for the most part like Gildas's, though in various little ways it differs, chiefly in that it has romantic additions and is more circumstantial. Especially is it so when Nennius comes to the story of British victo-

[1] There is no trouble in reconciling the few references to the Saxon Conquest which occur in works of the fifth and sixth centuries, if we accept 428 or 429 as the year in which the Saxons made their first settlement in Britain. The references seem contradictory, if we take this year to have been 449. Cf. Thurneysen, *op. cit.*, *Englische Studien*, xxii, p. 177.

[2] "Guorthigirnus . . . urgebatur a metu Pictorum Scottorumque, et a Romanico impetu, nec non et a timore Ambrosii." Nennius, § 31.

ries, the chief of which was at Mount Badon. He tells us that in these the Britons were commanded by a general (" dux bellorum ") named Arthur, who was successful in twelve battles. The first was fought at the river Glein ; the second, third, fourth, and fifth, at the river Dubglas ; the sixth, at Bassas ; the seventh, at the wood of Celidon ; the eighth, at Castellum Guinnion — " and in this battle Arthur carried upon his shoulders the image of the Holy Virgin Mary, and the pagans were put to flight on that day, and there was a great slaughter of them through the favor of our Lord Jesus Christ and through the favor of his Holy Mother Saint Mary; " the ninth was at the city of Legions ; the tenth, at the river Tribuit ; the eleventh, at Mount Agned ; the twelfth, at Mount Badon, " where there fell by Arthur's own hand in one day nine hundred and sixty of the heathen." [1]

Nennius makes still further mention of Arthur in a later part of the work attributed to him, which gives an account of certain wonders (" mirabilia ") of Britain.[2] Among these is a mound of stones in the district. of Buelt, the present Builth. It seems that Arthur's dog, Caval, left a footprint on a stone one day when Arthur was hunting the wild boar Troynt. Arthur, accordingly, placed the stone on top of a cairn which he built and named Carn Caval. You may carry away the stone with the dog's footprint as often as you please, but the next day it is always back on the cairn. Another wonder is found in the region called Ercing. Near a fountain there is a funeral mound named Licat Anir, in memory of Anir, the son of Arthur. Arthur himself is said to have slain the youth and buried him.

---

[1] *Historia Britonum*, § 56.   [2] *Op. cit.* § 73.

Men who come to measure the mound find it some-
times six feet long, sometimes nine, sometimes fifteen,
but never twice alike. " And I have tried it," says
Nennius ("et ego . . . probavi"). Whether it was
before or after dinner, the monk does not say.

These tales, of course, are not to be considered
in determining the existence of Arthur. The account
of him as a successful general, however, deserves
consideration. What, then, was Nennius's authority
for it?

The importance of Nennius's mention of Arthur as
a general has recently been considered by three Euro-
pean scholars — Professors Zimmer and Thurneysen
in Germany, and L. Duchesne in France. It is not
necessary to lose ourselves in the labyrinth of their
arguments, which make out that Nennius — whose ex-
istence, like Arthur's, has been doubted — did exist,
and that his mention of Arthur points probably to a
real person. The gist of it all is that Nennius, who
wrote in the first quarter of the ninth century, almost
certainly was not composing an original work, but was
making over an historical account written about the
year 679. This historical account furnished the *His-
toria* proper of Nennius, to which he added other
material, making a sort of composite that included,
besides the history of Britain, historical sketches of
some of the Germanic kingly families, or " Saxon Ge-
nealogies," an account of some of the principal towns of
Britain, and the Wonders, or "Mirabilia Britanniae."
The seventh-century history, which seems to have been
the foundation of Nennius's work, gave in all proba-
bility substantially the same account of Arthur and his
twelve battles as Nennius's made-over history. What

is more, this older work was, not improbably, a making over of a work of the first half of the seventh century. In other words, it is not impossible that Nennius's mention of Arthur as a victorious general comes ultimately from a similar mention of him in a kind of history composed within a hundred and fifty years of the battle of Mount Badon; it is tolerably certain to come from literary mention of Arthur in the last quarter of the seventh century, that is, within two hundred years of the battle of Mount Badon; and so Professor Zimmer and other scholars of the present day are generally agreed that Arthur is an historical personage.[1] Even so, though we may, with some probability, place the mention of Arthur a little more than a century after his own lifetime, still there is the fact confronting us that Gildas, writing possibly while Arthur was yet alive, makes no mention of him. Gildas's failure to mention Arthur must be disposed of, therefore, before we can accept the notice of him in Nennius as proving his existence.

Professor Zimmer has shown why the omission of Arthur's name in Gildas is unimportant. Gildas wrote not a history, but a jeremiad, a warning to the nobles and clergy of Britain. He himself called it (§ 1) "epistola" and "admonitiuncula" — an epistle and admonition. The second part of his work was, as we have seen, the main part. He prefaced it with his historical sketch only to make clear his point, that the

[1] The authorities which discuss the existence of an historical Arthur are: Heinrich Zimmer, *Nennius Vindicatus*, Berlin, 1893. L. Duchesne, *Nennius Retractus, Revue Celtique,* xv, p. 174 ff. R. Thurneysen, *Über Zimmer, Nennius Vindicatus, Zeitschrift für deutsche Philologie,* xxviii, p. 80 ff. Cf. also W. W. Newell, *Publications of the Modern Language Association,* xx, p. 622 ff.

Britons were more inclined to vice and civil strife than to making war against foreign enemies. He is not writing of the brave deeds of the Britons, but of their shortcomings; and therefore he makes as unimportant as possible everything which reflects credit on them. Moreover, he is vague in his statements and exceedingly chary of proper names. In speaking of the Romans' first coming to the island, he does not call Cæsar by name. He refers to the revolt of Queen Boadicea, but does not name her. Nor does he name Vortigern,[1] or Hengist, or Horsa. His failure to mention Arthur, then, means nothing.

There was yet further reason for Gildas to omit any account of Arthur. Gildas continually shows a Roman bias; he manifestly belonged to a party in Britain which still cherished the memory of Roman dominion. Of the Romans he speaks always as our "illustrious defenders." He speaks of the Britons as obtaining all their benefits from their Latin conquerors. And, finally, after the Saxons had arrived, when the Britons achieved some success, it was under "Ambrosius Aurelianus, a worthy man, who of all the Roman nation was then in the confusion of this troubled period by chance left alive." His descendants, though degenerated from the worthiness of their ancestors, in Gildas's own day still sometimes "by the goodness of our Lord won victories over the Saxons."

Now the feeling between those who had not ceased to long for the Roman connection and those who rejoiced that it had terminated was perhaps still bitter. We have seen that Nennius[2] makes the one success-

---

[1] This name is not found, at least, in the best manuscript.
[2] Nennius, § 43. Cf. p. 16 of this chapter.

ful British leader before Arthur a man with the Cel-
tic name of Vortimer rather than Ambrosius Aurelia-
nus, and that he mentions civil strife in the first half
of the fifth century, apparently between the pro-Roman
party and the anti-Roman. There is further notice
of this about the year 440, when, according to the
Annales Cambria, there was war in Britain between
two chieftains — one named Ambrosius, perhaps the
Ambrosius of Gildas, and the other, Guitolinus, from
his name evidently a native Briton. The descendants
of the two parties probably cherished something of the
old hostile feeling in the sixth century; and it is possi-
ble that Arthur belonged to the party opposed to Gil-
das, that is, to the patriotic British party. At least, a
twelfth-century Welsh tradition argues such a state of
affairs. In the *Life of Gildas* (*Vita Gildae*), attri-
buted to a Welsh priest, Caradoc of Lancarvan, about
1150, we learn that Gildas's brother was at feud with
Arthur and was slain by him. And towards the end
of the same century Giraldus Cambrensis writes: [1] —

"With regard to Gildas, who inveighs so bitterly against
his own nation, the Britons affirm that, highly irritated at
the death of his brother, the Prince of Albania, whom King
Arthur had slain, he wrote these invectives, and upon the
same occasion threw into the sea many excellent books, in
which he had described the actions of Arthur, and the cele-
brated deeds of his countrymen; from which cause it arises
that no authentic account of so great a prince is anywhere
to be found."

Plainly a twelfth-century creation, this last, as it
stands, it may be founded, nevertheless, on ancient
tradition.

[1] *Description of Wales*, bk. ii, ch. 2.

On the whole, therefore, we may believe in a real Arthur, but an Arthur very different from the king of mediæval romances or the ideal monarch of Tennyson. Indeed, Nennius implies that Arthur was no king at all. " He fought," says Nennius, " in company with the kings of the Britons, but he himself was *dux bellorum*," that is, a general.[1] Again, when Nennius mentions Arthur in connection with the wonders of Britain, he calls him each time "miles," which is equivalent to "knight" or "warrior." And so Arthur was probably not of royal blood ; he was only a brave leader, perhaps one of considerable military genius, though we may suppose of comparatively slight civilisation, a half-barbarous chieftain, attached to the party of Britons who had viewed with joy the departure of the legions. Long after Arthur's time the Britons were still pretty barbarous. The codes of law of Howell Dha, which assign so carefully the place of the bard in the king's household, show such a condition ; and in the twelfth century, too, when Giraldus was travelling in Wales, the country was far behind England in civilisation. The dress of a young Norman or French prince or noble of the time, or even of an English gentleman, was very different from that of the son of Rhys, a reigning Welsh prince, described by Giraldus.

" This young man was of fair complexion, with curled hair, tall and handsome ; clothed only, according to the custom of his country, with a thin cloak and inner garment, his legs and feet, regardless of thorns and thistles, were left bare." [2]

[1] Professor Rhys, *Arthurian Legend*, ch. 1, thinks that the title does not preclude Arthur's being of princely blood.
[2] *The Itinerary through Wales*, bk. ii, ch. 4.

And in his "Description of Wales" [1] Giraldus sketches the interior of a fairly comfortable Welsh mansion as follows : —

"The kitchen does not supply many dishes. . . . The house is not furnished with tables, cloths, or napkins. . . . The guests being seated in threes instead of in couples as elsewhere, they (that is, the host and hostess) place the dishes before them all at once upon rushes or fresh grass, in large platters or trenchers. . . .

"While the family is engaged in waiting on the guests, the host and hostess stand up, pay unremitting attention to everything, and take no food till all the company are satisfied ; that in case of any deficiency it may fall upon them. A bed made of rushes and covered with a coarse kind of cloth . . . is then placed along the side of the room, and they all in common lie down to sleep ; nor is their dress at night different from that by day, for at all seasons they defend themselves from the cold only by a thin cloak and tunic. The fire continues to burn by night as well as by day, at their feet, and they receive much comfort from the natural heat of the persons lying near them ; but when the under side begins to be tired with the hardness of the bed, or the upper one to suffer from cold, they immediately leap up and go to the fire, which soon relieves them from both inconveniences ; and then returning to their couch, they expose alternately their sides to the cold, and to the hardness of the bed." [2]

---

[1] Bk. i, ch. 10.

[2] Compare the description of Welsh houses in *The Welsh People*, J. Rhys and D. Brynmor-Jones, pp. 199 ff. Another interesting comparison is found in the description of a Highland house in Smollett's *Humphry Clinker*, published in 1771. In that novel Jerry Melford, writing from "a gentleman's house near the town of Inverary," says : —

"Our landlord's housekeeping is equally rough and hospitable, and savours much of the simplicity of ancient times. The great hall, paved with flat stones, is about forty-five feet by twenty-two, and

Such was the life in the twelfth century, not of the Welsh princes, who had begun to imitate the Norman nobles in building castles, but of the lesser nobility. In the sixth century, in Arthur's time, Welsh life was not more refined; and Arthur, we must remember, was probably not a prince, but only a brave and successful general. The real Arthur, then, was very far from being the magnificent king, outshining Capets and Plantagenets, whom chroniclers and romancers have imagined. He probably never went to battle on a finely caparisoned charger, but, like the Highland chieftains of later days, ranged the forest, followed by a dog whose name may or may not have been Caval. He never in his life wore such a panoply as clothes the noble ideal statue of Arthur by the Emperor Maximilian's tomb in the church at Innsbruck. In that Arthur you have the romantic Arthur. Rather he traversed the country, like the Welsh prince whom Giraldus met, with arms and legs bare, and no armor but a rough buckler and shield and sword. In a rude hall like that described by Giraldus, Arthur probably held his feasts. If he ever celebrated them in a more elegant banqueting-hall, it must have been one of an old Roman villa which, in the troubled conditions of the time, had come into his possession.

serves not only for a dining-room, but also for a bedchamber to gentlemen-dependents and hangers-on of the family. At night half a dozen occasional beds are ranged on each side along the wall. These are made of fresh heath, pulled up by the roots, and disposed in such a manner as to make a very agreeable couch, where they lie, without any other covering than their plaid."

III

THE ARTHUR OF POPULAR STORY

AND so Arthur seems to have been a real man, who led his countrymen to victory over the invading English about the year 500 — the best fighter, perhaps, on the British side. How his fame grew until he became a great romantic king, we cannot definitely say; the history of the Arthurian legend at first is entirely obscure. We are sure, though, that popular tales were early connected with it. There is one in the history of Nennius,[1] in which, not many pages before the mention of Arthur's victories, is an account of a castle which Vortigern, the British king, tried to build as a stronghold against his enemies. When the foundations had sunk from sight on three successive nights, Vortigern asked his wise men what the matter was. They told him that the only way to make the foundations lasting was to sprinkle them with the blood of a boy who had no father. Vortigern sent his messengers through the land in search of such a remarkable boy, whom they thought they had finally found in a young Ambrosius, whose mother maintained that she had never known mortal man. The boy was accordingly taken to Vortigern and about to be slain, when he declared that the wise men were entirely at fault. To prove his assertion, he challenged them to tell what was under the ground on which the foundations of the

[1] Nennius, §§ 40–42.

citadel rested. They could not tell. There was a pond, Ambrosius informed them; and on taking away the earth, Vortigern's workmen found the pond, sure enough. What was under the pond? said Ambrosius. Again the wise men could not tell. Two vases, said Ambrosius; and so there were. In them, he said, would be found a tent; and when it was opened, two dragons,[1] one red, the other white, which would fight with each other. So they did; and from their fight, in which the red dragon was the victor, Ambrosius was able to foretell the future victories of the British over the Saxons.

Now here in the history which first gives us the name of Arthur is this manifest bit of popular tradition,[2] which, like the mention of Arthur himself, occurs in that part of the history which seems the oldest. Besides, in a probably later part, we have seen attributed to Arthur connection with two of the so-called marvels of Britain. The more famous Arthur became, the more such tales would cluster round him; for it is the regular tendency of men to make their heroes loom large in a haze of popular story. We see instances of this even in recent times. In the very first life of George Washington, written within a few years of his death by a clergyman well acquainted with the Washington family, appears, complete in every detail, the story of the cherry-tree which the youthful George cut down with his little hatchet, a story since pronounced by the best authorities purely apocryphal. In the last

[1] *Vermis* is the word in Nennius's account as given among the chronicles *Auctorum Antiquissimorum*, 1898, vol. xiii. The *vermes* are said to be symbolical of dragons.

[2] It is common in Celtic tales to find one thing shut up in a series of others, as in this tale of Vortigern and Ambrosius.

quarter of the nineteenth century a good many shrewd, common-sense sayings have been attributed to Abraham Lincoln which in the first quarter of that century would probably have been attributed to Benjamin Franklin, and, a hundred years before, to somebody else. In earlier stages of civilisation than ours, popular tales would be likely to contain supernatural incidents ; the farther back we go, the more supernatural material there would be. Of this, in the years directly after Arthur lived, there was a great deal in floating folk-tales, which would be likely, sooner or later, to crystallise about him. For the sole literary mention of Arthur by Nennius in connection with marvels, we may safely postulate a hundred folk-tales which connected him with similar marvels. A few of these, most scholars think, may have endowed him with attributes which ages before had been given to a Celtic god; and some scholars, like Professor Rhys, are of the opinion that many deeds of the romantic Arthur are to be explained by the fact [1] " that besides a historic Arthur

[1] J. Rhys, *Studies in the Arthurian Legend*, Oxford, 1891, chs. i and ii.

Arthur, at times, according to Professor Rhys, is to be regarded as a culture hero, one of whose notable exploits was the invasion of Hades. On this, it would seem, directly or indirectly, was founded Arthur's subjugation of western Europe. Arthur's death at the hands of Mordred, in distinct contradiction to the story of his going to Avalon, Professor Rhys thinks may possibly be traced to the death of the real man Arthur at the hands of a real nephew.

In some instances, Professor Rhys believes, the culture hero has " been thrust forward into the position of " a Celtic Zeus. This confusion explains Arthur's incest with the Queen of Orkney. In other ways Arthur appears as a Celtic Zeus, but on the whole he seems to have been more of a culture hero.

To sum up his discussion of the historical and mythological elements in Arthur, Professor Rhys concludes " that there was a historical Arthur, who may have held the office . . . known as that of the

there was a Brythonic divinity named Arthur, after
whom the man may have been called, or with whose
name his, in case it was of a different origin, may
have become identical in sound, owing to an accident
of speech . . ."

However that may be, by the beginning of the ninth
century — that is, three hundred years after Arthur's
victories — the so-called history of Nennius shows us
that a romantic hero-story of Arthur had got started
among the British Celts. There was still no sign, so
far as we can see now, that it would become a story
of world-wide fame; nor are we able to see, in the
next three hundred years, the changes and additions
which made it so. When we do get sight of it again,
it is already fully developed — that is, when Geoffrey
of Monmouth, in the fourth decade of the twelfth
century, compiled his famous *History of the Kings
of Britain.* From some source which has never been
determined, we may imagine that he received a fairly
comprehensive story of Arthur, already adorned with

Comes Britanniae; that he may . . . have been partly of Roman de-
scent; that Maelgwn was his nephew, whom Gildas accuses of slaying
his uncle; that his name *Arthur* was either the Latin *Artorius,* or else
a Celtic name belonging in the first instance to a god Arthur. . . . In
either case, the name would have to be regarded as an important factor
in the identification or confusion of the man with the divinity. The
latter, called Arthur by the Brythons, was called Airem by the Goi-
dels, and he was probably the Artæan Mercury of the Allobroges of
ancient Gaul. His rôle was that of the culture hero, and his name
allows one to suppose that he was once associated, in some special
manner, with agriculture, over the entire Celtic world of antiquity.*
On the one hand we have the man Arthur, whose position we have
tried to define, and on the other a greater Arthur, a more colossal
figure, of which we have, so to speak, but a *torso* rescued from the
wreck of the Celtic pantheon." *Arthurian Legend,* pp. 47–48.

---

* Cf. the root *ar.*

historical and popular additions. To these he made
further additions — some legendary, some of his own
invention. The result was an Arthur no longer the
half-barbarous British general in rude armor, with
arms and legs bare, but the Arthur of Innsbruck, the
monarch in full mediæval panoply, whose armies sub-
dued every land from Rome to Iceland, the Arthur
who for eight hundred years has been the greatest
romantic king of the world.

Geoffrey of Monmouth, who started the literary fame
of this king, was probably the son of a man named
Arthur, for which reason he has sometimes been called
Geoffrey Arthur, rather than derisively, as has been
asserted, by those who doubted the wonderful history
which he wrote.[1] He was born about the end of the
eleventh century, in Monmouthshire. We may assume,
therefore, that there was Welsh blood in him. Perhaps
there was also Norman blood. His connections, at
least, were influential enough to secure him a position
of importance at the Norman court, probably that of
clerk or secretary to various princes of the blood, who
were sometimes in England, sometimes on the Conti-
nent. In 1152 Geoffrey was ordained priest and made
Bishop of St. Asaph's in Wales. He died in 1155.
Beyond these few facts, nothing is known of his life.

Though some scholars have thought Geoffrey's
History his first work, more have supposed that his

---

[1] Cf., however, Dr. Sebastian Evans, *Geoffrey of Monmouth*, London,
1904, pp. 329–330. Dr. Evans says, " It is incredible that a writer named
Arthur should create a literary hero also named Arthur unless the
two circumstances were in some way connected." I see no need of
assuming further connection than the fact that Arthur was a name in
his own family quickened Geoffrey's interest in the legendary history
of the British hero.

literary fame began about 1135, with the appearance
of his *Prophecies of Merlin*, a work in Latin based
on Nennius's tale of Vortigern and the boy Ambro-
sius. According to Geoffrey, the full name of Ambro-
sius, whom he represents not as a boy but as a young
man, was Ambrosius Merlinus, which Geoffrey soon
shortened to Merlinus. The name seems taken from
that of Myrddhin, a famous Welsh bard. Merlin's
prophecies, which follow the fight with the two dra-
gons, are far more extensive than in Nennius's account.
Though exceedingly obscure, they had, so far as one
can make head or tail of them, mostly come true.
Geoffrey accordingly made a name for himself.

If this was Geoffrey's first literary venture, prob-
ably its success encouraged him to compose the greater
work in which the earlier was included. The result
was the *Historia Regum Britanniae*, which appeared
about 1137, a chronicle of the British kings from
"Brute, the first King of the Britons," down to a
period later than the Saxon conquest. Many stories
now took literary form for the first time which have
given material to poets ever since. The story of King
Lear, for instance, and his three daughters is told
with considerable detail. When Geoffrey comes to the
reigns of Uther Pendragon and his son Arthur, his
history grows much more circumstantial than either
before or afterwards. He tells at length of Arthur's
birth — how Uther, loving Igerna, wife to the Duke
of Cornwall, made her, by the enchantments of Merlin,
take him for her husband, and so begat Arthur. Then
he tells of Arthur's childhood, and of his conquests
abroad and his return to Britain, to take vengeance on
his nephew, Mordred, for his usurpation of the throne

and adultery with the Queen. In a great battle Arthur
killed Mordred, but was himself mortally wounded.
Nevertheless, Geoffrey adds in apparent contradiction,
Arthur was carried to Avalon to be healed of his wounds.
His cousin, Constantine, succeeded him as king.

There is one other work attributed to Geoffrey in
which Arthurian characters appear, the *Vita Merlini*,
a Latin poem composed probably before 1150. This,
dealing chiefly with Merlin, gives us nevertheless a
little more circumstantial account of the end of Ar-
thur. In a boat steered by the Irish Abbot Barinthus,
whose account of a paradise far in the ocean sent St.
Brandan voyaging in search of it, Arthur, after his
last battle, was carried to the Island of Apples, that
is, Avalon, the happy other-world of the Celts, there
to be tenderly cared for by Morgan and her sisters.

It is in the events of his stories that the interest
of Geoffrey lies, not in his style, which is without ani-
mation, as one might expect in a work written in a
tongue several centuries dead. But Geoffrey's narra-
tive, if not vivid, has some mediæval picturesqueness.
So far as he gave the narrative a setting, it was one
of Anglo-Norman magnificence. You may take it
whichever way you will — a proof of great imagina-
tion in Geoffrey, or of the lack of it, that he saw all
his stories as contemporary.

A more certain sign of imagination is the fact that
Geoffrey was able to weld together old and new stories
quite disconnected, — for such must have been his
sources, — some fact, some fiction, into one connected
history. An instance of this ability is found in his
account of Helena, the mother of Constantine. An
historical character who has been canonised, Saint

Helena was born, probably of humble parents, in Asia Minor. In Geoffrey of Monmouth she becomes the daughter of a king of Britain named Coel, none other than " the merry old soul," with his pipe and his bowl and his fiddlers three, of the nursery rhyme.

It is not remarkable that Geoffrey chose for his work the form of history, for in his day that was the commonest form of literary expression in England. Geoffrey had been preceded by several chroniclers in the Anglo-Norman period ; and while he lived, two men were writing who were of more literary importance than any of the earlier ones — William of Malmesbury and Henry of Huntingdon, both of whom made only the briefest mention of Arthur. All these historians had stuck generally to facts. Now Geoffrey was not an historian in spirit, but something of a poet. Had he lived a generation later, or had he lived in southern France of his own time, he might have tried his hand more than he did at poetry. Living in England in a barren literary period, when literary energies were turned chiefly to historical writing, he naturally wrote history, or at least alleged history, to which he gave the semblance of reality by weaving into it real dates, events, and people. On the whole, his literary skill is most noticeable in his ability to impart historical verisimilitude to a conglomeration of unhistorical matter.

Though Geoffrey's popularity was great and instantaneous, contemporary scholars doubted him, and the learned people of the later part of his century never put much faith in him. Probably their feelings are shown by a yarn, as remarkable as any of Geoffrey's, which Giraldus Cambrensis spins in his

Journey through Wales.[1] He says that in the City of Legions there lived at his time a Welshman, Meilyr, who had a peculiar power of knowing when any one spoke falsely in his presence, for he saw a little devil exulting on the tongue of the liar. If he looked on a book containing anything false, he could point out the passage with his finger. Sometimes, in the presence of such a book, evil spirits would swarm on his person. If they oppressed him too much, the Gospel of St. John was placed on his bosom, when they immediately vanished; but when on one occasion that book was removed, and the history of Geoffrey placed there, the devils reappeared in greater numbers and remained a longer time than ever before, both on his body and on the book.

Nor were Geoffrey's own statements about the sources of his history calculated to allay doubt. His assertion in his first chapter was that Walter, Archdeacon of Oxford, had given him " a very important and very ancient book in the British tongue," from which he got his material. In his conclusion, he advised William of Malmesbury and Henry of Huntingdon not to mention the kings of Britain, since they have not " the book in the British tongue," which Walter brought out of Britain. These references to his source, especially the latter, which is probably facetious, have not inspired belief in " the book in the British tongue."

A book which Geoffrey must have been acquainted with is the *Historia Britonum* of Nennius; whether he knew any other is questionable. It is a question, too, if he knew no other, from what source Geoffrey

---

[1] *Itinerarium Cambriae*, i, ch. 5.

got his material, of which only the least little bit is in Nennius. Did he invent much of it? Did he find what was not his invention on the Continent or in England?

The chances are that Geoffrey did invent a considerable part of his history. He wrote, presumably, to be popular at court. Perhaps that is why he made the setting of his story Anglo-Norman; and since reminiscences of Norman history would enhance the popularity of his work, it is natural that Geoffrey should have worked in recent historical events. In Arthur's war with Ireland, Professor Zimmer accordingly sees a recollection of the trouble between the Normans and the people of Dublin. In the assistance given to Arthur by Hoel of Brittany and in Arthur's division of his conquests among tributary princes, Professor Zimmer sees references to William the Conqueror's Breton allies, and to his distribution of English land among his nobles. Then, too, the chief cities of Arthur are cities in some way or other important in twelfth-century England. Carlisle becomes one of the great king's capitals, a town established and fortified by William Rufus. Winchester is another frequent residence of the British king, a city which was not only of consequence traditionally as the capital of the old West Saxon kingdom, but which both the Conqueror and Stephen held in high favor. Among other favorite cities of Arthur are York, London, and Lincoln, all important in early Norman as they had been in later Saxon days. In fact, the only frequent seat of Arthur which was not an important English city is Caerleon-on-Usk, a town in Geoffrey's native Monmouthshire, and one, moreover, which may have been famous as a seat of Arthur in Welsh legend.

Much of Geoffrey's history, however, perhaps the greater part, was not his own fabrication. Though he gives us the first detailed account of Arthur, it is evident that he did not invent the glory of that hero. William of Malmesbury, writing his chronicle about 1125, speaks of stories of Arthur as being frequently told ; and they seem to have been well known likewise, as early as 1113, when nine monks of Laon in northern France travelled in England, one of whom, on returning to his monastery, recorded some of their experiences. In Cornwall, he says, they saw rocks bearing the names " Arthur's Seat " and " Arthur's Oven ; " and they found a tradition, as firmly established there as in their own home, that Arthur was still alive and would come again to his people. Moreover, church records testify that in the last years of the preceding century, children in the south of Italy were baptised from time to time with names of Arthurian heroes. It is evident that Geoffrey in his *Historia* was using stories already widely current.

The question of where Geoffrey found these, brings up the whole question of the popular sources of Arthurian romance. What would seem true of Geoffrey's sources would seem true of the sources of other twelfth-century writers ; for with the exception of the chroniclers, the later twelfth-century poets did not borrow their material from Geoffrey. It is fair to assume, then, that they derived the tales which they wove into their books from sources substantially the same in nature as Geoffrey's own. What these were must remain largely a matter of conjecture. Still, a certain degree of probability regarding them may be established.

At present there are two conflicting views on the question. Professor Zimmer, Professor Foerster, and others — mostly German scholars — have thought that the chief source of the Arthurian romances and pseudo-chronicles was continental. The kernel, at least, was Celtic; and it began to germinate in Brittany, where it had been carried from Britain in the great migration of southwestern Cymri in the second half of the sixth century. From Brittany, after taking on various legendary additions, the Arthur-story spread to the Normans; and from them over all northern France. On its native heath, however, the Arthurian hero-story remained comparatively undeveloped; there it got but little beyond the stage at which it appears in Nennius. The Britons who remained at home, with the very present English power always near by, were too much bound by sense of fact to give rein to their imagination. They were surprised, accordingly, when the Normans brought the developed Arthurian legends to England, but delighted as well. The romantic stories took immediate hold on the island; and the rapid spread of their popularity is shown by the report of those French monks who travelled in southwestern England in 1113. While the writers holding this view are inclined to minimise the Celtic element in the Arthurian romances, they differ considerably as to its importance. Professor Zimmer, for instance, sees a great deal that is Celtic. He seems to think that the romances of Chrétien de Troies, the greatest of the early French Arthurian writers, have substantially the same relation to the original Celtic tales as Shakespeare's plays to those " novels " which gave him so much dramatic material. Professor Foerster, on the other hand, sees much less that is Celtic ; and some scholars would see little more of a Celtic element than a few names of people and of places. The Arthurian romances, they hold, came almost wholly from general European folklore, and from the invention of French writers, conscious literary artists, especially of Chrétien de Troies.

Professor Gaston Paris and other scholars — French, English, and American — have held a different view. They think that the French gave literary finish to the Arthurian stories, but little else. Incidents, often plots, sometimes even the spirit of a romance, they regard as Celtic. The stories took shape, they think, not so much among the northern French as among the Anglo-Normans, that is, in England. Before the conquest, the Saxons had got the stories to some extent from the Welsh, among whom the stories were fairly well developed ; and the Saxons gave them to the Normans. Still larger were the contributions of the Welsh to the Normans, for the Welsh felt a great and immediate interest in the conquerors of their traditional English enemies. At a very early period, moreover, Norman nobles settled in South Wales. Insular proper names, correct English geography, occasional English words,[1] and the connection of the chief Arthurian writers with England — all these point to an insular development of the stories more than to a continental. Yet Paris would not deny that there was some growth of the Arthurian romances in Brittany.

[1] *Lovendrenc,* love potion, occurs in the earliest fragment of the Tristram romances, and *nihtegale,* nightingale, and *gotelef,* goat-leaf, in the *lais* of Marie de France. *Nihtegale,* to be sure, occurs in a *lai* which does not treat an Athurian theme. Compare, however, the discussion of the importance of the *lais* in the next chapter.

The antecedent probability seems to be that there is truth in both theories; there is no reason why a story should not flourish in the land in which it was born and in that to which it has been transported. This probability becomes stronger when we compare the conditions regarding the popular sources of Arthurian romance with those of English popular traditions in our own time — that is, of children's games and nursery tales — in the two great divisions of the English world. Every American, I suppose, who travels in England, on coming to Banbury, thinks of Banbury Cross, where the old woman got on a white horse, with rings on her fingers and bells on her toes. American children to this day play " London Bridge is falling down," rather than Brooklyn Bridge, or any other bridge of the western hemisphere. It is evident, moreover, that such nursery lore is still current in the old country no less than in the new. *Alice's Adventures in Wonderland* and *Through the Looking Glass*, books based on just such lore, have an equal popularity on both sides of the Atlantic. The case of the old British popular tales is parallel. Why should they not have grown on both sides of the Channel, in Brittany and in Britain, when the nature of the people and of their traditions was the same in both, and have been transmitted by the Celts of both lands to their neighbors? As a matter of fact, from the time of William I of Normandy, the ancestor of the Conqueror, down to the time of Geoffrey, the great-great-grandson of the Conqueror, who married Constance of Brittany, unhappy mother of the murdered Arthur, the Norman ducal house was often allied to. Breton families. The forms of many proper names in Round

Table romances of the twelfth century point to a Breton rather than a Welsh origin. The only way to explain Arthurian proper names in the south of Italy at the beginning of this century, is that the Arthurian stories were carried there by the Normans who conquered Sicily about the middle of the preceding century. The conclusion seems inevitable, therefore, that the Normans knew Arthur and his knights before they went to England, where the legend of the hero had had independent growth. Their conquest of the land which he was fabled to have held quickened greatly their interest in the stories, which they found already widely current among the Anglo-Saxons, as well as among the Welsh. The testimony of the monks of Laon points clearly to such being the case. It would be almost impossible for a story carried to England by the Normans and made known there first in 1066 to be so firmly rooted in remote Cornwall in 1113 as to have become a part of local tradition. At that time the Arthurian legend had probably been known for generations both in Cymric and in Saxon Britain. So eager were the Normans in seizing on the Arthurian material which they found in their new realm, that before long the insular contributions to Arthurian stories exceeded those of the Breton peninsula.

Not all the Celtic material in Arthurian legends came from the Britons; some of it came from the Irish. The more mediæval literature is studied, the more it becomes evident that Ireland had considerable influence in shaping the Round Table stories. It is easy to see how this might be. From earliest times, the Irish and the British Celts, either by commerce or in warfare, seem to have been in close connection. We have seen that the Scots, coming from Ireland, harried the Britons even in the Roman days. At the time of Arthur they occupied a good deal of the western seaboard of Britain, whether by recent conquest or not, cannot be definitely said ; some historians think that the Gaelic settlements in the west point to a former occupation of the larger part of Britain by the Irish, whence they had been forced into Ireland by the arrival of the British Celts from Gaul. However that may be, in the fifth and sixth centuries, Gaelic settlements existed among the Cymric Celts. Moreover, in the years immediately succeeding, up to the beginning of the ninth century, when the Northmen came down upon them, the Irish enjoyed a peace rare at that time among western European peoples. As a result, Ireland in the seventh and eighth centuries was a famous seat of learning. Irish monks went forth from it as missionaries, not only to Britain, but also to the Continent of Europe, founding monasteries as far east as Bavaria. Young Englishmen flocked to Ireland to study.[1] And later on, from the eighth century to the fourteenth, Irish minstrels frequently crossed the sea to wander about England and the northwestern part of the Continent.[2] The Irish and the British, furthermore, were somewhat akin. Naturally, the farther back we go, the nearer alike we find them, the nearer their manners and customs ; and consequently the nearer would be the similarity in their popular tales.

[1] Cf. H. Zimmer, *Ueber die Bedeutung des Irischen Elements für die mittelalterliche Cultur, Preussische Jahrbücher*, 1887, pp. 27–59; translated by Jane Loring Edmonds, *The Irish Element in Mediæval Culture*, New York and London, 1891.

[2] Cf. O'Curry, *Manners and Customs of the Ancient Irish*, i, p. dxix.

It would not be strange, therefore, for the ever-growing
Arthurian story to draw to itself Irish folk-tales of
greater or less length, both while it was confined to
the Celts, and later in the first years of its popularity
among the French and the English.

There are instances to show that what might thus
be expected actually happened. Irish influence on the
Arthurian legends appears in many proper names.
Even Arthur's sword, the famous Excalibur, seems to
have come from Ireland. The name for this in native
Welsh stories is Caledvwlch. Now an Irish champion,
Fergus, is said to have had a wonderful sword named
Caladbolg, which came to him from fairyland, even as
Excalibur came to Arthur from the ladies of the lake.[1]
Stray incidents, too, of Arthurian romance are par-
alleled in Irish story. The hideous damsels that Per-
ceval meets in the Grail romances, some of whom,
apparently, can change at will into creatures of radi-
ant beauty, are the counterparts of Irish hags who are
resplendent fairies in disguise. And, finally, several
whole stories connected with Arthur appear to have
come from Irish sources. That excellent story of the
Green Knight; the tale, likewise, of the knight who
was changed into a were-wolf; and the story of the
Marriage of Sir Gawain, best known as Chaucer gives
it in *The Wife of Bath's Tale*—all these are mani-
festly of Irish origin.

So now we have some idea of the popular beginnings
of the Arthurian legends. The historical hero, a semi-
barbarous British warrior, became a romantic hero
through the tendency of human nature to fasten
stories to noted characters. Once he had attracted a

---

[1] Cf. H. Zimmer, *Gött. gel. Anz.*, 1890, pp. 516–517.

few stories to himself, he attracted tales more and
more marvellous. As the hero-story went on growing,
it attracted popular material of all kinds. British in
the beginning, and keeping its chief elements British-
Celtic, it took to itself in time much that was not
British. Perhaps the next most important element
was the Irish-Celtic. Then, as the legend grew, stories
and historical events were attached, not Celtic at all—
some of Germanic origin, which the Saxons or the de-
scendants of the Franks may have introduced; others
of Oriental origin, which returning Crusaders may have
brought from the East. Thus on both sides of the
British Channel, but probably more in the British Isles
than on the Continent, there grew up a conglomerate
mass of romantic material, which has given us the
stories of Arthur as we know them. The Celts, more
than any other people, have given us the material, but
it is the early French writers who have given us the
stories in their enduring literary form. It is a question
whether they would have done so had not Geoffrey
first given the stories literary fame in Latin.

IV

THE CHRONICLES AND THE LAIS

WE have seen that Geoffrey, whose so-called history is the first extensive literary treatment of any part of the Arthurian stories, by no means invented the fame of Arthur and his knights. What he did was to give the stories literary dignity and consideration which they had not enjoyed before. When William of Malmesbury mentions the stories, writing some ten years before Geoffrey, he speaks of them as tales old wives might tell. Ten years after Geoffrey's history appeared they were above such scorn; and by the end of the century they had become, as they were to remain, the greatest mediæval hero-saga. So important were they that you will find some mention of Arthur in the pages of almost every chronicler down to the Elizabethan Holinshed, who gives, much abbreviated, what is substantially the same account as Geoffrey's. Of all these pseudo-historians, only two contributed materially to the development of the Arthurian stories; in the works of the others, virtually nothing new appears. The two important chroniclers are Wace, a Norman, who wrote within twenty years of Geoffrey, and Layamon, an Englishman, who wrote fifty years after Wace.

Wace, born in the island of Jersey about 1100, seems to have entered the church, and to have been interested early in literature. He decided to translate Geoffrey's history into Norman-French, and completed the work, which he dedicated to Eleanor, Henry II's queen, in the year 1155. Wace is more interesting than Geoffrey because of the greater picturesqueness of his narrative; his imagination sets forth at times vividly the magnificence of Arthur's court, especially the presents which tributary princes offer the king, of armor, steeds, brachets, greyhounds, furs, silks, satins, brocades, and all kinds of precious stones.[1] Wace is interesting, besides, because his is the earliest complete work on Arthur extant in a popular tongue.[2] And finally, he is interesting because the Round Table, that institution of Arthur's so important in later poetry, appears in his pages for the first time. This was instituted, Wace says, in the years of peace which intervened between Arthur's early conquests and his successful campaign against Lucius of Rome. All the barons and knights of the civilised world, together with their ladies, flocked to Arthur's court, and [3]

"For the noble barons, each of whom held himself better than any other, and was unwilling to take a place lower than any other, Arthur made the Round Table, of which the 'Bretons'[4] tell so many stories. At this table his vassals sat in equal dignity. They sat in perfect equality, and they were served in perfect equality. Not one of them could boast of sitting higher than his peers. All were seated with the same honor; no one was distinguished."

In two other places Wace mentions the Round Table, but he adds nothing to this vague account of

[1] For such vividness in Wace, see ll. 10875 ff.
[2] A few fragments of Arthurian romances in French are older than Wace's historical account.
[3] Lines 9994 ff.
[4] The word may mean the people of either Brittany or Britain, or of both.

its institution. Why, therefore, it was established, we cannot certainly say; though there is nothing in Wace's verse to prevent our surmise that it was established in order to settle the question of precedence.

Layamon, the other historian who is important, was a priest of Arley Regis, a village in Worcestershire on the right bank of the Severn. This district — so near to the Welsh border that its people might well be familiar with Welsh tales — was yet open to Norman influence, for the Norman law was enforced strongly on the Marches in order to keep the wild Welsh quiet. And so, forty or fifty years later than Wace, Layamon, coming across a copy of the *Roman de Brut*, the name commonly given to Wace's work,[1] decided to turn it into English. In doing so, he amplified Wace's work to the extent of nearly doubling it. Wace himself had nearly doubled Geoffrey's.

To English readers Layamon is more interesting than Wace. His *Brut*, composed in the first years of the thirteenth century, is the first English treatment which we have of any Arthurian story; it is, moreover, thoroughly English. Modelled metrically on Anglo-Saxon alliterative verse, — verse, as Layamon uses it, of spirited rhythm and considerable dignity, — the history contains no little poetry. Moreover, it shows that the old hostility between Saxon and Celt had virtually died; for Arthur — according to tradition, the greatest foe whom the English met in their conquest of Britain — now becomes an English king and hero: and ever since, all the way down to Malory, and from him to Tennyson, Arthur

---

[1] This name was given on account of Brutus, the pretended ancestor of the Britons, who was fabled to descend from Trojan Æneas.

has remained thoroughly English. Then again, Laya-
mon's few additions to the story, that must have come
from oral or written sources (we cannot tell which),
are even more interesting than Wace's; especially the
much more circumstantial account of the founding of
the Round Table.[1]

At a great feast of Arthur's, the English poet says,
among the assembled folk

"was mickle envy, for the one counted himself high, the
other much higher. Then men blew the trumpets and
spread the tables. They brought water in golden bowls;
they brought cloths of white silk. Then Arthur sat down,
and Wenhaver, his queen. Next sat the earls, then the
barons, and after them the knights; all his men sat. And
high-born men bare meat to the knights, then to the thanes,
then to the swains, then to the porters, forth at the board.
The people became wroth, and blows were rife. At first
they threw loaves of bread, . . . then the silver bowls filled
with wine, and then fists met necks. Then leapt forth a
young man that came out of Winetland; he was given to
Arthur to hold as a hostage. He was Rumaret's son, the
king of Winetland. Thus said the young knight to Arthur,
the king : —

"'Lord Arthur, go quickly to thy chamber, and thy queen
with thee, and thy kin, and we will decide this combat with
these outland warriors.'

"Even with the words, he leapt to the board where lay
the knives, before the king. Three knives he grasped, and
with one he smote that knight in the neck who first began
the fight, so that his head fell on the floor. Soon he slew
another, the same man's brother. Before the swords came,
seven he felled. Now the fight waxed great. Each man
smote some other: blood flowed: mischief was in the hall.

[1] See Sir Frederic Madden's edition of Layamon's *Brut*, vol. ii,
pp. 532 ff.

Then came the king out of his chamber, with him a hundred knights with helms and with burnies. Each bare in his right hand a white steel brand. Then called Arthur, noblest of kings : —

" 'Sit ye quickly, each man on his life: whoso will not, shall soon meet death. Take for me the same man that first began this fight: put a withey on his neck, and drag him to the moor, and put him in a low fen where he shall lie : and take all his nearest kin that ye may find, and strike off their heads with your broadswords. And cut off the noses of the women that ye may find, and their beauty shall perish utterly. So will I destroy all that be of his race. And if ever I hear that any of my folk, of high or low degree, stir up strife for this fight, there shall avail him neither gold nor jewels, neither fine horse nor rich mail, that he be not dead, or with horses drawn to pieces. That is the law for each. Bring now the relics, and I will swear, as shall ye knights that were at this fight, earls and barons all, that ye break not your oaths.'

" First swore Arthur, noblest of kings : then swore the earls, then the barons, then the thanes, then the swains, that they never more would stir up strife. Then men took the dead and carried them off. Then they blew trumpets with merry sound. Were he glad, were he sad, each one there took water and cloth, and then they sat down in peace at the board, all for dread of Arthur, noblest of kings. Cup-bearers thronged round them ; gleemen sang : harps resounded ; the people were in joy.

" Afterwards, it saith in the tale, the king fared to Cornwall. There came to him one, he was a crafty workman, and greeted the king fairly : —

" 'Hail to thee, Arthur, noblest of kings ! I am thine own man. Over many lands have I fared : I know of carpentry wonderful craft. I have heard beyond the sea strange tidings, that thy knights fought at thy board on a midwinter day. Many fell there : for their great pride they made slaughter : and for their high birth each would be within [that is, apparently, near the table or near the king]. But I will make thee a board exceeding fair, so that there may sit sixteen hundred or more, all turned about, so that none be without, but all without and within, man against man. When thou dost ride, thou mayest carry it with thee, and set it where thou wilt, after thy will. Thou needst never dread, to this world's end, that ever again proud knights fight at thy board: for there shall the high be even with the low.'

"They had the wood brought, and the board begun. In four weeks it was done. On a high day the folk were called, and Arthur himself came to the board; he bade all his knights to the board forthwith. When all were seated, knights to their meat, then spake each with the other as if it were his brother. All they sat about, there was not one without. A knight of whatever kin was there well placed : all they were seated together, the high and the low: no man might boast of other kind of drink than that of his fellows who were there at the board. This was that same board that the Britons still tell of, and they tell many tales of it about Arthur the king."

This account which Layamon gives of the Round Table seems to make clear what Wace hints at, that it was instituted to avoid a fight for precedence. Professor Brown, who has recently investigated the subject,[1] has come to the conclusion that in Layamon's tale we find a " transcript of ancient Welsh tradition." The excessive brutality, the " murderous combat with carving knives at the table of the king," make plain that the tale could not spring from the " imagination of a writer of the age of chivalry, anxious to invent a new story about the famous Arthur, whom he regarded as a national hero." Moreover, there is reason to believe that the savage tale reflects ancient Celtic customs.

[1] A. C. L. Brown, *The Round Table before Wace; Harvard Studies and Notes in Philology and Literature,* vol. vii, p. 183.

In Gaul, for instance, Posidonius found a similar tendency among the warriors to quarrel at feasts; and in olden times, he says, the strongest warrior received a particular portion, for which he was ready to fight if his right was disputed. Posidonius says, too, that in his time the Celts sat together in circles at their banquets.[1] And in early Irish literature there are instances of quarrels at feasts, at which the warriors and their ladies were present together, as at Arthur's great festivals.

When MacDatho, in the *Book of Leinster*, killed his famous pig in honor of Conchobar, King of Ulster, and Ailill, King of Connaught, who, with their courts, were to dine with MacDatho, the question arose at the banquet who should carve. After some dispute among the champions, Cet of Connaught seated himself by the pig, knife in hand, and challenged any one to displace him. Nor did any one, till Conall the Victorious, coming in, threw at Cet the head of the great champion, Anluan, which he was carrying in his belt, with so much force that the blood spurted from Cet's mouth. Then Cet went from the pig, and Conall sat down by it, and took its tail in his mouth, and carved. When the men of Connaught found that Conall had given them only the two forefeet, the result was a bloody Donnybrook Fair.

" It appears then," Professor Brown concludes, "from sources so widely separated as classical antiquity and Irish saga, that a tendency to quarrel about precedence at feasts was a universal Celtic failing, and that the use of a round table, possibly to obviate these disputes, was widely known, and probably also Pan-Celtic."

---

[1] Would it appear that one of their number sat in the middle? Posidonius says that the bravest took his place like the leader of a chorus.

There can be little doubt, therefore, that Laya-
mon, in his account of the Round Table, has preserved
a bit of ancient Welsh tradition. It may be taken as
one sign of the growth of the Arthurian stories in the
British Isles.

One other addition of Layamon to the earlier stories
is worth noting: he tells with some detail of Arthur's
departure for Avalon, which Geoffrey had related so
baldly in his *Vita Merlini*. After the king had com-
mended his realm and people to his kinsman, Constan-
tine, he said to him: —

" ' And I myself will go to Avalon, to the most beauteous
of women, to the queen Argante, an elf wondrous fair: and
she will heal me of my wounds, and make me quite well
with a healing drink. Afterwards I will come again to
my kingdom, and dwell among the Britons in great bliss.'
While he was saying this, a little boat came, borne by the
waves. There were two women therein, of marvellous
beauty. They took Arthur and laid him in the boat, and
sailed away. Then was fulfilled what Merlin had said of
yore, that there should be mighty grief at Arthur's forth-
faring. And the Britons believe yet that he is alive, and
dwells in Avalon with the fairest of elves ; and the Britons
still look for his coming again."

We see here that the passing of Arthur has taken
its first step towards the mystic poetry of Malory and
Tennyson.

It was not only the pseudo-histories that increased
the dignity of the Arthurian legends. Within a cen-
tury of Geoffrey's death, *lais*, metrical romances, and
prose romances had helped likewise to establish these
legends in their exalted position and to spread know-
ledge of them far and wide. Both the *lais* and the

metrical romances became important in the twelfth
century; the principal prose romances were the pro-
duct of the thirteenth century.

Lai is the French name for a particular kind of
poem, which may be described briefly as one that might
serve for a chapter in a romance. Nearly all the *lais*
extant in French are in octosyllabic couplets. Love
and adventure are their usual subjects; the hero is
generally a knight; almost always some supernatural
being appears; there is more or less magic. In short,
most of the *lais* are fairy-tales for grown-up readers.

A woman wrote the best *lais;* Marie de France, as
she is called, because she tells us that France was her
native country.[1] In the reigns of Henry II and Rich-
ard I she seems to have lived much in England, where
she composed her poems. She was apparently fond of
literature and a woman of education, for besides the
Lais she wrote a collection of *Fables* and the *Pur-
gatory of St. Patrick*, all in finished verse; and she
intimates in her Prologue [2] to the *Lais* that she knew
Latin. The *Lais* themselves point to an understanding
of English also,[3] and perhaps of Breton or Welsh,
or possibly both. We may reasonably surmise that
Marie was a lady of high birth; otherwise she would
not have been likely to know Latin. Besides, she is
at home in the high society which she portrays in her
poems; she knows the castles and palaces of which
she writes. Then, too, she dedicates her *Lais* to one
whom she calls "noble king, chivalrous and cour-
teous," — very likely Henry II of England. A woman

---

[1] *Epilogue to Marie's Fables*, 1, 4.   [2] Line 30.
[3] At least, the English words *nihtegale* and *gotelef* occur in her *Lais*.
Cf. ch. 10, p. 167.

of low birth would hardly have ventured to dedicate a work of hers to such a great monarch. And a contemporary [1] of Marie calls her Lady Mary (Dame Marie), and says that she is among the most esteemed writers of the time; counts, barons, knights, and ladies all take great pleasure in her stories.

How many *lais* Lady Mary composed is uncertain ; only twelve of those extant can surely be ascribed to her, but it is probable that at least two or three others were from her pen. The best way to make clear the nature of a *lai*, is to summarise one certainly composed by Marie, *Bisclavret*, or *The Were-Wolf*.

A good knight of Brittany, wedded to a fair lady, vexed her by going away three days every week, no one knew whither or why. After the lady had tried often to make him tell, at last he said : —

" Lady, three days in the week I am a were-wolf, and run in the forest, and live like the other wolves by prey."

Then loathing came over the lady, but she gave no sign of it, but asked her lord if he changed into a wolf clothed or naked.

" Lady," he said, " stark naked."

Then she besought him for God's mercy to tell where he left his clothes.

" Lady, that I may not say, for if I lost them, I should be a were-wolf the rest of my life."

But the lady ever besought him to tell her, saying that she loved him more than all the world, and that a husband should hide nothing from his wife. And so at last he said : —

---

[1] Denis Pyramus, who wrote, in the twelfth century, the *Vie de St. Edmond*.

" Lady, in the wood by the road where I go, once stood a chapel. At that place is a broad stone, and in the hollow under the stone, I leave my clothes."

The next time the knight went away, the lady sent for another knight who had loved her long, and she told him that if he would steal her husband's clothes from under the broad stone in the wood, her husband must be a wolf in the forest all his days. So the knight stole the clothes, and the lady's husband was ever a were-wolf.

For a year this good knight and baron of Brittany, whose name was Bisclavret, ranged with the pack, and then it chanced one day, when the king was hunting, that the king's hounds almost ran the wolf down. In danger of being caught, he ran to the king, and licked his feet, and crouched before him, and howled pitifully.

" Come, my lords," cried the king, " and see what marvel is here. The beast cries for mercy as if he were a man. It were great wrong to kill him."

Then the king took the wolf to his castle, and kept him as a pet. The wolf was gentle to all till one day the knight came to the king's castle who had married Bisclavret's wife. No sooner did the wolf see him than, growling and showing his teeth, he sprang at the knight, and would have torn him to pieces had not the king threatened the wolf with a rod. Twice that same day the wolf tried to spring on that same knight, and the king and his people wondered. And so they tied up the wolf till the knight had gone back to his own castle.

Not long afterwards the king went to that part of his land where he found the wolf. There Bisclavret's wife came in great estate to pay court to the king. When Bisclavret saw her, no man could hold him. He ran towards her in fury, and springing on her, tore the nose from her face.[1] At this the king and his people wondered again, and his counsellors said : " Sire, this is the wife of the baron you held once so dear, who has long been lost, no one knows how. Only this lady and the knight who is now her husband has the wolf attacked. Keep the lady till she tell what reason this wolf has to hate her. We know that many marvels before this have happened in Brittany."

And they kept the lady till she told the whole story, — that she and the knight had stolen her husband's clothes, and that her husband had been a were-wolf ever since. Then they bade her bring her husband's clothes to the king, and so she did. The king himself put the clothes before Bisclavret, but he looked at them not at all. Then one of the counsellors said : " Sire, we are not wise to stand by. He is ashamed to make the change before us." So they left the wolf and the clothes in the room together. And when the king looked in after a while, there was the good knight Bisclavret, in his true shape. And the false wife and the false knight were driven from the country.

This story is likely to strike a reader to-day as a kind of mediæval *Dr. Jekyll and Mr. Hyde.* Some irrepressible beastly longing forces the good baron to assume his wolfish shape, just as the demon nature of the esteemed Dr. Jekyll changes him into the

---

[1] Compare the punishment that Arthur threatens in Layamon's account of the Round Table to the kinswomen of those knights who had fought at his feast.

brute Hyde. But though we nowadays may see this resemblance, it is doubtful if Marie herself was interested enough in the psychology of her characters to wish any such meaning read into her story. And though we cannot help feeling that it was natural for the wife to have an unconquerable aversion to her husband, after she knew that he was a raging beast in the forest for three days every week, Marie certainly wished our sympathies to go out to the betrayed Bisclavret. Whatever in the man's nature forced him periodically to run with the pack, Marie would have us overlook it on his resuming his proper form.

Another characteristic *lai* is *Guingamor*, not certainly Marie's, yet in subject-matter and in treatment so like her own that Gaston Paris pronounced it all but surely hers.

Guingamor, the favorite nephew of a king of ancient Brittany, was loved at the court and among the people above all young knights. One day, when the king and most of his barons were hunting, Guingamor remained behind to play chess with the seneschal, and the queen saw him, and was filled with love for him. But Guingamor would not listen to the words of the queen, for he was loyal to the king, his uncle. And so when she asked him for his love, he started from her in great shame.

Then the queen was frightened, for she thought that Guingamor would tell the king what she had said. And so that evening, when the court was returned, and all the knights and ladies were sitting together, she said to the knights : —

" There is one adventure for which none of you are brave enough. You dare not hunt in the forest where the white boar wanders. Yet great praise would be his who should take that same white boar."

The king was angry, for he wished no more of his knights to go out in search of the white boar. Already ten of his bravest young men had ridden forth to take the white boar, and not one of them had come home. But Guingamor knew why the queen spoke as she did, and so he said to his uncle, —

"Sire, grant me a boon."

The king did so. Then Guingamor told his uncle that he wished to hunt the white boar in the forest, and to borrow the king's horse and bloodhound and brachet, and pack of hounds. Much against his will, the king had to keep his promise and give Guingamor leave to take his favorite horse and his brachet to go forth to hunt the boar.

At first the hunt went well. Then Guingamor lost sight of the boar, and lost the brachet of his uncle, the king, and wandered a long time hither and thither, not knowing where he was. At last he came to a river, and crossed it, and saw before him a palace of green marble with a tower which seemed to him of silver. The palace doors were of ivory, inlaid with gold. It was the fairest palace Guingamor had ever seen, and he paused to look at it before he went back to his hunt. Then he left the palace, and wandered hither and thither again, till he came to a spring in which was a beautiful damsel, bathing, and an attendant was combing the damsel's hair. The fairness of the damsel fired Guingamor, and seeing her garments on a bush, he seized them, to put them high up in the fork of an oak-tree, where she could not reach them. But the damsel chided him, saying that was an unknightly deed

he did, and she begged him to leave the clothes where
they were, and invited him to return to the palace
which was hers and lodge there. " And no one can tell
thee," she said, " but me, how thou canst find the
brachet which thou hast lost." And gladly the knight
said that he would go with the damsel.

Then she came out of the bath, and dressed herself,
and returned with Guingamor to the palace. In it
were three hundred or more knights, each one with
his lady; and there Guingamor lived in great joy and
delight, in love with the damsel, for three days. Then
he wished to return to his uncle, and asked the damsel
to give him the head of the white boar, and the brachet
which he had lost, and let him go back across the river
to his own country.

" Thou wilt go hence for naught," said the damsel.
" It is three hundred years since thou camest hither,
and all thy kinsmen are dead." But Guingamor would
not believe the damsel. And so she set him on a
steed, and gave him the boar's head, and the brachet
in leash, and had him put across the river to his own
land. But before he went, she warned him neither to
eat nor drink, whatever his need, until he came to her
again.

The first man Guingamor met in his own country
was a charcoal-burner. When he asked for his uncle,
the king, the charcoal-burner looked on the knight in
wonder, and said that the king had been dead three
hundred years, and that his cities and castles were
in ruins. Then great sadness came over Guingamor
for his uncle and his friends whom he had lost; and
he said to the charcoal-burner, " I am he, that great
king's nephew, who went hunting in this forest."

Then he gave him the boar's head, that the charcoal-burner might tell the people of the land that the old king's nephew had really come back. Then Guingamor turned to ride to the palace of his lady.

As he did so, he saw some apples growing on a tree by the road, and he was hungry. Forgetful of the lady's warning, he plucked three apples and ate them. Straightway he fell from his horse, such an old, old man that it seemed to the charcoal-burner the knight could not live till evening. But then came riding two fair maidens, who dismounted by Guingamor. Chiding him that he had heeded not his lady's word, they lifted him to his horse, and gently led him to the river, where they put him in a boat and ferried him over. And there, we may suppose, he was restored to youth, and lived happily ever after with his lady in fairyland.

These two *lais* are typical of Marie's work. Her stories are generally folk-tales, sometimes, as in *Guingamor*, with a suggestion of myth. Her verse is always smooth; and so far as she introduces detail, it pictures the life of polite society of her own time. In her men and women, fairy-tale puppets though they are, there is some fidelity to human nature. Moreover, in all her *lais* but two,[1] and in most of those of unknown authorship, there is no mention of Arthur or of his knights. And yet the *lais* are important in the development of the Arthurian stories.

They are important, because it is probable that the few which we have represent many which have been lost, and many more which never took literary form

[1] The two are *Lanval*, in which Arthur and Gawain figure, and *Chievrefoil*, in which Tristram and Iseult figure.

at all. They show us, probably, the nature of the stories told by the Celtic minstrels — Breton, Welsh, or Irish — who wandered about England and France in the eleventh and twelfth centuries, harp in hand, chanting and reciting their tales of wonder. Gaston Paris has thought that the minstrels generally chanted their stories in their native tongue. Probably the stories were often likewise translated, and were frequently preceded by short prose introductions. In fact, so far as can be made out to-day, the *lais* of these minstrels generally combined prose and verse, and in every one was at least some verse that was chanted.

The recitation and chanting of such *lais* was one of the great forces contributing to the literary development of the Arthurian story about the time of Geoffrey of Monmouth. Many of the *lais* now lost, like most of those which have been preserved, probably did not concern Arthur at all. Many others did. In time those which originally made no mention of him may to a greater or less degree have been associated with him. Thus a version of the were-wolf story, not written by Marie, makes the transformed knight one of Arthur's barons instead of a baron of a nameless king. Marie herself, in her *lai*, *Lanval*, suggestive of *Guingamor*, makes the hero a knight of Arthur's court. In a similar way, no doubt, many stories were changed that they might be attached to the ever-growing Arthurian story. The *lais*, therefore, more than anything else, probably spread the stories of Arthur before they took literary shape. How early the *lais* began to do so, no one knows. It was probably as far back as those days in which the hero-story of the brave warrior Arthur was scarcely distinguished above a score of other British hero-stories. The tale of Vortigern and Merlin, which appears in Nennius's history, might have formed the subject of a *lai*. It is easy to see how the *lais* might contribute to larger compositions, such as the pseudo-chronicles and the romances; several *lais*, more or less skilfully patched together, would produce a long poem, like the *lais* in tone and substance;[1] and such seems to have been the genesis of not a few metrical romances. But on the whole, the romances, which we may thus regard as an outgrowth of the *lais*, were more rational and less poetical.

And so the *lais* antedate the metrical romances and pseudo-histories both, though by accident they did not take literary shape till Geoffrey and Wace had written their chronicles, and Chrétien de Troies was making himself famous with his *Tristan* and his *Érec*.

[1] Gaston Paris, "Lanzelet," *Romania*, x, p. 466, says: "Plusieurs . . . lais, rapportés au même personnage, finissent par lui faire une sorte de biographie poétique; telle paraît être l'origine des romans consacrés à Tristan, les plus anciens peut-être qui aient paru en vers français."

V

CHRÉTIEN DE TROIES AND THE ROMANCES

CHRÉTIEN DE TROIES, the most gifted and the most fa-
mous among French writers of Round Table romances,
is the earliest whose work has survived in anything
but fragmentary form. As his name implies, he was
probably a native of Troies in the province of Cham-
pagne. He must have been a man of good education,
for he imitated in French parts of Ovid. For a time
he lived at the courts of Champagne and of Flanders,[1]
and was apparently a favorite at both, for at one the
countess supplied him with material for a story, at
the other, the count. This is all we know certainly of
Chrétien — the stranger, because as a writer he must
have been in high esteem from the first; otherwise it is
hard to explain his boast in the introduction of *Érec:*

> " Des or comancerai l'estoire
> Qui toz jorz mes iert an memoire
> Tant con durra crestiantez ;
> De ce s'est Crestiiens vantez." [2]

Chrétien wrote six Arthurian poems. The first was
the story of Tristram, composed about 1160 or earlier.
Though it has been lost, it is the surmised source of a

---

[1] Edward Wechssler thinks Chrétien composed his *Conte del Graal*
in Paris. Cf. E. Wechssler, *Die Sage vom Heiligen Gral*, Halle, 1898,
pp. 45, 152.

[2] *Érec*, ll. 23–26. " Now I am going to begin the story which shall
always be remembered as long as Christianity lasts. On this Chrétien
prides himself."

later prose romance which was the source of much of Malory's Tristram material. His next Arthurian story was *Érec et Énide*, known best to-day through Tennyson's *Marriage of Geraint* and *Geraint and Enid*, of which Chrétien's poem was indirectly the source. His third Arthurian romance, *Cligès*, made up of two distinct stories inartistically put together, shows that all sorts of tales were attracted to the growing Arthurian legend. The first part, a pretty love-story of contemporary French life, apparently Chrétien's own invention, tells of the courtship and marriage of Alexander, Prince of Greece, and Soredamor, the parents of the hero ; the second part, a tale of oriental origin, concerns Cligès himself, and tells a story like that of Romeo and Juliet, with the difference that all ends happily. Chrétien's next Arthurian poem, written about 1170, was the rather confused *Conte de la Charrette*, or *Le Chevalier de la Charrette*, which tells of the loves of Lancelot and of Guinevere, and of her abduction by a prince, son to the king of the land whence no man returns, — a romance highly important in the history of the Lancelot legend. *Yvain*, or *Le Chevalier au Lion*, was Chrétien's fifth Arthurian romance.[1] Its basis seems to have been a Celtic fairy-tale, in which a water-fairy is obliged to marry any man who can successfully defend the fountain over which she presides against all comers. To this slight *motif* are added various adventures. Finally, about 1175, Chrétien wrote his last Arthurian poem,

[1] It probably appeared soon after *Le Conte de la Charrette*, to which there are frequent allusions in *Yvain*. Opinions differ as to the dates of Chrétien's last compositions. Cf. G. Paris, *Litt. Française au Moyen Age ;* Foerster's introductions to Chrétien's works; E. Wechssler, *op. cit.* pp. 148–152.

Perceval, or *Le Conte du Graal*, which he left unfinished. This gives us the first literary mention of the Holy Grail.

Not one of the stories just mentioned is found in the work of Geoffrey of Monmouth or of any other pseudo-chronicler. It is Chrétien, therefore, who gives us the earliest literary versions of several stories now of world-wide fame. Chrétien is interesting, besides, because he has carried on the work begun by Geoffrey, of giving contemporary setting to the old stories which make up so much of the Arthurian legends. Geoffrey, we have seen, made some effort to picture contemporary society realistically; he tried to make the background of his generally dull narrative vivid, and occasionally he succeeded; but his characters remained wooden. Wace, without making his characters more alive than Geoffrey, made his background more realistic. He worked in so much color and detail that his pages are splendid with Anglo-Norman magnificence. Marie de France, in her *lais*, made the old Celtic tales yet more vivid pictures of contemporary French life; she created not only a realistic background, but also characters who are to some extent alive. Finally, Chrétien, painting his background as brightly and truly as either Wace or Marie, took more interest in his characters than either of them; and so he has given us, on the whole, the best pictures which exist of the upper classes in France in the Middle Ages. For this reason, Chrétien, more than any other author, may be said to have established the Arthurian stories in that dignity and popularity which they enjoyed till the Renaissance. Because he did so, and because of his influence on subsequent writers, both in the material he gave them and in the treatment of it, Chrétien is the principal figure among mediæval Arthurian romancers.

Opinions regarding the literary ability of Chrétien vary. In our own day, Professor Wendelin Foerster and one or two others count him the greatest poet who has ever told the Arthurian stories, not even excepting Tennyson. On the other hand, such a competent critic as James Russell Lowell seems to have rated Chrétien pretty low. " What are the 'Romans d'avanture,'" he says in his essay on Chaucer, " the cycle of Arthur and his knights, but a procession of armor and plumes, mere spectacle, not vision like their Grecian antitype, the *Odyssey*, whose pictures of life, whether domestic or heroic, are among the abiding consolations of the mind ? An element of disproportion, of grotesqueness, earmark of the barbarian, disturbs us, even when it does not disgust, in them all." Though Lowell does not expressly mention Chrétien here, neither does he expressly except his works from this general depreciation of Arthurian romances. What Lowell says is true of many of them. It is true of Wace's pseudo-chronicle, which on the whole is " but a procession of armor and plumes, mere spectacle," though, to be sure, extremely brilliant spectacle. It is true, too, of the works of other writers before and after Chrétien, and to a certain extent even of Chrétien's. Lack of proportion there is in his romances ; there is too much minuteness, there is not enough emphasis on important parts, and consequently there is some monotony. Yet Chrétien's romances are at times skilfully composed, and far from monotonous ; he can, at his best, make his story move with considerable rapidity and animation.

One merit of Chrétien's verse is its smoothness and dignity. Another is its extreme fluency, for Chrétien had a facile pen — to him, as to writers of lesser note, not always an advantage, since it led him now and again into unnecessary diffuseness. In these respects he was either inferior to Marie de France, or in no way superior. What did make him superior to her was his wider view of life. She was content merely with an interesting tale, a good plot, which she worked over as realistically as she could. Chrétien was not satisfied unless he gave his old fairy-tale some moral and psychological substance. In every one of his Arthurian poems, his interest is in the characters even more than in the events, with the result that he makes his people fairly real. We read *Érec* and *Yvain* with interest, not so much because Chrétien handles the plots well, as because he makes Erec and Yvain living mediæval barons, and Enid and the Lady of the Fountain tolerably real women — real, that is, so far as they go, for they are never thoroughly vitalised. Contrast them with some of Chaucer's characters in the *Canterbury Tales* — the Squire or the Parson, the Prioress or that very living woman, the Wife of Bath — and you will see the difference; Chrétien's characters, by comparison, are sketchy. But Chaucer is almost unique among poets for graphic delineation of character; the great novelists have not excelled him in making their personages alive.

Chrétien, then, was a realist only to a limited extent; but with literary sensitiveness and with romantic and poetic feeling he did combine a certain amount of realism. Such being the case, it would be remarkable if he offered us nothing but " mere spectacle; " and,

Lowell to the contrary, Chrétien has given us more. That there is much " spectacle " in his pages we must admit: there naturally would be, for twelfth-century life was far more spectacular than life to-day, and that is one reason why we like to read about it; but in Chrétien's pages there are likewise not a few pictures of human life eternally true. And what, after all, constitutes " vision," as Lowell uses the word, in contrast to " mere spectacle," if not true pictures of human life?

Eternally human is the spoiled child, Perceval, who rides out into the world against his mother's will, breaking her heart; but who, in spite of this selfish, thoughtless beginning, turns out a good and useful man at last. Human, too, is the frailty of Yvain, who lets himself be led away from his wife, the Lady of the Fountain, by his unmarried friend, Gawain, promising to come back on a certain day after he has fought at tournaments at Arthur's court, as he did in his bachelorhood. " But I think he will forget," Chrétien says slyly, " for Messire Gawain will treat him so well that he will not think of going back. For the two will go about to jousts and tourneys wherever jousts and tourneys are held." And so they do; and Yvain almost forgets that he is married, like many another husband who has left his own hearth for a little entertainment among his old friends. And finally, there is no episode which is more human, which opens wider "visions," than that of Gawain's meeting in *Perceval* with the girl known as " The Maid with the Narrow Sleeves." She is a child approaching womanhood, who has received her odd name because, though large sleeves are the fashion for grown-up ladies, she herself, hardly yet out of the nursery, wears narrow sleeves. At her father's castle there is a tournament in which the knight distinguishes himself who is the lover of the little maid's elder sister. As the ladies sit on the battlements of the castle, looking down at the knights in the plain below them, the girl sees Gawain, who happens to be travelling through the country disguised as a merchant; for certain reasons make it wiser for him not to be known or to engage in tournaments. Merchant though he seems, the little maid, pointing to him, says that there is a knight better than her sister's lover. The elder sister flies into a passion, and gives the little maid a slap in the face, which leaves its finger-marks on her cheek; and when the little maid persists in declaring Gawain the better knight, the ladies in attendance on the sisters have difficulty in keeping the elder from slapping her sister's face again. That evening the girl steals away to the house where Gawain is lodged, at the foot of the castle hill, and begs him of his courtesy to appear in the lists the next day as her champion, and prove that she was right in picking him out as better than any knight who had jousted during the day. Gawain's courtesy and kindness persuade him, at whatever inconvenience and risk to himself, to do as the girl requests. She promises, therefore, to send him a sleeve as her token, that he may wear it in the tourney. And so when she gets back to the castle, with the help of her father, whom she has taken into her confidence, she has a gorgeous sleeve prepared, made in the latest fashion, for she is ashamed to send one of her narrow ones. The next day Gawain, wearing the sleeve, overthrows all opponents in

the lists,[1] and proves that the little maid was right in
selecting him for her champion. And to justify her,
he does not ride farther on his way till he has pro-
claimed to all in the castle that he is Gawain, Arthur's
nephew, knight of the Table Round.

Gawain appears nowhere in a better light than here;
nothing sweeter is told of him than his kindness and
courtesy to the little maid. Once you have read this
incident, it sticks in your mind. True, it is not
grandly poetic, like the incidents in the *Iliad* and the
Odyssey, for Chrétien was not a Homer, but it is vivid
and human. You are as likely to forget Helen on the
walls of Troy, arousing the admiration of Priam's
aged counsellors, as those two sisters, one just arrived
at womanhood, the other just outgrowing the nursery,
who sit there on the battlements of that gray little
French burg, their ladies, gorgeous in brocades and
jewels, about them, and quarrel over the knights in the
green meadow beneath. By such pictures as these,
which give to the Arthurian stories their final touch
of interest and realism, Chrétien shows himself the
greatest French poet of the Middle Ages.

There were other metrical romancers than Chrétien
in the twelfth century, and others in the thirteenth.
None of them, however, made any important contri-
bution to the Arthurian stories as the world knows
them best to-day, except Robert de Boron, probably a
Norman knight settled in Hertfordshire,[2] who seems
to have composed his romances in the first years of
the thirteenth century. According to Gaston Paris,

---

[1] This episode may have influenced the author who first told of
Lancelot's wearing the sleeve of Elaine of Astolat.

[2] Gaston Paris thought him of the Franche-Comté. *Op. cit.* p. 99.

Boron wrote a trilogy — *Joseph d'Arimathie*, *Merlin*,[1] and *Perceval*. The first of these three poems tells the early history of the Holy Grail and of its bringing to England. The *Merlin* combines the old story of Merlin's wonderful birth with prophecies of Arthur's sage about the miracles of the Grail, and thus becomes a sort of link between the *Joseph d'Arimathie* and the *Perceval*, which recounts the Quest of the Grail. Only the *Joseph* and part of the *Merlin* are extant in verse; the metrical *Perceval* is entirely lost. We know, however, the substance of all three, for they were early turned into prose and exist as prose romances.

The prose romance was the last literary form which the Arthurian stories assumed. First, it must be remembered, were the *lais* circulating by oral transmission, and not taking literary shape till the middle of the twelfth century or later. Earlier in the century came the pseudo-chronicles, probably to a considerable extent made up from *lais*. From the chronicles, so constituted, it was an easy transition to metrical romances, pieced together likewise, for the most part, from *lais*, but differing from the pseudo-chronicles in that they made no claim to be regarded as history. Nevertheless, some of the characters figuring in the metrical romances were supposedly people who had actually lived. In other words, a metrical romance was probably regarded more or less as an historical novel is regarded to-day. We do not doubt the existence of Richard Cœur de Lion or of Louis XI of

[1] Mr. W. W. Newell doubts Boron's authorship of the *Merlin*. Cf. W. W. Newell, *The Legend of the Holy Grail*, Cambridge, Mass., 1902, p. 32.

France because Scott has associated a fictitious Ivan-
hoe with the one and a fictitious Quentin Durward
with the other. No more did mediæval readers doubt
the existence of Arthur, King of Britain and conqueror
of western Europe, because Chrétien invented as one
of Arthur's knights the Grecian Cligès.

There is no reason to suppose that the prose ro-
mances — the last of the principal literary forms of the
Arthurian stories to take shape — were not regarded
in much the same way as the metrical romances; in
fact, they often told the same stories. Sometimes
composed independently of the metrical romances
which they paralleled, at other times they were mani-
festly prose paraphrases of stories told originally in
verse, for frequently the verse shows through the prose.
Such is the case in the earliest prose romances which
recount the stories of Perceval and of Lancelot; in
each may be detected as a basis Chrétien's poem on
the same subject. Still again, prose romances grew
up, even in substance, independently of any metrical
tales now known. Why they came to supersede met-
rical romances in favor, it is difficult to say. The
fact remains that they did, and that after the first
part of the thirteenth century, they were, in French
at least, the most popular form which the Arthurian
stories assumed. Though appearing first in France,
in translation they reached almost every country of
western Europe.

In these prose romances, for the first time, stories
about the various heroes of Arthur's court were woven
together in accounts which made some attempt to be
comprehensive, including, as they did, the principal
feats of the King and his knights from the early days

of Arthur's father, Uther Pendragon, down to his own departure for Avalon. Of these stories the centre was substantially the same as the one Geoffrey had told in his pseudo-chronicle, — that is, the Arthur-story proper, — the account of the great King's birth and childhood, his winning the throne of Britain, his marriage, and his wide conquests, terminated suddenly by the fatal treachery of his nephew, Mordred. With this were worked in other stories of all sorts.

Though the prose romances often differ in regard to these other stories which they include, most of them show at least some traces of four important stories besides the Arthur-story proper. These are the Arthurian stories best known to the world to-day. Naming the four in the order in which, having attached themselves to the original hero-tale, they became integral parts of the greater Arthurian legend, they are the story of Merlin, the story of Lancelot, the story of the Holy Grail, and the story of Tristram and Iseult.

VI

MERLIN

THE story of Merlin, we have seen, appears as far
back as the time of Nennius in fairly close connection
with the story of Arthur; that is, only a few para-
graphs before the account of Arthur's twelve battles.
It tells of the boy of marvellous birth, whose name,
according to Nennius, was Ambrosius, and according
to Geoffrey, Ambrosius Merlin, and then simply
Merlin.

How a closer union of this story and the Arthur-
story came about cannot be said; but by the time
Geoffrey of Monmouth writes, Merlin was already an
important personage at Arthur's court, a sage revered
for his prophetic powers. The first time the enlarged
story of Merlin takes definite independent shape, with
Merlin as the central figure, is in the *Merlin* of Rob-
ert de Boron, which seems to have borrowed a good
deal of its material from Geoffrey's account. This
poem, which was soon turned into prose, dealt not only
with Merlin's life, but also with Arthur's career up to
his coronation. For some reason or other, romancers
whose names are not certainly known decided to carry
the adventures of Merlin beyond that point; accord-
ingly, early in the thirteenth century there were com-
posed two different continuations to the prose version
of Robert de Boron's poem. One of these, because
it had the greater currency, is commonly called the

ordinary, or vulgate, *Merlin ;* the other, the *Suite de Merlin.*[1]

Only a few incidents in the Merlin romances have considerably influenced the development of the Arthurian stories as a whole. These romances give an account of the Round Table different from that of Wace and Layamon, but more in keeping with the courtly and religious tone which the Arthurian stories were assuming at the end of the twelfth century. According to the *Merlin*, Uther Pendragon established the Round Table by the advice of his sage, in commemoration of the table of the Last Supper. It was the second table so instituted; for Joseph of Arimathea, years before in his travels to Britain, had likewise established a Round Table. Uther gave the table to Leodogran, King of Cameliard, who on the marriage of his daughter, Guinevere, to Arthur, sent it to him as a wedding present.

A more important addition of the *Merlin* to the Arthurian stories is that which makes Arthur the father of Mordred. When the wife of King Lot of Orkney, daughter of Igerna by her first husband, the Duke of Cornwall, came to pay her respects to the newly crowned Arthur, he fell in love with her, and not knowing his parentage, persuaded her to yield to his desire. So Mordred was born; and so there is poetic justice in Arthur's betrayal at Mordred's hands: his death is the result of his own misdeeds. How this episode got into the stories cannot be said.[2] In the

---

[1] These two continuations and the prose version of Robert's poem were all used by Malory in the first books of his *Morte Darthur.* For versions of *Merlin*, see the Huth *Merlin*, G. Paris and Ulrich, Paris, 1886.

[2] J. Rhys (*Arthurian Legend*, Oxford, 1891, pp. 20 ff.) thinks the incest comes from confusion of Arthur with a culture hero of Celtic

pseudo-histories there is no suggestion of it; in them Arthur is almost as blameless as in Tennyson's *Idylls*.

The most famous incident of all the Merlin romances is the seer's own enchantment, which is related differently in the two versions of the Merlin story, the *Vulgate* and the *Suite*. According to the latter, the version which Malory's *Morte Darthur* has followed, Merlin was "assotted and doted" on a "damosel of the lake," Ninien, or Nimue, which name in later versions got changed to Vivien.[1] Merlin and this damsel were travelling together in Brittany, when they came into the forest of Broceliande, always a forest of wonder, and there they found a great chamber built in a rock, where lay the bodies of two lovers who had formerly used the chamber for a meeting-place. The damsel declared that she would pass the night in that rock chamber, and Merlin declared that he would stay there with her. When evening came, he fell into a deep slumber; and Vivien, rising, at once wove about him the spells which, through her blandishments, she had persuaded him to teach her, so that he could move neither hand nor foot. Then she had the chamber closed by putting a stone before its entrance, for she was tired of the sage's love-making, now that she had learned his magic; and after that no one saw Merlin more.

In the vulgate *Merlin* the account is more poetic. As the sage and Vivien are travelling in this same marvellous forest, the damsel begs him again and again to

mythology who had himself in some way become confused with a Celtic Zeus.

[1] The change from *m* to *n* and so to *v* might easily occur through the carelessness of scribes.

teach her some of his craft. " ' Well,' " said he, accord-
ing to an English translation of *Merlin* of about 1450,
" ' I will do your pleasure.' Then he began to devise
the craft unto her, and she it wrote all that he said.
And when he had all devised, the damsel had great
joy in heart, and he her loved more and more, and she
showed him fairer cheer than before. And so they
sojourned together long time, till it fell on a day that
they went through the forest hand in hand, devising
and disporting, and this was in the forest of Broce-
liande, and found a bush that was fair and high of
white hawthorn full of flowers and there they sat in
the shadow; and Merlin laid his head in the dam-
sel's lap, and she began to taste [1] softly, till he fell on
sleep. And when she felt that he was on sleep she
arose softly, and made a cerne with her wimple all
about the bush and all about Merlin, and began her en-
chantments such as Merlin had her taught, and made
the cerne IX times, and IX times her enchantments.
And after that she went and sat down by him, and
laid his head in her lap and held him there till he did
awake; and then he looked about him, and him seemed
he was in the fairest tower of the world, and the most
strong, and found him laid in the fairest place that
ever he lay before. And then he said to the damsel :
' Lady, thou hast me deceived, but if ye will abide
with me, for none but ye may undo this enchantment;'
and she said : ' Fair sweet friend, I shall often times
go out, and ye shall have me in your arms, and I you ;
and from henceforth shall ye do all your pleasure.'
And she held him well covenant, for few hours there
were of the night nor of the day, but she was with

[1] That is, stroke.

him. Nor ever after came Merlin out of that fortress that she had him in set; but she went in and out when she would."[1]

[1] This is quoted, with only the spelling and some of the punctuation modernised, from the prose romance of *Merlin* written between 1450 and 1460, edition of the Early English Text Society, London, 1899, p. 681.

For the history of the legend of *Merlin*, see the introduction to this edition by Professor W. E. Mead.

This English prose *Merlin* makes Nimiane (that is, Vivien) originally not a lady of the lake, as in Malory, but daughter of a nobleman, Dionas; Merlin taught her necromancy. There is no doubt, however, that she was originally a fairy. Professor Rhys (*Arthurian Legend*, p. 284) identifies her with Morgan le Fay.

VII

LANCELOT

THOUGH the Lancelot story was not at first so closely connected with the Arthur hero-legend as the Merlin story, it influenced it in the end far more. In the principal English versions of the legend — Malory's *Morte Darthur* and Tennyson's *Idylls of the King* — the guilty love of Lancelot and Guinevere has become the centre of interest.

The first literary mention of Lancelot is in Chrétien's *Érec*,[1] where the poet tells us that Lancelot was the third best knight of the Round Table — surpassed only by Gawain, who was the first, and Erec, who was the second. This is equivalent to saying that Lancelot was the second, if not the first; for Gawain's supremacy does not militate against Lancelot's; Gawain was always the first knight in Chrétien's time; and always next to him was the hero of the particular romance in which Gawain had been introduced. We should expect Gawain and Erec, therefore, both to be classed ahead of Lancelot in *Érec et Énide;* his position just after them is as high as could be expected. Lancelot is mentioned again in Chrétien's *Cligès*,[2] where it is recounted that he was overthrown by the hero of the romance. This, again, is not at all to Lancelot's discredit, for Chrétien's heroes regularly

---

[1] Professor W. Foerster's edition, 1. 1694.
[2] Between 1. 4765 and 1. 4799.

overthrow every one but Gawain, with whom the fight is generally undecided ; and in this very *Cligès*, Perceval met a fate similar to Lancelot's. Thus Chrétien's two preliminary mentions of Lancelot show that he was a warrior worthy of becoming himself the central character of a story, as Chrétien made him in his *Conte de la Charrette* or *Chevalier de la Charrette*, frequently called the *Lancelot*.

Though this is the earliest Lancelot romance extant, a version of the story anterior to it is preserved in the *Lanzelet* of Ulrich von Zatzikhoven, a Swiss poet. Ulrich, who like so many other Arthurian poets, wrote in the last years of the twelfth century, translated into his own tongue a book which, he says, was brought to Germany by Hugh de Morville — one of the seven English gentlemen who were hostages for Richard I when he was released from captivity by the German emperor, Henry VI.[1] As Morville went to Germany in 1194, his book, which contained the Lancelot story, must have been written earlier, very likely before Chrétien's *Charrette*.

According to Ulrich's rough and confused poem, Lancelot, when still a baby, was carried away from his mother, widow of the king of Benwick,[2] by a fairy, who took him to her land in the midst of a lake. Her purpose was to train him that in time he might kill a giant, the arch-enemy of her son. When Lancelot

---

[1] According to Gaston Paris, this Hugh de Morville has apparently another claim to distinction in being one of the four knights who murdered Becket in Canterbury Cathedral. Compare, however, H. H., *Gentleman's Magazine*, xlv, New Series, pp. 380 ff. According to this article, Becket's assassin probably died in 1177. The hostage for Richard I was a Lord de Burgh of Cumberland, who was a relative of the assassin.

[2] I use the form of the name given by Malory.

was fifteen years old, the fairy, thinking him ready to become versed in knightly deeds of arms, sent him into the world in search of adventure. Like Perceval, in Chrétien's later Grail romance, Lancelot went out a raw, ignorant youth; and like Perceval, he found a kind baron who instructed him in knighthood. Then he entered on a course of strange adventures, in which he was married at least twice, to say nothing of one or two amours besides. He killed, moreover, two giants, — one of them the enemy of the fairy's son, — achievements which in each case immediately won him the love of the victim's daughter; for in this romance, killing a father was one way to a daughter's heart.

It was much against his will that Lancelot fought with his second giant; for Mabuz, the son of the fairy, had a castle, like so many others in mediæval romance, with a strange "custom." Every knight, no matter how valorous, became cowardly the instant he entered the castle gate. Accordingly, Lancelot, who had hitherto shown remarkable bravery, submitted to all sorts of indignities from the inmates of the castle; and when the giant presented himself before the gate, refused to go out to fight him. Mabuz, therefore, had Lancelot armed and set on his horse forcibly, and fairly dragged outside. Then Lancelot, now himself again, killed the giant, whose daughter Iblis speedily became Lancelot's wife; and so she remained throughout the poem.

Soon after this adventure, the Lady of the Lake, the water-fay who had abducted Lancelot, sent word to him that he should go to Arthur's court, for his mother was Arthur's sister; moreover, he was destined in time to recover his own realm of Benwick. Scarcely had Lancelot, following the fairy's behest, introduced himself as a nephew to King Arthur, who made him a knight of the Round Table, when news came that there was a queen of Pluris whom no hero might marry unless he overthrew the hundred knights who guarded her. Lancelot, though married, and apparently happily, decided to try the adventure for the honor of it. He came near getting more honor than he desired, for when, after defeating the knights, he wished to return to his wife, he found that the queen insisted that he should take the promised reward of her hand and heart. On his refusal, she threw him into a prison, whence he made his escape only when the Lady of the Lake sent four of Arthur's knights to Lancelot's rescue.

The next adventure which Lancelot undertook he was urged to by his wife, Iblis. She told him of a serpent that had attracted considerable attention in the neighborhood while he had been away. It was a terrible creature, that demanded a kiss from every knight it met, which no one yet had been brave enough to give. Lancelot immediately went to the forest and complied with the monster's strange request, where-upon there stood before him a fair woman. She was a princess of Thule, who had been enchanted and doomed to retain her foul shape till some knight should be bold enough to kiss her.

So his adventures continued, till in time Lancelot went back to Benwick, to the great joy of his mother, who had long thought him dead. In his own land he was crowned in the presence of Arthur and many of his court, who went to honor the coronation. And there Lancelot and Iblis both lived to a good old age, and there finally both died on the same day.

Of all the adventures in this loosely constructed romance, the one most important in the subsequent development of the Arthurian legend remains to be mentioned. This was Lancelot's assisting Arthur in the rescue of Guinevere from a king who abducted her. The king was named Valerin; and at the time when Lancelot first came to Arthur's court, before he had revealed himself as the great king's nephew, Valerin was making a claim that Guinevere was rightly his, on the ground that her hand had been promised to him before it was given to Arthur. Valerin agreed, however, to waive his pretensions to the queen, if he was defeated in single combat. Lancelot offered himself as Guinevere's champion, and by defeating Valerin, seemed to render her position at the court secure. Valerin, however, was not true to his word. While Lancelot was off on the adventure of the queen of Pluris, Valerin appeared again, and this time carried off Guinevere while a hunting party engaged the attention of most of Arthur's court. Having taken her to a remote place, encircled by a thick wood full of terrible serpents, he there threw her into a magic slumber. Then Arthur set out to rescue the queen, accompanied by a few of his best knights, among whom was Lancelot. Though a magician, Malduc, was of most service in rescuing Guinevere, for it took his spells to disperse the serpents, Lancelot played a fairly important part.

In this story of Ulrich's, it will be seen there is no hint that Lancelot was the lover of Guinevere. Such a relation appears first in Chrétien's *Conte de la*

Charrette. According to this, on Ascension Day, when Arthur was holding court at Camelot,[1] most romantic of all capitals of Arthur, because more than any other difficult to take out of the nowhere of poetry and locate definitely in this working-day world, — on Ascension Day, there came before Arthur a knight in full armor, by name Meleaguant, boasting that in the land of his father, King Bademaguz, certain knights and ladies of Arthur's court were held captive. He promised to free them, if one of Arthur's knights could overcome him in single combat. But if he himself was victorious, he was to lead away captive another lady, greater than any held in his father's land, the Queen herself.

Now Arthur had recently granted his seneschal, Sir Kay, a boon without any knowledge of its terms — an act of folly which experience never taught Arthur to desist from, though boons with conditions not stated were forever getting him into trouble. Kay, on hearing Meleaguant's challenge, decided that his boon should be nothing less than the privilege of defending Guinevere. He accordingly offered himself as her champion, much to the regret of the court, for Kay, a churlish, unloved knight, was notoriously a bad fighter. He was defeated, as every one expected he would be, and Meleaguant departed for his own land with Kay and Guinevere both.

At this juncture Gawain set out to rescue his sovereign lady. He had gone but a little way when he met a knight, with visor down, whom he did not recognise, though it was Lancelot, who seems to have been away

---

[1] Spelled Camaalot, this place seems to make its first appearance in literature in l. 34 of this poem.

from the court on Meleaguant's arrival, just as he was in Ulrich's poem, when Valerin carried off the queen. Lancelot, having borrowed a horse from Gawain, for his own was spent, spurred off furiously in pursuit of Guinevere and her captor. Gawain, following on, presently found Lancelot's horse killed, apparently in a fight between his rider and the men of Meleaguant, and Lancelot himself going on foot. Soon the two knights met an ill-favored dwarf driving a cart or tumbril, such as that in which criminals were carried to execution.[1] Lancelot directly asked the dwarf if he knew anything of the Queen. The dwarf replied that he would give news of her if Lancelot would get into the cart and ride with him. For a brief moment Lancelot hesitated to do so, thinking it unknightly to proceed even a short distance in such a base convey-ance. Love for the Queen, however, speedily prevailed; he got up beside the dwarf, who said that Meleaguant and his captives had gone the very way they were going. So they went on, Lancelot in the tumbril with the dwarf and Gawain riding, till all three came to a castle — Lancelot, the while, jeered at by knights and ladies whom he met, who called him mockingly "The Knight of the Cart," whence the name of the poem.[2]

When Lancelot and Gawain departed from the

[1] Lines 325 ff. Chrétien says that in Lancelot's time each town had but one cart — that which carried the criminals through the streets previous to punishment.

[2] Gawain likewise asked the dwarf if he knew anything of the Queen. The dwarf replied to him that if he wanted news of her, he might mount the cart, too: but Gawain, apparently thinking that foolish, when he had his horse to ride on, refused. It does not appear that the dwarf, after all, told Lancelot anything very definite of the Queen, though he did indicate the way her captor had taken.

castle the next morning, they learned from a damsel that the Queen had been carried to the land from which no man returns. It lay beyond a deep river, which could be crossed only by two bridges — one a keen-edged sword two lances in length,[1] the other through the waves, with as much water above as below. The two knights set out to reach the apparently inaccessible land, and both succeeded in getting over the river — Gawain by the bridge under the waves, from which he came out almost half drowned, and some time earlier Lancelot, who crawled over the sword bridge. Though his hands and feet were terribly cut, he had no hesitation in engaging the next morning in combat with Meleaguant, whom he defeated.

After this, at the command of Meleaguant's father, Bademaguz, who is represented as a kindly old king, Lancelot presented himself to the Queen to tell her that she was free. To his surprise, she received him coldly, and Lancelot, like a dutiful lover, was in despair; but the next time he met her, there was a reconciliation.[2] She let him know that her coldness was occasioned by his hesitating even for a moment to mount the cart, though how she knew of his hesitation is by no means clear. He had no business, she urged, to consider his own reputation in the least when it was a question of rendering service to her. However, as a token of her forgiveness, she appointed a meeting for that night. At the time set, Lancelot climbed up

[1] Line 3039.

[2] Before the reconciliation there was a rumor of Lancelot's death. This caused the Queen to grieve so for her unkindness to him that a rumor got abroad of her death. Hearing this, Lancelot wished to kill himself, but was prevented. After being alarmed by these false rumors, both lovers found it easy to become reconciled.

on a ladder to Guinevere's window, which was guarded by iron bars. These he tore away from the masonry, and so passed the night with her.

There were traces of blood in her chamber which came from his hands, that were cut as he tore away the bars; and so Meleaguant, when he visited the Queen the next morning, made charges against her, which both she and Lancelot could honestly declare untrue, for Meleaguant suspected the wounded Kay of passing the night with Guinevere. Lancelot thereupon offered himself as the Queen's champion, declaring that the question of her virtue should be settled in single combat between him and Meleaguant. As in their former fight, Lancelot was victor. Still, Meleaguant insisted on another single combat, to be fought later at Arthur's court. In the mean time, he tried to prevent Lancelot from presenting himself on the appointed day; but Lancelot overcame Meleaguant's plots, and defeated and slew the treacherous prince.

Such, roughly, is Chrétien's *Lancelot*.[1] Of most of this, there was probably nothing in the original Lancelot story, which, we may surmise, concerned itself with Lancelot's abduction by a fairy and his performance of some great adventure for her, in the course of which he won the love of a damsel, whom he married, and with whom he lived happily. To this simple tale were added the other adventures which made up the rambling, disconnected *Lanzelet* of Ulrich von Zatzikhoven.[2]

---

[1] Chrétien for some reason did not finish the poem. The last thousand (or a little less) of the 7134 lines were written by a clerk, Godefroi de Leigny. See ll. 7124 ff.

[2] Probably Ulrich's French originally " offrait des lacunes : l'embarras du traducteur est visible en plus d'un endroit." G. Paris, " Lanzelet," *Romania*, x, 471. Cf. Maertens, *Rom. Stud.*, v, 689.

Among these added adventures, the most important in its subsequent influence was that which Lancelot shared with Arthur, when they went to bring back Guinevere from her abductor. Almost every account of the Queen which is anything like comprehensive has her carried off by somebody; and in this persistent story of her abduction is one of the most likely traces, in the whole mass of Arthurian romance, of Celtic mythology. According to Chrétien, Meleaguant is son to the king of that land from which no man returns, that is, a god from the other world. In the nineteenth book of Malory's *Morte Darthur* the same prince carries Guinevere off while she is maying, an abduction suggestive of the rape by Pluto, god of the other world, of Proserpina when she was picking flowers in Sicily. Probably Guinevere's husband originally got her back unaided, as Orpheus regained his lost Eurydice — though only to lose her again. A trace of this earlier form of the story seems to persist in a Welsh tradition incorporated in the *Life of Gildas* (*Vita Gildae*), which has been ascribed to Geoffrey of Monmouth's contemporary, Caradoc of Lancarvon ; though, according to Gaston Paris, it is doubtful if the work is really so old. Whatever its age, it serves to preserve an ancient Welsh legend, which makes out that Guinevere was carried away by a certain king, Melwas,[1] to Glastonbury, whence she was restored to her husband without bloodshed through the mediation of St. Gildas. This seems to be a vari-

---

[1] It preserves, at any rate, a very old tradition, for Chrétien de Troies mentions King Maheloas of the Isle of Glass, — Isle de Voirre, that is, the other world (*Érec*, l. 1946), — who seems to be the same person as Guinevere's abductor in the *Life of Gildas*.

ant of the story told by Chrétien in his *Lancelot*. Paris takes Melwas to be a name from the same root as the French Meleaguant,[1] and Glastonbury to be synonymous with Avalon, with which in local traditions the place was associated; for in the twelfth century the Saxon meaning of the name "town of Glaestings" was generally forgotten, and by false etymology Glastonbury was understood to be "town of glass." This is one reason why it became confused with the Welsh Ynys Witryn, translated into French as Ile de Verre, one of the names given to the Celtic Island of the Blessed. The situation of Glastonbury, a pleasant group of hills rising from flat marsh land, which even now in winter is sometimes covered a foot or two deep by water, no doubt made the confusion easier.

This old Welsh tradition, then, seems to show in fairly primitive form an instance of Guinevere's abduction by a god from the other world. Doubtless some such legend of a great queen, or perhaps a goddess, stolen from her husband, was current among the Celts in the earliest times. Probably a variant of the legend caused an early teller of the Tristram story to make an Irish warrior carry Iseult off from Mark's court, and to have her rescued by Tristram before she was taken beyond the sea; for by the British Celts, Ireland, a mysterious land of the West, separated by a great water, was sometimes looked on as the other world. Probably a Gaelic variant of the same legend is the Irish story, in the *Book of the Dun Cow*, of

[1] Celtic scholars are virtually agreed that Chrétien's Meleaguant and his Maheloas are variants of the same noun, though he himself was ignorant of the fact, and are both from the same root as Melwas.

the abduction of Etain, wife of the mortal king Airem, by the fairy king Mider. And so Gaston Paris was justified in saying that the story of Guinevere's abduction may have been sung in Britain and Gaul, though with other names than those of Arthur and Guinevere, long before Cæsar had marched his legions beyond the boundaries of the Roman province.[1]

[1] For a discussion of the Lancelot legend and Guinevere's abduction, consult the two articles of Gaston Paris in the *Romania*, vol. x, p. 465, and vol. xii, p. 459. For the Irish analogue of the abduction of Etain, compare J. Rhys, *Arthurian Legend*, pp. 25 ff.

It seems next to certain that the abduction of Etain and the abductions of Guinevere and Iseult are variants of one and the same early Celtic legend. The name Etain, according to Professor Rhys, means " dawn " or " the shining one ; " and another name for Etain was " Be Find," the white or fair woman. Now Guinevere itself is said to mean " white vision." Moreover, the root *ar* in Arthur is very likely to be connected with the root *air* in Airem ; and both, it may be, have to do with the Indo-European root *ar*, meaning " plough." And so both Arthur and Airem may represent culture heroes. Moreover, the Irish Mider who abducts Guinevere evidently has a name related to the Welsh form of Mordred, that is, Medrod. And Mordred — or, more correctly, Modred — is the earliest abductor of Guinevere of whom we hear after the literary development of the Arthurian romances has begun ; that is, he figures in Geoffrey's account and in the other chronicles as Guinevere's only abductor.

A still further coincidence is that we hear in the Irish story of three Etains ; that is, Etain, the wife of Airem, is in her second existence, having been re-born since she was another Etain, originally in the possession of the very Mider who abducts her. The third Etain is the daughter whom she bears in the course of nature to her husband Airem. Now the Welsh triads, preserving, apparently, a Welsh legend of great antiquity, speak of three Guineveres, all in time married to Arthur. Such is the confusion of this account in the Welsh legend that the principal romancers did not see fit to make use of it.

A parallel of this, probably, is the appearance of three Iseults in the Tristram legend. One of these Tristram loves; another he marries ; and the third, the queen of Ireland, mother of Iseult the Blonde, plays, in the first part of the romance, as important a part in healing Tristram's wound as her daughter, the heroine of the story.

The abduction of Guinevere, suggestive of both the abduction of Proserpina and the recovery from the other world of Eurydice, is

All this gets us far enough away from Lancelot as Guinevere's lover. How, now, did he come to stand in this relation? We may surmise as follows: Some early teller of the episodic Lancelot story, wishing to enhance the fame of his hero by the introduction of some new adventure, made him, as he appears in Ulrich's *Lanzelet*, an assistant in rescuing Guinevere from her other-world abductor. In time he became her sole deliverer because, as the hero of the whole poem, he was made the hero of every incident. But always he went to her rescue, we may presume, from the same motive as Gawain in Chrétien's *Conte de la Charrette*, that is, out of the purest loyalty to the queen of his sovereign lord.

Perhaps at this stage in the development of the story, the incident of the cart was introduced for a different purpose from that which Chrétien assigns. As Malory tells the adventure,[1] Lancelot, after his horse was killed, got tired from walking in his heavy armor; and so, when the cart came along, he mounted it through fatigue, but with more or less attendant disgrace from faring in a vehicle which often carried criminals. As Chrétien tells it, we have seen that the fatigue disappeared, though the disgrace remained. Thus the dwarf made his invitation to Lancelot to get into the cart virtually a test of the knight's love.

There are various reasons why this love might have come into the Lancelot legend. In the early Arthurian stories there are two conflicting views of Guinevere's

only one of many Celtic tales reminiscent of Greek. Cf. the Celtic god, Lug, who resembles in some ways Hermes, Bellerophon, and Perseus. See *Cours de Littérature Celtique*, vol. ii, and John Rhys, *Celtic Heathendom* (Hibbert Lectures), London, 1888.

[1] *Morte Darthur*, bk. xix.

character. All Chrétien's romances but his *Char-rette*, and those of a good many other poets, represent Guinevere as an ideal queen, a gracious, dignified consort to Arthur, and a sweet womanly wife. There can be little doubt, however, that the old mythological story of Guinevere's abduction gave wide currency to a tradition of her faithlessness. That this was independent of her amour with Lancelot is proved by the fact that in some parts of Wales, to call a girl Guinevere has been as much as to say that she was no better than she should be;[1] and yet Welsh romance has never known anything of the Queen's love for Lancelot.[2] Many early accounts of Guinevere, therefore, make her fickle if not unfaithful. In Geoffrey and the other chroniclers, she is more than semi-acquiescent in her adultery with Mordred. In Marie's *Lanval*, Arthur's queen — here nameless, to be sure, but probably by many readers unconsciously identified with Guinevere — is unblushingly faithless. And so it would not have been difficult for Chrétien, or any other romancer, to give Guinevere a lover, if he saw fit.

Two reasons may have determined him to do so. One was the great popularity of the Tristram story, the essence of which was the love of a queen for the best knight of her husband's court. Why not introduce a similar element of interest into the Lancelot story? A yet weightier reason was the peculiar nature of fashionable love in northern France in the second half of the twelfth century.

[1] J. Rhys, *Arthurian Legend*, p. 49.

[2] Nor apparently of Lancelot himself. As Professor Wendelin. Foerster says (*Karrenritter*, Introduction, p. xxxix), " Lancelot ist den Kymren gänzlich unbekännt." In many ways, however, he resembles heroes who are known to the Welsh, as Perceval, in Welsh, " Peredur."

Fashionable or courtly love — *l'amour courtois*, the French called it — seems to have come from the Provençal poets, who represented love as something conventional, governed by so many rules that spontaneous passion was hidden under an artificial system. The troubadour lyrics, which express this system, became popular in the North at the time of Chrétien's literary fame ; and Chrétien, Gaston Paris thinks, was one of the first, perhaps the very first, who imitated in the "langue d'oil," or northern French, the lyric poetry of the "langue d'oc." Three extant songs of his are thoroughly in the spirit of the Provençal love lyrics. "No one," he says in one of the songs, "can know the first principle of love, who is not himself courtly and well informed : " —

> "Nuls, s'il n'est cortois et sages,
> Ne puet riens d'amors aprendre."

These lines set forth the essence of the Provençal theory of love which became *l'amour courtois* of northern France, that only a polished man of the world could be an ideal lover. He must know how to conduct himself in the presence of his lady according to rules of etiquette as definite as those for a courtier in the presence of his sovereign. He was also to be the unquestioning servant of his lady. Whatever she bade him do, he did. Whatever sacrifice she called for, he made without hesitation.

Such a conception of love naturally appealed to that talented, imperious, and rather amorous queen, Eleanor of Aquitaine, who on her marriage to Louis VII of France sought to make popular at the French court the love system of her native South. In all the intri-

cacies of the system Eleanor instructed the Princess
Marie, her daughter by Louis VII. This princess,
on her marriage with Henry, Count of Champagne,
became Chrétien's sovereign lady. By that time she
had become likewise one of the first leaders of fashion
in northern France, having succeeded in a way to the
position her mother had held ; for Marie inherited both
the worldly and the literary tastes of her mother, with
whom she probably remained in as close communi-
cation [1] as the times would permit, even after Eleanor,
divorced from Louis, had taken for a second husband
Henry II of England, a youth eleven years younger
than herself. More than any one else Marie de Cham-
pagne, Chrétien's liege lady, seems to have made fash-
ionable in the North that system of courtly love which
had been familiar to her mother, Queen Eleanor, from
the time that she could first read.

Proof both of the artificiality of the system and
of Marie's importance as an authority on it is found
in a book written early in the thirteenth century
by André le Chapelain, entitled *Flos Amoris*, or *De
Arte Honeste Amandi*, which might be translated
The Art of Loving "à la Mode." It contains many
rules for the conduct of a lover, such as: On account
of marriage no one is excused from being in love.
Every lover has always before his eyes, even in absence,
his loved one. He is inclined to be suspicious and

---

[1] Intercourse between Eleanor and her daughter Marie seems prob-
able, even without specific record of it, because friendly relations
existed between the families of Eleanor's first husband, who, like her,
married again, and her second husband. Marie's half-sister, Marga-
ret of France, married Marie's half-brother, Prince Henry of England ;
and another French half-sister of Marie was at one time betrothed to
Prince Richard of England, subsequently Richard I.

jealous. He is always in a state of fearful uncertainty. He sleeps and eats less than other people. At the sight of his lady he turns pale. If he beholds her suddenly, his heart palpitates; he almost faints.

Besides setting forth these rules and others for unquestioning obedience in a lover, the *Flos Amoris* explains the system of courtly love by considering disputed questions. In one place it recounts a fictitious interview between a knight and a lady whose love he sought. She was inclined to reject the knight's suit on the ground that, loving an excellent husband and being loved by him, she could love no one else. The knight, after maintaining stoutly that the love she bore her husband was not true love, persuaded the lady to refer the question to the Countess Marie de Champagne. The Countess decided for the knight, declaring that true love between husband and wife was impossible; there was no credit in love to which people were bound by marriage vows, though there was credit in a love which, if detected, would cause danger and disgrace; nor was there uncertainty in the fixed condition of marriage, and uncertainty and jealousy were both necessary to true love. Her opinion, the Countess said, was given after mature reflection, and was confirmed by the advice of several well-informed ladies to whom she had submitted the matter.

The same book records other judgments of disputed love questions. Three are given by the Countess of Narbonne, three by the Countess of Flanders, three by the Queen of France, who was Marie's sister-in-law, four by the Queen of England, Marie's mother, and seven by Marie de Champagne herself. On courtly love she was thus presumably the greatest authority.

This brings us to the question, had Marie, steeped in such a system of love, a considerable part in introducing into the Arthurian legends the love affair of Lancelot and Guinevere? That she would have approved it there can be no doubt, for Lancelot's love in the *Conte de la Charrette* is quite fashionable love. When he and Gawain, for instance, looking from a castle window, caught an unexpected glimpse of the Queen as she was led captive by Meleaguant, Lancelot nearly fell to the ground, and trembled so that Gawain thought his companion would faint.[1] Again, in his journey to the land whence no man returns, Lancelot came to a spring by which lay a golden comb with a few hairs in it, so radiantly golden that gold a hundred thousand times refined were to them as dark night to the most brilliant day in a whole summer. The damsel who accompanied him told him that the hairs were from the head of Guinevere, who had recently used the comb. At this Lancelot, who had got down from his horse at the damsel's request to pick up the comb for her, felt such weakness that he had to catch hold of the pommel of his saddle to keep from falling. He turned pale, and could not speak. The damsel, in fear for him, quickly got off her horse, and went to the knight's aid. Somewhat ashamed then of the emotion he had shown, he asked the damsel roughly why she had dismounted. To take the comb from him, she said tactfully, because her eagerness to possess it was so great that she could not wait for him to give it to her. He accordingly gave her the comb, but removed the golden hairs, which he kissed over and over again and pressed against his face and finally

[1] *Charrette*, lines 569 ff.

placed in his bosom, where he would have kept them, even had any one offered him in exchange a cartload of emeralds and carbuncles and other precious stones.[1] Lancelot could not have acted more in accord with the strict etiquette of courtly love, had he committed to memory, " Omnis consuevit amans in coamantis aspectu pallescere," " In repentina coamantis visione cor tremescit amantis," and all the other rules of the *Flos Amoris*.

These two instances are enough to show that Lancelot in the *Conte de la Charrette* is an ideal courtly lover. Now the Countess Marie, according to Chrétien's own account, gave him the material and the spirit (*matiere et san*)[2] of his story. Gaston Paris has concluded, therefore, that Chrétien, in telling an old tale of Lancelot's rescue of Guinevere, in which the knight did his duty in Platonic fashion as the loyal servant of the queen, deliberately changed their relations, and at the suggestion of Marie de Champagne made Lancelot Guinevere's lover.[3]

An objection to this theory is that Chrétien nowhere hints that he is telling a new story; he seems to take knowledge of the love affair for granted. This Paris explains by saying that Chrétien's desire was to mystify his readers as much as possible, as he shows by

[1] Lines 1396 ff.

[2] Line 26.

[3] Professor Rhys (*Arthurian Legend*, ch. vi, p. 135) disagrees with this view. He thinks " that Lancelot's passion for the queen was not so much the result of invention on the part of Chrétien as of blundering of his own or of those who gave him his materials." According to Professor Rhys (*ibid*. ch. vi), Lancelot and the Welsh hero, Peredur, were originally identical. Peredur (cf. story of *Peredur* in Lady Guest's *Mabinogion*) loved an indefinite " empress," who was confounded by French romancers with Guinevere.

concealing the name of the Chevalier de la Charrette till line 3676 of the poem. In the meantime the fact that the love of the unrevealed knight for the Queen was mentioned as a well-known affair would pique the curiosity of readers still further.

To many of us the Arthur legend is more interesting because more human, if we think that the love of the Queen and her knight owes something to the desire of a royal princess of long ago to see in verse, if nowhere else, the devoted love which she and other great ladies of her time longed for but found not in their exalted life. There is no reason why those who like the fancy should not indulge it. At the same time, it cannot be said that Gaston Paris has proved the origin of Lancelot's love to be what he himself, like so many of us, was pleased to imagine it. Nevertheless, the fact remains that no mention of Lancelot's guilty passion has been found earlier than Chrétien's *Conte de la Charrette*. And further, even if it had got into the Arthurian stories before, it had probably not taken on fashionable, courtly form. This peculiarity of Lancelot's love is due, almost undoubtedly, to Chrétien, acting at the command of his liege lord's wife, and so indirectly to the Countess Marie herself. Because courtly love at the time was so much the fashion, it became immensely popular in the Lancelot story. Once introduced there, it could not be forgotten; and so it bound the Lancelot story inseparably to the greater Arthur story. The more this grew, the more important Lancelot's passion became; till in time some writer, feeling called on to recount at length the first meeting of Lancelot and Guinevere, invented that episode of Galehault's introducing the knight to the

Queen, after they had long looked on each other with eyes of love. In the presence of his lady, the knight, true to the traditions of the courtly lover, was so timid that finally the Queen herself had to make the first advance, and taking him by the chin, she gave him the first kiss.

The German *Lanzelet* shows that other stories than Chrétien's concerning Lancelot were current in the twelfth century. Early in the thirteenth, some unknown writer gathered various of these into a prose romance combined with parts of the Perceval story. This enlarged *Lancelot* was further developed by the addition of more extraneous matter. Many manuscripts still existing, not only in French, but in most languages of western Europe, testify to the popularity of these later versions of the romance. Probably it was some form of this enlarged *Lancelot* which, coming into the hands of Dante,[1] led him to make the story of Lancelot's first meeting with Guinevere that which Paolo and Francesca were reading when they confessed their love for each other. And so the influence of Chrétien, and through him, that of Marie de Champagne — dreaming of such devotion as no woman ever had, or if any had, she would find cloying — reached to Dante, as it has reached since to Malory and Tennyson.[2]

[1] *Inferno*, V.

[2] The curious system of "l'amour courtois," which seems to have interested the ladies of the time so much, presents a love altogether different from that in many parts of the romances. Often that love is a mere animal passion, something enjoyed as a right of hospitality, as is the custom among certain savage tribes to-day; that is, a knight comes to a castle, makes his suit to the lady who for the moment takes his eye and who grants him her favors, and rides off the next day, or perhaps only a few hours later, never to see her again. In other

parts of the romances, love appears as an honest and ennobling natural passion, sometimes unlawful, as that of Tristram and Iseult, or again, wedded love, as that of Erec and Enid. The courtly love — " l'amour courtois " — was not like either of these. Artificial and absurd in contrast with the simple love of Erec and Enid or Tristram and Iseult, it was yet superior to brute passion. No doubt it did much to refine the relations of the sexes in mediæval France and England; but if more refined than gross desire, it was too apt to become a hypocritical cloak for license.

VIII

THE HOLY GRAIL

INTERWOVEN with the Lancelot story in its later forms, though at the opposite pole in spirit, is the mystical legend of the Holy Grail. Of this we owe the earliest extant form, again, to Chrétien de Troies. He is said to have written his *Perceval* or *Conte du Graal* at the request of Count Philip of Flanders, from whom Chrétien got the material of the story, and at whose court he spent the last years of his life.[1]

The hero of the *Conte du Graal*, Perceval, was brought up by his widowed mother in a lonely forest, where she went to live after the good knight, her husband, had been slain. By keeping her son, who was her only child, from all knowledge of knighthood, she hoped to save him from its dangers. But one day, when the grass was green and the trees were blossoming and the birds were singing, the boy met five knights in shining armor, who had lost their way. At first he

[1] The lines of the *Perceval* which state that Count Philip requested the poet to compose the romance are not regarded by all the authorities as Chrétien's own. It is worthy of mention, at least, that the Count of Flanders had been in England only a short time before Chrétien composed the *Graal*. This may point to an insular source of Chrétien's story. For the discussion of the Grail legend, see Alfred Nutt, *Studies on the Legend of the Holy Grail*, London, 1888; E. Wechssler, *Die Sage vom Heiligen Graal*, Halle, 1898; and W. W. Newell, *The Legend of the Holy Grail*, Cambridge, 1902, papers reprinted from the *Journal of American Folk-Lore*.

In these books will be found references to other studies of the legend.

thought them angels; then when he found out that they were earthly men and knights, he wished to become a knight. So, in spite of the remonstrances of his mother, Perceval rode away into the world, an ignorant lad in rough clothes of canvas and deerskin fashioned by his mother's hand. His mind was all on the great king's court at Carlisle, where he hoped to receive knighthood; and even when he looked back and saw his mother fallen on the ground in her sorrow, as if dead, he only spurred his horse on more eagerly.

Thus Perceval came to Arthur's court, a raw youth in rough clothes, clamoring to be made a knight. Riding up to the king in his hall, Perceval turned his horse so clumsily that he brushed Arthur's bonnet from his head. Nevertheless the king promised courteously to make Perceval a knight. At this a damsel of the court laughed with joy. Then Kay, the royal steward, whom Chrétien makes out generally crabbed and discourteous, struck her on the cheek; and he kicked the court fool because he had been wont to say that the damsel would never laugh till she saw the man who was to be the flower of chivalry. Perceval marked Kay's rudeness, but because he wished to wear red armor, he rode off without stopping longer in pursuit of a Red Knight who had insulted Arthur and the Queen just before Perceval entered their hall, by snatching a goblet from the royal table. With a dart the youth pierced the knight's eye and brain, striking him dead. Then with the help of Gawain's squire, who stole out after Perceval, wishing to see his meeting with the Red Knight, the youth got himself into the knight's armor and rode on his way.

It is not necessary here to mention all Perceval's adventures. In time he came to the castle of a kindly baron, Gonemans, who instructed him in knighthood and other ways of the world. Going thence, Perceval met with various adventures and overthrew many knights whom he sent to Arthur's court, always with the message: " Yield thyself to the damsel whom Kay buffeted, and tell her that God will not let me die till she is avenged." After defeating the enemy of a maiden, Blanchefleur, who would have married her against her will, Perceval tarried for a while in the lady's castle as her lover. Then he rode forth again, wishing to return to his mother, whom he remembered now ever oftener and oftener as he left her, prostrate in her sorrow on the ground.

One evening, while Perceval was looking for a place to spend the night, he saw a river deep and wide, and a skiff with two men in it, one of whom was fishing. They told the young man that he might lodge in a castle near by, to which he soon made his way. When he went from his chamber into the great hall, he found the fisherman, who was the lord of the castle, lying on a couch in front of the fire, with a sable cap on his head, clad in a robe of the same stuff lined with purple. He did not rise to greet the young man, excusing himself because he suffered from lameness. Presently a page entered, bearing a sword, which the host presented to his young guest, who straightway girded it on to try it, and then returned it to the page. Scarcely was this done when another page entered, carrying a lance, with which he passed between the fire and the couch on which the lord of the castle rested. Perceval noticed that from the point of the lance continually flowed a drop of blood. Following the lance-bearer, after a few minutes, came two youths with golden ten-branch candlesticks. With them came a damsel, bearing in her two hands a grail, which gave out such light that it dimmed all the candles in the hall. After her came a second damsel with a silver tray; and both damsels, like the lance-bearer, passed between the fire and the couch. Then the damsel bearing the grail, which was covered all over with precious stones, carried it into a side room, where it seemed to serve somebody with food; and later on, with every course of the supper, the grail was carried in and out of the same room. The youth wondered continually what these marvels meant; and he was often on the point of asking, but he refrained; for when he first went into the world, he asked too many questions, and the baron who gave him instructions advised him especially, to think before he spoke. And so the young knight went to bed, still wondering what the candlesticks and the sword might mean, and the bleeding lance and the shining grail.

Next morning, when Perceval woke, he seemed to be alone in the castle, for no servant came to his call. Marvelling at this, he made his way downstairs. He found his horse waiting at the door, saddled, and his lance and shield leaning against the wall. He mounted, and had scarcely got to the end of the drawbridge when it seemed to rise of itself. Wondering still more, he rode into the wood, where presently he found a damsel lamenting over a dead knight. She asked him what had been his hostel; and when she learned, she told the young man that he had been at the castle of the rich Fisher-King. Because the king had been wounded with a dart in both haunches, he was lame and could enjoy no sport but fishing. Then the damsel asked Perceval if he had inquired the meaning of the bleeding lance and the shining grail. Hearing he had not, she asked the knight what might be his name. When he told her that he was called Perceval the Welshman, she said rather Perceval the Worthless, for he should have inquired what the wonders of the castle meant. Had he done so, the king would have recovered from his lameness, and good would have come to the land round about the castle. But now woe would follow, because Perceval had not asked concerning the wonders that he saw. The reason for his failure to ask was his sin to his mother, who died of grief when the boy rode away from her. Then the damsel revealed herself as Perceval's cousin, and she said that the body over which she was lamenting was that of her own true love. Nor would she go from that place till she had buried the body.

The subsequent adventures of Perceval are not of so much interest. After some time he was found by Arthur, who had gone forth with all his court to seek the knight who sent so many captives to the damsel that Kay had insulted. Arthur came upon Perceval one morning when he was in a revery caused by three drops of blood which had fallen from a wild goose, wounded by a falcon, on the fresh snow; the blood and the snow reminded him of the red and white complexion of Blanchefleur, the lady whom he loved. When Kay, whom Arthur sent out to rouse Perceval from his revery, came to the young knight, he addressed him so rudely that Perceval, at once angered, fought with him and overthrew him; and so he was avenged

for the insult which Kay had long before offered the
damsel for Perceval's sake in Arthur's court. But
when Sir Gawain went out to rouse Perceval, he
accosted the young knight so courteously that soon
the two were making their way to Arthur's tent, arm
in arm like firm friends.

Perceval now dwelt at Arthur's court in great favor,
till one day there appeared on a tawny mule a damsel
so hideously ugly that the knights could imagine no
fiend in Hell uglier. The first words she spoke were
in denunciation of Perceval, because he had not asked
concerning the grail and the other wonders in the
castle of the Fisher-King. She bade Perceval, there-
fore, ride forth at once and rest not till he came to the
castle again and asked the appointed question. Then,
after telling of certain feats of arms awaiting brave
knights, she rode off as suddenly and mysteriously as
she had come. Sir Gawain set out at once to perform
one of the feats which the loathly damsel mentioned;
two other knights started on other adventures; and
Perceval declared that he would not lie two nights in
the same place until he should have found out who was
served with the grail, and why the lance dripped blood.

From this point the story seems to have been divided
between the adventures of Gawain and Perceval.
Taking up those of the former, it relates the charm-
ing incident of Gawain and the Little Maid with
the Narrow Sleeves. Then after a while it reverts to
Perceval, who, in desperation at causing his mother's
death and his apparent inability to find the Grail
Castle again, almost loses his mind. He rides, fully
armed, on Good Friday, unaware of the sacrilege he
is committing, until he meets some knights and ladies

in penitential garb, who chide him for forgetting the
solemn day and advise him to go to a hermit near by
for absolution. This hermit, who turns out to be Per-
ceval's uncle, tells the young man that he is at last
absolved from his sin in causing his mother's death;
and he encourages Perceval in his search for the grail,
about which the hermit gives some information. The
lame Fisher-King is the hermit's nephew, and there-
fore cousin to Perceval himself; it is the Fisher-King's
aged father, Perceval's uncle, who is fed with the
grail; the vessel contains nothing but one small wafer,
with which the aged king has been kept alive for
twenty years, so spiritual is the king himself, and so
holy is the grail. With this information Perceval goes
on his way, more determined than ever to find the
Grail Castle again.

The story, at this point, goes back to Sir Gawain,
in narrating whose adventures it stops in the middle
of a sentence. Apparently Chrétien died in the midst
of his work.

Chrétien's poem was not to remain unfinished.
Probably soon after his death, a poet named Gaucher,
or Gautier, added more than 20,000 lines [1] to the
10,601 which the earlier poet left. But Gaucher
himself was not to finish the poem; for some reason
or other he left it incomplete. And so it fell to a cer-
tain Mennessier, or Manessier, to conclude it, bring-
ing the whole poem to something upwards of 45,000
lines. He wrote at the command of the Countess Joan
of Flanders, a great-niece of the Count Philip for

[1] The first part of this is not certainly Gaucher's. Gaston Paris
thinks that up to the conclusion of Gawain's adventures it was writ-
ten by some anonymous writer.

whom Chrétien began the poem; and from internal evidence we know that he wrote about the year 1220. Still another author, Gerbert, wrote another conclusion of 15,000 verses about the same time, which some later copyist stupidly inserted between Gaucher's continuation and Mennessier's conclusion. Thus the *Conte du Graal*, with these additions and the interpolations to them, became a rambling metrical romance of over 63,000 lines.

In Chrétien's account of the grail, the earliest which we have, nothing definite is said of its sacred Christian character.[1] A magical vessel it is, for it feeds the old king of the castle; but it seems to be held in no greater reverence by the inmates of the castle than the lance which drips with blood; nor does it rouse in Perceval any other sentiment than that which the lance arouses, namely, curiosity, which Perceval feels may be impertinent. Moreover, in mentioning the mysterious vessel, Chrétien does not make it a proper noun. It is not *the* Grail, but *a* grail, which is evidently a dish or cup.

With Chrétien's continuators, however, the nature of the vessel changes. It becomes an object of Christian significance, *the* Grail, a proper noun; and the lance and the sword which accompany it are made holy objects. Thus, in the first part of that portion of the poem which is ascribed to Gaucher, Gawain, who has come to the Grail Castle, on asking about the lance, is told that it pierced the side of the Son of God.[2] Later on, we learn that the Grail caught

[1] Even when the hermit explains its unusual power to Perceval, it is an indefinite " holy " vessel.

[2] Cf. John xix, 34, " But one of the soldiers with a spear pierced his side, and forthwith came there out blood and water."

the blood from Christ's wounds on the day he was crucified : —

> " . . . c'est icel Graal por voir
> Que nostre Sires tant ama
> Que de son saint sanc l'onora
> Au jor que il fu en croix mis."

Mennessier gives the same account of the Grail, adding that the lance pierced Christ's side. Gerbert is nowhere so explicit.

It is probable that Gaucher's explanation of the sanctity of the Grail, which is lacking in the most important manuscript of Gaucher's addition to the *Conte du Graal* was after all not his, but an interpolation made after Robert de Boron wrote his poems on the Grail. These, we may say with tolerable certainty, were composed in the last years of the twelfth century, that is, within twenty years of Chrétien's death. It is likely, then, that Robert de Boron, and not Gaucher, first gave the Grail Christian significance. However that may be, it is certain that Boron was the first to attach the fully developed legend of the Grail to the Arthurian cycle.

Boron, we have seen,[1] wrote a trilogy — *Joseph d'Arimathie*, *Merlin*, and *Perceval*. The *Joseph*, more than any continuation of Chrétien's *Graal*, makes the vessel sacred, for it was used by Christ himself at the Last Supper. And afterwards a soldier[2] of Pontius

---

[1] Cf. ch. v, p. 76.

[2] The Gospels give no hint of Joseph's being a soldier. According to Matthew, he was "a rich man of Arimathea, . . . who also himself was Jesus' disciple." According to Mark, he was "an honorable counsellor;" according to Luke, "a counsellor . . . a good man, and a just;" according to John, he was "a disciple of Jesus." Even in the apocryphal Nicodemus, Joseph was a "a counsellor of Arimathea, a city of the Jews, a good and just man, who did not consent

Pilate, Joseph of Arimathea, who loved Christ, and took His body down from the cross, caught His holy blood in it when, as Joseph and Nicodemus [1] washed the Saviour's body, His wounds began to bleed afresh.

Boron's *Joseph* is concerned chiefly with showing how the Grail was carried to Britain. His *Merlin* sketches the history of Joseph's descendants down to the time of Arthur, thus forming a link between the *Joseph* and the *Perceval*. This differs from Chrétien's poem in that the hero is already a knight of Arthur's court when he sets forth in quest of the Grail. Nor does he first happen on the Grail Castle by accident: he comes to it on a quest of which the castle is the end and aim, for a voice has declared at Arthur's court that the Rich Fisher shall not be healed till the best knight in the world ask him concerning the vessel in his keeping. As in Chrétien's story, because the knight fails to ask the question, the castle vanishes the next day from his sight. More than seven years later, he comes to the castle again, having overcome many foes and resisted carnal temptation; and this time he asks the question which heals the king. The latter proves to be Perceval's grandfather, who soon after his healing is carried up to heaven by angels.

Still another *Perceval* was composed early in the thirteenth century, probably, unlike the others, originally in prose.[2] In the confused tale which it tells,

to their counsels nor deeds, and who himself expected the kingdom of God."

[1] Cf. John xix, 39: Nicodemus assists Joseph in burying Jesus.

[2] This *Perlesvaus*, as the author wrote the name, has been admirably translated by Dr. Sebastian Evans into English modelled on Malory's, under the name of *The High History of the Holy Grail*, London, 1898 and 1899.

Lancelot is a prominent figure ; and much is made 'of the fact that he may not ask concerning the Grail on account of his love for Guinevere.

The *Quest of the Holy Grail*, or *Quête du St. Graal*, was composed in prose probably after all these,[1] for it seems to show traces of most of the earlier versions of the story. The authorship of the romance has not been determined. It has been ascribed to Robert de Boron, and also — and more often — to an English clergyman, courtier, and writer, Walter Map,[2] archdeacon of Oxford, who lived in the reigns of Henry II, Richard I, and John. Like the three poems of Boron already mentioned, the *Quest* made the Grail a vessel used at the Last Supper, in which later Joseph collected the blood of Christ when He was taken from the cross. But in the *Quest* a new character appeared, whose introduction made it distinct from an earlier form of the story. For some reason or other Perceval was no longer the hero. He was superseded by a hitherto unknown knight, Galahad,[3] son of Lancelot and the daughter of King Pelles, the Fisher-King, of the family of Joseph of Arimathea.

With this appearance of Sir Galahad for the first time in literature, the *Joseph* of Robert de Boron became an unsatisfactory introduction to the quest proper, for it prophesied Perceval as the hero of the quest. Accordingly a new introduction was composed to suit the new quest with its new hero, Galahad. This revised early history of the Grail is commonly

---

[1] About 1220, Gaston Paris thinks : *Littérature Française*, p. 251.

[2] According to Paris, Map " a écrit . . . beaucoup de contes singuliers, mais aucun qui touche au cycle d'Arthur." *Op. cit.* p. 102.

[3] Apparently Boron knew no such person.

called, on account of its bulk, the *Grand St. Graal*. Its basis is Robert's *Joseph*, which has been amplified and changed, especially in foretelling Galahad as the perfect knight who shall at last be Keeper of the Grail.[1]

Though these earliest French accounts of the Holy Grail differ in many details, from them all we can make up a story somewhat as follows: Joseph of Arimathea, after taking Christ's body from the cross, collected His blood in the Grail, a dish or cup which our Lord had used at the Last Supper. Then, because Joseph had buried Christ reverently, he was thrown into prison by the angry Jews, who tried to starve him; but Joseph was solaced and fed by the Grail, miraculously presented to him by Christ in person. Released after forty years, Joseph set out from Jerusalem with his wife and kindred, who, having accepted his faith, were ready to follow him and his sacred vessel to far-off lands. He went through various adventures, principally conversions of heathen, the most important being of the king of Sarras and his people.[2] Near this city, too, Joseph acquired miraculously the spear which had pierced Christ's side, or at least one symbolical of it. After remaining in Sarras some time, where the Grail was kept in such honor that Sarras became a holy city, Joseph and his company set out to travel westward. According to one account, before Joseph's death, according to another, after it,

---

[1] The order of composition of these romances is not certain. That which I have given conforms in general to the chronology of Gaston Paris, *op. cit.* pp. 98 ff. Compare, however, Alfred Nutt, *Legend of the Holy Grail*, London, 1888, p. 95; G. McL. Harper of Princeton, *The Legend of the Holy Grail*, Baltimore, 1893; and W. H. Schofield, *English Literature from the Norman Conquest to Chaucer*, New York and London, 1906, pp. 240 ff.

[2] The *Grand St. Graal* derives the Saracens from the city of Sarras.

the Grail and lance and their attendants arrived at last in Britain after many adventures.

The *Grand St. Graal* relates a miracle that occurred when the company with the Grail came to the shore, ready to pass over the sea to Britain. On their lamenting that they had no ships, Joseph rebuked them, saying that those might cross safely who were chaste ; whereupon four hundred and sixty confessed to lechery. Then Josephes, the son of Joseph, took the shirt from his back and, spreading it on the water, said that all the pure in the company might cross on it. So they did without difficulty except two, who, apparently not so pure as they had declared, narrowly escaped drowning. Thanks to the prayers of Josephes, the four hundred and sixty, who had not attempted the crossing, were brought over in time in Solomon's ship and warned against falling into sin again.

There followed many conversions of the British heathen, and more than one miracle like that of the loaves and fishes. Once, for instance, the whole company of Joseph and Josephes, after going without food for a day, came to the hut of a poor woman who had only twelve loaves. Josephes broke each loaf into three pieces, and having put the Holy Grail at the head of the table, made the bread suffice for more than five hundred people. Another time Joseph's nephew, Alain, according to the *Grand St. Graal*, but according to Boron's *Joseph*, Joseph's brother-in-law, Brons, caught a big fish, which, placed on the table along with the Grail, fed a multitude, except such as were hardened sinners.[1] Ever after, Brons

---

[1] According to the *Grand St. Graal* (see Nutt, *The Legend of the Holy Grail*, p. 62), the fish, through the prayers of Alain, feeds the

or Alain, according to which version we read, had the title of the Rich Fisher or the Fisher-King, and so had all subsequent keepers of the Grail. These were always chosen from the descendants of Brons, or Alain, — that is, from the race of Joseph of Arimathea, — and they lived in the Grail Castle, happy and holy men, till finally one of them was wounded in a fight — no adequate explanation is given for the incident — through both thighs or haunches, from which wound he could not be healed until the good knight should come to the castle to ask certain appointed questions.[1]

This good knight was the raw youth of the *Perceval* story. After learning the evil occasioned by his failure to ask the necessary question in the Grail Castle, he set out to find the castle a second time. In the course of his wanderings, his moral character was more or less tested, especially, in the later versions of the legend, with regard to virginity. When he came to the castle again, he asked the fated question ; his quest was crowned with success ; and in time he himself became the Keeper of the Grail.

Such is the Legend of the Holy Grail, as you may construct it in its simplest form from the conflicting versions now extant ; and to some such conclusion, no doubt, Chrétien would have brought his *Conte du Graal*, had he lived to complete it. Taken in its entirety, the legend might have been composed by some monastic Christian poet, especially in the form best known to English readers to-day, which makes

sinners themselves. The others had been nourished by the passing of the Grail through the company.

[1] According to Malory (ii, chs. 15 and 16) the wounded king was Pellam, who later (xvii, chs. 19 and 20) seems to have been living in the castle of Carbonek with King Pelles, grandfather of Galahad.

the maiden knight, Galahad, its hero. But when one comes to study the legend carefully, two perplexing questions arise, which make one doubt its original Christian character. How came Perceval and Galahad both to be heroes of the quest? Which was the original hero?

Of the earliest French versions of the Grail legend, which we have mentioned in this chapter, only two, and those apparently the latest, make Galahad the hero. On the other hand, four — or, if we choose to count the three continuations of Chrétien's *Graal* as distinct poems, seven — make Perceval the hero. Moreover, in the stories which make Galahad the hero, Perceval is a prominent character, only second in importance to Galahad himself. In the stories which make Perceval the hero, there is no mention of Galahad. One can hardly doubt, then, that the original hero was Perceval. And what was his character as compared with Galahad's? Certainly not ideal according to monastic mediæval standards, for Perceval was a worldly knight, whose virginity was not insisted upon. An ascetic Christian poet, sitting down deliberately to construct the legend of the Holy Grail, would never have made Perceval the successful quester.

Still another question might occur to one interested in the legend: Was it originally one, or does it consist of two distinct stories, that of the early history of the Grail, and that of the quest? In no one of the earlier French versions is the whole story told: they all relate either one part or the other. The majority deal with the quest of the Grail; only two tell circumstantially of its journey from Jerusalem to Britain. Furthermore, the stories dealing with the quest are

complete, they come to a logical end. The two stories
of the journey of the Grail to Britain, on the contrary,
stopping in the midst of things, — and one, the *Grand
St. Graal*, with a lamed king who is to be healed
by a promised knight, — obviously call for a sequel.
It looks, then, as if the original part of the legend
were the quest, and as if the early history had been
subsequently added as an introduction. Now the older
part of the complete legend, the story of the quest,
which is the more important, is the less Christian,
both in substance and in spirit. We have already
seen that Perceval, the original hero, was less Christian
in character, according to monastic standards, than
Galahad, the later hero. The natural conclusion, there-
fore, is that the Grail legend, apparently the conscious
invention of mediæval monasticism, was not so in real-
ity. Rather it took the form in which we know it best
to-day accidentally and gradually.

From what we have seen of the Celtic origins of
Arthurian stories, we shall not be surprised at finding
tales in Irish and Welsh both, which will make us
think the earliest sources of the Grail legend pagan
rather than Christian. In an Irish legend of the elev-
enth century, we find that the Irish fairies (the Tuatha
de Danann) cherished four talismans — a so-called
stone of fate, a spear, a sword, and a cauldron from
which no man ever went away unsatisfied. The stone
of fate, according to tradition, is none other than the
Lia Fail, that sacred stone on which the Scottish kings
were crowned ; that same stone which Edward I car-
ried away from Scone, because of the reverence in
which the Scots held it, believing the old saying that
wherever the stone went, the Scottish race should rule ;

that same stone which was set in the coronation chair at Westminster, where some three hundred years later the saying was verified, when a prince of the Scottish race was crowned James I of England.[1] The stone itself has obviously no parallel in the Grail legends, but the three attendant talismans, the lance, the sword, and the life-giving vessel, all have their parallels in the objects which made the self-conscious young knight wonder, though he did not speak, in the castle of the Fisher-King.

Welsh tradition, as well as Irish, knew mystical objects suggestive of those in the Castle of the Grail. In the story of *Branwen, the Daughter of Llyr*, there is a magic cauldron which had the power of restoring the dead to life,[2] " as good as before, except that they were not able to speak." In the same tale, the head of Bran, carried about for fourscore and seven years by Bran's followers, had the power of keeping them alive without food and always in joy and mirth. And Bran, it is at least worth noting, had been wounded in the foot with a poisoned dart, as the Grail king had been wounded in the thighs. Still again, in *Kilhwch and Olwen*[3] the father of the damsel, Olwen, stipulates that before the youth, Kilhwch, shall wed her, he must procure a certain vessel never without food, " the basket of Gwyddneu Garanhir." " If the whole world should come together, thrice nine men at a time, the meat that each of them desired would

---

[1] Scholars, however, doubt whether the coronation stone can be traced from the Lia Fail. See Charles Squire, *Mythology of the British Islands*, London, 1905, p. 71; and W. F. Skene, *The Coronation Stone*.

[2] A translation of this is found in Lady Charlotte Guest's *Mabinogion*. Cf. Alfred Nutt's edition, London, 1902, p. 39.

[3] Cf. translation in *Mabinogion*.

be found within it." [1] If nothing more, it is an inter-
esting coincidence that the owner of this vessel was
the owner also of a marvellous fish-weir, and that the
lord of the Grail Castle found his chief solace in
fishing, and was known as the Rich Fisher, or the
Fisher-King.

Not only in ancient Celtic story are found such
correspondences with parts of the Grail romances ; in
modern Celtic folk-lore, likewise, a striking parallel
is found in a tale which within a few years was still
popular in the Scotch Highlands. The common name
of it is *The Lay of the Great Fool*.[2] A boy, born
after his father's death, is sent away by his mother to
be brought up in the wilderness, that he may escape
his father's enemies. When he is approaching man-
hood, he goes, clad in the hide of a deer which he
himself has killed, to the court of a king, much as
Perceval goes to Arthur's court in the rude clothes
made for him by his mother. The Great Fool, as the
boy calls himself when asked his name, soon after
coming to the court slays a prince who jeers at him,
as Perceval slays the Red Knight. After this fol-
low various adventures, including a stag hunt, which
bears some resemblance to a stag hunt that Perceval
undertook at the command of a beautiful damsel whom
he met in one of the many castles to which he came.
Among other adventures, the Great Fool loses his legs
through the enchantment of a magician. He finally
succeeds in unspelling a brother of his who was des-
tined to remain under spells until he found the Great
Fool. The latter, meantime, has his legs restored by

[1] Alfred Nutt, edition of the *Mabinogion*, p. 123.
[2] Alfred Nutt, *Legend of the Holy Grail*, London, 1888, Index.

the newly discovered brother, who happens to be the owner of a magic cup. And so ends the story, full of correspondences, sometimes far from close, again very close, to incidents of the Grail legend.

The Lay of the Great Fool suggests many Celtic stories, and indeed stories of all the Indo-European peoples, in which a youth punishes some hereditary enemy. Generally, in order to do so, he seeks and ultimately finds appointed weapons or talismans. There are also many stories in Celtic lands and others in which a hero disenchants a person or persons by consciously or unconsciously performing some act. A fusion of two such tales would make the latter part of the Grail legend, that is, the quest. At the beginning, the vengeance story manifestly predominates, introducing talismans which somehow were made the subject of the all-important unspelling question. Proof that a vengeance tale was the basis of this part of the legend seems to appear in the fifteenth-century English poem, *Sir Perceval of Galles*.[1] In this the Red Knight, whom Perceval slays, has slain the hero's father. No Grail figures in the story. The end of it is, that after rescuing a lady from a hostile " Sowdane," who would force her to be his wife, a service similar to that which Chrétien's Perceval renders Blanchefleur, Perceval marries her himself, and then returns to his home to find his mother still alive.

Thus various Celtic folk-tales apparently combined to form the tale which Chrétien did not finish. Whether he intended to introduce the Christian

---

[1] The Thornton manuscript, in which this is found, is of about 1440. The story may be much older. It was edited by J. O. Halliwell in 1844.

significance of the legend must remain uncertain. Though he mentions the Grail with almost enough reverence to make possible such intention, there is no direct statement to that effect. The nearest approach to it is in the information which the hermit uncle gives Perceval about the Grail, saying that it is a very holy vessel. Nor does its Christian significance appear in the Welsh story of Peredur,[1] which is so nearly related to Chrétien's poem that the Welsh author must have been familiar either with Chrétien's work itself, or with its principal source — perhaps with the tale contained in that book which the poet received from Count Philip of Flanders, and which inspired him to write his *Perceval*. In *Peredur* there is no Grail at all, but in its place a head carried on a salver, which has the same power of sustaining life as the Holy Grail, and as the head of Bran in that other Welsh tale of *Branwen*. Whatever Chrétien might have revealed about the nature of the Grail had he lived, we have seen that Robert de Boron made it a most holy object. By 1200 it had become the cup of the Last Supper, which subsequently received Christ's own blood; the lance had become that of Longinus, which pierced Christ's side; and later, the sword became that which beheaded John the Baptist.[2] Then, in order to explain how these sacred objects came to Britain, some poet composed the elaborate early history of the Grail; but even here, full as the poem is of Christian monastic spirit, the pagan Celtic influence

[1] Translated in Lady Charlotte Guest's *Mabinogion*.

[2] Opinion differs more or less as to the date of Robert de Boron's poems. The earliest date conjectured for them is just before 1190, the latest 1215. The weight of opinion seems to be that Boron wrote in the last decade of the twelfth century.

is still apparent. The two earliest Grail-Keepers bear such Celtic names as Alain and Brons. We have seen that the owner of the life-sustaining basket in *Kilhwch and Olwen*, who owns also a fish-weir, bears some resemblance to the Grail-King, forever fishing in the river or lake near his castle. And the life-restoring cauldron of Welsh tradition was kept at Caer Pedryvan, which Professor Rhys identifies with the Castle of Carbonek, where the Grail was kept.[1]

It is impossible to say exactly how Christian significance was given to the Celtic legends which seem thus to have made up the Grail stories. An explanation both ingenious and plausible is offered by Mr. Nutt in his *Studies on the Legend of the Holy Grail*.[2] In Robert de Boron's *Joseph*, which is the older form of the early history, Joseph himself appears never to reach Britain. That land is converted mainly by his brother-in-law, Brons. Here Mr. Nutt thinks is a clue to the way in which the Christian element came into the stories. An old Welsh legend made a certain British king, Bran, — the same name as the French Brons, — a captive in Rome for seven years, where he learned the faith of Christ, which he was the first to preach in Britain. Now Bran was also the name of a heathen god of the other world, who owned a cauldron which restored the dead to life.[3] A confusion of these two Brans, which might arise from the similarity of name,

---

[1] Professor Rhys, *Arthurian Legend*, ch. xiii, gives his opinion that the Grail, as we know it, is a combination of the cauldron of Pwyll, Head of Hades, and the basket or vessel (Welsh Mwys) of Gwydno Garanhir.

[2] Pages 218 ff.

[3] Cf. Bran, king of Britain, whose head, cut off from his body, sustained his followers for eighty-seven years.

would make the first Christian in Britain the owner of a magic vessel.

There was another conversion legend current in Britain, where for some reason the apocryphal gospel of Nicodemus was well known very early;[1] at least, traces of familiarity with it are found in England in the last quarter of the eighth century. This gospel, in recounting Joseph of Arimathea's imprisonment for Christ's sake and his release by Christ himself, tells of miracles like those that struck Arthur and his knights dumb with amazement before the dazzling light of the Grail. According to Joseph's own narrative, his imprisonment, which seems to have lasted only over the Sabbath, was terminated as follows: —

"And when midnight came, while I stood and prayed, the house wherein ye shut me was suspended by the four corners, and there was a flashing of light in mine eyes, and I fell trembling upon the ground. Then one lifted me up from the place where I had fallen, and poured abundance of water upon me . . . and put about my nostrils the fragrance of wonderful ointment, and rubbed my face with the water, as if washing me, and kissed me, and said to me, 'Joseph, fear not, but open thine eyes, and see who it is that speaketh to thee.' And looking, I saw Jesus, and being afraid, I thought it was an apparition. . . . And he took hold of me with his hand, and put me in the midst of my house, the doors being shut, and he put me in my bed, and said to me, 'Peace be to thee!' "[2]

Compare with this Malory's story of the appearance of the Holy Grail at Arthur's court: —

[1] It was not widely known on the Continent till about the twelfth century.

[2] Apocryphal Gospels, translated by B. H. Cowper, fifth edition, London, 1881, Latin Gospel of Nicodemus, p. 341.

" Then anon they heard cracking and crying of thunder, that them thought the place should all to-drive. In the midst of this blast entered a sunbeam more clearer by seven times than ever they saw day. . . . Then there entered into the hall the Holy Graile covered with white samite, but there was none might see it, nor who bare it. And there was all the hall full filled with good odours, and every knight had such meats and drinks as he best loved in this world : and when the Holy Graile had been borne through the hall, then the holy vessel departed suddenly that they wist not where it became. Then had they all breath to speak." [1]

The gospel of Nicodemus makes no mention of Joseph's travels after he was released from prison, or of his brother-in-law, Brons. It cannot certainly be said, therefore, to have given rise to an early tradition that Joseph somehow reached Britain, and converted its people to Christianity. Still, the widely diffused knowledge in Britain of the apocryphal story of Joseph may have been the origin of such a legend, which existed in the island in the twelfth century. This would conflict with the Welsh legend, already mentioned, of Bran as the converter of Britain, for it would put in the field a rival claimant to the sacred honor of first preaching the gospel in the island. Now it would be natural to try to harmonise the two legends, to construct some relation between the two converters. Accordingly Bran, changed in French into Bron or Brons, was made the brother-in-law of Joseph; and the magic vessel with which Bran, by virtue of his original character as a heathen god, was still endowed, became associated with Joseph, who had himself been closely associated with Christ. Its magical properties could no longer be explained by whatever pagan sym-

[1] *Morte Darthur*, bk. xiii, ch. 7.

bolism clung to it; they must be explained by Christian symbolism. Thus, at last, a magic vessel of pagan Celtic imagination became a cup from which Christ had drunk and which had caught His blood, a cup symbolical of the Holy Communion. With this last change, that part of the Grail legend was complete which deals with the early history of the Grail.[1]

Long before this early history was constructed, with its highly sacred sacramental cup, the original folk-tale of Perceval was circulating. This also, we have seen, was made up of two parts — a vengeance story introducing certain talismans, and a story of disenchantment. These talismans were a lance, a sword, and a magic vessel, perhaps in primeval Celtic folk-lore identical with Bran's cauldron. The fact that the talismanic vessel of the Perceval story bore some resemblance to the sacred cup of the conversion legend may have led some one to put the two legends together. With a little doctoring at the end, the conversion story made a good introduction to the quest. Then it was necessary merely to give Christian meaning to sword and lance, and the Grail legend was complete.

Still it would not be in the form which is best known to-day, that in which the hero is Galahad, a virgin knight. The change necessary to give the legend this final form was far-reaching as compared with the

---

[1] If nothing more, it is an interesting coincidence that Robert de Boron connects the early keepers of the Grail with Avalon, and that Joseph of Arimathea takes the Grail to Glastonbury, which we have already seen twelfth-century tradition confused with Avalon. Glastonbury, Professor Rhys conjectures, which was one of the earliest Christian towns in Britain, may have been the site of a sacred heathen town with a temple to the god of the other world, who originally owned the life-giving cauldron.

others. With it the legend took on a completely new spirit, as did the Lancelot story when some one (perhaps Chrétien de Troies, to gratify the whim of a worldly-minded princess) invented the love of the great Queen and Arthur's favorite knight.

This last change in the spirit of the Grail story was but natural. When the Celtic pagan talismans first acquired their Christian significance, they were still associated with a hero not strikingly Christian. The need was felt, accordingly, of making over the hero, for the Grail, typical of the sacramental cup, was a most sacred object. Now the worldly but energetic and courageous Perceval was an unpromising hero to accord with ascetic Christian ideals. According to Chrétien, with whom the Grail, as we have seen, is probably not Christian, Perceval is no better than he should be : he is kind-hearted, daring, energetic, honest, an agreeable companion, a good knight, and a young man of judgment, but one who would enjoy such good things of this world as might offer themselves. When the damsel Blanchefleur throws herself in his way, he is no Joseph in his relations with her. In Gaucher's continuation of the story, Perceval's conduct is the same ; and this is one of the signs that Gaucher's continuation was written before the Christian spirit had materially modified the legend. Wolfram's *Parzival*, which, like the Welsh *Peredur*, was influenced by Chrétien's own poem or one very like it, makes the hero marry the lady who corresponds to Blanchefleur. But even if Perceval had finally legalised his relations with Blanchefleur by marriage, as indeed he does in Gerbert's continuation of the *Perceval*, he would still not have been an ideal holy knight, for by the monastic standards an ideal holy man was a celibate.[1]

An attempt to make such a man out of Perceval appears already in Boron's poem, in which Perceval's love adventures disappear. True, he is at first in love with Aleine, Gawain's niece, and then with a damsel who sends him to hunt the white stag; but before he returns with the stag, he is told by his hermit uncle never to lie with woman. Perceval therefore refuses the damsel's love when she offers it later, and subsequently refuses to take a wife. In the prose *Perceval*,[2] or *Holy Grail* of the thirteenth century, love is directly condemned; it is Lancelot's love for Guinevere which prevents him from seeing the Grail. Then came a later writer, his head full of the monkish confusion of celibacy with chastity, who found it difficult to forget the wife or mistress whom the earlier stories had given Perceval, and so he superseded Perceval with a new hero, whom he called Galahad,[3] who should be ever virginal. Thus was created the famous Sir Galahad, youngest and purest knight of the Round Table, a son of the good worldly knight

[1] Gerbert writes, it is true, as if he thought the previous relations of the lovers entirely innocent.

[2] The *Perlesvaus* previously referred to, translated by Dr. Sebastian Evans under the title of *The High History of the Holy Grail*.

[3] The origin of the name is uncertain: it looks Welsh. In *Kilhwch and Olwen*, one of the many warriors invoked by Kilhwch is Gwalhaved, the son of Gwyar: *Mabinogion*, Alfred Nutt's ed., London, 1902, p. 113. Cf. Rhys, *Arthurian Legend*, pp. 168–169. Professor Rhys thinks " the name is probably to be analysed into Gwalchhaved, from gwalch, 'a hawk or falcon,' and a vocable derived from hâv or hâf, 'summer.' The whole word may . . . be interpreted as meaning the Hawk of Summer and forming a sort of synonym of Gwalchmei," the Welsh form of Gawain, " 'the Hawk of the month of May.' "

Lancelot and of the Lady Elaine, daughter of the Grail-Keeper, King Pelles,[1] of the family of Joseph of Arimathea.

With this change of the story to its final mediæval form, which nineteenth-century poets have made so familiar to English readers, we see the complete transformation of a Celtic folk-tale to a legend apparently wholly and peculiarly the fruit of mediæval Catholicism. A Christian poet used pagan symbols for his Christianised story in the same way that the early Church made use of the pagan festivals in honor of the spring and of the turning of the sun at the winter solstice, for the great Christian feast-days of Easter and Christmas. The fact that the earliest version of the Grail stories gave no Christian significance to the vessel is strong proof of the soundness of this theory ; and so is the fact that the two versions most nearly related to the earliest, the Welsh *Peredur* and Wolfram's *Parzival*, know nothing of the Grail as a sacramental cup. In one, we have seen, there is properly speaking no grail, but a salver containing a man's

---

[1] Pelles himself, like every other keeper of the talismans in the more or less inaccessible Grail Castle, seems to have been a king of the other world. So was King Pellam, the keeper of the sacred spear with which Balin smote the dolorous stroke. According to Professor Rhys, *Arthurian Legend*, p. 268, the sympathy is not with Balin, who represents a sun god, for the following reason : —

"Suppose the rays of the sun . . . to be let in on " the other world, "the whole is clean gone as in a fairy-tale. . . . The visit of the solar hero has annihilated a whole landscape of enchantment in the twinkling of an eye. Balyn, with one thrust of his long lance, has undone a whole world : why should not the curse of its fall pursue him evermore ? "

Rhys, *ibid.*, pp. 273 ff., equates Pellam with Peleur, the name in the Welsh Seint Greal of the Maimed King, or lord of the Grail Castle. He is brother to Peles (French, Pelles), the Fisher-King.

Compare the destruction of Klingsor's castle in Wagner's *Parsifal*.

head, and the talismans that appear with it have no
Christian significance. In the other, the Grail is a
precious stone sent from heaven.

The peculiar spirit of the later Grail legends reveals
itself clearly in the prose *Perceval*, translated from
the French into beautiful archaic English by Dr. Se-
bastian Evans under the title, *The High History of
the Holy Grail*.[1] " Hear ye the history of the most
holy vessel that is called Graal," the first " branch "
of the romance begins, " wherein the precious blood of
the Saviour was received on the day that He was put
on rood and crucified in order that He might redeem
His people from the pains of hell." And a little far-
ther : " The High Book of the Graal beginneth in the
name of the Father and of the Son and of the Holy
Ghost. These three persons are one substance, which
is God, and of God moveth the High History of the
Grail." Then follows a confused account of the King
Fisherman, descended from the race of Joseph of
"Abarimacie," and of Perceval, Gawain, and Lancelot,
and their adventures, concluding with the passing of
the Grail from mortal ken, and the departure of Per-
ceval himself in a ship with a white sail and a fair red
cross thereon, " and within . . . the fairest folk that
ever he might behold . . . all robed in such manner
as though they should sing mass." Singular enough
it seems to one who reads to-day, the union of the
sacred and the fantastic in this *High History*, but the
author was conscious of no irreverence. He believed
all he wrote. In connecting the sacred names of the
Trinity with Celtic fairy-tales, he was only giving ex-
pression to the mixture of ignorance, superstition, and

[1] See p. 115, note 2.

simple, zealous faith characteristic of mediæval Catholicism.

The *High History* is identical in spirit with the still later Galahad romances, which many regard as the fairest flower of the whole Arthurian cycle, for in them the Grail seems symbolical of the highest spiritual ideal. Beauty there certainly is in this latest form of the Grail legend. A fairer picture was never painted than that of Galahad in his red cloak, led in by a white-haired old man to Arthur's court, to sit among the wondering knights, purest and youngest of them all, in the Siege Perilous, long destined for him. But Galahad is beautiful here with the innocent beauty of childhood; and except for his martial prowess, he remains a child; he never becomes a perfected man. He preserves his innocence because he seems not to feel human temptations; and one cannot but think that he does not feel them because he scarcely feels human sympathy. His thoughts are too much on the glory of achieving the Grail, and not enough on relieving the wounded Fisher-King from pain. Perceval's sister, who died from loss of her own blood that a sick lady might be healed, had a better right to the Grail than Galahad, according to modern Christianity, when it is really what we complacently fancy it. Holy according to mediæval standards, he is often selfish according to ours. The opening lines of Tennyson's exquisite *Sir Galahad* —

> " My good blade carves the casques of men,
> My tough lance thrusteth sure,
> My strength is as the strength of ten,
> Because my heart is pure " —

bring out at once Galahad's virtue and Galahad's

fault. If they testify to his purity, they show that he knew little of humility.

Nor can Galahad, whether imagined by Tennyson or by a mediæval romance writer, be called other than fanatical. As he rides round the world singing, —

> "I yearn to breathe the airs of heaven
>   That often meet me here,"

he is either not normal and healthy or not honest. His only real joy comes to him in his visions of the Holy Grail.

> "When down the stormy crescent goes,
>   A light before me swims,
> Between dark stems the forest glows,
>   I hear a noise of hymns.
> Then by some secret shrine I ride ;
>   I hear a voice, but none are there ;
> The stalls are void, the doors are wide,
>   The tapers burning fair.
> Fair gleams the snowy altar-cloth,
>   The silver vessels sparkle clean,
> The shrill bell rings, the censer swings,
>   And solemn chaunts resound between.

> "Sometimes on lonely mountain-meres
>   I find a magic bark ;
> I leap on board ; no helmsman steers ;
>   I float till all is dark.
> A gentle sound, an awful light !
>   Three angels bear the Holy Grail ;
> With folded feet, in stoles of white,
>   On sleeping wings they sail.
> Ah, blessed vision ! blood of God !
>   My spirit beats her mortal bars,
> As down dark tides the glory slides,
>   And starlike mingles with the stars."

In these lines, for all their beauty, Galahad shows himself after all only a knightly brother of the revivalists who manifest their religion nowadays with so much noisy emotion and so little sanity. And no mediæval monk, however ascetic, could have been more firmly convinced than Galahad that women were put into this world to tempt men from the paths of virtue. In short, Galahad, beautiful in his innocence and admirable in his unswerving quest of that vessel which typified the monastic ideal of the Middle Ages, is nevertheless unhuman and unnatural.

There is more practical moral teaching in Chrétien's *Perceval* than in all the Galahad romances put together ; and there is still more, and of finer quality, in the German *Parzival*. One of the greatest virtues of the hero of this romance is his love for his wife. When he makes confession to his hermit uncle, he has two chief regrets, — one that he did not ask the appointed question at the Grail Castle, the other that he has been separated from his wife so long. Go back to her, says the hermit uncle in effect; it is better to seek her than the Grail ; and he tells Parzival that if he would live honorably, he must honor women.[1] Thus it is, when Parzival's thoughts at last are all on his wife, that Cundrie, the hideous maiden-messenger of the Grail, comes a second time to Arthur's court, not as formerly to denounce Parzival, but to say that he has been chosen king of the Grail Castle at Munsalvaesch in Spain, where he is to live in wedded happiness with his wife and their son Lohengrin.[2]

The author of this poem, Wolfram, commonly

[1] Bk. ix, ll. 2074 ff.   [2] Bks. xiv and xv.

called von Eschenbach, from the place of his birth, was a Bavarian, who wrote in the earliest years of the thirteenth century.[1] He seems to have come of a knightly family; and he was one of those poets who lived at the literary court which the Landgrave Hermann of Thüringen kept at the Wartburg, the castle which to this day rises in mediæval stateliness above Eisenach, the same castle where later Martin Luther threw his inkstand at the devil. According to Wolfram's own statement in the second book of his *Parzival*, he could neither read nor write, but whether he made the statement seriously or not is in doubt.[2]

If we are to believe Wolfram's assertion of illiteracy, we must regard his memory as wonderful even for those days of great memories, when minstrels learned such long stories by heart, for he seems to have known familiarly the French poem which gave him much of his own. This, if not Chrétien's *Perceval*, was very like it; otherwise it is difficult to account for the strong resemblance between parts of Wolfram's poem and Chrétien's.[3] There are impor-

[1] He composed *Parzival* probably before 1210.

[2] Professor G. McL. Harper of Princeton feels sure that Wolfram in declaring that he knew no letters was only joking. "It is preposterous to suppose that he was illiterate, and the connection in which the remark occurs is full of repartee." *The Legend of the Holy Grail*, Baltimore, Modern Language Association, 1893, p. 35. Cf. also E. Wechssler, *op. cit.* p. 178.

[3] Wolfram himself asserted that not Chrétien de Troies but a certain Kyot (Kiot) of Provence was the author of the French poem which was his source. Since no other reference to Kyot is known, since no trace of his writings has ever been found, most scholars have doubted whether Kyot's poem was anything but a fiction of Wolfram's. Others, however, have believed in the existence of Kyot, seeing no adequate reason for Wolfram to invent such an author. However that may be, Kyot's poem, if such ever existed, must have followed very closely Chrétien's *Conte du Graal*, for the resemblance

tant variations, however. Wolfram introduces a history of Parzival's father,[1] which has no parallel in any French romance. And he makes the Grail no longer a cup, but a precious stone which Wolfram seemed himself but imperfectly to understand. When it is borne in procession through the castle of Amfortas, the Fisher-King, it is honored by a much larger company than in the French poems. Like the French Grail, it yields food and drink to those about it — according to Wolfram, by virtue of a white wafer which a shining white dove brings from heaven and lays upon the Grail every Good Friday.[2] The holy stone has the power of keeping both men and women young. Angels are said to have brought it from heaven, and chosen knights guard it in the Grail Castle on the hill of Munsalvaesch. Only those who are pure in heart and steadfast in the Christian faith may behold the Grail; and so Parzival's half-brother, Feirefiz, although a true knight, may not see the holy vessel because he is a heathen. From time to time mystic writings appear on the Grail, announcing who shall serve it. The king of the Grail Castle himself may marry, but his attendant knights may not, except when they are called into foreign lands to do service to such as may need them there.[3] A knight of the Grail may stay in a foreign land only so long as no one asks him his name and race. Once so questioned,

between portions of Wolfram's narrative and Chrétien's is remarkable. Nevertheless, there is much in Wolfram's poem of which Chrétien knew nothing. From what source Wolfram (or Kyot) got this material is still a matter of conjecture.

Cf. Alfred Nutt, *Studies on the Legend of the Holy Grail*, G. McL. Harper, *op. cit.* pp. 32 ff.; and E. Wechssler, *op. cit.* pp. 164 ff.

[1] Bks i and ii.   [2] Bk ix, ll. 1100 ff.   [3] Bk. ix, ll. 1869 ff.

he must return directly to Munsalvaesch. Wolfram
explains this apparently unreasonable law by saying
that Amfortas, the Fisher-King, suffered so much on
account of an unasked question that all questions
became disagreeable to the Grail knights.

There is yet further difference between Wolfram's
romance and Chrétien's; in the German poem is a
moral meaning which is not in the French. The lamed
king, Amfortas, according to Wolfram, received his
wound because he took up arms in the cause of worldly
and unlawful love, going out to fight in the pride
and strength of his youth with "Amor" for his motto.[2]
For that reason he was wounded in the thighs and con-
demned to suffer till the chosen knight should release
him from his pain. Though it is still by a question
that the knight is to release the king, it is by a ques-
tion inspired not by curiosity but by sympathy. The
whole poem is thus on a loftier spiritual plane than the
French, in which the questions are merely why does
the lance bleed, and who is served with the Grail? In
the German poem Parzival learns from the damsel
Sigune,[3] whom he meets in the wood near the Grail
Castle, and from the hermit[4] later, that the appointed
question must be about the king's suffering. Even had
Parzival been so instructed when he first came to the
castle, he was, despite the teaching of Gurnemans,
the same kindly baron as Chrétien's Gonemans, — he

[1] Bk xvi, ll. 954–968.   [2] Bk. ix, l. 1380.

[3] " Iuch solt' iur wirt erbarmet hân,
      An dem got wunder hât getân,
      Und het gevrâget sîner not."

Bk. v, lines 947 ff.

Compare Cundrie's denunciation of Parzival in the sixth book.

[4] Bk. ix, l. 1215, and l. 1557, " Hêrre, wie stêt iuwer nôt? "

was a youth still too ill at ease in society, and too self-conscious to ask the natural questions, however much he might wonder at the marvels of the castle and at the lame king's evident suffering. But when he comes to the castle a second time, he is an older man, whose experience has taught him much of human pain, both physical and mental. His sympathy is so wide that quite unconsciously, with never a thought for the propriety of his conduct, he says, after praying for the king, "What ails you now, my uncle?" [1] And the suffering king is healed.

This question, so much finer in its significance than those of the French stories, seems to be more than an accidental change. It is Wolfram's inspiration, which has made his poem a sermon, though not offensively didactic, on that without which men are as sounding brass or tinkling cymbals. This, coupled with the strong, manly morality inculcated likewise in *Parzival*, raises Wolfram to as high a rank among poets as Chrétien's, despite his lack of Chrétien's grace and finish. The two, one filled with the romantic spirit of mediæval Germany, the other with the romantic spirit of mediæval France, are the greatest poets of the Middle Ages before Dante.

There is one more chapter, a brief one, in the history of the Holy Grail, and it is in the nature of an anti-climax. The sacred object is preserved at Genoa, where it may still be seen, in the words of Mr. F. J. Furnivall,[2] "a hexagonal green vessel said to be made of emerald." It was found at the capture of

[1] " Oéhéim, waz wirret dir ? " Bk. xvi, l. 269.
[2] *History of the Holy Grail*, Roxburghe Club, 2 vols., London, 1851, i, p. viii.

Cæsarea, and "was sent to Genoa in 1101 by Baldwin king of Jerusalem," who had recently come to his throne on the death of his elder brother, Godfrey of Bouillon, leader of the first Crusade. Baldwin presented the vessel captured at Cæsarea to some Genoese mercenaries to take to their native city in return for the good service they had rendered him. Once in Genoa, it is not difficult to see how this vessel came to be called the Holy Grail. According to one version of the legend, the Grail was last seen on earth in the Orient, at the city of Sarras. Though it went thence to heaven, there was no reason why it should always stay in heaven; and if it came back to earth, it might naturally reappear in the region where it was last seen. Nor was there any family to whom it would more naturally be revealed than the family of those princes who delivered the Holy Sepulchre, and who according to a tradition,[1] to be sure, not very widely known, claimed descent from Perceval.

When the name of the Grail came to be given to the Genoese vessel cannot be said with certainty. Reverent and enthusiastic mention of it as such is found in a French chronicle of the reign of Louis XII.[2] After this the Holy Grail is mentioned frequently as among the relics of the cathedral of San Lorenzo at Genoa. There it rested quietly till the

[1] Cf. Gerbert's continuation of Chrétien's *Conte du Graal*, Ch. Potvin's ed., Mons, 1866–70, vi, p. 210. Perceval's descendant, known as the Swan-Knight, is to be the ancestor of the Redeemer of the Holy Sepulchre. Godfrey and Baldwin themselves claimed descent from a Swan-Knight.

[2] D'Auton, *Chroniques de Louis XII*, Part iv, chs. xx and xxi. According to d'Auton, Christ made the Grail miraculously from "terre ville," having no rich vessel for the paschal lamb, and wishing to show His divine power.

Middle Ages, whose religious ideal it typified, had long passed, and from one end of Europe to the other, the mighty Corsican, self-made Emperor of the French, was throwing down the mediæval structures of government and society that seemed to him anachronisms at the beginning of the nineteenth century. The fate of the Holy Grail now was symbolical of that of other relics of the past. Disturbing its long rest, Napoleon carried it off to Paris, together with other booty which he took from Italy, for the adornment of his capital. After Waterloo it was returned to its old home, but, like the *ancien régime*, no longer a gem without flaw and of inestimable value. In the course of its travels it was broken, and the supposed emerald turned out to be green glass. The sacredness, however, which attached to it from long association with the cathedral caused the Genoese to mend it reverently, and the cracked Grail is still preserved among the relics in the sacristy of San Lorenzo. "A fine glass vessel," you will find it called in the latest Baedeker to Northern Italy. When the Holy Grail is thus patronisingly mentioned in a Baedeker, truly the days of its glory have departed.

IX

THE GRAIL AND THE SWAN-KNIGHT

In less than a hundred lines at the end of his *Parzival* Wolfram tells briefly, even sketchily, the story of Parzival's son, the famous Grail Knight, Loherangrin, as Wolfram spells the name, who has himself been the hero of long romances. This story of Lohengrin, the Swan-Knight, never more than slenderly connected with the Arthurian legends, is probably the best known tale of non-Celtic origin that became attached to that ever-growing cycle. The part played by the swan, a favorite bird of Germanic mythology, points to a Germanic origin; and so does the localisation of the story. The scene of action is generally in Low German territory, most often somewhere in the Netherlands, but sometimes as high up the Rhine as the city of Mainz. In its simplest form the story tells of a man, young, handsome, brave, who comes in a boat drawn by a swan to a strange land, where he releases from danger the lady of the country. He marries her; but on her asking a forbidden question, he is obliged to go to his own land again as mysteriously as he came, leaving her widowed, with a child from whom is to descend an illustrious race.

From various allusions to some such story as this, it is evident that it was well known in France in the second half of the twelfth century, where it probably came from Flanders. There seem on the whole to have been two main forms of the story, of one of which the hero was commonly called Helias or Elias; the hero of the other became best known as Lohengrin.

The story of Helias was the more popular in France and the more elaborated. It makes much of the birth and childhood of the Swan-Knight, who, it seems, was one of seven children, six boys and a girl, born at one birth of a fair young queen, who was the object of her mother-in-law's unreasonable enmity. This cruel mother-in-law persuaded her son that his wife had given birth to seven pups, and so the young queen was shut up in a gloomy tower and treated with every indignity. In the meantime the old queen had had her grandchildren, each one of whom was born with a silver chain round its neck, exposed in a dark, thick forest, where, thanks to a white she-goat and a pious hermit, the babes were carefully nourished. After several years, the old queen, learning that there were seven children in the wood with silver chains round their necks, feared that the children she had supposed dead were still living. Accordingly, she sent a servant to put them to death, commanding him to bring back the silver chains as proof that he had executed her orders. When the servant arrived in the wood he could find only six children, for one boy, Helias, had gone off with the hermit, with whom the children were living. Touched with compassion, the servant decided not to obey his cruel orders, but merely to take the chains back with him and say that he had murdered the children. And so he removed the chains from their necks, when, to his horror, all six turned into swans and flew away. Nevertheless, he took the chains to the old queen, saying that he had lost the seventh by the way. She, perhaps not quite trusting the messenger's story, sent the chains to a goldsmith to be melted into a cup, but when the smith melted one, it multiplied so much that it sufficed of itself for the cup; and he kept the other five.

Years passed, and Helias was grown to a strong, fair young man when the hermit, instructed by a vision, told the prince to go to his father's palace and see that justice was done to his long-suffering mother. Helias did as directed, the truth was made known at last, the mother was released from prison, and the smith gave the five chains he had been keeping so long to the king and queen, who "kissed them reverentlie . . . bewayling naturally theyr poore children." But then, to quote further from a version of the romance of about 1500,[1] "in the river that ranne about the kinges palays appered visibly the swannes before all the people. And whan Helias had seen them : he called diligentli the king and the queene his father and mother saiing. I pray you my lord and my lady that ye will lightly come and se your other notable children mi v. brethren and my sister. The which ben now presently arived upon the river that is about this palays. And incontinent the kynge and the queene descended wyth many lordes, knightes, and gentilmen, and came with great diligence upon the water syde, for to see the above sayde Swannes. The king and the queene behelde them piteousli in weeping for sorow that they had to se theyr poore children so transmued into swannes. And whan they saw the good Helias

<hr>

[1] W. J. Thoms, *Early English Prose Romances*, London, 1858, vol. iii, pp. 95 ff.

come nere them they began to make a mervaylous feast and reioyced them in the water. So he approched upon the brinke, and whan they sawe him nere them : they came lightli fawning and flikering about him making him chere, and he playned lovingli theyr fethers. After he shewed them the chaynes of silver, where by they set them in good order before him. And to five of them he remised the chaynes about theyr neckes, and sodeynlye they began to retourne in theyr propre humayne forme as they were before, and before al miraculsly they shewed them iiii. fayr sonnes and a doughter. To whome diligentlie the king and the queene ranne, and naturalli kissed them as their children, whereof everye man had mervaile, and ioyed of the divine miracle of God so notably shewed. And whan the other swanne (whose chaine was molten for to make the cuppes as afore is sayd) saw his brethren and his sister retourned into theyr humaine fourmes he lept agayn all sorowfully into the river, and for dole that he had he plucked almost al his fethers to the bare flesshe. And when the good Helias saw him so dolorously demeane himselfe ; he took him to weepe for sorow, and recomforted him sayinge. My dere brother my freende, have somwhat pacience, and discomforte you not. For I shall make so meeke and humble praiers unto God almighti for you, that yet I shall se you ones a noble knight. And than the swanne began to enclyne and bowe downe his head as in thanking him and syth plunged hymselfe all togyther in the water. And for him in likewise the kinge and the queene made moche lamentacion. But Helyas conforted them sweetly, and sayde to them that he wolde in suche wyse pray unto our lorde for him that

in shorte time he should retourne into his owne natu-
rall fourme. And thus they ceased somwhat of theyr
sorowe by the consolacion and goodly wordes of the
said Helias for theyr other sonne, wherfore than they
toke benignely the other v. children and ledde them
to the churche where they made them to be baptised.
And the mayden was named Rose, of whom after-
warde descended a noble lignage and worthy of prais-
ing. And the other sonnes were named and called at
the fonte after the good discrecion of the kinge and
the queene. The whiche sonnes also in lykewise were
ryght noble and vertuous knyghtes and beloved of
God. Than after their baptising thei were solempnely
conduited and ledde into the palays, and there feasted
in all joye as it apperteyned well. And thither cam
many for to see them in laudinge and magnifienge the
name of our almighty saviour, that so miraculously
shewed his great vertue."

One day, soon after this, Helias beheld on the river a
swan drawing a little boat. Realising that this must
be his enchanted brother and that some noteworthy
adventure would follow, Helias without hesitation got
into the boat to start for he knew not where. A voy-
age of five days brought him to the land of Bouillon,
whose duchess was looking for a champion to defend
her against the false claimant of her territories. Helias
valiantly did battle for the duchess, overcame her
enemy, and then married her daughter and only child.
After some years, through the malice of an envious
lady,[1] the young Duchess of Bouillon asked her hus-
band questions which on the eve of their marriage he
had forbidden her ever to put — that is, What was his

1 This lady's name varies in various versions of the story.

race, and what was his country? So questioned the stranger knight had to depart, and he went back sorrowfully to his own land, led again by his swan brother.

This brother, it seems, was soon to recover his proper shape. At the end of the return voyage, by prayer and the application of the cup which had been made out of his silver chain, the swan, placed upon a bed before the high altar of the cathedral, was at last restored to human form. And so the family of the swans, reunited, were all perfectly happy except Helias, who grieved for the wife and children he had to leave in a far-away land. He was comforted, though, by the thought that from a child of his should descend the valiant knight, Godfrey of Bouillon, the leader of the First Crusade.

Various explanations have been offered of the way in which this story came to be connected with so well known a character of history as Godfrey. A plausible one is that a remote ancestress of his married an adventurer, who, though brave, was of obscure origin. By becoming the hero of the swan story, this unknown husband of a Duchess of Bouillon received an ancestry which, however unusual, was at least one of which no knight need be ashamed.[1]

---

[1] For discussion of the origin of the Swan-Knight legend, see Baron de Reiffenberg, *Le Chevalier au Cygne et Godefroid de Bouillon*, 3 vols., Brussels, 1846; J. F. D. Blöte, *Zschf. f. rom. Phil.*, xxi, 176 ff., and xxv, 1 ff.; and Gaston Paris, *Rom.* xxvi, 580 ff., and xxx, 444.

Blöte concludes that the Swan-Knight story comes from no old legend. It is a poetical treatment of the deeds of Roger de Toéni, a Norman nobleman, grandfather to Godehilde, wife of Baldwin of Boulogne.

Roger de Toéni (ca. 1040) bore the image of a swan as his device. He freed from the attacks of the Saracens the widowed Countess of

The stories which follow this form of the Swan-Knight legend [1] do not in general make the hero a son of the Grail-King. Apparently the oldest romance to do so is Wolfram's *Parzival*, which follows the other form of the legend. In Gerbert's continuation of Chrétien's *Conte du Graal* there is a similar relation. Perceval, in a vision which comes to him on his wedding night, is told that he and his wife must remain virginal till he has won the Holy Grail.[2] Then he shall beget a son from whom shall descend the Swan-Knight,[3] and the redeemer of Jerusalem and the Holy Sepulchre.

The form of the story which Wolfram follows seems

Barcelona, whose daughter he married. He returned after a while to his native land. He may have affected to call himself the Swan-Knight rather than by his own name. Baldwin of Boulogne may have assumed, in lieu of any other emblem, the swan, one of the emblems of his wife's family, and so he, instead of his wife, was made to descend from the Swan-Knight. The ancestry ascribed to Baldwin would naturally in time be ascribed to his brother, Godfrey.

Paris could not agree to this theory, nor can one be surprised at his failure to do so. He thought the story of the Swan-Knight was "une ancienne légende lorraine, rattachée arbitrairement au XIIe siècle à la famille des rois de Jérusalem." It was probably a family tradition rather than mythological.

Cf. also A. H. Billings, *Middle English Metrical Romances*, New York, 1901, p. 228, and Jacob Nover, *Deutsche Sagen*, Giessen, 1895–96, ii, *Lohengrin*.

[1] Grimm's *Sechs Schwäne* is perhaps to be connected with it.

[2] Potvin's *Perceval . . . ou le Conte du Graal*, Mons, 1866–70, vi, pp. 207 ff.   Perceval is informed : —

> " Que nus hom ne doit atouchier
> Qu'à sa mollier fors saintement
> Et pour II choses solement :
> L'une si est por engenrer,
> L'autre por péchié eschiver ;
> Chà porte raison et droiture."

[3] **A knight**

> " Qui primes aura forme d'ome,
> Qui moult sera et gens et biax
> Et puis devenra il oisiaus."

to have been known chiefly in Germany, and is, on the whole, simpler than the one just outlined. Elsa, Duchess of Brabant, is left to the guardianship of Friedrich von Telramund, who, wishing to marry her for her lands, though she does not love him, pretends that she once promised him her hand. The German Emperor, to whom appeal is made, declares that the duchess must marry unless a champion will defend her against Friedrich. At this moment, far off on Munsalvaesch, the knights of the Grail hear the castle bells chiming, and they learn by writings on the Grail that their king's son, Lohengrin, must offer himself as Elsa's champion. His horse is brought, saddled and bridled, to the mounting-block, when suddenly on a stream in front of the castle appears a swan drawing a boat. The horse is led back to the stable, and Lohengrin confidently, without provisions or baggage of any kind, sets forth in the swan-boat. After five days, in which he eats nothing except part of a holy wafer that the swan takes in his beak from the waves, Lohengrin arrives at Antwerp.[1] From there he accompanies the young Duchess of Brabant to Mainz, where the Emperor is holding court, and in single fight with Telramund proves the untruth of his assertions. Then Lohengrin and Elsa are married, and they live in perfect happiness, till some spiteful lady persuades Elsa to put the forbidden question which sends her husband back to the Grail Castle.

In this simpler form of the story, it will be seen, there are no swan brothers or swan sister; and the Duchess herself, instead of the daughter of the Duchess, is the Swan-Knight's wife. Wolfram still further

---

[1] The place of arrival is not always the same.

simplifies the story. As he tells the tale, there was no false claimant to the Duchess's hand. She had resolved, contrary to the wishes of her people, never to marry, unless a husband was sent her by divine favor; and until she saw Lohengrin, who was so sent to her from the Grail, no knight could win her love.

Where Wolfram got the name Loherangrin for his hero is not known. Possibly he invented it, for he had a predilection for strange names.[1] It was contracted to Lohengrin in a long German romance written about 1280,[2] which made much more than Wolfram of Lohengrin's connection with Arthur's court. Arthur himself was now Lord of the Grail Castle, and Lohengrin, Parzival's son, was a knight of the Round Table who engaged in many chivalrous adventures with other knights; his service to Elsa was only one of many feats. This *Lohengrin* was the principal source of Wagner's opera of the same name.

Another romance, whose influence made itself felt in the opera, especially in the first part, is *Der Schwanritter*, by Konrad von Würzburg,[3] who died in 1287. True, the lady in dire need is not Elsa, but still a Duchess of Brabant: it is not herself but her daughter that the hero marries; and his name is not Lohengrin, nor is he a knight of the Grail. But the Emperor, as in the opera, is holding court on the bank of a river, — in this case the lower Rhine, — and as the two distressed ladies are making their complaint to

[1] J. Nover, *Deutsche Sagen*, ii, *Lohengrin*, p. 24, thinks that the name was suggested to Wolfram by that of the hero *Garin li Loherains*, Garin of Lorraine.

[2] Between 1276 and 1290, Paul's *Grundriss*, ii, i, 292.

[3] J. Nover, *op. cit.*, *Lohengrin*, p. 19, says *Der Schwanritter* was composed between 1260 and 1270.

him, he sees a white swan on the water drawing a little boat by a silver chain, and in the boat the ladies' Heaven-sent champion, a knight in full armor, sleeping with his head on his shield as if on his pillow. And when the boat comes to land and the knight awakes, he turns straightway to the swan, saying, like the hero of the opera, "Fly now on thy way, dear Swan, and when I need thee again, I will call thee."

X

TRISTRAM AND ISEULT

THE Tristram legend, the last of the chief stories of
the romances to be closely connected with the Arthur
story proper, is, with its overpowering passionate love,
and its wild, sea-washed Celtic lands, the most poetical
of them all. Unlike the other principal legends, it
comes to us in three literary forms; it is the subject
of three *lais*, and of metrical and prose romances
both.

The earliest extant Tristram narrative is from the
pen of an Anglo-Norman, or Norman, Béroul, who
wrote early in the second half of the twelfth century.[1]
Only fragments of his poem exist. The lost *Tristan*
of Chrétien de Troies, written shortly before 1160,
is thought to have followed the same version of the

---

[1] For the date and the composition of the so-called Béroul frag-
ments, see Ernest Muret, *Le Roman de Tristan*, Paris, 1903, pp.
lxiii–lxxii. M. Muret thinks that the fragmentary poem preserved
in MS. 2171 of the Bibliothèque Nationale was composed partly by
Béroul, between 1165 and 1170, and partly by an anonymous *jongleur*
(not unacquainted with Béroul, perhaps, though considerably younger),
who composed the latter part of the poem in the last decade of the
twelfth century. M. Muret is of the opinion that the authors may
have got their knowledge of Great Britain from their sources or from
hearsay; it is possible that neither of them was ever in England. A.
Bossert, on the contrary, *Tristan et Iseult*, Paris, 1902, p. 173, thinks
that if Béroul was not a native of Great Britain, he passed most of
his life there. Cf. also W. H. Schofield, *English Literature from the
Norman Conquest to Chaucer*, New York and London, 1906, pp. 201 ff.

legend as Béroul's.[1] An idea of what this would be,
if it existed entire, may be formed from the German
Tristrant, written by Eilhart von Oberge about 1170
or 1180.[2] Of Eilhart's original poem only fragments
remain, but the whole is to be found in a later re-
vised form; and there is a prose romance of the fif-
teenth century which is a making over of Eilhart's
story.[3]

About 1170 another poet, almost certainly an Anglo-
Norman,[4] composed a Tristram story which differed in
some important respects from the one told by Béroul
and Eilhart. This poet was a Thomas, commonly
called Thomas de Bretagne; and he tells us that he
got his material from one Bréri, whom Gaston Paris[5]
and others have taken to be a Welsh poet of the
reign of Stephen, mentioned by Giraldus Cambren-
sis.[6] Thomas's poem, like Béroul's, has not come to
us entire; there are only fragments of it, all of the

---

[1] A reason for supposing so is that the French prose romances about
Tristram give substantially the same version of the story as the Béroul
fragments. Since, in other cases, the French prose romances have
come more or less directly from Chrétien's verse, it is not unreason-
able to suppose that the Tristram prose romances likewise owed some-
thing to him. There is no good reason to believe, however, that
Chrétien's poem was the source of Béroul's. Cf. G. Paris, *Journal des
Savants*, 1902, pp. 296–302.

[2] The poem of Eilhart corresponds fairly closely to the part of the
French Tristram fragment certainly by Béroul in MS. 2171. At all
events, the so-called Béroul fragments and Eilhart's poem followed
substantially the same version of the story.

[3] Cf. Franz Lichtenstein's edition of Eilhart, *Quellen und Forschungen*,
xix, Strassburg, 1878.

[4] Cf. G. Paris, *Tristan et Iseult*, Paris, 1894, p. 30; and A. Bossert,
op. cit. chs. viii ff.

[5] *Littérature Française au Moyen-Age*, § 56.

[6] *Description of Wales*, bk. i, ch. xvii. Bledhericus is the name
Giraldus gives him.

latter part of the story.[1] We have the earlier part of
the legend, however, complete in the German adap-
tation of Thomas's poem, the *Tristan* of Gottfried von
Strassburg, who wrote about 1210.[2] A Norse prose
rendering of this version of the Tristram legend, writ-
ten in 1226, though much abridged, gives the whole
tale. There is also another form of this version in an
English poem, *Sir Tristrem*,[3] written by an unknown
author in the last decade of the thirteenth century,
which carries the story almost to the end. And Gott-
fried's incomplete poem received at least three contin-
uations, of which the two most important,[4] unlike the
poem which they concluded, follow the Béroul version
rather than that of Thomas.

The main incidents of the Tristram legend, as we
get them in the principal romances which tell the story,
are substantially the same. Tristram was the son of
the fair Blanchefleur, sister to King Mark of Cornwall,
and of a prince named Riwalin,[5] who, in the beauty
and strength of his youth, came to Mark's court from
some northern land not certainly identified. Tris-
tram's mother died at his birth, and, in several forms

[1] Cf. A. Bossert, *op. cit.* pp. 135 ff.; and Joseph Bédier, *Le Roman
de Tristan par Thomas*, 2 vols., Paris, 1902-05.

[2] Gottfried carried his poem just beyond the point at which the first
long Thomas fragment begins. He leaves Tristram pondering whether
he shall marry Iseult of Brittany.

[3] *Sir Tristrem*, edited by G. P. McNeill for the "Scottish Text
Society," 1886. The dialect of the poem is of the north of England or
the south of Scotland. Cf. A. H. Billings, *Middle English Metrical
Romances*, pp. 85 ff.

[4] The first of them was written by Ulrich von Türheim about 1240,
the second by Heinrich von Freiberg about 1300.

[5] The forms of this name vary in the different stories. It is Roland
in the English poem. According to Malory, it is Meliodas, and Mark's
sister is Elizabeth.

of the story, his father died before her.[1]   Tristram
was brought up, therefore, by a faithful baron of his
father's land, Roland, or in some of the French ro-
mances, Rual le Foi-tenant.   When Tristram had
grown to be a young man, he went to Cornwall,
where he made himself known to his uncle, whose
favorite he soon became.[2]

Just at this time an Irish warrior, Morolt, pre-
sented himself in Cornwall to exact the tribute which
Mark had been obliged to pay Ireland for years — a
tribute, like that which the Athenians in the story
of Theseus paid the Cretans, of youths and maidens,
whom Morolt[3] boastingly declared he would make his
slaves.   Tristram, thinking it shameful for Cornwall
to pay such tribute, challenged the Irish champion
to single combat.   If Tristram was defeated, the trib-
ute should be paid, as heretofore ; if Morolt was de-
feated, it should cease.   When the two met, Morolt
was slain by a wound in the head from his adversary's
sword, a piece of which remained in his skull, and
Tristram was so severely wounded that no leech or
surgeon could cure him.   Realising that poison from
the Irishman's weapon had got into his system, Tris-
tram decided at last to go to that country whence the
poison came, in the desperate hope that there, even
among the enemies of the Cornishmen, he might be
healed.   So he went to Ireland, giving himself out as a

[1] In the others, Tristram's father lives till Tristram is a grown
man.

[2] According to the Thomas version of the story, Tristram was car-
ried by Norwegian sailors, who had kidnapped him, to his mother's
country, Cornwall.   In the other version of the story, he went there
purposely to make himself known to his mother's brother, the king.

[3] His name is variously given.   Sometimes Morhalt, sometimes
Morold.   Marhaus is the name in Malory.

harper by the name of Tramtrist, — a disguise one would think sufficiently transparent — and soon attracted the attention of the Irish court by his harping, in which he excelled all men of his time. Queen Iseult of Ireland, who was skilled in medicine, and her daughter, the Princess Iseult, healed the strange harper; and then in return for their services the queen demanded that Tristram should give the princess music lessons. So Tristram did, with the result not uncommon when the teacher is a young man and the pupil a young woman. As Malory puts it, " Tramtrist cast great love to La Beale Isoud, for she was at that time the fairest maid and lady of the world. And there Tramtrist learned her to harp, and she began to have a great fancy unto him." [1] And then, feeling that it was dangerous to remain longer among the hostile Irish, and perhaps dangerous also to remain near La Beale Isoud, Tristram went back to his uncle's country.

He was destined soon [2] to make a second visit to Ireland. Mark, for reasons which vary according to different forms of the tale, [3] decided to take for his

[1] Malory, bk. viii, ch. 9. According to some older forms of the Béroul version, Tristram is healed without beholding the face of Iseult.

[2] The time varies according to the authors who tell the story.

[3] One story, manifestly of folk-tale source, was that a swallow one day flew to Mark's court with a hair in its bill of most brilliant gold. Mark declared then and there that he would marry the woman from whose head that hair came, and sent Tristram to seek her. She was Iseult.

The other story was that a few noblemen of Mark's court were jealous of Tristram, the king's nephew and favorite. Accordingly they wished Mark to have a son, so that Tristram might not inherit the throne. They wished, too, if possible, to get Tristram out of the world. They could think of no more dangerous mission than to send him to Ireland. So with a double purpose, they advised Mark to send Tristram to ask for the Princess Iseult in marriage.

wife this same Princess Iseult, famed far and wide for her beauty. He sent his nephew, accordingly, to persuade the princess to become queen of Cornwall — a mission fraught with danger on account of the law in Ireland that any Cornishman found there should be instantly put to death. And so Tristram went to Ireland again, this time disguised as a merchant. Fortune favored him in his mission, for he arrived when a dragon was devastating the land, a dragon so fierce that the king had promised that whoever killed him should have the hand of the beautiful maiden. Tristram, quite by himself, succeeded in slaying the monster, and then cut out the creature's tongue as proof of his achievement. But there was poison in the tongue ; and when Tristram wrapped it in his garments, the poison took away his strength, and he fell senseless by a spring which he had gone to for a drink of its cool waters.

Meantime the cowardly steward of the Irish king, who had hoped himself to win the hand of the princess, found the dragon dead, and cut his head off; and with that as proof of his daring, he presented himself at the court to claim the princess's hand. Both Princess Iseult and Queen Iseult felt sure that the craven could never have slain the dragon, and so they set out to find the real slayer, accompanied by the queen's favorite gentlewoman — in some forms of the story, kinswoman — Bragwaine.[1] They discovered a man lying by the spring, to their amazement no other than the minstrel Tramtrist, and restored him to consciousness by removing the tongue of the dragon from his

[1] Her name, like Morolt's, varies in the different forms of the story. Bragwaine is the form which Malory uses.

clothes. Then they took him to the palace and nursed him to recovery.

One day, during his agreeable convalescence, he came near losing his life. The princess drew his sword from the scabbard to clean it, and discovered a piece gone from it exactly like that which had been found in the skull of Morolt, the queen's brother, when his body was brought home from Cornwall. The princess thought first to kill her uncle's slayer, while he was weak and defenceless in his bath; but then she hesitated, apparently because she was already in love with him. Then the queen said that it would be foolish to slay the knight who alone stood between the Princess Iseult and the craven steward; and so, in the end, Tristram and the royal ladies swore peace.

When the day came for Iseult's hand to be awarded to the slayer of the dragon, the steward claimed it.

"What proof that thou didst slay the dragon?" asked the Irish king.

"Sire, this head," said the steward.

"Hold," said Tristram, "he hath spoken falsely. Bid thy men, Sire, open the dragon's jaws. They will not find the tongue in the mouth, for my squire hath it in that satchel. I cut it from the dragon's head, for I myself slew the dragon."

Thereupon the king's men opened the dragon's mouth and found no tongue; but Tristram's squire stepped forward with it, and it fitted into the mouth exactly, and the false steward was discredited. Then, to Iseult's regret, Tristram asked her hand, not for himself but for his uncle, King Mark, that there might be peace henceforth between Cornwall and Ireland. The Irish king granted Tristram's request, and said that, slayer of Morolt though he was, he should not suffer death, because he had freed Ireland from the dragon. Whether she would or no, the princess had to leave her own land, to marry a man whom she had never seen ; and her mother, fearing that the girl might give her love to Tristram, brewed a magic potion to be drunk by her and Mark on their wedding night, a potion of such effect that it should make the two forever after the fondest of lovers. This the queen entrusted to Bragwaine, who was to accompany the Princess Iseult to her new home.

The rest of the story is known to every one. As the vessel bearing the Irish princess was sailing over the sea to Cornwall, one hot day she and Tristram, being thirsty, sent an attendant for wine.[1] By accident the attendant brought the flask containing the magic potion. The knight and the princess drank, and the passion which they had mutually felt and concealed they now declared. Thenceforth Tristram and Iseult were bound in love, which could not cease, even after Iseult was married to Mark. It continued till all the court of Cornwall except Mark himself knew the truth. Finally even Mark was convinced of it, and Tristram was banished from the land. After various wanderings he came to Brittany,[2] where he found another Iseult, called Iseult of the White Hands, daughter to the duke of the country, a girl who reminded him

[1] Some forms of the story, including Malory's, make Tristram and Iseult find the wine themselves accidentally. Tristram says jestingly, "Madam Isoud, here is the best drink that ever ye drank, that dame Bragwaine your maiden, and Gouvernail my servant, have kept for themselves."

[2] Gottfried von Strassburg makes Arundel the land of Iseult of the White Hands.

faintly, and chiefly by her name, of Iseult of Ireland.
As Tristram was wont to sing lays in honor of his
own Iseult, with the refrain, —

> " Iseut ma drue, Iseut m'amie,
> En vous ma mort, en vous ma vie,"

no wonder the duke's daughter understood them as
composed in her honor and fell in love with him.
The result was that Tristram at last, scarce knowing
what he did, asked the hand of the girl in marriage.
But little happiness followed the bridal. Almost im-
mediately Tristram left his wife, and in time went
over to Cornwall to get stolen interviews with Iseult
of Ireland. Returning from one of his visits there,
he undertook an adventure in Brittany, — according
to one story, to help his brother-in-law in a love affair,
according to another to help a knight with his own
name of Tristram, — which proved to be his last. He
was wounded by a poisoned arrow; and feeling that
if anybody in the world could help him, it was Iseult
of Ireland, and that even if she could not, he must
see her before his death, he sent a trusty messenger [1]
with a ring, which she had given him for a token in
just such an emergency, begging her to come to him
in Brittany. Should the messenger bring Iseult back,
the ship's sails were to be white; should he not bring
her, they were to be black. Through accident, accord-
ing to some forms of the story, according to others,
through the malice of the jealous and injured Iseult
of Brittany, Tristram was told that the ship returned
with black sails. He turned over straightway and died ;
and Iseult of Ireland lived only long enough, after put-

[1] The messenger is frequently Tristram's brother-in-law.

ting foot on shore, to throw herself on Tristram's body.
Scarcely was she dead when Mark himself came in
haste, having learned at last through Bragwaine the
true story of the potion whose power had so long bound
the lovers. He had resolved to give up Iseult in favor
of Tristram ; but he came too late ; all he could do
was to take the bodies of the lovers back to Cornwall
and bury them in the royal chapel side by side.

Though all forms of the story are agreed in regard
to the main points, various forms differ in minor
details. The continuators, of Gottfried, for instance,
declare that a rose, planted by the tomb of one lover,
and a vine, planted by the tomb of the other, grew
towards one another till they intertwined affection-
ately.[1] And there is a pleasant little touch in the Eng-
lish *Sir Tristrem* which appears nowhere else. After
Tristram and Iseult drink the magic potion, they put
down the cup, which they have just drained, on the
deck ; and Tristram's faithful dog, Hodain, comes up
and licks it, and ever after is bound to his master
with a devotion unusual even in a favorite dog.

There are more important differences, running
through the various forms of the story, which divide
them, as a whole, into two groups or versions. One is
commonly called the Béroul version, from the name of
the writer who wrote the earliest form of it now extant;
the other, for a similar reason, is called the Thomas
version. The first important difference between the
two is that, according to Béroul, Tristram's native land
is Lyonesse, that unknown country of romance, with
which for most English readers he is forever associ-

---

[1] A similar miracle occurs in the ballad of *Lord Lovell*, and in
several other popular tales.

ated. In the Thomas version, on the other hand, it
is Ermonie, or as Gottfried von Strassburg calls it,
Parmenie, a land which, if we regard the middle syl-
lable as the root syllable of the word, is perhaps to
be identified with the Isle of Man.[1] Moreover, in the
Thomas version more is made of Tristram's childhood
than in the Béroul version ; and Tristram's father
dies while Tristram is still in his infancy, instead of
living to take a second wife, who in Malory becomes
the· devoted friend of her grown-up stepson. In the
Thomas version, too, the queen of Ireland plays a
more important part, though in each version it is she
who entrusts Bragwaine with the fateful potion. In the
Béroul version the power of this potion seems some-
what to abate in three or four years,[2] but in the Thomas

---

[1] Cf. W. H. Schofield, *The Story of Horn and Rimenhild, Publica-
tions of the Modern Language Association of America,* vol. xviii, No.
1, p. 25.

[2] Some commentators have written as if the power of the potion
came quite to an end, but one may argue, especially from certain
lines of Béroul in MS. 2171, that its power scarcely decreased appre-
ciably. Tristram seems anxious to renounce his forest life with Iseult
only on account of the hardships it brings on her. Cf. ll. 2179–2184
of Béroul : —

> " Et poise moi de la roïne,
> Qui je doins loge por cortine.
> En bois est, et si peüst estre
> En beles chanbres, o son estre,
> Portendues de dras de soie,
> Por moi a prise male voie."

In bidding Iseult farewell, Tristram declares ll. (2249–2250) : —

> " Roïne franche, ou que je soie,
> Vostres toz jors me clameroie."

And Iseult, in begging Tristram's dog, Hodain, as a last parting gift,
and in giving Tristram a ring, seems far from indifferent to him. Cf.
ll. 2696 ff. : —

> " Iseult parla o grant sospir :
> ' Tristran, entent un petitet :
> Husdent me lesse, ton brachet.
> Ainz berseret a veneor

version there is no hint that it diminishes in the least. Finally, and most important difference of all, in the Thomas version Mark is king of Cornwall and England; in the Béroul version Mark is king of Cornwall only, and one of the many tributary kings to the mighty Arthur. That is, in the Béroul version the Tristram legend is connected with the Arthur story; in the Thomas version, the legend is still independent. This fact shows beyond doubt that in this one respect the Thomas version preserves the older form of the story.[1]

About 1220 appeared a French Tristram romance in prose. It was attributed to a man named Élie de Boron, who called himself a relative of the famous Robert de Boron, but it is by no means certain that such a person as Élie ever existed. This prose romance, of

> Non ert gardé a tel honor
> Con cist sera, beaus douz amis.
> .   .   .   .
> Amis Tristran, j'ai I. anel:
> I. jaspe vert a u seel.
> Beau sire, por l'amor de moi,
> Portez l'anel en vostre doi;
> Et s'il vos vient, sire, a corage
> Que me mandez rien par mesage,
> Tant vos dirai, ce saciez bien,
> Certes, je n'en croiroie rien,
> Se cest anel, sire, ne voi.' "

But if she sees the ring, nothing shall prevent her from heeding Tristram's message. And so the two lovers exchange presents, and (ll. 2733–2734) —

> "Tristran en bese la roïne,
> Et ele lui par la saisine."

From all of which we may judge whether the power of the potion is exhausted or not.

The above quotations are from E. Muret's *Roman de Tristan par Béroul et un Anonyme*, Paris, 1903.

[1] Some indefinite Welsh association of Tristram with Arthur seems to have occurred pretty early, as the " Triads " show : i, 30; ii, 56; iii, 101. Cf. Professor Rhys, *Arthurian Legend*, pp. 12 and 378.

which very likely Chrétien's lost poem was an indirect
source, was made over and amplified more than twenty
times in the course of the thirteenth century. In these
amplifications the Tristram story came more and more
to be mixed with the other Arthurian stories, and
became popular in foreign countries. Thus Sir Thomas
Malory got a good deal of his material in the *Morte
Darthur* from the prose *Tristram* romances. Though
these follow the Béroul version more than the Thomas,
traces of the latter are to be found in them. In the
course of time, moreover, incidents got into them
which are not found in any early form, of the story.
For instance, the poetic tale of the death of the lov-
ers, through the mistake in the color of the sail, was
superseded by another which related that Mark killed
Tristram treacherously as the knight sat harping before
Iseult, and that Iseult herself died in a swoon upon
her lover's corpse.

Gaston Paris [1] thinks that *Tristram* more than
any other of the principal Arthurian stories shows its
Celtic origin. Important names, like Tristram and
Mark,[2] are Celtic : the former apparently Pictish, the
latter related to the word for horse in all Celtic tongues
— a fact to be in some way connected with the strange
story told by Béroul that Mark had horse's ears, which
he concealed under his long hair. The lands, likewise,
which are the scene of action — Cornwall, Ireland,
South Wales, Ermonie (which may be Man, or An-
glesey, Mona) and Brittany — are all Celtic. It is
scarcely to be supposed that they would be prominent

[1] *Tristan et Iseut*, Paris, 1894, *Extrait de la Revue de Paris du 15
Avril 1904*, pp. 9 ff. ; published also in *Poèmes et Légendes du Moyen-
Age*, Paris, 1900, pp. 113 ff.

[2] The more correct though the less common spelling is Marc.

in a story invented by a Frenchman, who knew his
Celtic coasts only at second hand. Then, too, the
barbarous state of society sometimes portrayed points
to Celtic sources. Tristram, in order to arrange meet-
ings with Iseult, sends chips as signals floating down
a brook, which in some of the earliest forms of the
legend seems to flow through her apartment. When
Tristram kills one of the treacherous barons who spy
upon him, hoping to surprise him with Iseult, he cuts
off two braids of hair, that hang on either side of the
baron's face, as trophies, and shows them proudly to
Iseult, who rejoices at the sight. Moreover, Tristram,
unlike a French noble, has no favorite horse, but, like
a Celtic chieftain, a favorite dog. Like a Celtic chief-
tain, too, he possesses wonderful skill as a harper.
And when the two lovers, banished from the court, flee
together into the woods, where for a time they lead an
idyllic life, it is a rough hut of branches, or a grotto,
in which they live. If a French poet of the twelfth
century had conceived the story, Paris observes, he
would have invented a remote, deserted manor in the
forest, which the lovers might come upon ; and sure
enough, in Malory's fifteenth-century version, they do
find " a fair manor," [1] in which they pass their time.

The characters, too, are strangely savage in their
feelings, even for mediæval romance. Mark, seemingly
without the least compunction, beheads the dwarf who
has rendered him conspicuous service, merely because
the dwarf has betrayed the secret that the king has
horse's ears. Even more incredibly cold-blooded is
Iseult's decision to have Bragwaine killed because that
gentlewoman knows so much which should not be di-

[1] Malory, viii, ch. 35.

vulged. From the first, Bragwaine has been the confidante of the lovers; and on Iseult's wedding night she sacrificed herself for her royal mistress, laying herself down, after the lights were carried out, a maid, by Mark's side in place of Iseult, who was a maid no longer. No other wrong she did Iseult, Bragwaine declares to the two men who lead her to a wood, following Iseult's commands to kill Bragwaine. " My lady and I had two smocks," she says, " snow-white. My lady's was soiled, and for her wedding night I lent her mine all clean." Touched by her beauty and her pleading, the men spare Bragwaine, much to Iseult's joy, who, with the caprices of a barbarous princess, hardly orders Bragwaine murdered before she repents of the command.

From all this it would seem that the story of *Tristram and Iseult* grew up in some Celtic region of Britain, possibly in Cornwall. And there are signs, apart from the localisation of so much of the story in Britain, which seem to indicate that it came into French verse through an English medium. Such are the words " gotelef," that is, honeysuckle, in a *lai* on Tristram written by Marie de France, and " lovendrenc" or " lovendranc," [1] meaning love potion, in the fragmentary poem of Béroul.

The story of Tristram and Iseult, quite as much as that of the Holy Grail, and certainly more than any of the other Arthurian legends, has profoundly impressed human imagination. One reason is its poetry, espe-

---

[1] The words for this in the poem of Béroul, E. Muret's edition, Paris, 1903, are " loucvendris " (l. 2138) and " lovendrant " (l. 2159). According to the glossary, the former is a corruption of " lovendrincs " or " lovendrencs," the nominative of " lovendrene " or " lovendrent."

cially that of the beginning, the poetry which symbol-
ises the mystery of the sea together with the mystery
of love, felt through the ages in the love potion; a
poetry so real that Tennyson, in his version of the Ar-
thurian legends, made the excuse for his lovers, Lance-
lot and Guinevere, virtually the same as that of Tris-
tram and Iseult. As the mystery of the sea brought
the Cornish prince and the Irish princess together be-
fore she had ever seen the man whose bride she was to
be, so before Guinevere had looked on Arthur to dis-
tinguish him from other men, she rode with Lancelot,
sent to fetch her to Arthur's court, through the magi-
cal, flowering spring; and so, through the witchery of
that fair season, they felt the witchery of love.

But there is more than this poetry which makes
Tristram remarkable among the Arthurian legends,
for none of them is without poetry. The Tristram
legend has impressed the imagination of centuries be-
cause in it, for the first time, romantic love [1] is the
central theme of a long story. Love, to be sure, comes
frequently into the great poems of classical antiquity;
and sometimes, as in the tragic stories of Antigone of
Thebes and Dido of Carthage, especially the latter, it
is romantic love. But the story of Dido is only an epi-
sode in the *Æneid ;* and the love of Antigone was less
important in the eyes of Sophocles than her sisterly
devotion. In no long story of classical antiquity is love
the chief interest, nor of the Middle Ages before *Tris-
tram.* True, we find love often the central theme in
the *lais ;* but the *lais* are all short, not longer, in most
cases, than the chapters, or episodes, which make up
the romances. In the great Germanic epic of *Sieg-*

[1] Cf. G. Paris, *Tristan et Iseult*, Paris, 1894, i.

fried, the theme is vengeance rather than love. It is in *Tristram* for the first time that love is the moving power of a long story.

A very animal passion it is, to be sure, in the earliest forms of the story, quite different from the courtly love of Lancelot and Guinevere. Arthur's Queen, in her love adventures, almost never appears in an undignified and unqueenly light; Iseult's adventures with Tristram, on the contrary, are often as broadly farcical as those in the coarsest mediæval *fabliaux*. So they are, for instance, in a curious French poem, *Le Donnei des Amants*, of the late thirteenth or early fourteenth century,[1] which relates that the poet went to walk one summer morning in his bare feet through the dewy grass for the sake of his health, thus showing himself a convert to the "Kneipp cure" of recent years five or six centuries ago. As he walked, he overheard a young man talking to the lady of his love, and he was not above eavesdropping. Since the lady was not willing to grant her favors, the young man recounted various persuasive instances of ladies who gave all for love, among them one in the history of Tristram and Iseult which might well have existed independently in the form of a *lai*. Iseult, sleeping one night in Mark's court, heard a nightingale singing outside, which by the intuition of love she knew at once to be Tristram, who had the power of imitating all the birds in the forest. She rose, accordingly, found the ten knights who were guarding her sound asleep, and was just slipping through the door, when the mischievous and always troublesome dwarf of Mark's court discovered her. After some argument,

[1] *Romania*, vol. xxv, pp. 497 ff.

since he continued to block her way, Iseult, with
strength which the most athletic " new woman " might
envy, gave him a blow that stretched him on the floor
and knocked out four of his teeth. The noise natu-
rally roused the whole court, who discovered Iseult in
her nightdress, slightly dishevelled by her sparring-
match. After hearing both sides of the story, Mark,
gullible as always, told the dwarf that his suspicions
were nonsense, that Tristram was nowhere in the coun-
try, and that the Queen should walk in the garden
if she pleased. And so Iseult passed on to the arms
of her expectant lover.

In others of the love-episodes, there is even more
horse-play and coarseness than here. They are full of
such adventures as very properly befall muleteers and
kitchen wenches in *Don Quixote*, or the robust trav-
ellers who put up at English inns in eighteenth-cen-
tury novels. Throughout the stories, moreover, there
is entire lack of moral feeling. Sometimes even the
Deity winks at the trickery of the lovers, as in the
chastity test to which Iseult [1] is subjected. She is to
swear before the bishops of England and the court of
Cornwall that no man except Mark has ever had her
in his arms. Then she is to take hold of hot irons,
which, unless she has told the truth, will burn her
hands to the bone. The place appointed for the test is
Caerleon, whither Iseult goes by boat. She has written
to Tristram to meet her at the shore, disguised as a
pilgrim from the Holy Land, and as the boat makes
fast, she points to him and says that she will be car-
ried ashore by no one except the holy man yonder. No
sooner has Tristram taken her in his arms than she

[1] This occurs in most forms of the story.

whispers to him to trip when he gets beyond the mud. He does so, and for a minute or two Tristram and Iseult lie side by side. Then when she is ready to take the oath, she says : " I should be foolish to say that no man save Mark has had me in his arms, for you have just seen that I have been in this holy man's and have lain by his side ; but truly I have lain in no other man's arms save my husband's." Then she takes the hot irons, and her hands are not burned.

Yet with all the immorality of it, with all the grossness of many of the adventures, the story of Tristram and Iseult is not degrading, for theirs was a love ever capable of sacrifices. One instance, somewhat childish though it be, is enough to show how each was always ready to give up happiness for the sake of the other. Tristram in South Wales became the owner of a little fairy dog named Petit-Criu, — his coat, of changing colors, red, green, and blue, softer than silk, — with a little bell on his neck of such power that whenever it rang, sadness passed from every one within hearing. Tristram therefore decided at once to send this dog with the magic bell to Iseult, whom he knew to be sorrowing for him. She received the dog, heard the bell ring, and felt her sorrows go from her ; but then she thought of Tristram, sorrowing apart from her, and she threw the bell into the sea.

And at the last nothing can be finer than Iseult's unselfish readiness to go to Tristram on receiving the message from his sick-bed. Without stopping to change her garments, with never a thought of what men may say, or of what danger may ensue, she leaves the lights and the warmth of the royal hall, and in the scourging midnight rain hurries down from the rock of Tintagel to the ship that has borne Tristram's messenger, and sets out on the stormy sea for Brittany. The account of her landing there, as Eilhart von Oberge gives it, just too late to see Tristram again in life, is impressive in its simplicity.

"Then, when the queen came ashore and heard the great lamentation, her grief was heavy. 'Alas!' she said, 'woe is me! Tristram is dead.' But she turned neither red nor white, nor wept any more, though in her heart was great woe. Hear now what she did. Silently she went to the chamber where the knight lay on his bier. And close by stood his wife, who wept and lamented sorely. The queen said to her : 'Lady, thou shouldst stand aside, and let me come nearer : I have better cause to weep than thou, that mayest thou well believe. He was dearer to me than ever he was to thee.'

"With that she turned back the covering that was on the bier, and pushed Tristram's body a little farther over. Then she sat down by the knight, and spake never a word more, but laid herself close beside him and was dead." [1]

A recent writer, Mr. Lauriston Ward, in the *Harvard Monthly*,[2] a Harvard undergraduate magazine, has caught the spirit of this self-sacrificing love so accurately in a little poem, *Tristan* [3] *in Brittany*, that I take the liberty of quoting the greater part of it. As Tristram tosses on his bed, longing to hear whether the ship from Cornwall will show a black sail or a white, he muses and dreams, —

[1] Eilhart v. Oberge, *Quellen und Forschungen*, xix, ll. 9417 ff.

[2] March, 1902.

[3] It is to be wished that Mr. Ward had translated the name of his hero into the English form, Tristram.

"The fire waxes hotter in my veins,
  The restless soul tugs at the tortured body,
  Fretful to leave — around me falls the dark.

  O Mark, you have your will — Iseult is yours.
Sweet be the strained joy you get of her!
Sweet be the loveless kisses from those lips
That once took fire at mine! Sweet be the thoughts
Of that dark goblet, and the draught it held,
And all the after days!

  Yours is the triumph, yet not all the triumph.
The slow years hasten, and your life's spent torch
Flares to the socket. Think you after death
To keep Iseult? No, by the Holy Rood!

  For when my breath is sped, my struggle done,
My fevered clay securely housed at last,
To rest in unforgetful quietness —
Then shall my fair soul take its upward flight
To the blue towers and courts of Paradise.
And my great love shall make me unafraid,
Though I rise like wafted incense through the air
Tremulous with aureoles of adoring saints,
And hear the everlasting anthems swell,
Where Michael and the countless hosts of Heaven
Praise God continually. Onward through the throng
Shall I press fearless, as befits a knight,
Until I reach the Blessed Virgin's throne.
There, kneeling, shall I kiss the broidered hem
Of her bright robe, and humbly pray forgiveness —
Begging her for the love of her dear Son,
When he was crucified, to have compassion
On us, who sinned by reason of our great love.

  And she shall hear me there and raise me up,
Saying 'Sir Tristan' (and her voice will be
Like cloister bells for sweetness), 'Tristan, rise.
Were your sins great as Heaven, yet your love,
Being greater still, should burn your guilt away.'"

This is after all the essence of the story, that the love of Tristram and Iseult was great enough and steady enough to burn their guilt away. This it is which has made the wild Celtic tale of passion, immoral and barbarous, into a love-romance that is immortal.

XI

THE MOULDING OF THE LEGENDS

THUS there are five stories which make up the great mass of Arthurian romance as we to-day know it — the hero-story of Arthur himself in the pseudo-chronicles; the story of Mage Merlin, "assotted" at last and doating on a damsel of the lake;[1] the story of Lancelot, "the truest lover . . . that ever loved woman;"[2] the story of the Grail, illumined with mystic, holy light; and the story of Tristram and Iseult, the first great love-story of the world. We have seen that these and tales of lesser import clustered about a British chieftain of the fifth and sixth centuries, who, becoming a national hero, attracted to himself stories from all sources, but chiefly from British or Irish, till he was known over Europe as the greatest king of romance. We have seen that Geoffrey of Monmouth was the first to tell at length in literature the story of the great King. But we have not seen why men of letters told it first in the twelfth century rather than in the eleventh or the thirteenth; nor have we considered how much we are indebted to the French for fixing the Arthurian legends in the permanent literature of the world.

One great reason why these became popular with poets just when they did was the Norman Conquest,

[1] Malory, bk. iv, ch. 1.   [2] *Ibid.*, bk. xxi, ch. 13.

whose part in making the legends imperishable is clearly shown by that zealous student of folk-lore and mediæval romance, Mr. Alfred Nutt. Among the great and varied issues of the Conquest, he says, " most important from the standpoint of general European literature have been the rise of a sixth-century Roman-British chieftain to the type and model of Christian heroic achievement, the coalescence and flowering of a mass of Celtic fairy-tales into one of those supreme legends in which mankind sums up and sets forth its ideal.

" The Conquest, which left the Duke of Normandy vassal to the King of France whilst it gave him a position of equal power and influence, contained all the germs of the secular rivalry of the two countries, a rivalry which only began when England, ceasing for a time to be English, became, as far as literary and social ideas were concerned, French. The new race of kings must needs have its own heroic legend, its *Matière de Bretagne* to rival the *Matière de France*, full as that was of the glory and might of old-time rulers of France. The Arthur legend lay ready to hand. It was welcomed much as the new family might welcome the old portraits, long relegated to the attics, of a yet earlier race than the one it had dispossessed, a race in connection with which it might seek other title-deeds than those of force. And as French rulers of England were among the foremost personalities of the twelfth century, the body of imaginative literature which they patronised was bound, on that score alone, to flourish and prosper." [1]

[1] *Celtic and Mediæval Romance*, by Alfred Nutt, London, 1899, pp. 11–12.

Even without the Norman Conquest, French litera-
ture must have inclined to the stories of Arthur; its
older romances were too rough for polite society of the
twelfth century. As James Russell Lowell says in his
essay on Chaucer, " who, after reading the *Chansons
de Geste* — even the best of them, the *Song of Roland*
— can remember much more than a cloud of battle
dust, through which the paladins loom dimly gigantic,
and a strong verse flashes here and there like an angry
sword ? " Such martial tales could no longer satisfy
French society, for now, as Mr. Nutt says further,[1]
" the patronage of literature was abruptly shifted from
the one sex to the other. The poet no longer sang
solely for men, but mainly for women. In the early
part of the century changes in feudal custom granted
to women the rights and privileges of feudal inherit-
ance, and thereby made the heiress a factor of first-
rate importance in the social and political life of the
times. The student of twelfth-century England needs
only to recall the *rôle* of Matilda and of Eleanor of
Aquitaine. The material and moral enhancement in
the status of the great heiresses reacted upon that of
all women of the aristocratic class. Throughout the
century we find women among the most powerful and
influential patrons of certain kinds of literature; we
find them, too, actively promoting an attempt to reor-
ganise social life and social morality in accordance
with the ideals set forth in the literature they favoured.
Here . . . the Crusades were a contributory cause.
When the husband was away, it might be for years,
fighting the Paynim, power and influence fell to the
stay-at-home wife; nor, human nature being what it

[1] *Celtic and Mediæval Romance*, pp. 16–18.

is, can it be subject for astonishment that prolonged
absence led frequently to mutual infidelity, the very
circumstances of which would tend to heighten and
diversify the emotions of love and the modes through
which they are manifested. For the husband's lady-
love would often be a daughter of that older, mysteri-
ous civilisation with which he was brought into con-
tact, a civilisation which had systematised love between
the sexes into an inextricable blend of animalism, legal
pedantry, and mysticism ; whilst the wife's lover might
be a cleric, with whom love had the attraction of the
forbidden, or a minstrel, or one of the pages or knights
of her household, her inferior, therefore, in station,
wealth, or knowledge of life.

"Thus a new literature was inevitable, and, equally
inevitably, it had to possess certain characteristics.
It had to be distinct from the *Matière de France ;* it
had to recognise the change in the circumstances of
Christendom and to cease harping upon feelings that
were partly outworn ; it had to take into account
the new ideal of adventurous knighthood ; it had to
give full prominence to the elements of mystery and
sorcery ; above all, it had to please women and to
give expression to a new conception of the relations
between the sexes.

"These requirements were fulfilled by the French
Arthurian romance . . . because the older Celtic
legends out of which that romance grew contained in
germ all the elements which the twelfth century de-
manded and which it could have found nowhere else.
The Celtic genius was reincarnated in twelfth-century
France because the times were favourable ; it took
the world by storm because it contained incidents,

personages, traits of feeling and character which were susceptible of embodying the most perfect form of the twelfth-century ideal."

In order to do so, however, the Celtic genius had to suffer considerable modification. When established in the highest favor among the French and the Normans, it had materially changed its form.

We have already seen that so far as the French altered the Celtic personages whom they borrowed for their romances, they made them men and women of their own time. Strange antiquated figures, sometimes almost monstrous, of Celtic fable or history, or it might be even of mythology, emerged from the French rejuvenating cauldron rationalised enough, but not too much, to live for centuries with readers to whom reason does not mean everything; and the more the French worked the stories over, the more contemporary they made the setting for these figures. Thus the earliest Tristram fragments, which probably represent a stage of French adaptation nearer to Celtic sources than most romances, show a correspondingly more barbarous, British state of society than the poems of Chrétien and of Robert de Boron. These, based probably on earlier French romances now lost, represent a stage of adaptation more remote from Celtic sources, and make Arthur's court one which might have existed at the time in either London or Paris.

Then the French modified the geography, probably already confused, of the stories they borrowed. They carried Arthur and his knights to places which the Celtic prototypes of these heroes had never known, and they made his capitals and castles French or

Anglo-Norman. In the places which they chose thus to make over, one may see proof again that the insular contribution of the Arthurian legends was greater than the continental. Arthurian geography, so far as it is fixed, seems to show that the French picked up the greater number of Celtic stories, which they appropriated, in the island of Britain, and most of the others in Brittany. Nearly all the Arthurian places of importance may be included in one of two classes — those of note historically in twelfth-century England, or earlier in Celtic lands; and those, either in Celtic lands or in England, of poetic or legendary interest.

Arthur's principal capitals among notable places of English history are London, the chief city of the Norman kings; Lincoln and York, both seats of church dignitaries and towns of consideration even in Roman times; Winchester, the ancient capital of the West Saxon monarchs; Chester, an old Roman town, later strongly fortified to overawe the turbulent Welsh; and Carlisle — in French, Carduel — in the extreme north-west of Cumberland, founded by William Rufus as a bulwark against the Scots. Of Arthur's capitals in Celtic lands, the most important are Nantes, for a time the capital of Brittany; Cardigan, among the Welsh hills looking out to the waters of Cardigan Bay; and Caerleon, a wealthy British city in the later Roman days, subsequently the see of a bishop, and widely known in Welsh history and tradition. Apart from these associations, Caerleon might have won a name for itself in poetry on account of its picturesque site on the muddy Usk, where it twists down from the Welsh mountains through a fair wooded valley, to join the " yellow sea "[1] of Severn, four miles below the town.[2]

Other important Arthurian places are known almost all for their appeal to poetic or legendary imagination. Most famous of them on the Continent is the enchanted Forest of Broceliande in Brittany, gloomy now, as when Chrétien wrote, with its ancient thorn-trees — the forest where Ivein came to the fountain of Barenton, whose water, dashed on the stone near by, instantly caused a terrific storm of rain and hail and wind and lightning. No wonder that belief in the rain-making property of the fountain lasted long among the Breton peasants. The Atlantic makes the climate of Broceliande so moist that still a dash of Barenton water on the stone is as likely, as in Ivein's time, to be followed by rain within a few hours.

Justly prominent among the more poetic Arthurian places in Britain is Lancelot's castle of Joyous Gard, most often identified with Bamborough Castle in Northumberland. Bamborough, though not famous in British story, because from the earliest Angle settlement it was never held by the Britons, is so situated that few places on the eastern coast would be more likely to impress English or Anglo-Norman poets. High on its bare rock, it looks south and west over a flat, wind-swept, almost treeless country ; north and east it looks out to sea. The power and chill of northern seas are everywhere; hardly in mid-Atlantic do

[1] Tennyson, *The Marriage of Geraint*, l. 829, and elsewhere in the *Idylls*.

[2] Many of these cities Geoffrey of Monmouth makes important. Cf. ch. iii, p. 41, of this book.

[3] Joyous Gard is sometimes identified with the Duke of Northumberland's imposing Alnwick Castle.

you feel them more. The surf pounds on the beach; and in the little village at the back of the castle, and in the little churchyard where Grace Darling lies, the scraggy trees are all bent in the same direction by the sea-winds. From the pleasaunce you see nothing but the gray German Ocean; and as you stand there, you wonder why the old romancers named the place Joyous Gard; you would have to be in very merry company, or a love-sick Tristram just fled hither to Lancelot's hospitality with your Iseult, to think it other than Bleak Gard.

Glastonbury, famed as the spot to which Joseph of Arimathea carried the Holy Grail, and sometimes said to be the burial-place of Arthur, owes its celebrity to tradition and situation both. Its church is said to have been one of the three ancient British churches — the other two were Amesbury and Bangor — in which there was continuous service. Hence its holy name.[1] It is also the most conspicuous place in middle Somerset, for the town stands on the northwest slope of a group of hills culminating in the steep Glastonbury Tor, a landmark for miles around. Except for a little space toward the east, where the land rises a few feet higher than on the other sides, and where the railway now comes, the hills and the town of Glastonbury are encircled by rich, level meadows, crossed by hedges and ditches and dotted with trees. At varying distances beyond the smooth green fields rise hills of varying height, except where the flat country stretches like a floor northwest to the Bristol Channel. Sometimes in winter the meadows are still covered by water;

[1] Glastonbury may have been sacred in pagan times. Cf. ch. viii, p. 129, n.

and years ago, when they were unreclaimed marsh-
land, they were covered so often that Glastonbury was
frequently almost an island. Partly from this fact, as
we have seen,[1] came its confusion with Avalon; and one
can imagine that without modern engines of warfare
it would have been an excellent place for Melwas to
stand a siege after carrying off Guinevere.

A short twenty miles southeast of Glastonbury,
there rises abruptly from the garden-like country of
Somerset, over the little village of South Cadbury, the
steep hill called Cadbury Castle. Strong by nature, it
was made stronger years ago by fortifications. The top,
a level space of about thirty acres, was surrounded by
four walls of earth and brown stone, still in places dis-
tinctly marked, and outside of each wall a deep ditch,
the whole forming a rough parallelogram, not so reg-
ular as that of a Roman camp, but curving a little to
conform to the configuration of the hilltop. Whether
or not the place actually was a Roman camp, as local
tradition has it, there is no doubt that it was a Brit-
ish fort, which the Britons must have found of great
service in resisting the Saxons; and it may have been
the scene of a fierce battle, perhaps of a British victory,
which lived in British legend. Now the best identifi-
cation of romantic Camelot [2] is with Cadbury Castle;

[1] Cf. ch. vii, p. 94.

[2] We have seen (ch. vii) that there seems to be no earlier men-
tion of Camelot than in Chrétien's *Charrette*. This of all Arthur's
capitals has the least certainly been identified. Professor Wendelin
Foerster unhesitatingly accepts the identification, which on the whole
seems most likely, with Cadbury Castle in Somerset. Cf. Sir Edward
Strachey's edition of the *Morte Darthur*, Introduction, p. xvi. So far
as known, the name Camelot appears in mediæval romance only in
certain French romances, and in the *Green Knight* and Malory's *Morte
Darthur*.

and therefore its poetic fame may rest, like Arthur's, on historical foundation. Needless to say, however, the Camelot of literature is purely fictitious. The real Camelot, if at Cadbury, could have been nothing but a fort, and never a many-towered city with palaces and churches and a river close by, down which Ladies of Shalott might float.

Finally, on the Cornish coast is that remarkable promontory, Tintagel. As you drive towards it from the railway station, you wonder why poets should have celebrated the place, for the Cornish country, rolling in low hills crossed by hedges and stone walls, is treeless, desolate, unfriendly ; but when you come to the sea, all is poetic. You walk down a steep little " combe " between the cliffs to the very edge of the water, and before you, almost an island, is the great rock of Tintagel. From the chasm which parts it from the mainland cliff, you follow a rough path up its precipitous sides to a gate in what little remains of the old castle wall; and passing through that to the grassy, uneven plateau of Tintagel Head, you feel for the moment alone with the sea. On three sides it stretches before you ; the air is charged with its salt smell and cool breath. Then, turning to the north, you see far off the Isle of Lundy, light blue. Beyond it, a mistier blue, the Devon coast runs out in a long point. Nearer are the dark Cornish cliffs, with the sea washing and breaking below them, always more distinct in color and outline as the eye follows them from the distance to the deep chasm between the Head and the mainland ; and then to the southwest, the cliffs again, now curving inward round a bay, then thrusting out to a bare headland, with here and there a needle-rock rising from the sea in front of them, to mark where the headlands once reached. There is no sound but the breaking of the waves — a swish and a roar — never-ceasing, and the occasional screech of a gull, or, if the breeze is from the land, the cawing of rooks.

Stupendous as Tintagel is in storm, loud with wind and wave, and dark with mist and driving rain, you must see it on a bright day if you will feel its peculiar charm, which lies in color. Probably there is no place in the British Isles where color will impress you more. Landward, the greenish brown fields, sprinkled plentifully with yellow gorse, and occasionally a little patch of purple heather. Then the line of the slaty cliffs, black, brown, or gray — sometimes dark purple in shadow, and in the full sunlight, olive green or lilac. And below them, the surf-edged Cornish sea — against it here and there a white sail or a gull — shades from deep, dark blues to lighter blues, brilliant as tropical waters, which turn to lavender when the clouds pass over the sun, and change in the coves to opal green, always with a heaving lace-work of white, where the foam flows back from the breakers at the foot of the crags.

These are the places, all in one way or another stirring the imagination, that figure most prominently in the Arthurian legends. Others which appear, whether of historical, legendary, or poetic interest, are less important, probably because less known to the Cymric Celts. And yet several of them deserved the wider celebrity which they might have enjoyed had they been better known, as Dublin, Iseult's birthplace, on the quiet Liffey near Dublin Bay, with bold Howth Head to the north, and away to the south,

beyond green shores, the graceful Wicklow Hills.
Still less known places figuring in the Tristram ro-
mances are the shadowy Ermonie, Tristram's native
land in one version of the legend; and in the other,
the even more shadowy Lyonesse, probably never any-
thing but a realm of romance.

Though all these give us enough real geography to
point to the sources of the stories, yet, as we might
expect of writers who seldom or never knew at first-
hand the places which they named, the French have
altogether confused their geography. Erec's father, for
instance, in Chrétien's *Érec*, is the king of Outregalles,
a part of Wales, but his capital is Nantes in Brittany.
Ivein finds it an easy ride from Carlisle in Cumber-
land [1] to the Breton forest of Broceliande. In the
Chevalier de la Charrette, it is not such a very long
journey from Camelot to the land whence no man
returns.[2] And in most of the romances, a few hours
from the palace of Arthur, wherever at the time he
may be holding court, will bring a knight to enchanted
castles and mysterious forests full of giants, robbers,
dragons, and what not, of all of which neither Arthur
nor the knight has ever heard.

So the French considerably modified the people and
the places of the legends which they made their own;
and to the original people and places they added many
that were new. Incidents, too, they changed, though
not so much, inclining on the whole to rationalise
them; and they added many from non-Celtic sources.

---

[1] " An Gales," Chrétien says in the seventh line of *Ivein*.

[2] This land, called by Chrétien Gorre, Professor Rhys, *Arthurian
Legend*, pp. 329 ff., identifies with the peninsula of Gower in Glamor-
ganshire. If Camelot is South Cadbury, the journey would not be so
very great, though longer than Chrétien makes it.

But they did not add to the poetry of the old stories, for they could not. What they did was to put them into something less remote from classical form, showing sensitiveness alike to form in detail, for their verse is almost invariably smooth, and to form in a larger way, for in a measure, but not sufficiently, the French authors bridged the gaps of the folk-tales which came to them and cut out irrelevant matter. French sense of proportion and French clarity made the old stories more coherent, more reasonable, more intelligible than they had been before, with the result that the romances, though never quite without irrelevant material, and at their worst exceedingly jumbled, are at their best good compositions, and some of the *lais* have taken a form which is final. There are, then, two very important contributions which the French made to the old Celtic tales. They gave them a contemporary setting and they gave them literary form; that is, in polished, courtly verse they related stories made fairly organic which pictured feudal society with some vividness.

In order to see what the Arthurian stories would have remained, had they not been reincarnated among the French and the Normans, it is necessary only to look at the *Mabinogion*,[1] a collection of mediæval

[1] The name *Mabinogion*, as applied to the whole collection, is a misnomer. There are only four tales to which it properly belongs: *Pwyll, Prince of Dyved ; Branwen, the Daughter of Llyr ; Manawyddan, the Son of Llyr ; Math, the Son of Mathonwy*. The name *Mabinogion* has been commonly misunderstood. It was thought after Lady Charlotte Guest's translation to mean a collection of fairy-tales. As a matter of fact, it means the stories which in mediæval Wales were given to a bard's apprentice to work over. Mabinog was Welsh for a would-be bard, a young man studying with a bard for his master, Mabinogi meant the material given to such an apprentice for practice, and Mabinogion is the plural of Mabinogi.

Welsh tales delightfully translated by Lady Charlotte Guest.[1] One of the most charming of them, and the most important Arthurian story in Welsh virtually untouched by French influence, is *Kilhwch and Olwen*. The hero, Kilhwch, Arthur's cousin, is in love with the damsel Olwen, to win whose hand he seeks the aid of Arthur and his knights. One of the prettiest and most fanciful parts of the story is that which recounts the young man's ride from his home to Arthur's castle.

"And the youth pricked forth upon a steed with head dappled grey, of four winters old, firm of limb, with shell-formed hoofs, having a bridle of linked gold on his head, and upon him a saddle of costly gold. And in the youth's hand were two spears of silver, sharp, well-tempered, headed with steel, three ells in length, of an edge to wound the wind, and cause blood to flow, and swifter than the fall of the dewdrop from the blade of reed-grass upon the earth when the dew of June is at the heaviest. A gold-hilted sword was upon his thigh, the blade of which was of gold, bearing a cross of inlaid gold of the hue of the lightning of heaven; his war-horn was of ivory. Before him were two brindled white-breasted greyhounds, having strong collars of rubies about their necks, reaching from the shoulder to the ear. And the one that was on the left side bounded across to the right side, and the one on the right to the left, and like two sea-swallows sported around him. And his courser cast up four sods with his four hoofs, like four swallows in the air, about his head, now above, now below. About him was a four-cornered cloth of purple, and an apple of gold was at each corner, and every one of the apples was of the value of an hundred kine. And there was precious gold of the value

---

[1] Lady Charlotte Guest made her translation in 1838. The tales with one exception — *Taliesin* — are from *The Red Book of Hergest*, a fourteenth-century manuscript. Older forms of many of them exist.

of three hundred kine upon his shoes, and upon his stirrups, from his knee to the tip of his toe. And the blade of grass bent not beneath him, so light was his courser's tread as he journeyed towards the gate of Arthur's Palace.

"Spoke the youth, 'Is there a porter?' 'There is; and if thou holdest not thy peace, small will be thy welcome. I am Arthur's porter every first day of January. And during every other part of the year but this, the office is filled by Huandaw [1] and Gogigwc, and Llaeskenym, and Pennping-yon, [2] who goes upon his head to save his feet, neither towards the sky nor towards the earth, but like a rolling stone upon the floor of the court.' 'Open the portal.' 'I will not open it.' 'Wherefore not?' 'The knife is in the meat, and the drink is in the horn, and there is revelry in Arthur's hall, and none may enter therein but the son of a king of a priv-ileged country, or a craftsman bringing his craft. But there will be refreshment for thy dogs and for thy horses; and for thee there will be collops cooked and peppered, and lus-cious wine and mirthful songs, and food for fifty men shall be brought unto thee in the guest-chamber, where the stran-ger and the sons of other countries eat, who come not unto the precincts of the Palace of Arthur. Thou wilt fare no worse there than thou wouldest with Arthur in the Court. A lady shall smooth thy couch, and shall lull thee with songs; and early to-morrow morning, when the gate is open for the multitude that came hither to-day, for thee shall it be opened first, and thou mayest sit in the place that thou shalt choose in Arthur's Hall, from the upper end to the lower.' Said the youth, 'That will I not do. If thou open-est the gate, it is well. If thou dost not open it, I will bring disgrace upon thy Lord, and evil report upon thee. And I will set up three shouts at this very gate, than which none were ever more deadly, from the top of Pengwaed in Corn-wall to the bottom of Dinsol, in the North, and to Esgair Oervel, in Ireland. And all the women in this palace that are pregnant shall lose their offspring; and such as are not

[1] Sharp-Eared.   [2] Horny-Head.

pregnant, their hearts shall be turned by illness, so that they shall never bear children from this day forward.' ' What clamour soever thou mayest make,' said Glewlwyd Gavaelvawr, ' against the laws of Arthur's Palace shalt thou not enter therein, until I first go and speak with Arthur.'

" Then Glewlwyd went into the hall. And Arthur said to him, ' Hast thou news from the gate? ' — ' Half of my life is past, and half of thine. I was heretofore in Kaer Se and Asse, in Sach and Salach, in Lotor and Fotor; and I have been heretofore in India the Great and India the Lesser; and I was in the battle of Dau Ynyr, when the twelve hostages were brought from Llychlyn. And I have also been in Europe, and in Africa, and in the islands of Corsica, and in Caer Brythwch, and Brythach, and Verthach; and I was present when formerly thou didst slay the family of Clis the son of Merin, and when thou didst slay Mil Du the son of Ducum, and when thou didst conquer Greece in the East. And I have been in Caer Oeth and Annoeth, and in Caer Nevenhyr; nine supreme sovereigns, handsome men, saw we there, but never did I behold a man of equal dignity with him who is now at the door of the portal.' Then said Arthur, ' If walking thou didst enter in here, return thou running. And every one that beholds the light, and every one that opens and shuts the eye, let them show him respect, and serve him, some with gold-mounted drinking-horns, others with collops cooked and peppered, until food and drink can be prepared for him. It is unbecoming to keep such a man as thou sayest he is, in the wind and the rain.' " [1]

And so the youth was admitted to the king's presence, whereupon he declared that he had not come to the court to stay, but only to beg a boon of the king. Then Arthur replied : [2] —

---

[1] The *Mabinogion*, translated by Lady Charlotte Guest, edited by Alfred Nutt, London, 1902, *Kilhwch and Olwen*, pp. 103 ff.

[2] *Ibid.* pp. 106 ff.

"'Since thou wilt not remain here, chieftain, thou shalt receive the boon whatsoever thy tongue may name, as far as the wind dries, and the rain moistens, and the sun revolves, and the sea encircles, and the earth extends; save only my ship; and my mantle; and Caledvwlch,[1] my sword; and Rhongomyant, my lance; and Wynebgwrthucher,[2] my shield; and Carnwenhau,[3] my dagger; and Gwenhwyvar, my wife. By the truth of Heaven, thou shalt have it cheerfully, name what thou wilt.' 'I would that thou bless my hair.' 'That shall be granted thee.'

"And Arthur took a golden comb, and scissors, whereof the loops were of silver, and he combed his hair. And Arthur inquired of him who he was. 'For my heart warms unto thee, and I know that thou art come of my blood. Tell me, therefore, who thou art.' 'I will tell thee,' said the youth. 'I am Kilhwch, the son of Kilydd, the son of Prince Kelyddon, by Goleuddydd, my mother, the daughter of Prince Anlawdd.' 'That is true,' said Arthur; 'thou art my cousin. Whatsoever boon thou mayest ask, thou shalt receive, be it what it may that thy tongue shall name.' 'Pledge the truth of Heaven and the faith of thy kingdom thereof.' 'I pledge it thee, gladly.' 'I crave of thee then, that thou obtain for me Olwen, the daughter of Yspaddaden Penkawr; and this boon I likewise seek at the hands of thy warriors. I seek it from Kai, and Bedwyr,'"

and from various other warriors whom he named, giving a list that covers eight or nine pages. The result was that Arthur called on the best of them to aid Kilhwch, among them Kai, who had the peculiarity that when

"it pleased him he could render himself as tall as the highest tree in the forest. And he had another peculiarity — so great was the heat of his nature, that, when it rained hardest, whatever he carried remained dry for a handbreadth

[1] Hard-Breacher.   [2] Night-Gainsayer.   [3] White-Haft.

above and a handbreadth below his hand; and when his
companions were coldest, it was to them as fuel with which
to light their fire." [1]

Arthur and Kilhwch and the others journeyed to
the castle of Olwen's father, Penkawr, who promised
the girl's hand to the youth if he would comply with
certain conditions which it takes nine or ten pages to
enumerate. One was to procure "the basket of Gwyd-
dneu Garanhir," which, we have already seen, some
scholars suppose to be a Welsh original of the Holy
Grail.[2] A still more difficult condition which Pen-
kawr imposed, and the hardest for his would-be son-
in-law to fulfil, was to get the comb and scissors which
were between the two ears of the Twrch Trwyth, a
remarkable wild boar, in order that Penkawr might
arrange his hair. This was so rank that with no
other comb and scissors could Penkawr arrange it.
Through the assistance of Arthur and his dog Cavall,
and of warriors from the three Islands of Britain,
and the adjacent Isles, and France, Armorica, Nor-
mandy, and the Summer Country, the Twrch Trwyth
was hunted over Ireland, Wales, Devon, and Cornwall,
until at last the comb and the scissors were obtained.
And when Kilhwch had given them and other marvels
to Penkawr, then

"Kaw of North Britain came and shaved his beard, skin,
and flesh clean off to the very bone from ear to ear. 'Art
thou shaved, man?' said Kilhwch. 'I am shaved,' an-
swered he. 'Is thy daughter mine now?' 'She is thine,'

[1] *Kilhwch and Olwen*, p. 115. With this peculiar heat of Kay is to
be compared that of the Irish champion, Cuchullin.

[2] Cf. Rhys, *Arthurian Legend*, p. 316. Professor Rhys thinks that
Garanhir means "Long Crane" or "Tall Heron," and so is another
name for the Fisher-King of the French romances.

said he, ' but therefore needest thou not thank me, but
Arthur who hath accomplished this for thee. By my free
will thou shouldest never have had her, for with her I lose
my life.' Then Goreu, the son of Custennin, seized him by
the hair of his head, and dragged him after him to the
keep, and cut off his head, and placed it on a stake on
the citadel. Then they took possession of his castle and
of his treasures.

" And that night Olwen became Kilhwch's bride, and she
continued to be his wife as long as she lived. And the hosts
of Arthur dispersed themselves, each man to his own coun-
try. And thus did Kilhwch obtain Olwen, the daughter of
Yspaddaden Penkawr."

This story is of interest as pointing to the steady
cherishing of the Arthurian legends in Wales inde-
pendent of French influence, for this wild boar is none
other than that Troynt which Arthur was hunting, in
the pages of Nennius. It is also a charming, fanciful
tale, full of two traits which Matthew Arnold cites as
characteristic of the Celtic literary genius, in his inter-
esting *Essay on the Study of Celtic Literature*. One
of these Arnold calls a " turn for style," by which he
means an exalted poetic style. " The Celt's quick feel-
ing for what is noble and distinguished " has given
his poetry this style, which is so clearly shown in the
passages just cited as to need no further explanation.
The other trait Arnold calls the

"gift of rendering with wonderful felicity the magical
charm of nature. The forest solitude, the bubbling spring,
the wild flowers, are everywhere in romance. They have a
mysterious life and grace there; they are Nature's own
children, and utter her secret in a way which makes them
something quite different from the woods, waters, and plants
of Greek and Latin poetry. Now of this delicate magic,

Celtic romance is so pre-eminent a mistress, that it seems impossible to believe the power did not come into romance from the Celts. Magic is just the word for it, — the magic of nature ; not merely the beauty of nature, — that the Greeks and Latins had ; not merely an honest smack of the soil, a faithful realism, — that the Germans had ; but the intimate life of Nature, her weird power and her fairy charm." [1]

A subtle, elusive quality this, commonest, outside of Celtic romance, as Arnold observes, in English poetry. It is " expressing almost the inexpressible," [2] putting into words the magic of skies and seas that you behold in the melting light of the West, as you look out from one of the heather-covered headlands of Scotland or Ireland or Wales. It is putting into words what Turner put into the skies and seas on his canvases, what Reynolds put into the smiles of the children he painted. Sometimes in poetry the effect is produced by the introduction of actual magic in the landscape ; as in Chaucer's *Wife of Bath's Tale*, the hero rides up to question four-and-twenty ladies whom he sees dancing on the green under a forest-side ; but when he comes to the dance, lo ! it has vanished, and there sits on the green only a hideous hag, the most revolting in her ugliness that any man could imagine. By this transformation the green and the forest-side are changed from commonplace to a green and a forest-side of magic. Again, the charm may be felt without the introduction of actual magic, as in the oft-quoted description of Olwen, the heroine of the tale just referred to : " More yellow was her hair than the flower of the broom, and her skin was whiter than the foam

---

[1] *Celtic Literature*, p. 120. [2] *Op. cit.* p. 93.

of the wave, and fairer were her hands and her fingers than the blossoms of the wood-anemone amidst the spray of the meadow fountain; " and in the moonlight scene in *The Merchant of Venice*, which Arnold cites as a supreme instance of " the sheer, inimitable Celtic note : " —

> " The moon shines bright. In such a night as this,
> When the sweet wind did gently kiss the trees,
> And they did make no noise, in such a night
> Troilus, methinks, mounted the Trojan wall
> And sigh'd his soul toward the Grecian tents,
> Where Cressid lay that night.
>
> "... in such a night
> Did Thisbe fearfully o'ertrip the dew —
>
> "... in such a night
> Stood Dido, with a willow in her hand,
> Upon the wild sea-banks, and waved her love
> To come again to Carthage."

Kilhwch and Olwen, a typical Celtic tale, is full of "natural magic," of " turn for style," and of quaint humor; and for all its diffuseness, the story is interesting in itself. But beyond its charm and its historical interest for a student of literature, *Kilhwch and Olwen* is not noteworthy. It is not a tale to impress human imagination for centuries, like the legends of Lancelot, Perceval, and Tristram and Iseult, for it is after all best characterised by that adjective which Matthew Arnold applies to Celtic art in general, " ineffectual." [1] Celtic art, he says, so long as it remained

---

[1] Arnold sees a third characteristic in Celtic literature, which he calls its " Titanic melancholy," but in regard to this his assertion seems not so well founded as his others. Such a widely-read Celtic scholar

purely Celtic, has never profoundly impressed the world like Greek or Roman art, or the best German, French, English, Spanish, and Italian art. Now it was because French art was able to join reason and significance to the fantastic poetry of such Celtic tales as *Kilhwch and Olwen*, to give the old charming but "ineffectual" stories substantial meaning, that they have become effectual and permanent contributions to the literature of the world.

So we see what a great debt of gratitude poetry owes the French romancers of the twelfth and thirteenth centuries. After Geoffrey of Monmouth they were the first literary explorers of the newly discovered "perilous seas, in faëry lands forlorn;" and they found many pleasant bays and headlands and faëry isles which Geoffrey never saw. Moreover, they showed the way which many might follow. The earlier Celtic bards had sailed these seas aimlessly, faring whither their fancy led, or driven by the winds hither and yon, caring for no map to guide to a definite port. The French charted these seas so well that ever since poets have sailed on none more gladly.

as Professor F. N. Robinson of Harvard tells me that though he agrees with Arnold in applying the term "Titanic melancholy" to much of Ossian, certainly to the famous passage about the desolation of Balclutha, which Arnold cites as an instance of this quality, yet he cannot see it in Celtic literature in general. Often, to be sure, it has a gentle melancholy, such as you see in some of the *lais*, notably *Guingamor*, but not Titanic melancholy. In regard to natural magic, however, Professor Robinson feels that Arnold was wholly right. It is to be found in the literature of every branch of the Celts, Breton, Welsh, Irish, and Scottish.

XII

FROM LAYAMON TO MALORY

ONCE they had taken definite shape in French, the Arthurian legends speedily found their way into other languages. Next to French, the early German treatment of the stories was the most important, not because of far-reaching changes made in them, but because of the high merit of several of the poets who treated them, especially Wolfram and Gottfried. Less important was their development in Spanish, Italian, Scandinavian, and Dutch. English treatment of the stories, on the contrary, has been very important. Taking them in the organic form which the French had given them, the English, by steadily cherishing the stories, have done more than any other people to keep them alive.

The first Arthurian poet writing in English, Layamon, who wrote his *Brut* shortly after 1200, made, as we have seen, three important contributions to the legends. He gave a circumstantial account of the founding of the Round Table; he gave a more detailed account than the earlier writers of the departure of Arthur for Avalon; and he made Arthur, who had already changed from a British chieftain to a French or Anglo-Norman king, into a king with a good deal of English blood in him. After Layamon, it was to be long before an English poet should make any notable

addition to the Arthurian legends, for though most
chroniclers from him to Holinshed said something of
Arthur, their pseudo-histories, in the main, merely
condensed the story which Geoffrey first told.

The English chronicle-stories of Arthur, romantic
as they were, always pretended to be history; hence
they may be regarded as different from those works
which were avowedly romances. The earliest of these
which we know in England is the *Sir Tristrem* of the
last years of the thirteenth century. With that begins
the English development of Arthurian romances as
distinguished from the Arthurian pseudo-chronicles.

At first sight it may seem strange that no earlier
Arthurian romance is to be found in English, espe-
cially if we accept the theory that England had so
much to do with the twelfth-century development of
the Arthurian stories. The fact, however, is easily
explained. For two hundred years after the Norman
Conquest, the works composed in English were chiefly
religious and historical. Those in England who read
romances, which were the novels of the day, for the
most part either knew French as their native lan-
guage, or understood it with ease. Now, as we know,
plenty of French Arthurian romances were composed
all through this period, some actually in England,
and others apparently of English sources. Moreover,
during this same time, there is a dearth of English
romances concerning such undoubtedly English cham-
pions as Guy of Warwick, Havelock the Dane, and
Bevis of Hampton, but there are stories about all
three in French. There is an English *Gest of King
Horn* in the thirteenth century and a French *Horn et
Rimenhild* in the twelfth century. It was not until

French was losing its vitality in England that the English production of romances which have lasted began on a large scale. Once begun, however, it went on continuously throughout the Middle Ages, and even since then it has not ceased.

Among the mediæval Arthurian stories, whether verse or prose, there is, in temper and intrinsic interest, little variety. One of the last was the Scotch metrical romance, *Lancelot of the Laik*, at the end of the fifteenth century. Of English Arthurian romance from *Sir Tristrem* to this *Lancelot*, — and in this generalisation we may include the chronicles, too, — it may be said, as of most English literature of the same time, that it is insensitive. It has next to none of Arnold's "turn for style," which does appear in Layamon, and not enough of the varied smoothness of French verse. It is generally insensitive, too, to life and nature; much less than contemporary French or German literature, it mirrors the society of chivalry, and it pays little attention to nature except in praise of early summer, especially of the month of May, which tends to become conventional. English mediæval fiction, then, is mostly bald statement of fact told in monotonous verse with stock epithets and stock rhymes. If ladies are not "fair," they are pretty sure to be "bright of ble"[1] or "bright in bower;" heroes are almost always "hend and fre."[2] If you have a line ending with *ride*, *side*, or some other word in *ide*, the chances are good that the rhyming word will be *tide*, in its old sense of *time*; if a line ends in *other*, you may pretty safely lay a bet that its rhyme will

---

[1] Complexion or color.
[2] Courteous and generous.

be *brother*. Two stanzas taken from *Sir Tristrem* are a sample — extreme, it is true — of this English mediæval fiction.

> " Moraunt was vnfayn
> And fauȝt wiþ al his miȝt;
> Þat tristrem were y-slayn
> He stird him as a kniȝt.
> Tristrem smot wiþ main,
> His swerd brak in þe fiȝt
> And in morauntes brain
> Bileued [1] a pece briȝt
> Wiþ care;
> And in þe haunche riȝt
> Tristrem was wounded sare.

> " A word þat pended [2] to pride
> Tristrem, þo spac he: —
> ' Folk of yrland side,
> Zour mirour ȝe may se.
> Mo þat hider wil ride,
> Þus grayþed [3] schul ȝe be.'
> Wiþ sorwe þai drouȝ þat tide
> Moraunt to þe se
> And care.
> Wiþ ioie tristrem þe fre
> To mark, his em, [4] gan fare."

There are exceptions, of course, to this insensitiveness. In various authors there are traces of the sincere fondness for outdoor nature which fills Chaucer, and which has been so conspicuous in later English poetry. There are traces, too, of the robust, healthy, humorous realism which appears in Chaucer again, and later in Shakspere and Fielding. Here and there, even, there

---

[1] Remained or stuck.   [2] Belonged.
[3] Hurt.   [4] Uncle.

is spirit in the verse. But for the most part, English literature from Layamon to the Renaissance is a dreary waste. Once, however, there is an exception, not only in individual authors but in a whole period, which is lifted high above the general dulness — the second half of the fourteenth century, or the age of Edward III.[1] To this we owe *Piers Plowman*, the correct verse of the "Moral Gower," Wiclif's Bible, and the poems of Chaucer.

Chaucer unfortunately tells none of the Arthurian stories; for some reason they did not attract him. True, he places the scene of his *Wife of Bath's Tale* at Arthur's court, but for the sole reason, apparently, of giving the tale a picturesque background. Its connection with Arthurian romance is of the slenderest, though in other forms of the same tale, which make Gawain the hero,[2] the connection is close. And yet Chaucer must have been familiar with the Arthurian stories. In his *Sir Thopas*, he mentions both Sir Libeaus, the son of Gawain, and Sir Perceval. In the *Nonne Prestes Tale*,[3] his reference to Lancelot shows that Chaucer knew this knight as the beau ideal courtly lover.

> "This storie is also trewe, I undertake,
> As is the book of Launcelot de Lake,
> That wommen holde in ful gret reverence."

And again in the *Squieres Tale* :[4] —

> "Who coude telle yow the forme of daunces,
> So uncouthe and so fresshe contenaunces,

[1] Edward III died, to be sure, in 1377, but the principal writers who had distinguished themselves in his reign lived on till the end of the century.

[2] *The Marriage of Sir Gawaine* and *The Weddynge of Sir Gawen and Dame Ragnell.* See ch. xviii.

[3] Lines 391 ff.   [4] Lines 283 ff.

> Swich subtil loking and dissimulinges
> For drede of Ialouse mennes aperceyvinges?
> No man but Launcelot, and he is deed."

We may surmise that Chaucer had no very high opin-
ion of Lancelot. His reference to Gawain, however,
is truly appreciative. The young man, in the *Squieres
Tale*, who came with the wonderful steed of brass to
the Tartar King, Cambynskan, on entering the great
hall, saluted king, queen, and court

> " With so heigh reuerence and obeisance
> As wel in speche as in contenaunce,
> That Gawayn, with his olde curteisye,
> Though he were come ageyn out of Fairye,
> Ne coude him nat amende with a word." [1]

It is a pity that Chaucer, with this better idea of
Gawain, did not see fit to make the once peerless
nephew of Arthur the hero of a Canterbury Tale.

Yet, curiously, this time when Chaucer, the greatest
poet of his age, and Gower, that pattern of correct
verse, were scorning the Arthurian legends, was the
time of the chief development of Arthurian metrical
romance in England. It came with the revival of the
old-fashioned alliterative verse, one of the signs of
the English renaissance in Edward III's reign,[2] when
at last French ceased to be the language of polite soci-
ety, parliament, the courts, and the schools. Now in
England, least Germanic of all Germanic countries,
this oldest and most idiomatic form of Germanic verse
was employed for the last time, except as antiquarian
scholars have experimented with it since. Though
confined to parts remote from the influence of the

---

[1] Lines 93 ff.   [2] 1327-1377.

court, that is, the west and north, and to southern
Scotland, in these regions the alliterative revival en-
joyed considerable favor, and in two or three instances,
at least, produced poetry of excellence. The most pop-
ular hero of the alliterative romances was Sir Gawain.
So many of the stories told about him were localised
in the Lake Region and the country on the Scottish
border just north of it, that it would almost seem as if
there had been an independent growth of the Arthurian
legends there, or at all events of the Gawain legend.
Nor is it unreasonable to suppose that since this re-
gion remained Celtic to a comparatively late period,
traditions connected with the historical Arthur did
develop there independently and uninterruptedly, as
they seem to have done in Wales and Brittany.

In these alliterative and other romances of the north-
west, Carlisle, as we might expect, figures extensively.
The chief town of Cumberland and strongly fortified,
it was rather poetically situated, with its pleasant out-
look north over the curves of the River Eden to the
blue Scottish hills, and southeast to the nearer Cum-
berland Fells, and south to Skiddaw and Saddleback
— or more melodiously Blencathara — and the other
mountains of the Lake Country. Famous, too, was
Inglewood Forest, which once covered the plain of
northern Cumberland from Carlisle to Penrith, a dis-
tance of about twenty miles. As the name implies, it
was early the scene of Angle settlements in this Cel-
tic region. Its importance as a favorite hunting-place
of Arthur comes, no doubt, from the fact that through-
out the Middle Ages it was a much esteemed hunting-
ground and a royal domain, as indeed it remained till
William III gave it to his friend, the Earl of Portland.

Why a diminutive lake like Tarn Wadling, nearly in the centre of the forest, should have been almost as famous as Carlisle or the forest itself, is less easy to understand. Yet it was at Tarn Wadling that Arthur, in the *Weddynge of Syr Gawayne and Dame Ragnell*, met a gigantic baron, who would have taken the king's life but for the self-sacrificing courtesy of Gawain. The title of a fourteenth-century romance, in which Gawain and Guinevere are confronted by a grisly spectre at the edge of the lake, is *The Auntres of Arthur at the Tarnewathelan*. And in *The Avowynge of King Arthur*, Gawain takes a vow to watch all night by the same sheet of water. This romantic interest, whatever its origin, is now lost, for the little tarn has long since been drained; it is to-day only a sedgy swamp where cattle feed. About it are green fields, with the neat little village of High Hesket, on an eminence above it, less than half a mile away. Farther off, in all directions, are hills. Only some dark, bristling pines on the edge of the tarn remain to suggest wildness. All around, the country is beautiful and the land open, except where, now and then, a few fine old oaks and chestnuts remind you that this was once Inglewood Forest.[1]

---

[1] Metrical romances celebrating Gawain, which either placed the scene in the northwest of England or were composed thereabouts, are as follows : —

Sir Gawain and the Green Knight, probably of the western Midlands, about 1360, with the scene in Lancashire or Westmoreland.

The Grene Knight, found in the *Percy Folio Manuscript* in a southern dialect, but telling substantially the same story as *Sir Gawain and the Green Knight*.

Golagrus and Gawain, composed in southern Scotland in the second half of the fifteenth century. The scene of the story is on the Continent. Arthur is on his way to the Holy Land.

The Auntres of Arthur, composed in a dialect of northwest Lanca-

The best of the alliterative poetry is the romance entitled *Sir Gawain and the Green Knight*, written by an unknown author between 1350 and 1375. Three other poems, *The Pearl, Cleanness*, and *Patience* have been ascribed to the same writer. All three are religious and didactic poems, which, though in skilful verse, lack the interest of *The Green Knight*.

This, which Gaston Paris called the gem of English mediæval literature, tells the story of a redoubtable champion of more than human size, who appeared mysteriously at Arthur's court, clad all in green and mounted on a green horse. It was the Yuletide feast, and the Green Knight came riding boldly into Arthur's hall to propose what he called a Christmas jest, — a grim one it proved, — that he should bend his neck for a stroke of the huge battle-axe which he carried, to be given by any knight of the court, provided that a year later the same knight should meet him at

shire, Westmoreland, or Cumberland in the second half of the fourteenth century. The scene is Cumberland.

The Avowynge of Arthur, in the same handwriting, dialect, and manuscript as the *Auntres of Arthur*. It is supposedly of the same date.

The Morte Arthure, in a border dialect, possibly Scottish, with some English forms. It was composed between 1350 and 1400.

The Turk and Gowin. The dialect is of the north, the date late fifteenth century. The scene is in the north of England and Isle of Man.

The Carle of Carlile. The dialect is of the north of England. The date is probably early fifteenth century. The scene is chiefly Cumberland, though Arthur holds court in Wales.

The same story is told with few variations in the *Percy Folio Manuscript* of the seventeenth century.

The Weddynge of Sir Gawen and Dame Ragnell. Though the dialect is mixed, the scene of the story is Cumberland. The date is late fifteenth century.

Substantially the same story is told in a ballad in the *Percy Folio Manuscript, The Marriage of Sir Gawaine*.

the Green Chapel, and receive from his hands a like stroke. Gawain accepted the challenge, cut off the knight's head, and then to his horror saw the headless body take up the head with one hand and ride away, the eyes rolling horribly and the lips moving to remind Gawain to keep his pledge at the Green Chapel on the next New Year's Day.

The year following was an anxious one for Gawain. As early as November he set out in search of the Green Chapel, and after various adventures — climbing cliffs from whose crests the cold water leapt or hung in hard icicles over his head, sleeping on bare rocks almost slain with the sleet — he came to a castle at Christmastide, whose lord told him that the Green Chapel was but two miles away. And so Gawain gladly said yes to the baron's bidding to stay at the castle for the next three days ; and, because he was tired from his journey, he preferred to rest rather than go out each day with his host, who was a famous huntsman. Just for sport, the host said, they would make a bargain : at nightfall each should give the other what he got through the day. And so each evening the baron gave Gawain the spoils of the chase ; but Gawain had nothing to give except one kiss on the evening of the first day, two kisses on the second evening, and three kisses on the third. He won these from the wife of the baron, who came every morning to Gawain's chamber while he was still in bed, tempting him to make love to her. But she never got anything more from him than loveless kisses. The third day, however, Gawain got that from her which he did not give up. Just at parting she offered him the green and gold lace which she had girt round her waist, saying that whoever wore it could receive no wound. No wonder Gawain, remembering that the next day he must stretch out his neck for a blow from the Green Knight's axe, did not give his host the lace.

Before the next sun had risen, Gawain bade farewell to the lord and lady of the castle and set out for the Green Chapel. When he entered the wild glen where it stood, — it was only a mound with a hole at either end, hollow, and overgrown with grass, — he heard the sound of one sharpening an axe, as if whetting it on the grindstone. It was not a comforting sound ; nor was it a comforting sight when, directly, the Green Knight appeared, as green as the day he rode into Arthur's court, and his head as firmly on his shoulders. Still Gawain shrank not from keeping his word ; he knelt and bared his neck ; but then, as the knight was about to drop the axe, he could not forbear flinching slightly. The Green Knight taunted Gawain with this sign of fear. " I will not flinch a second time," said Gawain ; nor did he when the knight brought the axe down. The knight did not strike, however, this time, but only made a feint at doing so. The third time, he struck in truth, but so gently that the axe made only a skin wound on Gawain's neck. Up jumped Gawain at once ; never since the day of his birth had he been so glad. " I have stood my test," he cried ; " if thou dost offer another blow, I will give thee as good."

But the Green Knight had no thought of offering another blow. He explained that he himself had been Gawain's host, and that his lady had tempted Gawain through his own connivance. He had given Gawain the flesh-wound because Gawain, untrue to their covenant, had kept the green and gold lace on the third evening instead of surrendering it. And he had appeared at Arthur's court, the Green Knight said, through the enchantments and machinations of Morgan Le Fay, Arthur's malicious sister, who had sent him thither to terrify Guinevere.

Shamed, Gawain rode sadly back to the court, where he told the whole story. But no one else thought that he ought to feel shamed; and Arthur bade that in future, to commemorate Gawain's faith, the whole court should wear green laces.[1]

This story is told in long stanzas of varying length, but of unvarying metrical ease, each concluding with a tag like the following, which concludes the whole poem:

> " I-wis
>
> Many a venture here beforn
> Hath fallen such as this;
> May He that bare the crown of thorn
> Bring us into His bliss."

But the writer was something more than a smooth versifier; he knew how to tell a straight story, and how to give it a moral meaning without turning it into a sermon. He had, besides, unusual appreciation of nature; many descriptions, especially of Gawain's journey to the north and of the Green Knight's hunting, could not be bettered. What is more, the writer knew human nature; he knew well the rougher aristocratic life, that which was remote from the influence of London and the court. In the story of Gawain's visit at the Green Knight's castle, it is not too much to say that country-house life appears in English fic-

---

[1] See Jessie L. Weston, *Sir Gawain and the Green Knight, Retold in Modern Prose*, London, 1899.

tion for the first time in a way which is persuasively real. The author of *The Green Knight* was an early predecessor — perhaps the earliest — of all those who, from the time the Spectator went visiting Sir Roger de Coverley, have gladdened thousands of readers with wholesome pictures of English country-house life.

Apart from its interest as a story, *Sir Gawain and the Green Knight* is interesting to a student of comparative literature; it is the best known instance in mediæval romance of the transmission of a tale from Irish to English. Not that the direct source of *The Green Knight* was Irish ; the story probably came from Ireland to the author through various French adaptations, and the direct source has not been discovered. It is interesting to note, furthermore, that the hero of the adventure in Irish is Cuchullin, whose deeds so often resemble Gawain's.

According to the Irish tale, Bricriu, of venomous tongue, gave a feast to the king and nobles of Ulster, which they would attend only on condition that he himself should not be present to stir up strife. To this he agreed, but beforehand he secretly advised Cuchullin, Loegaire, and Conall each to claim the champion's portion at the feast,[1] and he advised each hero's wife likewise to claim precedence. The result was such dispute that, in order to prevent bloodshed at the feast, the king of Ulster sent the three champions to various judges to decide which was the best. In one of their tests the three champions were challenged by a gigantic warrior to exchange sword strokes, as Gawain was challenged by the Green Knight. Both Loegaire and Conall, after cutting off the man's head, failed to

[1] Cf. A. C. L. Brown, *The Round Table before Wace*, p. 192.

keep the appointment; but Cuchullin did not shrink
from the return blow, not even when the huge chief-
tain bade him stretch out his neck as long as he could
that it might be easier to cut. The giant, however, like
Gawain's Green Knight, made only three feints with
his axe, and then pronounced Cuchullin the chief hero
of Ulster.[1]

It is not worth while to name here all the Ar-
thurian metrical romances extant in English of the
fourteenth century; a list of them is to be found in
Middle English Metrical Romances, by Anna Hunt
Billings.[2] Two or three, however, are worthy of spe-
cial mention.

About 1350, or possibly earlier, was composed *Sir
Launfal*, an adaptation by Thomas Chestre of the
Lanval of Marie de France, which has much in com-
mon with her *Guingamor*. Needless to say, Chestre's
Launfal and Lowell's, the hero of the *Vision*, have
nothing in common but their name.

Probably somewhat later was composed the *Morte
Arthure*, an alliterative poem telling of Arthur's con-
quest of Rome, Mordred's treachery, and Arthur's
death. Its lines have a better swing than those of most
alliterative poems of the time, perhaps because alliter-
ative verse is better suited to martial narrative than to
romantic adventure. The romance is spirited and has
a good deal of poetic feeling. It has been attributed
to a Scotch poet named Huchown, who, it is known,
wrote a *Great Geste of Arthur*, which a Scotch chron-

---

[1] Cf. *Histoire Littéraire de la France*, vol. xxx. Anna Hunt Billings,
Middle English Metrical Romances, p. 163. J. L. Weston, *The Legend
of Sir Gawain*, London, 1897, pp. 92 ff. Ernst Windisch, *Irische Texte*,
Leipzig, 1880, i, pp. 236 ff. George Henderson, *Irish Texts Society*, ii.

[2] New York, 1901.

icler of the early fifteenth century, Andrew Wyntoun,
alludes to in terms of high praise. The *Morte Arthure*
in question is not undeserving of the praise, as an ex-
tract will show, but its dialect is rather of the north
of England than of the south of Scotland. With the
knowledge at present obtainable, it is hardly safe to
go beyond ten Brink's conjecture,[1] that a portion of
the *Great Geste of Arthur* was the source of the *Morte
Arthure*, and that Huchown's verse, so far as it may
have been preserved in the poem, has been Anglicised
by some Northumbrian scribe. The opening lines of
the *Morte Arthure* give a good idea of its style : —

> " Here begynnes Morte Arthure.
> In nomine Patris et Filij et Spirituc Sancti
> Amen pur charite. Amen.

" Now grett glorious Godde, thurgh grace of hym seluen,
And the precyous prayere of hys prys [2] modyr,
Schelde vs fro schamesdede and synfull werkes,
And gyffe vs grace to gye,[3] and gouerne vs here,
In this wrechyde werlde thorowe vertous lywynge,
That we may kayre [4] til hys courte, the kyngdom of hevyne,
When oure saules schall parte and sundyre fra the body,
Ewyre to belde [5] and to byde in blysse wyth hym seluen;
And wysse [6] me to werpe owte [7] som worde at this tym,
That nothyre voyde be ne vayne, bot wyrchip till hym selvyn,
Plesande & profitabill to the pople þat them heres.
ʒe that liste has to lyth,[8] or luffes for to here,
Off elders of alde tym and of theire awke [9] dedys,
How they were lele in theire lawe, and louede God Al-
myghty,

-----

[1] *History of English Literature*, vol. iii, bk. v, ch. 11.
[2] Precious, estimable.   [3] Guide.   [4] Go.   [5] Dwell.
[6] Teach.   [7] Utter.   [8] Listen.   [9] Strange.

Herkynes me heyndly [1] and holdys ȝow styll,
And I sall tell ȝow a tale, þat trewe es and nobyll,
Off the ryeall renkys [2] of the rownde table,
That chefe ware of cheualrye and cheftans nobyll,
Bathe ware in thire werkes and wyse men of armes,
Doughty in theire doyngs, and dredde ay schame,
Kynde men and courtays, and couthe of courte thewes ; [3]
How they whanne wyth were wyrchippis many,
Sloughe Lucyus þe lythyre, [4] that lorde was of Rome,
And conqueryd that kyngryke thorowe craftys of armes.
Herkenes now hedyrwarde, and herys this storyé.
Qwen that the kynge Arthur by conqueste hade wonnyn
Castells and kyngdoms, and contreez many,
And he had couered [5] the coroun of the kyth [6] ryche,
Of all that Vter in erthe aughte in his tym,
Orgayle and Orkenay, and all this owte-iles,
Ireland vttirly, as Occyane rynnys ;
Scathyll [7] Scottlande by skyll he skyftys [8] as hym lykys,
And Wales of were he wane at hys will,
Bathe Flaundrez and Fraunce fre til hym seluyn ;
Holaund and Henawde they helde of hym bothen,
Burgoyne and Brabane, and Breytan the lesse,
Gyan and Gothelande, & Grece the ryche.
Bayon and Burdeux he beldytt full faire,
Turoyn and Tholus with toures full hye ;
Off Peyters and of Prouynce he was prynce holdyn,
Of Valence and Vyenne, off value so noble,
Of Eruge & Anyon, thos erledoms ryche.
By conqueste full cruell þey knewe hym fore lorde
Of Nauerne and Norwaye, & Normaundye eke,
Of Almayne, of Estriche, and oþer ynowe ;
Danmarke he dryssede [9] all by drede of hym seluyn,
Fra Swynn vnto Swetherwyke, with his swerde kene." [10]

---

[1] Courteously.   [2] Men.   [3] Customs.
[4] Wicked.   [5] Recovered.   [6] Country.
[7] Hostile.   [8] Disposes.   [9] Ruled.
[10] *Morte Arthure*, ed. by Mary Macleod Banks, London, 1900, ll. 1 ff.

Another poem with similar name, *Le Morte Arthur*,
though probably composed in the fourteenth century,
has come to us in a manuscript written about the mid-
dle of the fifteenth century [1] in rough eight-line stanzas
of octosyllabic verse, with alternate lines rhyming.
Since alliteration shows through the verse here and
there, scholars have suspected that the poem was
originally alliterative. The romance tells the story of
Lancelot and Elaine, — with the events less skilfully
arranged than by Malory and Tennyson, — of Arthur's
discovery of Guinevere's love for Lancelot, of the
subsequent enmity between Arthur and his favorite
knight, and of Mordred's rebellion and Arthur's death.
The story is sometimes vivid and rapid, though with-
out the poetic feeling which is in the alliterative poem
of similar name. An extract from *Le Morte Arthur*,
telling of Bedivere's return of Excalibur to the Lake
and of Arthur's passing to Avalon, is of interest as
showing that Malory sometimes followed the poem
closely in making his compilation.

> " Whan the kynge had swounyd there,
>   By an Auter vp he stode,
>   Syr lucan that was hym dere
>   Lay dede, and fomyd in the blode ;
>   Hys bold brother syr Bedwere,
>   Fulle mykelle mornyd in hys mode,
>   For sorow he myȝte not nyghe hym nere,
>   But euyr wepyd As he were wode.[2]
>   The kynge tornyd hym there he stode
>   To syr Bedwere, wyth wordys kene,
>   ' Have Excalaber, my swerd good,

---

[1] A. H. Billings, *Middle English Metrical Romances*, p. 208; F. J.
Furnivall, *Le Morte Arthur*, London, 1864 ; preface, p. xv.

[2] Mad.

A better brond was neuyr sene,
Go, Caste it in the salt flode,
And thou shalt se wonder, as I wene,
Hye the faste, for crosse on Rode
And telle me what thou hast ther sene.'
    The knyght was bothe hende and free; [1]
To save that swerd he was fulle glad,
And thought, whethyr I [2] better bee
Yif neuyr man it After had;
And I it caste in to the see,
Off mold [3] was neuyr man so mad.
The swerd he hyd vndyr A tree,
And sayd, 'syr, I ded as ye me bad.'
' What saw thow there?' than sayd the kynge,
' Telle me now, yiff thow can;'
' Sertes syr,' he sayd, 'nothynge
But watres depe, And wawès wanne.'
' A, now thou haste broke my byddynge!
Why haste thou do so, thow false man?
A-nother bode [4] thou muste be [5] brynge.'
    Thanne careffully the knyght forthe Ranne,
And thought the swerd yit he wold hyde,
And keste the scauberke in the flode,
' Yif Any Aventurs shalle be-tyde,
There-by shalle I se tokenys goode.'
In-to the see hee lette the scauberke glyde;
A whyle on the land hee there stode;
Than to the kynge he wente that tyde
And sayd, 'syr, it is done by the Rode.'
' Saw thow Any wondres more?'
' Sertys syr, I saw nought.'
' A! false traytor,' he sayd thore,
' Twyse thou haste me treson wroght;
That shalle thow rew sely [6] sore,
And be thou bold it shalbe bought.' [7]

----

[1] Courteous and noble.   [2] Miswriting of " it."   [3] Of earth.
[4] Message.   [5] Miswriting of " me."   [6] Very.
[7] And be confident that you shall pay for it.

The knyght than cryed, 'lord, thyn ore,' [1]
And to the swerd sone he sought.
Syr bedwere saw that bote [2] was beste,
And to the good swerd he wente ;
In-to the see he hyt keste ;
Than myght he see what that it mente ;
There cam An hand, wyth-outen Reste,
Oute of the water, And feyre it hente, [8]
And brandysshyd As it shuld braste,
And sythe, as gleme, A-way it glente. [4]

To the king A-gayne wente he thare
And sayd, 'leve syr, I saw An hand ;
Oute of the water it came Alle bare,
And thryse brandysshyd that Ryche brande.'
'Helpe me sone that I ware there.'
He lede hys lord vnto that stronde ;
A ryche shyppe wyth maste And ore,
Fulle of ladyes there they fonde.
The ladyes, that were feyre and Free,
Curteysly the kynge gan they fonge, [5]
And one, that bryghtest was of blee,
Wepyd sore, and handys wrange,
'Broder,' she sayd, 'wo ys me ;
Fro lechyng hastow be to longe,
I wote that gretely greuyth me,
For thy paynès Ar fulle stronge.'

The knyght kest A rewfulle rowne, [6]
There he stode, sore and vnsownde,
And say, 'lord, whedyr Ar ye bowne,
Allas, whedyr wylle ye fro me fownde ? '
The kynge spake wyth A sory sowne,
'.I wylle wende A lytelle stownde
In to the vale of Avelovne,
A whyle to hele me of my wounde.'
Whan the shyppe from the land was broght,

---

[1] Mercy.
[2] Amends.
[8] Caught.
[4] It passed like a flash.
[5] Receive.
[6] Speech.

Syr bedwere saw of hem no more,
Throw the forest forthe he soughte,
On hyllys, and holtys hore ;
Of hys lyffe Rought he Ryght noght,
Alle nyght he went wepynge sore,
A-gaynste the day he fownde ther wrought
A chapelle by-twene ij holtès hore." [1]

That this second half of the fourteenth century is
the most important period of the Middle Ages for
English metrical Arthurian romances, is plain from
the fact that about half of those now extant were
composed in these years.

Chaucer died in 1400, Langland about the same
time, Gower a few years later, and the first brilliant
period of English literature came to an end. A bar-
ren period followed ; the Renaissance of letters which
had apparently begun in England proved to have
been premature. Interest in the fine arts declined
under the unkindly influences of a disputed succession
and civil war. Had the barrenness been confined to
Arthurian literature, it would not have been surpris-
ing, for we have seen that the fashionable poets of
Chaucer's day turned away from Arthurian romance ;
but lack of interesting literary production was now
general ; and when writing of romances began again,
Arthurian themes instead of being the least liked
were the most liked. Taste turned to them, probably
because the Wars of the Roses brought back among
English readers a fondness for tales of adventure ;
and so it came about that the years from 1450 to
1500, roughly speaking, were almost as productive of
Arthurian stories as those from 1350 to 1400. But

[1] F. J. Furnivall, *op. cit.* line 3438 to line 3525.

now the generally martial taste of society made these stories, which before had flourished chiefly in the west and northwest, more popular in regions nearer to the court; and the best work now was not verse but prose.

In this period it is not worth while, more than in the earlier, to mention all the romances. A metrical *Holy Grail* of some interest deserves notice, and a metrical *Merlin*.[1] Between 1450 and 1460 was written that prose *Merlin* which tells the tale of Merlin's enchantment already quoted.[2] Parts of the romance are good reading to this day, though never with the flow of Malory's narrative. In the latter quarter of the century, several short verse romances were composed, of which Gawain was the hero.[3] And finally, after the Renaissance had begun, came the Scotch *Lancelot of the Laik*, which virtually marks the end of English mediæval romance. But of course the principal Arthurian product of the time is the prose *Morte Darthur*, completed by Sir Thomas Malory in 1469 or early in 1470, and printed by William Caxton, the first English printer, in 1485. Not only is it the English work of the fifteenth century of most literary beauty, but it is the most famous Arthurian romance of the Middle Ages. What is more, it is the only romance of mediæval England which is widely read to-day.

[1] Both by Herry Lonelich between 1450 and 1460.
[2] Page 82.
[3] Several of these have been mentioned in the note on Gawain stories of the northwest of England.

XIII

SIR THOMAS MALORY

REMARKABLE as it is that the author of so important a work as the *Morte Darthur* should till recently have been known only by name, such is nevertheless the case. You will search the *Dictionary of National Biography* in vain for definite information about him. It remained for Professor Kittredge of Harvard University to discover, not many years ago, the few facts that are known regarding this writer of the most popular mediæval romance. In setting them forth I cannot do better, for the most part, than quote directly from Professor Kittredge's article, *Who Was Sir Thomas Malory?* [1]

After showing that no one previously put forward as claimant of this honor has been justly entitled to it, Professor Kittredge says : —

" If a Sir Thomas Malory can be discovered who fulfils all the conditions required, such a person may reasonably be advanced as the writer of the *Morte Darthur*, at least till some other claimant offers. What the required conditions are, may be seen from the three places in the work which mention the author :

" (1) Caxton's preface, in which he says he has printed ' after a copye vnto me delyuerd, whyche copye Syr Thomas Malorye dyd take oute of certeyn bookes

[1] *Harvard Studies and Notes*, vol. v, p. 85.

of frensshe and reduced it in to Englysshe ' (Som-
mer, p. 3).[1]

" (2) The concluding words of the last book :
' I praye you all Ientyl men and Ientyl wymmen
that redeth this book of Arthur and his knyghtes
. . . | praye for me whyle I am on lyue that god
sende me good delyueraunce | & whan I am deed I
praye you all praye for my soule | for this book was
ended the ix yere of the reygne of kyng edward
the fourth | by syr Thomas Maleore knyght as Ihesu
helpe hym for hys grete myght | as he is the seruaunt
of Ihesu bothe day and nyght | ' (Sommer, p. 861).
These are obviously not the words of Caxton, as Dr.
Sommer takes them to be, but the words of Malory
himself.

" (3) Caxton's colophon, which says that the book
' was reduced in to englysshe by Syr Thomas Malory
knyght as afore is sayd[2] | and by me deuyded in to
xxi bookes chapytred and enprynted | and fynysshed
in thabbey westmestre the last day of Iuyl the yere
of our lord M | CCCC | lxxx | v ' (Sommer, p. 861).

" From these passages it appears that any Sir
Thomas Malory advanced as the author of the *Morte
Darthur* must fulfil the following conditions : —

" (1) He must have been a knight ;[3] (2) he must
have been alive in the ninth year of Edward IV,
which extended from March 4, 1469, to March 3, 1470
(both included) ; (3) he must have been old enough
in 9 Ed. IV to make it possible that he should have

---

[1] This reference and others to H. O. Sommer are to his edition of
Malory's *Morte Darthur*, 3 vols., David Nutt, London, 1889–1891.

[2] " That is, in Caxton's preface."

[3] " ' Sir *priest* ' is out of the question, though some have absurdly sug-
gested it (see the reference in Sommer, ii, 2, n. 1)."

written this work. Further, Caxton does not say that he received the 'copy' directly from the author, and his language may be held to indicate that Malory was dead when the book was printed. In this case he must have died before the last day of July (or June),[1] 1485, and we have a fourth condition to be complied with.

"All these conditions (including the fourth, which can hardly be regarded as completely imperative) are satisfied by a fifteenth-century Warwickshire gentleman, an account of whose career, in outline, has for many years been accessible to all in Sir William Dugdale's [2] *Antiquities of Warwickshire*.[3] I refer to that Sir Thomas Malory, knight, of Newbold Revell (or Fenny Newbold), who was M. P. for Warwickshire in 1445.

"(1) This Sir Thomas was certainly a knight.[4]

"(2) He survived the ninth year of Edward IV, dying March 14, 1471 (11 Ed. IV).[5] This fits the closing passage in the *Morte Darthur*.

"(3) He was quite old enough to satisfy the conditions of the problem, for he was not under fiftyseven at the time of his death, and he may have been seventy or above.

"(4) He died some years before the *Morte Darthur* was published.

"So far as can be seen, there is nothing against

---

[1] "As to the question whether *Iuyl* in Caxton's colophon is *July* or *June*, see Sommer, iii, 336. The point is of no consequence in the present discussion."

[2] 1605–1686.

[3] Vol. i, p. 83. "First published in 1656. I have used the second edition, revised by the Rev. Dr. William Thomas, London, 1730."

[4] "*Rot. Fin.* 23 Hen. VI, m. 10 (Dugdale, *l. c.*)."

[5] See NOTE at end of this chapter.

our ascribing the *Morte Darthur* to this Sir Thomas Malory. He belonged to that class to whom the Arthurian stories directly appealed; he was a gentleman of an ancient house and a soldier.[1] His ancestors had been lords of Draughton in Northamptonshire as early, apparently, as 1267–68, and certainly earlier than 1285; and the Malores had been persons of consequence in that county and in Leicestershire from the time of Henry II or Stephen. Sir Peter Malore, justice of the common pleas (1292–1309) and one of the commission to try Sir William Wallace, was a brother of Sir Stephen Malore, the great-grandfather of our Sir Thomas, — that Sir Stephen whose marriage with Margaret Revell brought the Newbold estates into the family. Thomas's father, John Malore, was sheriff of Leicestershire and Warwickshire, Escheator, Knight of the Shire for Warwick in the Parliament of 1413, and held other offices of trust. It is not to be doubted, then, that Sir Thomas received a gentleman's education according to the ideas of the fifteenth century, which are not to be confounded with those of an earlier, illiterate period. That he should learn to read and write French, as well as to speak it, was a matter of course."

Malory appears to have been born about 1400. An interesting fact in regard to his youth is that he served in the French wars with Richard Beauchamp, Earl of Warwick. As Dugdale says, — I quote Professor Kittredge again, —

---

[1] " Cf. Caxton's Preface: 'Many noble and dyuers gentylmen of this royame of England camen and demaunded me many and oftymes wherfore that I haue not do made & enprynte the noble hystorye of the saynt greal and of the moost renomed crysten kyng . . . kyng Arthur.' "

" ' Thomas . . . in K. H. 5 time, was of the retinue
to *Ric. Beauchamp* E. Warr. at the siege of Caleys,
and served there with one lance and two archers; re-
ceiving for his lance and 1. archer xx. *li. per an.* and
their dyet; and for the other archer, x. marks and no
dyet.'[1] I can find no siege of Calais in Henry V's
time. Perhaps the agreement was merely to serve *at
Calais*. In that case, the likeliest date for Malory's
covenant is perhaps 1415, when Warwick indented
' to serve the King as Captain of Calais, until *Febr. 3.
An.* 1416 (4 *Hen. 5*). And to have with him in the
time of Truce or Peace, for the safeguard thereof,
Thirty Men at Arms, himself and three Knights ac-
counted as part of that number; Thirty Archers on
Horsback, Two Hundred Foot Soldiers, and Two Hun-
dred Archers, all of his own retinue. . . . And in
time of War, he to have One hundred and forty Men
on Horsbak,' etc."[2]

This service of Malory with Richard of Warwick is
" peculiarly significant in view of the well-known char-
acter of the Earl. No better school for the future
author of the *Morte Darthur* can be imagined than a
personal acquaintance with that Englishman whom
all Europe recognized as embodying the knightly ideal
of the age. The Emperor Sigismund, we are informed
on excellent authority, said to Henry V ' that no
prince Cristen for wisdom, norture, and manhode,
hadde such another knyght as he had of therle War-
rewyk; addyng therto that if al curtesye were lost,

---

[1] "*Warwickshire*, i, 83. Dugdale's authority is a roll which I have
not identified. (*Rot.* in Bibli. *Hatton.*) Perhaps it was a retinue roll.
He gives no date."

[2] G. L. Kittredge, *op. cit.*

yet myght hit be founde ageyn in hym; and so ever
after by the emperours auctorite he was called the
Fadre of Curteisy.' [1]

"The history of Warwick's life, as set down by
John Rous, chantry priest and antiquary, and almost
a contemporary of the great earl, reads like a *roman
d'aventure*. One exploit in particular might almost
have been taken out of the *Morte Darthur* itself.[2]
'Erle Richard,' we are told, '... heryng of a greet
gaderyng in Fraunce, inasmoche as he was capteyn
of Caleys he hied him thidre hastely, and was there
worthely received; and when that he herd that the
gaderyng in Fraunce was appoynted to come to Ca-
leys, he cast in his mynde to do sume newe poynt
of chevalry; wheruppon,' under the several names of
'the grene knyght,' 'Chevaler Vert,' and 'Cheva-
ler Attendant,' he sent three challenges to the French
king's court. 'And anone other 3 Frenche knyghtes
received them, and graunted their felowes to mete at
day and place assigned.' On the first day, 'the xii
day of Christmasse, in a lawnde called the Park
Hedge of Gynes,' Earl Richard unhorsed the first of
the French knights. Next day he came to the field in
another armor and defeated the second French knight,
'and so with the victory, and hymself unknown rode
to his pavilion agayn, and sent to this blank knyght
Sir Hugh Lawney, a good courser.' On the third
day the Earl 'came in face opyn ... and said like as

---

[1] "John Rous, *Life of Richard Earl of Warwick*, as printed from
MS. Cotton. Julius, E. IV, by Strutt, *Horda Angel-cynnan*, 1775–76,
ii, 125, 126. Rous died Jan. 1492; Beauchamp May 31, 1439."

[2] "For similar incidents in romance, see Ward, *Catalogue of Ro-
mances*, i, 733 ff., with which cf. Malory's *Morte Darthur*, bk. vii, chs.
28, 29, Sommer, i, 257 ff."

he hadde his owne persone performed the two dayes afore, so with Goddes grace he wolde the third, then ran he to the Chevaler name[d] Sir Colard Fymes, and every stroke he bare hym bakwards to his hors bakke ; and then the Frenchmen said he was bounde to the sadyll, wherfor he alighted down from his horse, and forthwith stept up into his sadyll ageyn, and so with worshipe rode to his pavilion, and sent to Sir Colard a good courser, and fested all the people ; . . . and rode to Calys with great worshipe.' (Strutt, *Horda*, ii, 124, 125.)

" This romantic adventure cannot be dated with any certainty. The *days* are settled by the text of Rous ; they are January 6, 7 and 8 (Twelfth Day and the two days following), but the *year* is not easily fixed. By a process of elimination we may arrive at the date 1416 or 1417, either of which may be right. One likes to imagine Thomas Malory as serving in Warwick's retinue on this occasion, and I know of nothing to forbid our indulging so agreeable a fancy." [1]

The father of our author, Sir John Malory, " seems to have died in 12 Hen. VI (1433 or 1434), and Sir Thomas succeeded to the ancestral estates. . . . In the twenty-third year of Henry VI (1445) we find him a knight and sitting in Parliament for his county. Some years later he appears to have made himself conspicuous on the Lancastrian side in the Wars of the Roses, for in 1468 ' Thomas Malorie miles ' is excluded, along with . . . several others, from the operation of a pardon issued by Edward IV. We know nothing of the matter except this bare fact. Whether or not Malory subsequently obtained a special pardon,

[1] G. L. Kittredge, *op. cit.*

cannot now be determined. If he did not, we must suppose that he was relieved by the general amnesty of 1469, since, on his death in 1471, there seems to have been no question as to the inheritance of his estate. Malory died, as has been already noted, March 14, 1471, and, when Dugdale wrote (about 1656), lay 'buryed under a marble in the Chappell of St. Francis at the Gray Friars, near Newgate in the Suburbs of London.' [1] He left a widow, Elizabeth Malory, who lived until 1480,[2] and a grandson, Nicholas, about four years of age. This Nicholas was alive in 1511.[3] He died without male heirs." [4]

As Professor Kittredge says, this Malory was just the man to write the *Morte Darthur*. His birth, education, and training fitted him to do so. Excluded from the pardon issued by Edward IV, he had to keep out of public life, even in his native Warwickshire. Under such conditions an elderly gentleman with the literary taste which Malory must have had, would have been likely to seek literary diversion. It is difficult not to agree with Professor Kittredge's conclusion that " we have before us a Sir Thomas

[1] " Dugdale, *l. c.* referring to MS. Cotton. Vitellius, F. 12 (which contains a 'registrum eorum, qui sepeliuntur in ecclesia et capellis fratrum minorum London '), (*Cat.*, 1802, p. 432). In Stow's list of 'the defaced (*i. e.*, destroyed) monuments' in this church I find: 'Thomas Malory, Kt. 1470,' *Survey of London*, ed. Strype, 1720, bk. iii, ch. 8, p. 134 (ed. 1754, i, 632)."

[2] " The *inquisitio post mortem* on the estate of ' Elizabetha quae fuit uxor Thomae Malory militis ' was taken in 20 Ed. IV (Calend. iv, 400). It declares the heir to be Nicholas, son of Robert, son of Sir Thomas, and gives his age as thirteen and more on Sept. 30, 1479. See Dugdale, *Warwickshire*, i, 83; Nichols, *Leicestershire*, iv, 362; Bridges, *Northamptonshire*, ed. Whalley, i, 603."

[3] " See Nichols, iv, 233."

[4] G. L. Kittredge, *op. cit.*

Malory who, so far as one can see, fulfils all the conditions required of a claimant for the honor of having written the *Morte Darthur*. There is absolutely no contestant, and until such a contestant appears, it is not unreasonable to insist on the claims of this Sir Thomas." [1]

Fortunately for English literature, Malory, so well fitted to produce the *Morte Darthur*, lived at a time which demanded it. We have seen that about the middle of the fifteenth century the Arthurian stories were very popular in England. And yet, outside of the chronicles, which omitted many of the most romantic and interesting adventures in the Round Table stories, there was in English nothing like a comprehensive history of Arthur and his knights. Malory, doubtless long familiar with most of the stories, decided now to write such a history. Accordingly he set to work, we may imagine, to acquaint himself with stories which he did not know, and to make selections for his new compilation from French romances and English, chiefly from the former. [2] His principal sources were the French *Merlin*, *Tristram*, and *Lancelot* romances in prose (the last including the stories of the Grail, of Elaine of Astolat, and of Arthur's death), the English alliterative *Morte Arthure*, and *Le Morte Arthur* in English octosyllabic verse.

Malory was not the first to collect disconnected Round Table stories in one volume. The prose *Lancelot* and the prose *Tristram* of the thirteenth cen-

[1] *Op. cit.*

[2] For a full discussion of Malory's sources, see *Studies on the Sources of Le Morte Darthur*, H. O. Sommer's ed. of Malory, iii. Cf. also, J. L. Weston, *The Legend of Sir Lancelot du Lac*, London, 1901, especially pp. 187–188 and 205.

tury made in their later forms some attempt to bring various Arthurian stories together.[1] In the latter part of the same century,[2] Rusticiano da Pisa made a still more comprehensive collection of Round Table stories — that Rusticiano, who, finding himself in a Genoese jail in 1298, took down from the lips of a fellow prisoner, Marco Polo, the famous story of his adventures in Tartary and China. Rusticiano's Arthurian compilation, which included several of the most important tales of the Round Table, is said to be one of the most stupidly composed of the whole cycle.[3] It is full of signs of haste ; the different stories are so badly joined that adventures of Tristram's maturity are followed by adventures of his father's youth. Yet Rusticiano's work, both in French, in which it was originally composed, and in Italian, into which it was translated, had considerable literary influence. Prior to Malory's richer compilation, it was the most important Arthurian work of its kind.[4]

---

[1] In the French prose *Tristan,* for instance, there is an adventure at the Isle of the Fountain, imitated from Chrétien's *Chevalier au Lion.* Tristram is the hero. (See E. Löseth's *Tristan,* p. 249.) There is also much about Erec, and an account of his meeting with Enide, which differs from Chrétien's.

[2] About 1270.

[3] Paulin Paris, *Manuscrits Français,* Paris, 1838, ii, 358.

[4] The following preamble of Rusticiano's book (quoted from E. Löseth's *Le Roman en Prose de Tristan . . . et la Compilation de Rusticien de Pise . . . ,* Paris, 1890, p. 423) gives an idea of the purpose of Rusticiano's work : —

" Seigneurs empereurs et princes et . . . tous les preudommes . . . qui avez talent de vous deliter en rommans, si prenez cestui et le faites lire de chief en chief ; si orrez toutes les grans aventures qui advindrent entre les chevaliers errans du temps au roy Uter-pendragon jusques au temps au roy Artus, son fils, et des compaignons de la Table Reonde, et sachiez tout vraiement que cist livres fut translatez du livre monseigneur Edouart, le roi d'Engleterre, en cellui temps que

More than in his plan, Malory was original in
the execution of it. He was original in emphasising
Arthur as the central figure of his tale. Though
he takes the Merlin legend for the source of his first
books, he does not go back to the very beginning, as
many mediæval writers would have done, and tell what
happened to Merlin and Vortigern long before Arthur
was born. Instead he begins with the meeting of
Uther Pendragon, king of all England, and the lady
Igraine, whom he loved, and on whom — in the shape of
her husband, the Duke of Cornwall, assumed by Mer-
lin's magic aid — he begot the mighty Arthur. And
after the great King's death, Malory delays his con-
clusion only to narrate the death of Guinevere in the
nunnery at Almesbury and her burial beside the king,
and Lancelot's death in the monastery at Glastonbury

il passa oultre la mer . . . pour conquester le saint sepulcre, et
maistre Rusticiens de Pise . . . compila ce rommant. Car il en trans-
lata toutes les merveilleuses nouvelles et aventures qu'il trouva en
cellui livre et traita tout certainement de toutes les aventures du
monde, et si sachiez qu'il traittera plus de monseigneur Lancelot du
Lac et de monseigneur Tristran, le filz au roy Meliadus de Loonnois,
que d'autres, pour ce qu'ilz furent sans faille les meilleurs chevaliers
qui a ce temps furent en terre, et li maistres en dira de ces deux
pluseurs choses et pluseurs nouvelles que furent entre eux que l'en
trouvera escript en tous les autres livres . . ."

At present it seems impossible to determine the exact form of Rus-
ticiano's work. E. Löseth says (*Tristan*, p. 473) : —

"Suivant toute probabilité, Rusticien ne s'est pas borné a transcrire
. . . le manuscrit du roi d'Angleterre (cf. l'epilogue) ; il a sans doute
ajouté du sien, mettant a profit les romans en prose ordinaires.
. . . Mais nous ne saurions déterminer la part qui lui revient dans
le fouillis des manuscrits ; le titre de ' maistre ' se trouvant le plus
souvent sous l'addition du nom de Rusticien, nous devons même nous
demander si tel ou tel episode ne provient pas d'une rédaction tout
autre que l'œuvre du Pisan : les scribes-remanieurs du moyen âge ne se
gênaient pas pour jeter pêle-mêle des débris de *livres* qui, composés
par des auteurs différents, dérivaient des sources ordinaires auxquelles
puisaient les romanciers."

and his burial at Joyous Gard. It is no violation of unity thus to bring these two, like every fair lady and brave knight, to the grave, for the interest of the book is in them as much as in the King.

Malory showed some originality, too, in the selection of his stories, and of the incidents in them — an originality not always commendable. Though it is impossible to know how wide his acquaintance was with Arthurian romances, it is reasonable to suppose that he had knowledge of more than he included in his compilation. Either through choice or ignorance he left out some very good stories, like that of the Green Knight; and he sometimes made use of the poorer versions of those which he included, as in narrating the death of Tristram, who, according to Malory, was treacherously slain by Mark while harping before Iseult.[1] Besides, when he took his *Morte Darthur* out of " certain books of French and reduced it into English," [2] he did not " reduce " enough. There are too many inconsequent adventures, too many tournaments and single combats of similar nature. When one chapter is headed " Yet of the same battle," it seems unnecessary to follow it by two, each headed " Yet more of the same battle." But a critic should remember the difficulties that confronted Malory, and the perplexing number of stories and the confusion of the long, rambling narratives from which he had to select.

In still another way Malory was original, though not conspicuously so, because he was but doing what

---

[1] This, we have seen (ch. x, p. 165), is the common story of Tristram's death in the French prose romances. (See E. Löseth's *Roman en Prose de Tristan*, Paris, 1890, p. 383.) Cf. Malory, bk. xix, ch. 11.

[2] Caxton's Preface.

others had done before him. All the English Arthu-
rian writers had Anglicised their Celtic-French mate-
rial. Malory, at the end of the line of mediæval
romancers, was near enough to our own time to make
the England of his Arthur, when not altogether unreal,
something like the England we know. The Archbishop
(or Bishop, as Malory calls him) of Canterbury plays
as important a part as he might play in the reign of
an historical English sovereign. Queen Guinevere's
excuse to put off her nuptials with Mordred, that she
had to go up to London " to buy all manner of things
that longed unto the wedding," makes her almost a
bride of to-day.[1] Then her conduct when once in Lon-
don, throwing herself into the Tower and sustaining a
siege from Mordred, recalls Margaret of Anjou, who,
in Malory's own time, had shown herself a woman
of similar martial spirit in opposing the forces of
Edward IV. And as the climax of Malory's realistic
Englishing, there is that beautiful English Maying
of immortal freshness : " So it befell in the month of
May, Queen Guenever called unto her knights of the
Table Round, and she gave them warning that early
upon the morrow she would ride on maying into woods
and fields beside Westminster. ' And I warn you that
there be none of you but that he be well horsed, and
that ye all be clothed in green, either in silk, either in
cloth, and I shall bring with me ten ladies, and every
knight shall have a lady behind him, and every knight
shall have a squire and two yeomen, and I will that
ye all be well horsed.' So they made them ready in

---

[1] Both this excuse and the Bishop of Canterbury's hostility to
Mordred appear in the octosyllabic *Morte Arthur*, but without seem-
ing so real as in Malory.

the freshest manner, and these were the names of the knights: Sir Kay the Seneschal, Sir Agravaine, Sir Brandiles, Sir Sagramor le Desirous, Sir Dodinas le Savage, Sir Ozanna le Cure Hardy, Sir Ladinas of the Forest Savage, Sir Persant of Inde, Sir Ironside that was called the knight of the red lawns, and Sir Pelleas the lover, and these ten knights made them ready in the freshest manner to ride with the queen. And so upon the morn they took their horses, with the queen, and rode on maying in woods and meadows, as it pleased them, in great joy and delights; for the queen had cast to have been again with King Arthur at the furthest by ten of the clock, and so was that time her purpose. . . .

" So as the queen had mayed and all her knights, all were bedashed with herbs, mosses, and flowers, in the best manner and freshest . . ." [1]

I have quoted this not only for its fresh English treatment of nature, but also for its liveliness and picturesque mediæval vividness — qualities which go far towards making Malory's *Morte Darthur*, more than four centuries and a quarter after its composition, a book which publishers find profitable to bring out. No one can read Malory long without feeling that vividness is one of the distinguishing qualities of his style. Not that he paints realistic pictures on a large scale; only small ones he could paint well: but with distinct little pictures his *Morte Darthur* is filled. I do not mean the conventional pictures, such as you find in the narration of single combats ; — how the two knights come together like thunder so that their horses fall down, how they avoid them lightly, and then rush at

[1] Book xix, chs. 1 and 2.

one another like boars, racing, tracing, and foining,
either giving other sad strokes the while, till one knight
is overcome. This may seem vivid the first time you
read it, but it is less so the second, and not at all so
the twentieth time. There are other miniatures, how-
ever, always vivid, never monotonous, because, besides
being as specific as the formula just cited, they are
individual. "And in the midst of the lake Arthur was
ware of an arm clothed in white samite, that held
a fair sword in that hand." [1] "Now . . . speak we of
Sir Launcelot du Lake that lieth under the apple tree
sleeping. Even about the noon there came by him four
queens of great estate; and, for the heat of the sun
should not annoy them, there rode four knights about
them and bare a cloth of green silk on four spears,
betwixt them and the sun, and the queens rode on four
white mules." [2] "Sir Tristram . . . came a soft trot-
ting pace toward them." [3] "Queen Guenever . . .
let make herself a nun, and wore white clothes and
black, and . . . lived in fastings, prayers, and alms-
deeds, that all manner of people marvelled how virtu-
ously she was changed." [4] Such concrete bits, though
making Malory's *Morte Darthur* a succession of won-
derfully vivid little pictures, nevertheless do not make
it real as a whole. The Britain which it presents has
reality here, and again there, but never continuous,
logical reality like Homer's heroic Greece, or Dickens's
middle-class England, or Hawthorne's Puritan New
England. Britain with Malory, as with the Arthurian
writers before him, is after all a romantic nowhere.

[1] Book i, ch. 25.   [2] Book vi, ch. 3.
[3] Book x, ch. 85.
[4] Book xxi, ch. 7. The white clothes and black are mentioned also
in the octosyllabic *Morte Arthur*.

The characters in this nowhere, like the background, are real only at times, but then very much so. Lancelot, for instance, is thoroughly alive when, on one of his visits to a well in Windsor Forest, where he liked to " lie down, and see the well spring and bubble, and sometime he slept there," he is unfortunate enough to encounter a lady of no more accurate aim than many others of her sex. While he slept one day, this lady, who, Malory says, was " a great huntress," aiming an arrow at a hind, by misfortune overshot the hind, and " the arrow smote Sir Lancelot in the thick of the thigh, over the barbs. When Sir Lancelot felt himself so hurt, he hurled up woodly,[1] and saw the lady that had smitten him.[2] And when he saw that she was a woman, he said thus, Lady or damsel, what that thou be, in an evil time bare ye a bow, the devil made you a shooter." When Iseult was tired of disputing with Palamides, "then La Beale Isoud held down her head, and said no more at that time."[3] When Lancelot had overcome Meliagrance, and looked to Guenever to see what she would have done with the caitiff, " then the queen wagged her head . . . as though she would slay him. Full well knew Sir Lancelot by the wagging of her head that she would have had him dead."[4] And often these knights and ladies speak as well as move like real people, though never with marked individuality.

Yet with all their external reality, Malory's characters are only partially alive, for Malory had but little psychological interest in them and but little invention. Accepting his people as he found them, he did not develop them further. One result of thus

---

[1] Madly.
[2] Book xviii, ch. 21.
[3] Book x, ch. 77.
[4] Book xix, ch. 9.

taking them from his sources unchanged, is that his characters are full of incongruities. Such is Malory's Gawain, who, in his attitude toward Guinevere and Lancelot, is more like the noble Gawain of the twelfth-century French romances and of the Gawain poems of northwestern England, than that Gawain in the earlier pages of Malory, who is as base to Pelleas, in his relations with Ettard, as Tennyson's Gawain.

But though Malory's characters are more or less contradictory, though you may read for pages without feeling one character distinct from another, yet when you get to the end of the *Morte Darthur*, you find that the most important have taken on some individuality. Especially is this true of the three chief personages — Arthur, Lancelot, and Guinevere. Of them Arthur is the least distinct: though he takes shape as a right kingly king, he is conventionally so. He spends most of his time sitting on his throne, presiding at his feasts, cheering the knights who are about to start on their quests, or welcoming those who return. When he is active himself, he seems often less a free agent than a puppet in the hands of his advisers, as in his war against Lancelot. Only now and then is he independently active, as in his young days, when he so boldly asserts and confirms his right to his father's throne. Afterwards he seldom wins our sympathy, except occasionally when he flings out at some one in righteous rage, as at Sir Bedivere when he tells the King falsely that he has thrown Excalibur into the lake.

"Ah, traitor, untrue, said king Arthur, now hast thou betrayed me twice. Who would have wend that thou that hast been to me so lief and dear, and thou art named a noble knight, and would betray me for the riches of the sword. But now go again lightly, for thy long tarrying putteth me in great jeopardy of my life, for I have taken cold. And but if thou do now as I bid thee, if ever I may see thee, I shall slay thee with mine own hands, for thou wouldest for my rich sword see me dead." [1]

Lancelot is more individual than Arthur and more human, the strong man of noble feelings, in whom rages the conflict which will not end ; the knight whose word is ever truth, save when he declares that Guinevere has always been a true wife to Arthur ; the knight of greatest honor and greatest dishonor, for he was false to the friend who trusted him. And yet Malory's Lancelot is not so much to be condemned as Tennyson's, for though Arthur esteems Lancelot in the *Morte Darthur* as the first of his knights, there is not that remarkable love between the two which is one of the noble things in the *Idylls of the King*. Apart from his great fault, Malory's Lancelot, like Tennyson's, is all but faultless. With all his prowess, he has that virtue of humility which his son Galahad lacked, as witness the story of Sir Urre of Hungary.[2] This knight came to Arthur's court with " seven great wounds, three on the head, and four on his body and upon his left hand . . . so that he should never be whole, until the best knight of the world had searched his wounds." And then Arthur searched Sir Urre's wounds, and after him one hundred and ten knights of the Round Table, but to no avail. At last Arthur called Sir Lancelot, who had just ridden up to them, saying :—

" Ye must do as we have done. . . . Heaven defend me, said Sir Launcelot, when so many kings and knights have

[1] Book xxi, ch. 5.   [2] Book xix, chs. 10–12.

assayed and failed, that I should presume upon me to achieve that all ye my lords might not achieve. Ye shall not choose, said king Arthur, for I will command you for to do as we all have done. My most renowned lord, said Sir Launcelot, ye know well I dare not nor may not disobey your commandment, but and I might or durst, wit you well I would not take upon me to touch that wounded knight, to that intent that I should pass all other knights; heaven defend me from that shame. Ye take it wrong, said king Arthur, ye shall not do it for no presumption, but for to bear us fellowship, insomuch ye be a fellow of the Table Round, and wit you well, said king Arthur, and ye prevail not and heal him, I dare say there is no knight in this land may heal him, and therefore I pray you do as we have done. And then all the kings and knights for the most part prayed Sir Launcelot to search him, and then the wounded knight Sir Urre set him up weakly, and prayed Sir Launcelot heartily, saying, Courteous knight, I require thee for God's sake heal my wounds, for me thinketh, ever sithen ye came here my wounds grieve me not. Ah my fair lord, said Sir Launcelot, Jesu would that I might help you, I shame me sore that I should be thus rebuked, for never was I able in worthiness to do so high a thing. Then Sir Launcelot kneeled down by the wounded knight, saying, My lord Arthur, I must do your commandment, the which is sore against my heart. And then he held up his hands, and looked into the east, saying secretly unto himself, Thou blessed Father, Son, and Holy Ghost, I beseech thee of thy mercy, that my simple worship and honesty be saved, and thou, blessed Trinity, thou mayest give power to heal this sick knight, by thy great virtue and grace of thee, but, good Lord, never of myself. And then Sir Launcelot prayed Sir Urre to let him see his head; and then, devoutly kneeling, he ransacked the three wounds, that they bled a little, and forthwith all the wounds fair healed, and seemed as they had been whole a seven year. And in likewise he searched his body of other three wounds, and they healed in likewise. And then the last of all he searched the

which was in his hand, and, anon, it healed fair. Then king Arthur, and all the kings and knights, kneeled down, and gave thanks and lovings unto God, and to his blessed mother, and ever Sir Launcelot wept as he had been a child that had been beaten." [1]

Then, too, Lancelot is remarkably patient towards Guinevere. Without blaming the Queen for her whimsical tyranny, the natural result of her uncertain relations with Lancelot, we cannot help feeling that at times her knight had much to bear. When the Queen, for instance, at one moment upbraided him for having loved the maid of Astolat, and almost the next for not having loved her, we could have pardoned Lancelot a harsh reply instead of the gentle reproof : —

" Madam, . . . she would none other way be answered, but that she would be my wife, or else my love, and of these two I would not grant her ; but I proffered her, for her good love that she shewed me, a thousand pound yearly to her and to her heirs, and to wed any manner knight that she could find best to love in her heart. For, madam, said Sir Launcelot, I love not to be constrained to love ; for love must arise of the heart, and not by no constraint." [2]

And there is Guinevere herself, who, were she known nowhere else than in Malory's *Morte Darthur*, would be one of the great epic queens of the world. Of her it may be said, as of so many other women whose lives go to wreck, that had she but had children to take her love and attention, the tragedy might have been averted. Proud and passionate, unreasonable in her demands on Lancelot, vindictive, as when she wags her head to have Meliagrance killed, she can be, and generally is, sweetly gracious, womanly, and

[1] Book xix, ch. 12.   [2] Book xviii, ch. 20.

queenly. We can understand that Sir Pelleas, Sir
Ozanna le Cure Hardy, and the rest were willing to
risk their lives fighting for her in the forest against
the greater force of Meliagrance; not only was she their
queen, but a woman who in the best womanly way
would requite them for their services. When, sore
wounded, they were captives, like Guinevere herself, in
the castle of the craven prince, " in no wise the queen
would not suffer the wounded knights to be from her,
but . . . they were laid within draughts by her cham-
ber, upon beds and pillows, that she herself might see to
them, that they wanted nothing." [1] And when finally
shame and sorrow came, she was not only courageous
in her resistance of Mordred, but also firmly self-sac-
rificing in her refusal to live her last days in love
at Joyous Gard with Lancelot. When he went to the
nunnery where the Queen had taken refuge, to urge
her to go with him, —

"Then was queen Guenever ware of Sir Launcelot as he
walked in the cloister, and when she saw him there she
swooned thrice, that all the ladies and gentlewomen had
work enough to hold the queen up. So when she might
speak, she called ladies and gentlewomen to her, and said,
Ye marvel, fair ladies, why I make this fare. Truly, she
said, it is for the sight of yonder knight that yonder stand-
eth: wherefore, I pray you all, call him to me. When Sir
Launcelot was brought to her, then she said to all the ladies,
Through this man and me hath all this war been wrought,
and the death of the most noblest knights of the world; for
through our love that we have loved together is my most
noble lord slain. Therefore, Sir Launcelot, wit thou well I
am set in such a plight to get my soul's health; and yet
I trust, through God's grace, that after my death to have a

[1] Book xix, ch. 6.

sight of the blessed face of Christ, and at doomsday to sit on his right side, for as sinful as ever I was are saints in heaven. Therefore, Sir Launcelot, I require thee and beseech thee heartily, for all the love that ever was betwixt us, that thou never see me more in the visage; and I command thee on God's behalf, that thou forsake my company, and to thy kingdom thou turn again and keep well thy realm from war and wrack. For as well as I have loved thee, mine heart will not serve me to see thee; for through thee and me is the flower of kings and knights destroyed. Therefore, Sir Launcelot, go to thy realm, and there take thee a wife, and live with her with joy and bliss, and I pray thee heartily pray for me to our Lord, that I may amend my mis-living. Now, sweet madam, said Sir Launcelot, would ye that I should return again unto my country, and there to wed a lady? Nay, madam, wit you well that shall I never do: for I shall never be so false to you of that I have promised, but the same destiny that ye have taken you to, I will take me unto, for to please Jesu, and ever for you I cast me specially to pray. If thou wilt do so, said the queen, hold thy promise; but I may never believe but that thou wilt turn to the world again. Well, madam, said he, ye say as pleaseth you, yet wist you me never false of my promise, and God defend but I should forsake the world as ye have done. For in the quest of the Sancgreal I had forsaken the vanities of the world, had not your lord been. And if I had done so at that time with my heart, will, and thought, I had passed all the knights that were in the Sancgreal, except Sir Galahad my son. And therefore, lady, sithen ye have taken you to perfection, I must needs take me to perfection of right. For I take record of God, in you I have had my earthly joy. And if I had found you now so disposed, I had cast me to have had you into mine own realm. . . . But sithen I find you thus disposed, I insure you faithfully I will ever take me to penance, and pray while my life lasteth, if that I may find any hermit either grey or white that will receive me. Wherefore, madam, I pray you kiss me, and never do more. Nay, said the queen, that shall I never do, but abstain you from such works. And they departed. But there was never so hard an hearted man, but he would have wept to see the dolour that they made." [1]

Poor lady, who never found peace in her palaces of Westminster and Cardigan, Carlisle and Camelot, she found something of it finally, after she took her last leave of Lancelot, in this nunnery at quiet Almesbury, there to the southeast of Salisbury Plain in the valley of the Wiltshire Avon, with its stately trees, green fields, and low hills rising all around, where nothing seems to move but the cool, quick-flowing little river.

One reason that Malory's characters are only partially real is that he lacked the humor essential to the best realism. Such as he had is general, conventional, and broad. Lancelot, for example, like Fielding's equally chivalrous but less romantic Parson Adams, gets into the wrong bed, where he is surprised by the arrival of a knight, who takes him for quite a different person.[1] It is in short the humor of the practical joke, like that of so many of Shakspere's Falstaffian scenes, and of some in *Don Quixote* and most in *Peregrine Pickle*, though far less amusing. When Sir Dinadan, overthrown at jousting by Sir Lancelot disguised as a maid, is dressed in woman's garments and brought before Queen Guinevere, she laughs till she falls down ; and the same knight often diverts La Beale Isoud to a like degree ; but a modern reader can scarce smile faintly at his fun.

More intellectual humor is almost wholly wanting. Though Malory makes much of the lay which Eliot the Harper composed at the instigation of Sir Dinadan

[1] Book xxi, chs. 9–10. [2] Book vi, chs. 4 and 5.

to sing before King Mark, to the vast entertainment
of all Mark's enemies who heard it, he never quotes
so much as one word of the lay, which, had he been
really a humorist, he would probably have quoted
entire.[1] In fine, Malory gives no delicately humorous
touches to his narrative, with one or two possible ex-
ceptions. When the Bishop of Canterbury "does" his
threatened curse on the incorrigible Mordred, with
book, bell, and candle, it is "in the most orgulous
wise that might be done." Were this in Chaucer,
we should think it a hit at the self-importance of a
haughty church dignitary; but, being in Malory, the
passage is probably amusing not by intent, but only
on account of its quaint expression. This brings us
to the cause of much that seems humorous in Malory
to-day. For instance, Arthur's reply to King Ryence,[2]
who sends the extraordinary message that he wishes
Arthur's beard given him to trim his mantle, is humor-
ous chiefly because of its archaic language: " ' Well,'
said Arthur, ' thou hast said thy message, the which
is the most villainous and lewdest message that ever
man heard sent unto a king; also thou mayest see my
beard is full young yet to make a trimming of it. But
tell thou thy king this: I owe him none homage, nor
none of mine elders; but or it be long he shall do me
homage on both his knees, or else he shall lose his
head, by the faith of my body, for this is the most
shamefulest message that ever I heard speak of.' "
Here the serious acceptance of an absurdly impossible
situation, not less than the phrasing, amuses the mod-

---

[1] The lay, to be sure, is not given in detail in the French prose
Tristram, nor do we get any definite idea of its contents, though enough
is said about it to excite our interest.

[2] Book i, ch. 26.

ern reader ; and it is these, his odd phrasing and his unnecessary seriousness, that produce one of Malory's charms, his quaintness.

Mere quaintness is not enough to keep a book alive for centuries ; and since both the characters and the background of Malory's narrative have only partial reality, one naturally asks, what is it further which has given the *Morte Darthur* its long life ? It cannot be excellence of plot, for we have already remarked that Malory, in " reducing from French to English," by no means got rid of all superfluous material, a fault which to some extent spoils the unity of his work. And yet when one considers that nearly every adventure is brought into some connection with Arthur, one must say that the book fails not so much in unity as in coherence. The chief trouble is that Malory has too many stories to tell, all of which he is so anxious to work in that he is seldom off with one before he is on with another. The result is often extreme confusion. Now and then, to be sure, a story stands out distinctly, as the tale of those unfortunate brothers, Balin and Balan,[1] or that of the young knight, Gareth, and the scornful damsel, Linet ;[2] but for the most part, no uninterrupted tale runs through a whole book. I myself do not altogether mind this weaving together of many threads. Though most of us are agreed, I suppose, that the secret of art is selection, there may be so much selection as to produce an effect of simplicity which no human being is likely to experience after childhood, and then only rarely. Malory is guilty of no such simplicity. In the suddenly interrupted companionships and friendships and loves of his knights

[1] Book ii.　　　　[2] Book vii.

and ladies, in their continual meetings with the unex-
pected, a reader who will may see something of the
confusion of actual life. Indeed, Malory has that with-
out which the highest art does not exist — a sense of
the mystery of life. He is as far from being con-
fined by fact as most writers of the eighteenth century
were from getting beyond it. From the beginning of
his tale, with the love of Uther Pendragon for the
Lady Igraine, to its conclusion, the death upon a Good
Friday in the Holy Land of the last four knights of
the Round Table, who have gone thither to do battle
" upon the miscreants or Turks," Malory is never
unconscious of the poetic wonder of this world, of
the truths which we feel rather than know.

For a wider circle of readers a great charm of
Malory's story is its rapidity; there is scarcely ever a
cessation of action. From the first sentence, which
tells of the war between Uther and the Duke of Tin-
tagil, to the author's valedictory, — " Here is the end
of the whole book of King Arthur . . . and . . . I
pray you all pray for my soul," — something is always
happening. Sometimes the action is too rapid; it takes
your breath away; but on the whole it is refreshing
in these days when morbid introspection and hesita-
tion too often prevent doing.

After all, though, the most potent charm of Malory
is his style. It is not a style suited to the essay, as
may be seen by looking at his childishly and delight-
fully ingenuous little chapter on true love and the
month of May, which begins : " And thus it passed
on from Candlemas until after Easter, that the month
of May was come, when every lusty heart beginneth
to blossom and to bring forth fruit; for like as herbs

and trees bring forth fruit and flourish in May, in likewise every lusty heart, that is in any manner a lover, springeth and flourisheth in lusty deeds ; " and soon runs its brief, illogical course, concluding : " Therefore all ye that be lovers call unto your remembrance the month of May, like as did Queen Guenever. For whom I make here a little mention, that while she lived she was a true lover, and therefore she had a good end." [1] After which comes the account of Guinevere's Maying, to which this chapter is leading up.

Now and then the style is tangled and inorganic, as in the sentence which tells of Sir Tristram's death : —

" Also that traitor king slew the noble knight Sir Tristram, as he sat harping afore his lady La Beale Isoud, with a trenchant glaive, for whose death was much bewailing of every knight that ever were in Arthur's days : there were never none so bewailed as was Sir Tristram, and Sir Lamorak, for they were traitorously slain, Sir Tristram by King Mark, and Sir Lamorak by Sir Gawaine and his brethren." [2]

But what if Malory sometimes writes sentences which would keep a boy from passing his college examinations? What if he is hopelessly unreasonable in the use of the connectives " and " and " so " ? In Malory's prose, as in that of few other authors, is there beautiful rhythm. Besides, he is dignified, simple, and generally direct ; excellently specific, as we have seen ; and now, after the lapse of years, charmingly quaint. It is the excellence of his style, in fact, that makes Malory the earliest English prose writer of whom we can read many pages at a time with pleasure. Except for the Book of Common Prayer, the *Morte Darthur* is the best known English prose before the King

[1] Book xviii, ch. 25.   [2] Book xix, ch. 11.

James Bible, whose style it frequently suggests ; and when you have added to these three the *Pilgrim's Progress*, you have virtually all the English prose before Queen Anne's day which is still widely read.

In fine, Malory lives because he is a great epic writer. He has the three epic traits which Matthew Arnold justly ascribes to Homer — swiftness, simplicity, nobility. Like Homer, he has swiftness only in detail ; he does not hurry us to the final catastrophe. Often he takes us aside, rather than ahead, but only for the moment ; he leads us after all pretty steadily towards his end. And always he is simple and noble in diction, and generally simple and noble in thought. If you will see Malory at his best, read the chapter which tells of Arthur's departure for Avalon. After Bedivere, finally obedient to his king, threw the sword, Excalibur, back into the lake, he took Arthur

" upon his back, and so went with him to that water side. And when they were at the water side, even fast by the bank hoved a little barge, with many fair ladies in it, and among them all was a queen, and all they had black hoods, and all they wept and shrieked when they saw king Arthur. Now put me into the barge, said the king : and so he did softly. And there received him three queens with great mourning, and so they set him down, and in one of their laps King Arthur laid his head, and then that queen said, Ah, dear brother, why have ye tarried so long from me ? Alas, this wound on your head hath caught over much cold. And so then they rowed from the land ; and Sir Bedivere beheld all those ladies go from him. Then Sir Bedivere cried, Ah, my lord Arthur, what shall become of me now ye go from me, and leave me here alone among mine enemies. Comfort thyself, said the king, and do as well as thou mayest, for in me is no trust for to trust in. For I will into the vale of Avilion, to heal me of my grievous wound. And if thou hear never more of me, pray for my soul. But ever the queens and the ladies wept and shrieked, that it was pity to hear. And as soon as Sir Bedivere had lost sight of the barge, he wept and wailed, and so took the forest, and so he went all that night, and in the morning he was ware betwixt two holts hoar of a chapel and an hermitage." [1]

Tennyson's *Passing of Arthur*, which this chapter inspired, is not nobler.

NOTE. — In quoting from Professor Kittredge's article, in all references to the year of Malory's death, I have changed 1470, the date which Professor Kittredge first took to be right, to 1471, which is the correct date. Professor Kittredge tells me that Dugdale, from whom he got the date, made an error in computation in passing from the year of our Lord to the year of Edward IV's reign. Dugdale should have called it "11" instead of "10 Ed. IV." An "inquisitio post mortem," dated November 6, 1471, places Malory's death in the preceding March ; and "in a manuscript" — I quote from a letter of Professor Kittredge's — "ca. 1533 (MS. Cotton. Vitellius, F. 12) which gives an account of the monuments in Gray Friars, near Newgate, we have : 'Sub 2ᵃ parte fenestre 4ᵉ sub lapide jacet dñs Thomas Mallere valens miles Qui obijt 14 die mensis Marcij Ao dñi 1470 de parochia de Monkenkirkby in comitatu Warwici." From this it would appear that *valens miles* was probably on Malory's tombstone. March 14, 1470, is of course March 14, 1471, according to our notation.

A second Thomas Malory, already rejected by Professor Kittredge, was suggested for our author by Mr. A. T. Martin in *The Identity of the Author of the "Morte d'Arthur*," published in 1898,[2] when Mr. Martin had not seen Professor Kittredge's article. Since this Thomas is designated in records as *armiger* and never *miles*, knight, there can be little doubt that the Sir Thomas Malory of whom Professor Kittredge writes was the author of the *Morte Darthur*. Mr. Martin first called attention to the "inquisitio post mortem," so important in fixing the year of Malory's death.

[1] Book xxi, ch. 5.   [2] *Archæologia*, vol. lvi.

XIV

CAXTON AND THE TRANSITION

WILLIAM CAXTON deserves some mention in any
history of Arthurian Romance, because, according to
the colophon of the *Morte Darthur*, it was by him
that this most important of English romances was
"deuyded in to xxi bookes chapytred and enprynted
and fynysshed in thabbey westmestre the last day
of Iuyl the yere of our lord MCCCCLXXXV." This
Caxton, born in Kent about 1422, after being appren-
ticed to a London mercer, removed to Bruges, then a
great mercantile centre of western Europe, where he
became so prominent among the many Englishmen
settled in the Netherlands that he was chosen the
Governor of the English Merchants in Flanders and
Brabant.

Caxton had considerable interest in literature, which
presumably his mercantile life did not give him time
to gratify to the full. At length, in 1468, he got more
time for literary interests. In that year Charles the
Bold of Burgundy married Princess Margaret of York,
sister to Edward IV of England. On her arrival in
the Netherlands, Caxton became a favorite with her,
and soon gave up his business to accept a position in
her household. Just at that time Bruges was feeling
the Renaissance. Books were numerous there; and
Caxton got hold of a French story of the Siege of

Troy, entitled *Le Recueuil des Histoires de Troyes*, compiled by Raoul Lefevre, who had been chaplain to Philip the Good of Burgundy. A translation of this by Caxton so pleased the Duchess Margaret that she gladly accepted the book as a gift. Her interest made it fashionable. Presently so many of her English lords and ladies, and of the English merchants in Bruges, too, were requesting copies, that it was impossible to supply the demand. Caxton accordingly consulted one Colard Mansion, a caligrapher in Bruges, about the new invention of printing. They studied its technicalities, and brought out, probably in 1474, the *Recuyell of the Historyes of Troye*, the first printed book in the English tongue.

The next year Caxton published the *Game and Playe of the Chesse*, translated from the French, which, like his *Historyes of Troye*, had a great success. The favor given to these first ventures in printing soon determined Caxton to introduce the new invention into his native country. He gave up his position at the Burgundian court, and went home to establish a printing-press close by Westminster Abbey, possibly in one of the connected buildings.[1] There Caxton printed seventy-one books. Malory's *Morte Darthur* was the fifty-second.

Though a man of literary feeling, Caxton was far inferior to Malory in literary ability. His *Charlemagne*, translated from the French and published in 1485, — the same year as the *Morte Darthur*, — and his *Four Sons of Aymon*, translated and published in 1489, are both now forgotten. It is fortunate, therefore, that Malory, and not Caxton, translated and

[1] Seven colophons say, "Printed in the Abbey."

abridged various French Arthurian romances. Had
Caxton done so, the work would probably not have
lived; though without Caxton to publish it, the work
might equally have perished.

Caxton brought out Malory's book because it was
his idea to publish books of various kinds in order to
satisfy various tastes. At first, however, he seemed to
think the Arthurian legends hardly worthy of his
attention, and he was apparently unwilling to trans-
late any French Arthurian romance himself. In his
preface to the *Morte Darthur* he says: "After that
I had accomplished and finished divers histories . . .
of great conquerors and princes, . . . many noble and
divers gentlemen of this realm of England came and
demanded me many and ofttimes, wherefore that I
have not do made and imprint the noble history of
the Saint Greal, and of the most renowned Christian
king, first and chief of the three best Christian, and
worthy, king Arthur, which ought most to be remem-
bered amongst us Englishmen tofore all other Chris-
tian kings. . . . To whom I answered that divers men
hold opinion that there was no such Arthur, and that
all such books as been made of him, be but feigned and
fables, because that some chronicles make of him no
mention, nor remember him nothing, nor of his knights.
Whereto they answered, and one in special said, that
in him that should say or think that there was never
such a king called Arthur, might well be aretted great
folly and blindness. For he said that there were many
evidences of the contrary. First ye may see his sep-
ulchre in the Monastery of Glastingbury. And also in
Policronicon, in the fifth book the sixth chapter, and
in the seventh book the twenty-third chapter, where

his body was buried, and after found, and translated
into the said monastery. . . . Also Galfridus in his
British book recounteth his life; and in divers places
of England many remembrances be yet of him, and
shall remain perpetually, and also of his knights.
First in the Abbey of Westminster, at St. Edward's
shrine, remaineth the print of his seal in red wax
closed in beryl, in which is written, *Patricius Arthu-
rus Britannie, Gallie, Germanie, Dacie, Imperator.*
Item in the Castle of Dover ye may see Gâwaine's
scull, and Cradok's mantle: at Winchester the Round
Table:[1] in other places Launcelot's sword and many
other things. Then all these things considered, there
can no man reasonably gainsay but that there was a
king of this land named Arthur. For in all places,
Christian and heathen, he is reputed and taken for
one of the nine worthy, and the first of the three
Christian men. And also, he is more spoken of be-
yond the sea, more books made of his noble acts, than
there be in England, as well in Dutch, Italian, Span-
ish, and Greekish, as in French. And yet of record
remain in witness of him in Wales, in the town of
Camelot,[2] the great stones and the marvellous works

[1] The Round Table to which Caxton refers still hangs on the wall
in Winchester Castle; and inasmuch as it was an object of curiosity
in Caxton's time, it is now a relic of undoubted antiquity. The story
of the guide to the castle is that the table was painted as it now
appears, at the command of Henry VIII. However that may be, it
is a curious-looking affair, eighteen feet in diameter, with the roses of
York and Lancaster united in the middle, or at the hub, as one might
say, — symbolical of the union of the two houses in the family of
Tudor, — and divided, like a wheel of fortune, into spaces, radiating
like spokes, alternately blue and white, with the name of the knight
at the head of each, who was supposed to sit there. The place for
Arthur himself is at the top of the table, as it now hangs on the wall.

[2] Caxton apparently confused Camelot and Caerleon.

of iron lying under the ground, and royal vaults, which divers now living have seen. . . . Wherefore . . . I have after the simple conning that God hath sent to me . . . enprised to imprint a book of the noble histories of the said King Arthur, and of certain of his knights, after a copy unto me delivered, which copy Sir Thomas Malorye did take out of certain books of French, and reduced it into English. And I, according to my copy, have down set it in print, to the intent that noble men may see and learn the noble acts of chivalry, the gentle and virtuous deeds that some knights used in those days. . . . For herein may be seen noble chivalry, courtesy, humanity, friendliness, hardiness, love, friendship, cowardice, murder, hate, virtue, and sin. Do after the good and leave the evil, and it shall bring you to good fame and renommee. And for to pass the time this book shall be pleasant to read in, but for to give faith and belief that all is true that is contained herein, ye be at your liberty. . . .

" And for to understand briefly the content of this volume, I have divided it into xxi Books, and every book chaptered, as hereafter shall by God's grace follow . . ."

Thus Caxton, though doubting at first the advisability of publishing an Arthurian romance, was at length persuaded to bring out the *Morte Darthur;* and thus to some extent he influenced the form in which it appeared, though probably, as he says, only by the division of the text into books and chapters. Nor can it be said that he deserves great credit for this division which sometimes seems unreasonable and arbitrary, in spite of his referring to it in both

preface and colophon. The books are of very une-
qual length. The tenth, which is the longest, consists
of eighty-eight chapters; the fifteenth, which is the
shortest, of six. Moreover, books xi and xiii, which
treat the same material, might have been combined
in one book. Nor is the division into chapters much
more skilful. Two or three times a chapter stops in
the middle of a sentence, as the fourth chapter of the
twenty-first book. " I would it were so, said the king,"
is the last of this chapter. The next begins: " but I
may not stand, my head works so."

The fact is significant that Caxton, the first Eng-
lish printer, printed the work of Malory, the last
English writer of note to express the mediæval spirit.
It means that we are at the passing of the Middle
Ages. With Malory we say good-bye to them; after
him we come to a time which seems comparatively
modern. Yet it is a mistake to hold, as some writers
do, that the people of the Middle Ages were utterly
different from ourselves. Their books show that their
life differed from ours superficially rather than funda-
mentally ; and, even superficially, not so much as some
people believe. Mark Twain, for instance, in his *Con-
necticut Yankee in King Arthur's Court*, in making
his knights and ladies of vastly different temper from
our own, is mistaken. He has much to say about their
lack of cleanness and their brutality to animals. In
point of fact, the knights of romance were as fond of
bathing as the athletic young gentlemen of our own
time. A bath was one of the first hospitalities offered
to a knight when he came to a strange castle ; and he
seldom passed a woodland pool in summer without a
refreshing dip. Sometimes, too, he happily found a fair

damsel laving her white form in the same cool water. As to animals, though in general they may have needed the protection of a society for the prevention of cruelty, plenty of individual pets received all the attention which such pampered favorites enjoy to-day. Many a knight had his favorite steed, as Gawain his Gringalet, which he cherished with all care and affection. Almost every romancer speaks of dogs in a way which shows sincere love for them, as witness Tristram's fondness for his hound Hodain, Guingamor's care for his uncle's hunting-dogs, and the many ladies who came to Arthur's court or went about their own castles fondling the brachets which they carried on their arms. Furthermore, in their relations with one another, these mediæval knights continually showed, in the words of Caxton, "humanity, love, courtesy, and very gentleness." [1] Few young men of any age could do better than cultivate those five virtues for which Gawain was conspicuous — frankness, fellowship, purity, courtesy, and compassion.[2] Gawain and Lancelot and Guinevere and many others might adapt themselves without great trouble to a modern drawing-room.

At the same time they would have much to learn. Their life of castles and pageants and tournaments, substantially the same in the pages of Geoffrey of Monmouth and three hundred and fifty years later in the pages of Malory, did of necessity differ in many ways from the life of ladies and gentlemen to-day, with their calls, receptions, dances, dinner-parties, concerts, and theatres. Then, too, in other than superficial ways,

[1] Preface to the *Morte Darthur*, last paragraph.
[2] See *Gawain and the Green Knight*.

mediæval people differed from ourselves. Their reli-
gion, summing up its narrow, unpractical spiritual
ideals in the mystical legend of the Grail, was nearer
superstition than religion is to-day. Lords and ladies
concerned themselves very little with the lower classes
except in individual cases. As you read the old ro-
mances, you hardly know that there was a populace
manufacturing in the towns, and tilling the soil and
tending the cattle in the country. But there were ad-
vantages in those less thoughtful days. Our mediæval
ancestors, who did not bother with problems of soci-
ety, did not concern themselves, either, with personal
problems. If a gentleman wanted a strong drink,
he drank it, worrying neither about the effect on his
own stomach, nor about the deplorable example he
might be setting his neighbor. If he could not accept
the mediæval church as he found it, he was less likely
to attempt reform of its abuses like Wicliff, than to
poke satirical fun at them like Chaucer. Life, in short,
was simpler and calmer than now; and so, as we emerge
from the Middle Ages into a period which, compared
with our own, is still simple, we find it, compared with
the older times, modern and complex : the period, that
is, of the early Renaissance, the immediate precursor
of the seething Elizabethan age.

The more we study this early Renaissance, the more
we feel that Malory wrote just in time. In Caxton's
preface is a hint that the great day for Arthurian
romance was passing ; a few years more, and it would
have passed. The changes which were now to crowd
thick and fast on Europe made thinking men even
more sceptical than Caxton as to the reality of Ar-
thur. In 1483, two years before the publication of

the *Morte Darthur*, Martin Luther was born, who was to strike the hardest blow at the mediæval church. In 1505, twenty years after the book was published, John Knox was born, whose stern Calvinism had little in common with mediæval romance. Again, only a few years after Malory's book appeared, some say in 1491 at Oxford, Greek was taught for the first time in England. Later, in 1497, Erasmus, the foremost scholar of his age, seems to have made his first visit to England, who, in the early years of the sixteenth century, was teaching Greek at Cambridge. And it was almost seven years to a day after the appearance of the *Morte Darthur*, — on the 3d of August, 1492, — that Columbus sailed on his momentous voyage from Palos to discover a new world beyond the western seas. Tudor England, that is, suddenly came face to face with two new worlds. Across the heaving Atlantic was an actual world of wonder, far beyond the sunset where the primitive Celts, gazing from the headlands of the west, had fancied Avalon to lie. In the new libraries lived again the old world of classical antiquity, past forever except in the books and statues and temples of Greece and Rome: a world known only imperfectly to the Middle Ages, which had made Alexander the Great and Julius Cæsar kings like Charlemagne and Arthur, which had dressed their followers and the champions of Athens and Thebes in mediæval armor, and which knew no incident in the Tale of Troy so well as the love of Troilus and Cressida, of which Homer never heard. Then hard upon these discoveries followed the defection from the Church of Rome, and the subsequent acquaintance of all reading England with the Old and New Testaments in the most beautiful and rhythmical of English prose. No wonder, with all these changes, that the greatest literary minds of England in the sixteenth century, as they sought inspiration for original work, drank commonly of other than mediæval springs.

Yet the old romances had by no means lost favor entirely. The Arthurian stories, among others, remained popular still, as various editions of Malory show; but for a century after his *Morte Darthur* came out, there was no new literary treatment of Arthurian material in England worthy of attention. Finally, as the sixteenth century drew to its close, notable Arthurian works began again. *Albion's England*, by William Warner, published in 1586, devoted several stanzas to Arthur's wars. The first Arthurian drama in English,[1] *The Misfortunes of Arthur*, was performed before Queen Elizabeth in February, 1588. And already a much greater work introducing Arthur had been begun, though no part of it was to be made public for two years yet — Spenser's *Faerie Queene.*[2]

[1] Hans Sachs (1494–1576) wrote a play in 1553, *Tristrant und Isolde.*
[2] Spenser seems to have had this in mind more than ten years before the first three books were published.

XV

SPENSER

Spenser is remarkable as one of the most inventive of our English poets, for he created his own poetic language and a stanza of unusual beauty. Born in London soon after 1550, he entered Pembroke Hall, Cambridge, in 1569, where he studied the classics diligently and formed an important literary friendship with Gabriel Harvey. Thanks to him, Spenser was subsequently introduced to some of the leading literary men in London, among them Sir Philip Sidney and Leicester. Probably through their influence, he was appointed Secretary to Lord Grey, who was sent as Lord Deputy to Ireland in 1580. Having got a grant some years later of a fairly large estate in the County of Cork, Spenser remained there the rest of his life, except for three visits to London. During one of these, in 1590, appeared the first three books of the *Faerie Queene*, containing so much praise of Elizabeth, to whom they were dedicated, that the poet received a pension of fifty pounds a year. In 1594 Spenser was married. The fourth, fifth, and sixth books of the *Faerie Queene* appeared in 1596. Before any more were ready, the Irish Rebellion of 1598 occurred, in which Spenser's house was burned, with his youngest child in it. He died in London, poverty-stricken (so the tradition is), in January, 1599.

The *Faerie Queene*, Spenser's great work, shows that interest in Arthurian romance was still alive, for the poet makes Arthur his hero ; but it is Prince Arthur, not King Arthur, and his adventures are mostly new to us. Fortunately, with the first three books of his poem, Spenser published a letter of explanation to Sir Walter Raleigh, with whom he became acquainted in Ireland, setting forth his plan clearly. It must be said that, considering the fragmentary condition in which Spenser left his poem, we should find the story hard to understand without this letter, which is in the main as follows : —

Sir,

Knowing how doubtfully all Allegories may be construed, and this booke of mine, which I have entitled *The Faery Queene*, being a continued Allegorie . . . I have thought good . . . to discover unto you the generall intention and meaning. . . . The generall end . . . is to fashion a gentleman or noble person in vertuous and gentle discipline. Which for that I conceived shoulde be most plausible and pleasing, beeing coloured with an historicall fiction [1] . . . I chose the historie of king Arthure, as most fit for the excellencie of his person, beeing made famous by many mens former workes, and also furthest from the danger of envie, and suspicion of present time. In which I have followed all the antique poets historicall : first Homer, . . . then Virgil, . . . after him Ariosto . . . and lately Tasso. . . . By ensample of which excellent Poets, I labour to pourtraict in Arthure, before he was king,

---

[1] In spite of this statement, there is little of the pseudo-historical Arthur in Spenser.

the image of a brave knight, perfected in the twelve
private morall vertues, as Aristotle hath devised; the
which is the purpose of these first twelve bookes:
which if I finde to be well accepted, I may be perhaps
encoraged to frame the other part of pollitike vertues
in his person, after he came to bee king.

. . . Arthure . . . I conceive, after his long edu-
cation by Timon [1] (to whom he was by Merlin deliv-
ered to be brought up, so soone as he was borne of
the Lady Igrayne) to have seene in a dreame or vision
the Faerie Queene, with whose excellent beautie rav-
ished, hee awaking, resolved to seeke her out: and so,
being by Merlin armed, and by Timon thoroughly in-
structed, he went to seeke her forth in Faery land.
In the Faery Queene I meane *Glory* in my generall
intention: but in my particular I conceive the most
excellent and glorious person of our soveraine the
Queene, and her kingdome in Faery land. And yet,
in some places else, I doe otherwise shadow her. For
considering shee beareth two persons, the one of a
most royall Queene or Empress, the other of a most
vertuous and beautifull lady, this latter part in some
places I doe expresse in Belphoebe. . . . So in the
person of Prince Arthure I sette forth Magnificence
in particular, which vertue, for that (according to
Aristotle and the rest) it is the perfection of all the
rest, and containeth in it them all, therefore in the
whole course I mention the deeds of Arthure appli-
able to that vertue, which I write of in that booke.
But of the twelve other vertues I make xii other
knights and patrons, for the more varietie of the his-
torie: Of which these three bookes containe three.

[1] Sir Ector in Malory.

The first, of the Knight of the Redcrosse, in whom I expresse Holinesse: the seconde of Sir Guyon, in whom I set foorth Temperance: the third of Britomartis, a Lady knight in whom I picture Chastitie. But because the beginning of the whole worke seemeth abrupt and as depending upon other antecedents, it needs that yee know the occasion of these three knights severall adventures. . . . The beginning therefore of my historie, if it were to be told by an Historiographer, should be the twelfthe booke, which is the last; where I devise that the Faery Queene kept her annuall feast twelve daies; uppon which twelve severall dayes, the occasions of the twelve severall adventures hapned, which being undertaken by xii severall knights, are in these twelve books severally handled and discoursed.

The first was this. In the beginning of the feast, there presented him selfe a tall clownish younge man, who falling before the Queene of Faeries desired a boone (as the manner then was) which during that feast she might not refuse: which was that hee might have the atchievement of any adventure, which during that feast should happen; that being granted, he rested him selfe on the floore, unfit through his rusticitie for a better place. Soone after entred a faire Ladie in mourning weedes, riding on a white Asse, with a dwarfe behind her leading a warlike steed, that bore the Armes of a knight, and his speare in the dwarfes hand. She falling before the Queene of Faeries, complayned that her father and mother, an ancient King and Queene, had bene by an huge dragon many years shut up in a brazen Castle, who thence suffered them not to issew: and therefore besought the

Faery Queene to assigne her some one of her knights
to take on him that exployt. Presently that clownish
person upstarting, desired that adventure; whereat the
Queene much wondering, and the Lady much gaine-
saying, yet he earnestly importuned his desire. In the
end the Lady told him, that unlesse the armour which
she brought would serve him (that is, the armour of a
Christian man specified by St. Paul, v Ephes.[1]) that
he could not succeed in that enterprise: which being
forth-with put upon him with due furnitures there-
unto, he seemed the goodliest man in al that company,
and was well liked of the Lady. And eftsoones taking
on him knighthood, and mounting on that straunge
Courser, he went forth with her on that adventure;
where beginneth the first booke, viz.

"A gentle Knight was pricking on the playne," etc.

The second day there came in a Palmer bearing
an Infant with bloody hands, whose Parents he com-
plained to have bene slaine by an enchauntresse called
Acrasia: and therefore craved of the Faery Queene,
to appoint him some knight to performe that adven-
ture, which being assigned to Sir Guyon, he presently
went foorth with that same Palmer: which is the be-
ginning of the second booke and the whole subject
thereof. The third day there came in a Groome, who
complained before the Faery Queene, that a vile En-
chaunter, called Busirane, had in hand a most faire
Lady, called Amoretta, whom he kept in most griev-
ous torment. Whereupon Sir Scudamour, the lover
of that Lady, presently tooke on him that adventure.
But beeing unable to performe it by reason of the

[1] Spenser should have written *vi* Ephes.

hard Enchauntments, after long sorrow, in the end met with Britomartis, who succoured him, and reskewed his love.

But by occasion hereof, many other adventures are intermedled; but rather as accidents then intendments. As the love of Britomart . . . the vertuousnesse of Belphoebe ; and many the like.

Thus much, Sir, I have briefly over-run to direct your understanding to the wel-head of the History, that from thence gathering the whole intention of the conceit, ye may as in a handfull gripe all the discourse, which otherwise may happely seem tedious and confused. So humbly craving the continuance of your honourable favour towards me, and th' eternall establishment of your happiness, I humbly take leave.

Yours most humbly affectionate,

EDM. SPENSER.

23 Ianuarie, 1589.

This letter testifies to Spenser's knowledge of romances. In his twelve knights, suggestive of the twelve peers of Charlemagne, we have one of the many instances in the *Faerie Queene* of reminiscence of the Charlemagne legends, whose influence came to Spenser, as he says, through Tasso and Ariosto. Strong, too, is the influence of the Arthurian legends, which Spenser evidently knew best through Malory. The association of Arthur with the Faerie Queene may have been suggested by Malory's association of Arthur with the Lady of the Lake, or by Arthur's connection with Avalon, whence came Excalibur, and whither he went himself after his last battle. Or, in view of Spenser's admiration for " Dan Chaucer, well of English unde-

fyled," it may have been suggested by the beginning
of the *Wife of Bath's Tale:* —

> "In tholde dayes of the king Arthour,
> Of which that Britons speken greet honour,
> All was this laud fulfild of fayerye,
> The elf-queen, with her Ioly companye,
> Daunced ful ofte in many a grene mede."

No thoroughgoing investigation of Spenser's relation
to Arthurian writers has yet been made. Thomas
Warton's *Observations on the Faery Queen*, first
published in 1754, is still the best authority on the
subject.[1]

Only the first quest in the *Faerie Queene* is strongly
reminiscent of any famous Arthurian quest. The ap-
parently clownish Red Cross Knight, given as a cham-
pion to the "gaine-saying" Una, inevitably suggests
Sir Gareth, who sets out with the unwilling Linet to
free Dame Liones from the Red Knight of the Red
Lawns, or that other young knight whose adventures
are like Gareth's, Libeaus Desconus, who rode with
the unwilling Elene to free from prison her lady of
Sinadoun.[2] Arthur himself, as Spenser introduces
him, is hardly recognisable as the older Arthur, nor do
you see him much in the *Faerie Queene*, though from
what the poet wrote to Raleigh, you would expect to
see him often.

The famous prince makes his entry into the poem
in the first book, when Una, having lost her Red

---

[1] Cf. Marie Walther, Malory's *Einfluss auf Spensers Faerie Queene*,
Eisleben, 1898.

[2] For a discussion of Libeaus Desconus, see W. H. Schofield,
Harvard Studies in Philology and Literature, Boston, 1895. Cf. also
A. H. Billings, *Middle English Metrical Romances*, New York, 1901,
p. 134.

Cross knight through enchantment, has long sought him in vain.[1]

29 " At last she chaunced by good hap to meet
    A goodly knight, faire marching by the way,
    Together with his squire, arayed meet:
    His glitterand armour shined far away,
    Like glauncing light of Phœbus brightest ray;
    From top to toe no place appeared bare,
    That deadly dint of steele endanger may.
    Athwart his brest a bauldrick brave he ware,
That shind, like twinkling stars, with stones most pretious
        rare :

30 " And in the midst thereof, one pretious stone
    Of wondrous worth, and eke of wondrous mights,
    Shapt like a ladies head, exceeding shone,
    Like Hesperus emongst the lesser lights,
    And strove for to amaze the weaker sights:
    Thereby his mortall blade full comely hong
    In yvory sheath, ycarv'd with curious sights;
    Whose hilts were burnisht gold, and handle strong
Of mother pearle, and buckled with a golden tong.

31 " His haughtie helmet, horrid all with gold,
    Both glorious brightnesse and great terrour bred ;
    For all the crest a dragon did enfold
    With greedie pawes, and over all did spred
    His golden wings : his dreadfull hideous hed
    Close couched on the bever, seemd to throw
    From flaming mouth bright sparkles fiery red,
    That suddeine horrour to fainte hartes did show,
And scaly tayle was strecht adoune his back full low.

    .   .   .   .

33 " His warlike shield all closely cover'd was,
    Ne might of mortall eye be ever seene ;

---

[1] Book I, canto vii.

Not made of steele, nor of enduring bras,
Such earthly mettals soon consumed beene;
But all of diamond perfect pure and cleene
It framed was, one massy entire mould,
Hewen out of adamant rocke with engines keene,
That point of speare it never percen could,
Ne dint of direfull sword divide the substance would.

34 "The same to wight he never wont disclose,
But when as monsters huge he would dismay,
Or daunt unequall armies of his foes,
Or when the flying heavens he would affray:
For so exceeding shone his glistring ray,
That Phœbus golden face it did attaint,
As when a cloud his beames doth over-lay;
And silver Cynthia wexed pale and faint,
As when her face is staynd with magicke arts constraint.

35 "No magicke arts hereof had any might,
Nor bloody wordes of bold enchaunters call;
But all that was not such, as seemd in sight,
Before that shield did fade, and suddeine fall:
And, when him list the raskall routes appall,
Men into stones therewith he could transmew,
And stones to dust, and dust to nought at all:
And when him list the prouder lookes subdew,
He would them gazing blind, or turne to other hew.

36 "Ne let it seeme, that credence this exceeds;
For he that made the same was knowne right well
To have done much more admirable deedes:
It Merlin was, which whylome did excell
All living wightes in might of magicke spell:
Both shield, and sword, and armour all he wrought
For this young prince, when first to armes he fell;
But when he dyde, the Faerie Queene it brought
To Faerie lond, where yet it may be seene, if sought."

This prince is both like and unlike Geoffrey's or Chrétien's or Malory's king. The precious stone, shaped like a lady's head, in the midst of his baldric is perhaps a reminiscence of the image of the Virgin on Arthur's shield or banner, in the chronicles.[1] The dragon, on his golden helmet, is manifestly reminiscent of a similar dragon in Geoffrey's account.[2] The sword, however, which Spenser gives Arthur — by name, as we learn later, Morddure[3] — is different from Excalibur, in that it will not harm its owner.[4] And his shield is unlike any that Arthur ever had before.[5] It is not beyond Merlin's powers, however, to have fashioned such a shield.

When Arthur has met with Una, he hears of her distress at losing the Red Cross Knight, whom he accordingly rescues from Giant Orgoglio's castle, and restores to the lady. As the three ride on together, the prince, who is ignorant of his parentage, tells what he knows of his history.[6] From this he goes on to speak of his love for the Faerie Queene, whom he has seen in a vision. Then after exchanging presents with the Red Cross Knight, he bids farewell to him and Una, and rides on his own quest.

[1] Cf. Dr. Sebastian Evans's *Translation of Geoffrey of Monmouth*, London, 1904, p. 232. "Upon his shoulders, moreover, did he bear the shield that was named Priwen, wherein upon the inner side, was painted the image of Holy Mary, Mother of God, that many a time and oft did call her back unto his memory."

[2] *Ibid.* "Arthur . . . did set upon his head a helm of gold graven with the semblance of a dragon."

[3] Book II, viii, 21.   [4] *Ibid.*

[5] Rather does it resemble the shield of Atlante, which Ariosto describes, *Orlando Furioso*, ii, 55 and 56, with an added power like that of the Gorgon's head.

[6] This turns out to be virtually that of his youth as related by Malory. See *Faerie Queene*, I, canto ix, stanzas 3, 4, and 5.

Thus Arthur comes and goes in the various books of the *Faerie Queene*. Appearing by chance, he rides along for a time with the principal personages, to whom he usually renders conspicuous service. Then he goes off on his own adventures.

Spenser makes use of Arthur's meeting with Sir Guyon,[1] the hero of the second book, to work into his poem a partial summary of Geoffrey's chronicle. The prince and the knight, who have come to the House of Temperance, where lives the Lady Alma, put to rout a savage band besieging her house. The lady, wishing to entertain them most hospitably, shows them over her castle. In a remote chamber they find an old, old man sitting amid books and scrolls, with a boy to wait on him, and they ask his permission to look over two books which seem to them of special interest. The one Sir Guyon reads is *Antiquitee of Faery Lond;* the one Arthur reads is

> " An auncient booke hight *Briton moniments*,
> That of this lands first conquest did devize,
> And old division into Regiments,
> Till it reduced was to one mans governementes." [2]

And then follows

> " A chronicle of Briton kings
> From Brute to Uther's rayne,"

in giving which Spenser makes brief mention of the Grail : —

> " He [3] dide; and him succeeded Marius,
> Who joyd his dayes in great tranquility.

---

[1] Arthur rescues Sir Guyon from two paynim knights. In the contest, his own sword is at first in the hands of one of these knights. Cf. Arthur's combat with Accalon : Malory, bk. iv, chs. 9 and 10.

[2] Book II, ix, 59.   [3] Arviragus.

> Then Coyll; and after him good Lucius,
> That first received Christianity,
> The sacred pledge of Christe's Evangely.
> Yet true it is, that long before that day
> Hither came Joseph of Arimathy,
> Who brought with him the holy grayle, (they say)
> And preacht the truth; but since it greatly did decay." [1]

Spenser breaks the chronicle off suddenly : —

> " After him Uther, which Pendragon hight,[2]
> Suceeding . . ."

Had he continued it, he must have mentioned Arthur's birth and parentage, of which it served the poet's purpose to keep the prince still ignorant.

But Spenser finds a chance to give the rest of the British History later. After Guyon and Arthur have left Alma's castle, they meet Britomart, the Knight of Chastity, the heroine — or hero, for she is disguised as a man — of the third book. Her story shows again Spenser's debt to Round Table romances.

Britomart was the only child of King Ryence [3] of South Wales, quite a different person from Malory's savage Ryence of North Wales, for Spenser's Ryence was a gentle monarch, fond of his daughter, and happy in enjoying the services of the great Merlin, who lived at Ryence's court instead of at Arthur's. The sage characteristically had constructed a wonderful looking-glass for the king, in which whoever looked could see everything in the world. In this the fair Britomart one day saw the image of a knight, Artegal, with whom she fell instantly in love. Since she could not rest till she found who the knight was, she went in disguise with her nurse to interrogate Merlin. The two

[1] Book II, x, 53.   [2] Book II, x, 68.   [3] Book III, ii, 18.

had not questioned him long, when he could not help laughing aloud on account of the ease with which he penetrated their disguise. Then, having revealed to Britomart that she was destined to marry Artegal, he went on to foretell the line of princes who should descend from them. And here Spenser finds his chance to take up once more Geoffrey's History, — interrupted at the reign of Uther Pendragon in the book that Arthur was reading in the house of Alma, — which he now turns to glorify Queen Elizabeth by making her descend from the ancient British kings : —

> "Begin, O Clio ! and recount from hence
> My glorious Soveraines goodly ancestrye,
> Till that by dew degrees and long protense,
> Thou have it lastly brought unto Her Excellence." [1]

In tracing this descent, Spenser has to alter a little the genealogy of the old kings as given by Geoffrey.

Artegal, Spenser's own invention, except in so far as he is a portrait of Lord Grey, is a son of Gorlois, Duke of Cornwall, and Igerna, and so half-brother to Arthur himself. Vortipore, who, in all the chronicle accounts succeeded Constantine, Arthur's successor, is made a grandson of this Artegal and therefore grandnephew to Arthur. Vortipore's descendants Spenser gives substantially as Geoffrey does, except that Spenser is able to carry the history of the British princes four centuries farther. After the last one flees to Brittany, and the Saxons make themselves masters of Britain, Spenser refers briefly to the Danish Conquest and the Norman Conquest, during which the Britons still suffer under the yoke of foreign rulers. But now in Spenser's time the day long-prophesied

[1] Book III, iii, 4.

has come when the British race shall rule again, for a princess of the Welsh house of Tudor is on the throne, the descendant of Geoffrey's fabled kings.

48 " Tho, when the terme is full accomplishid
   There shall a sparke of fire, which hath long-while
   Bene in his ashes raked up and hid,
   Bee freshly kindled in the fruitfull Ile
   Of Mona,[1] where it lurketh in exile ;
   Which shall breake forth into bright burning
   And reach into the house that beares the stile
   Of roiall majesty and soveraine name :
So shall the Briton blood their crowne agayn reclame.

49 "Thenceforth eternall union shall be made
   Betweene the nations different afore,
   And sacred Peace shall lovingly persuade
   The warlike minds to learne her goodly lore,
   And civile armes to exercise no more :
   Then shall a royall Virgin raine, which shall
   Stretch her white rod over the Belgicke shore,
   And the great Castle smite so sore withall,
That it shall make him shake, and shortly learn to fall." [2]

Having thus been told by Merlin of her husband and her descendants and their glory, Britomart arms herself like a knight, and, with her nurse disguised as a squire, rides forth to find Artegal. She is tolerably safe in doing so, for her spear has the power of unhorsing any knight whom it may touch. After various adventures in which there is nothing strikingly Arthurian, she finds her chosen knight, and plights her troth with him. Nor is there anything strikingly

[1] This refers to the mistaken statement that Henry VII, Elizabeth's grandfather, was born in the island of Mona or Anglesey. In point of fact, he was born at Pembroke Castle in South Wales.
[2] Book III, iii.

Arthurian in the prince's own adventures, in Book III, either when with Britomart or later, or in Books IV, V, and VI, in which, as in the earlier books, he appears from time to time. It is in Book V that he performs his most important enterprise, which he undertakes by himself; he frees the Lady Belge (the Netherlands) from the Tyrant (Spain) who had grievously oppressed her.

Among other Arthurian reminiscences in Spenser are matters of detail, such as certain names, which seem to have been borrowed from the old romances, like " Castle Joyeous," [1] — perhaps suggested by Lancelot's *Joyous Gard*, — a castle at which Britomart is entertained. Then in the sixth book appears the " Blatant Beast," [2] symbolical of slander, which recalls Malory's " Questing Beast." Like that, the Blatant Beast is pursued especially by certain knights, but according to Spenser, by Sir Pelleas and Sir Lamoracke, instead of Sir Pellinor and Sir Palamides, who pursue Malory's Questing Beast.[3] In the same book of the *Faerie Queene* [4] the Lady Briana has a whim like that of Malory's King Ryence of North Wales. She wishes to have a mantle with the " beards of Knights and locks of Ladies lynd," and accordingly persuades her lover, Sir Crudor, to compel all knights and ladies who pass to be shaven or shorn. Sir Callidor, the knight of Courtesy, at length puts an end to this discourteous custom. And in the sixth book, too, appears Tristram, at the age of seventeen, a pleasing, well-grown youth, versed, as we should expect, in hunting and harping. Spenser seems to have had no

[1] Book III, i, 31.　　　[2] Canto i, stanza 7, following.
[3] Book I, ch. xix.　　　[4] Canto i, 11 ff.

reason for introducing Tristram except to add to the general interest of his poem by bringing into it one of the best known heroes of old romance.[1]

There are other reminiscences of the Round Table legends in the *Faerie Queene*, but those mentioned, which are the most obvious, are enough to show Spenser's spirit in handling the legends. It is a spirit as far removed from Malory's as if Spenser were one of ourselves ; he is on our side of the gulf which separates us from the Middle Ages. The temper of his time we feel not essentially unlike that of our own, and our own is not a time in which a great romantic legend could develop. No more was Spenser's. The Elizabethan age could keep the old romances alive, but it could not give them the nourishment requisite for further growth. This fact means that we have passed beyond the constructive period of the Arthurian legends. From now on they are interesting, not for the addition of new incidents, but for the different ways in which new generations have regarded the old incidents. Their history is much like that of the force in literature which we call romanticism. When this is powerful, there is interest in the old stories; when romanticism has little strength, these receive little consideration. In short, from the Renaissance to the present time the

[1] Canto ii. Spenser's Tristram, like the mediæval, though descended from the royal family of Cornwall, has been brought up in Lionesse. He differs from the earlier Tristram, however, in being Cornish on his father's side rather than on his mother's. According to Spenser, moreover, he is the rightful heir to the Cornish throne, which has been unjustly seized by his uncle. It is the father of Tristram who dies when Tristram is still a babe ; the mother lives until her son is grown. Whether Tristram would have played an important part had the *Faerie Queene* been completed is of course an unanswerable question ; very likely he would not have appeared in the poem again.

Arthurian legends may serve as a touchstone of romanticism.

Full as Spenser was of our spirit, he may, nevertheless, not have realised, as have the principal Arthurian writers of the nineteenth century, that the day had passed for permanently changing the form of the old legends. He may have thought that the queen who should share Arthur's throne might for the rest of time be Gloriana instead of Guinevere. And this brings us to the greatest difference between Spenser's attitude towards the Round Table romances and Malory's. Heretofore the usual attitude of the reading public was to regard the old stories as so largely historical that authors dared not change the main incidents of them. True, there were unbelievers, and more at the end of the Middle Ages than earlier, as Caxton's misgivings about the popularity of the *Morte Darthur* testified. Moreover, when the Arthurian world was a comparatively new discovery, certain writers, especially Chrétien de Troies, had treated the old stories with considerable independence. Such free treatment, however, corresponded, as we have seen, to the free treatment of historical events and characters in what we know to-day as historical novels, as Scott's use of Richard I of England and Louis XI of France in *Ivanhoe* and *Quentin Durward*. But Spenser went beyond free treatment like this. He was not trying to retell the old stories at all, or to reproduce any of the old characters. His aim was to make up a brand-new story, for which he was willing to draw material from all possible sources. Many were accessible to him. He knew his classics, he knew his Bible with something of a Puritan's knowledge, he knew his

French, he knew his Tasso and his Ariosto: and whatever he knew he was ready and able to transform to his very own by his brilliant poetic imagination. It is on account of his bewildering wealth of material that he saw fit to use none of the old Arthurian incidents without change, and only a few of the old characters. Merlin and Tristram, but scarcely Arthur, are the only ones like the originals.

Spenser does show fidelity to the old romances, however, in one respect. His poem is full of the old romantic tone, and of such supernatural machinery as you find in mediæval Arthurian tales, albeit, as we have seen, with different places and different people. Mr. Mac-Callum[1] maintains that Spenser made so little use of the old knights because they were not suited for his personified vices and virtues. The reason is rather to be found in Spenser's extreme catholicity of taste and exuberance of imagination. The earlier Gawain, he of Chrétien's fancy and of *The Green Knight*, would have served as well as Callidor for the knight of Courtesy; and this Gawain Spenser may have known, though, to be sure, in Malory only the deteriorated Gawain appears. At all events, Spenser was familiar with Chaucer, and must have remembered the appreciative mention of Gawain's courtesy in the *Squire's Tale*. Then, again, Galahad would have made an excellent knight of Chastity, had Spenser wished to have him. It served his purpose better, of course, to make his knight of Chastity Britomart, a woman, that he might pay another compliment to the Virgin Queen. Still other Arthurian knights would have served for Spenser's personified qualities, had he wished to be faithful to

[1] *Tennyson's Idylls and Arthurian Story*, p. 132.

the old stories, but he did not. He regarded them
merely as a rich storehouse from which he might select
at will ornaments for his new poem, the magnificent
Renaissance palace which he, Prince of Poets, was
building, whose wide taste and great wealth rendered
accessible to him all the artistic material — Gothic,
Renaissance Italian, Moorish, Hebraic, Roman, Greek
— known to European civilisation.

In thus adorning and elaborating his new poetic
structure, Spenser showed the new spirit again in that
he inevitably became a more conscious artist than any
previous Arthurian writer. Between him and Malory
especially the contrast is striking; and it is a curious
literary coincidence that the beginnings of their two
romances differ in the same way as the beginnings of
two great epics of classical antiquity. Malory's tale
starts with even more directness than Homer's *Iliad ;*
in the very first sentence he has got his story under
way: "It befell in the days of Uther Pendragon,
when he was king of all England, and so reigned, that
there was a mighty duke in Cornwall that held war
against him long time." Homer begins: —

> Μῆνιν ἄειδε, θεά, Πηληϊάδεω Ἀχιλῆος,
> οὐλομένην, ἣ μυρί᾽ Ἀχαιοῖσ᾽ ἄλγε᾽ ἔθηκεν,
> πολλὰς δ᾽ ἰφθίμους ψυχὰς Ἄϊδι προΐαψεν
> ἡρώων, αὐτοὺς δὲ ἑλώρια τεῦχε κύνεσσιν
> οἰωνοῖσί τε δαῖτα, Διὸς δ᾽ ἐτελείετο βουλή,
> ἐξ οὗ δὴ τὰ πρῶτα διαστήτην ἐρίσαντε
> Ἀτρεΐδης τε, ἄναξ ἀνδρῶν, καὶ δῖος Ἀχιλλεύς.[1]

"Sing, goddess, the wrath of Achilles, Peleus' son, the
ruinous wrath that brought on the Achaians woes innumer-
able, and hurled down into Hades many strong souls of
heroes, and gave their bodies to be a prey to dogs and all

[1] *Iliad*, i, lines 1–7.

winged fowls; and so the counsel of Zeus wrought out its accomplishment from the day when first strife parted Atreidès, king of men, and noble Achilles."[1]

Homer's first sentence, impersonal like Malory's, gives us the fresh spring of the narrative, though the continuous flow does not begin till the eighth line.

With no such unconscious directness Virgil begins his epic, *Arma virumque cano*, — "Arms and the man I sing." That is, in the first four words of the Latin the "I" comes in, the poet is conscious of himself; and it is not till the thirty-fourth line that the story begins. So in Spenser the "I" appears in the first line:

"Lo I the man, whose Muse whilome did maske,
  As time her taught, in lowly Shepheards weeds,
  Am now enforst, a far unfitter taske,
  For trumpets sterne to chaunge mine oaten reeds,
  And sing of knights and ladies gentle deeds;
  Whose praises having slept in silence long,
  Me, all too meane, the sacred Muse areeds
  To blazon broade emongst her learned throng:
Fierce warres and faithfull loves shall moralize my song."

And there are three stanzas more before Spenser gets to the beginning of his tale, "A gentle Knight was pricking on the plaine."

Spenser shows the new spirit in still another way, though not so distinctively, in that he seeks, as far as he uses the Arthurian stories, to give them new meaning. True, he attempts this by allegory, a thoroughly mediæval device, but nevertheless his attempt is significant. Not that he was the first who sought to make his readers see in the stories more than a superficial

---

[1] Translation by Lang, Leaf, and Myers, 1883.

meaning : Chrétien understood how to show in them
something of the deeper significance of life ; so still
more did Wolfram von Eschenbach in his *Parzival*,
and the author of *The Green Knight*, with his poem
in which the sermon barely escapes being too promi-
nent. Even more than these, Spenser wished to teach
moral lessons ; and in so doing he hit upon one of the
ways to keep the old stories fresh. Dangerous as it
is to emphasise moral teaching in works of art, for
it is so easy to exaggerate the moral, still, the history
of Arthurian romances since the Renaissance will
show that it is successful attempts to give them new
moral meaning which have made alive the most famous
Arthurian stories of later times.

Spenser, then, in the history of Round Table ro-
mances, stands primarily for the change from the
mediæval spirit to the modern. Among the poets of
his time second only to Shakspere, he surpasses Shak-
spere in showing the catholicity of Elizabethan taste.
He shows that with the interest in mediæval allegory
and adventure there was in the land an interest,
sometimes Puritanical, in the teachings and stories of
the Bible, an interest in the problems of the day, and
an interest in the stories of classical antiquity. The
light which shines in his poem is by no means all
from heroic France and heroic Britain ; it shines, too,
from his own heroic England, and from Palestine and
Greece and Rome. By thus mingling what before had
been distinct, Spenser takes his stand with his suc-
cessors and not with his predecessors. And none of
his successors has gone beyond Spenser in the desire
to work contemporary moral lessons into the old ro-
mances, or in the free treatment of them.

XVI

FROM SPENSER TO MILTON

BEFORE Spenser, by his free treatment of the old stories, had made clear that belief in the reality of Arthur with his court of wonders was past, a poet of much less note had expressed similar scepticism. This was William Warner, of whom we know that he was a little younger than Spenser; that he was born in London and educated at Oxford; and that he died in 1609.[1] His principal work was *Albion's England*, the contents of which are set forth in the title : *Albion's England : A Continued Historie of the same Kingdome, from the Originals of the First Inhabitants Thereof : and Most the Chiefe Alterations and Accidents there Hapning : unto and in, the Happie Raigne of our now most Gracious Soveraigne Queene Elizabeth. With a Varietie of Inventive and Historical Intermixtures. First Penned and Published by William Warner : and now Revised, and Newly Inlarged by the same Author.* This metrical history was published in 1586, in which year it was seized, for reasons now unknown and unaccountable, and its sale forbidden, by order of the Archbishop of Canterbury.[2] The publication seems soon to have been permitted, for the book went through a fifth edition before its author's death.

---

[1] G. Saintsbury, *Elizabethan Literature*, London, 1887, pp. 132–134.
[2] *Ibid.*

Warner tells his tale in the English ballad metre of fourteen-syllable lines, with few rhetorical ornaments. Among his " Inventive Intermixtures " are tales from classical mythology and contemporary tales of the *fableau* type. In joining these with Geoffrey's history (for the earlier part of the poem is a condensation of the story in that " chronicle "), Warner shows himself a true Elizabethan in that he has something of Spenser's catholicity of taste ; but he is not a true Elizabethan in that he almost entirely lacks Spenser's poetical feeling. Eminently common-sense, he takes little interest in the more romantic incidents of Arthurian story; he tells nothing of Guinevere's faithlessness, of the king's departure for Avalon, or of the other incidents which readers and writers of poetic imagination have most liked. As he says distinctly, the only part of the old legend which seems to him worthy of notice is that which may be historical : —

"His [i. e. Arthur's] Scottish, Irish, Almaine, French, and
    Saxone battelles got,
Yeeld fame sufficient : these seeme true, the rest I credite
    not."

Fourteen stanzas and a half of this length suffice Warner for the whole story of Arthur, from Uther's love for the wife of Gorlois to Arthur's death.

Like Warner in disregarding the more marvellous parts of the legend is Thomas Hughes, whose *Misfortunes of Arthur*, acted before Queen Elizabeth in February, 1588, is the earliest Arthurian drama in our tongue. Of the author we know nothing beyond the fact mentioned in the introduction to his play, that *The Misfortunes of Arthur* was " reduced into tragical notes by Thomas Hughes, one of the society of Gray's

Inn." [1] The play makes Arthur's downfall the proper result of the sins of his house, as the chorus states explicitly at the end of the first act: —

> " In Rome the gaping gulf would not decrease,
>   Till Curtius corse had closed her yawning jaws :
>   In Thebes the rot and murrain would not cease,
>   Till Laius brood had paid for breach of laws :
>   In Britain wars and discord will not stent,
>   Till Uther's line and offspring quite be spent."

Whoever Hughes was, he must have been a faithful reader of Geoffrey of Monmouth's *Chronicle* and of Malory's *Morte Darthur*, for he keeps as close to the old stories as Spenser goes far from them. Like the romancers, he makes Mordred Arthur's son. Otherwise he agrees with Geoffrey, who says distinctly that the father of both Gawain and Mordred was King Lot.[2] In the drama, as in the pseudo-chronicle, their mother is named Anne, and not Morgawse, as in the *Morte Darthur*. Most of the characters are found in either the chronicles or the romances, though some, like the queen's sister [3] and the queen's attendant, seem to have been Hughes's invention. The story of the drama is set forth clearly in that part of the introduction entitled " The Argument of the Tragedy."

> " At a banquet made by Uther Pendragon for the solemnising of his conquest against the Saxons, he fell enamoured

---

[1] For information about Hughes and his collaborators, as well as the sources of the play, see *The Misfortunes of Arthur*, H. C. Grumbine, Berlin, 1900, *Litterarhistorische Forschungen*, xiv.

[2] Book ix, ch. 9.

[3] The name of the queen's sister, Angharat or Angarad, occurs in Geoffrey, ii. 8. It is given to one of the thirty daughters of Ebrauc, the founder of York.

of Igerna, wife to Gorlois, Duke of Cornwall, who, perceiving the king's passion, departed with his wife and prepared wars at Cornwall, where also, in a stronghold beyond him, he placed her. Then the king levied an army to suppress him, but waxing impatient of his desire to Igerna, transformed himself, by Merlin his cunning, into the likeness of Gorlois, and after his acceptance with Igerna he returned to his siege, where he slew Gorlois. Igerna was delivered of Arthur and Anne, twins of the same birth.[1] Uther Pendragon, fifteen years after, pursuing the Saxons, was by them poisoned. Arthur delighted in his sister Anne, who made him father of Mordred. Seventeen years after, Lucius Tiberius of Rome demanded a tribute, due by conquest of Cæsar. Arthur gathered his powers of thirteen kings besides his own, and leaving his queen Guenevera in the tuition of Mordred, to whom likewise he committed the kingdom in his absence, arrived at France, where, after nine years' wars, he sent the slain body of Tiberius unto Rome for the tribute. During this absence, Mordred grew ambitious, for th' effecting whereof he made love to Guenevera, who gave ear unto him. Then by th' assistance of Gilla, a British lord, he usurped, and for maintenance entertained with large promises the Saxons, Irish, Picts, and Normans. Guenevera hearing that Arthur was already embarked for return, through despair purposing diversely, sometimes to kill her husband, sometimes to kill herself, at last resolved to enter into religion. Arthur at his landing was resisted on the strands of Dover, where he put Mordred to flight. The last field was fought at Cornwall where,

[1] Geoffrey is contradictory in regard to the relation of Arthur and Anne. In viii, 20, he says that they were both children of Uther and Igerna, though he does not call them twins; but in the next chapter he speaks of Anne as the wife of Lot, though if she were full sister to Arthur, she could hardly be more than a child ; and in ix, 9, he says that she had been married to Lot " in the days of Aurelius Ambrosius," whose death it was that made Uther king (viii, 15). According to this statement, Anne could be only half-sister to Arthur, for Uther had been king some time when he met Igerna.

after the death of one hundred and twenty thousand, saving on either side twenty, Mordred received his death, and Arthur his deadly wound."

This story is told in five acts, with a " dumb show " before each, which is supposed to be symbolical of the action, and a chorus at the end of each to point the moral. For a reader to-day the interest of the drama lies chiefly in its being a literary curiosity; otherwise it is dull. As usual in the "Senecan tragedy," of which *The Misfortunes of Arthur* is a very good example, there is too little action and too much narration. Then, too, there are not enough women characters. The principal one, Guinevere, is unwisely withdrawn after the first act — that is, just at a time when she promises to be interesting. While she is on the stage, she shows herself not unlike the tragic epic queen whom we already know, though at the same time she is a queen of the French pseudo-classic drama, who never stirs without her confidante, into whose ear she pours her most intimate thoughts. The centre of interest is Arthur, and in depicting him with his conflicting emotions the dramatist had some success. The chorus is almost uniformly dull, and the dumb shows are nothing but amusing, even if Master Francis Bacon, as we read at the end of the play, did help devise them.

The chief merit of the tragedy is its unity of action. It begins with the ghost of Gorlois denouncing the family of Uther Pendragon for their lust, and threatening the downfall of Arthur, who is returning from his Roman war. It ends with the ghost of Gorlois rejoicing at the ruin of the sinful house. Though wanting strict unity of time and place, *The Misfor-*

tunes of Arthur, in its Senecan unity of tone as well as action, is more like the later pseudo-classic drama than the Elizabethan; but it is still Elizabethan in its conceits of both diction and dumb show, its flattery of the queen, with which it ends,[1] and the quality of its blank verse. This, generally smooth but without the roll of " Marlowe's mighty line," has at times considerable poetic merit, though it is never free from bom-

---

[1] The ghost of Gorlois, rejoicing at the downfall of the house of Uther, foretells the day when perfect peace shall come to Britain: —

> " Now rest content, and work no further plagues :
> Let future age be free from Gorlois' ghost :
> Let Britain henceforth bathe in endless weal.
> Let Virgo come from heaven, the glorious star,
> The Zodiac's joy, the planets' chief delight,
> The hope of all the year, the ease of skies,
> The air's relief, the comfort of the earth !
> That virtuous Virgo, born for Britain's bliss ;
> That peerless branch of Brute; that sweet remain
> Of Priam's state; that hope of springing Troy,
> Which, time to come and many ages hence,
> Shall of all wars compound eternal peace.
> Let her reduce the golden age again,
> Religion, ease and wealth of former world.
> Yea, let that Virgo come, and Saturn's reign,
> And years, oft ten times told, expir'd in peace.
> A rule that else no realm shall ever find,
> A rule most rare, unheard, unseen, unread ;
> The sole example that the world affords."

William Fullbecke, "gentleman, one of the society of Gray's Inn," wrote two speeches for the play, which we are informed were "pronounced instead of " the first speech and the last of Gorlois, "penned by Thomas Hughes." Fullbecke made Gorlois pay his tribute to Elizabeth as follows : —

> " Gorlois will never fray the Britons more :
> For Britain then becomes an angels' land.
> Both devils and sprites must yield to angels' power,
> Unto the goddess of the angels' land.
> Vaunt, Britain, vaunt of her renowned reign,
> Whose face deters the hags of hell from thee,
> Whose virtues hold the plagues of heaven from thee ;
> Whose presence makes the earth fruitful to thee ;
> And with foresight of her thrice-happy days,
> Britain, I leave thee to an endless praise."

bast. A fair sample is the messenger's description of
the fatal conflict between Mordred and Arthur : —

" At length, when Mordred spied his force to faint,
   And felt himself oppress'd with Arthur's strength,
   (O hapless lad, a match unmeet for him)
   He loathes to live in that afflicted state,
   And, valiant with a forced virtue, longs
   To die the death : in which perplexed mind,
   With grenning teeth and crabbed looks he cries,
   I cannot win, yet will I not be won.
   What ! should we shun our fates, or play with Mars,
   Or thus defraud the wars of both our bloods ?
   Whereto do we reserve ourselves, or why
   Be we not sought ere this amongst the dead ?
   So many thousands murther'd in our cause,
   Must we survive, and neither win nor lose ?
   The fates, that will not smile on either side
   May frown on both. So saying, forth he flings,
   And desperate runs on point of Arthur's sword !
   (A sword, alas, prepar'd for no such use),
   Whereon engor'd he glides till, near approach'd,
   With dying hand he hews his father's head.
   So through his own annoy he 'nnoys his liege,
   And gains by death access to daunt his sire.
   There Mordred fell, but like a prince he fell ;
   And as a branch of great Pendragon's graft
   His life breathes out : his eyes forsake the sun,
   And fatal clouds infer a lasting 'clipse.
   There Arthur staggering scant sustain'd himself ;
   There Cador found a deep and deadly wound ;
   There ceas'd the wars, and there was Britain lost !
   There lay the chosen youths of Mars, there lay
   The peerless knights, Bellona's bravest train,
   There lay the mirrors rare of martial praise,
   There lay the hope and branch of Brute suppress'd :
   There fortune laid the prime of Britain's pride,
   There laid her pomp, all topsy-turvy turn'd."

In spite of Arthur's fairly early appearance on the Elizabethan stage, he was not a popular subject for dramatists. They not infrequently alluded to him, however. He and the knights of his court are mentioned several times by Shakspere,[1] as when in *King Lear* the Fool gives his estimate of Merlin by saying, " This prophecy Merlin shall make ; for I live before his time."[2] Since the prophecy declares that

> " the realm of Albion
> Shall come to great confusion,"
> " When slanders do not live in tongues,"
> " When usurers tell their gold i' the field,"

and other like improbabilities come to pass, we may judge that Shakspere did not regard Arthurian romances seriously; or else, like contemporary dramatists, he felt little interest in them. Mr. MacCallum,[3] amplifying a hint from Mr. Swinburne,[4] suggests, as a reason for such lack of interest, that the Arthurian stories, a Celtic-French mixture, produced by poets of various lands, and not the native product of any one, were too unreal for dramatic representation. This is true to some extent; the Arthurian stories were better suited to fanciful poetry like Spenser's. Yet even the most fantastic of them might have taken on some reality if treated by the author of *A Midsummer-Night's Dream ;* and there·were episodes in them that would have offered good material to dramatists of less power. As Thomas Hughes has shown, the central theme of the whole legend offers serviceable dramatic

---

[1] See M. W. MacCallum for a very interesting discussion of Arthur and the Elizabethan dramatists, *Tennyson's Idylls and Arthurian Story*, ch. i.

[2] Act iii, scene 2.   [3] MacCallum, *op. cit.*   [4] Dedication to *Locrine.*

material; so does the story of Elaine of Astolat; and so
does the story of Tristram and Iseult, as Wagner was
to show three centuries later. The fact nevertheless
remains that even the incidents suited to dramatic re-
presentation did not commend themselves to the Eliza-
bethan dramatists. This is the more remarkable when
we consider that at no other time in the history of Eng-
lish literature has the drama been so much the normal
form of expression. The more fancifully poetic treat-
ment of the old themes Spenser gave, and so another
great Arthurian poem was not to be expected; nor
was another prose romance to be expected, for Malory's,
which had put the prose Arthurian romance into final
form, was accessible in several editions; [1] but it is
strange that in this greatest day of the English drama,
Thomas Hughes's work should be the only serious
dramatic treatment of an Arthurian subject. It is all
the stranger because the old stories must have been
widely known. Otherwise the Lady of the Lake would
not have been one of the characters to greet Elizabeth
on her famous visit to Kenilworth; Sir Philip Sid-
ney would not have referred casually, as he does in
his *Apologie for Poetrie*, to " honest King Arthur; "
nor would Roger Ascham have denounced the *Morte
Darthur* so fiercely, as finding its whole pleasure in
" slaughter and bold bawdrye; in which booke those
be counted the noblest knightes, that do kill the most
men without any quarrell, and commit fowlest adoul-
teries by sutlest shiftes! " [2] Besides, the Tudor family

[1] The second edition of Malory appeared in 1498: there was
another in 1529; another in 1557; and there were two about 1585.
Cf. H. O. Sommer, *Morte Darthur*, London, 1889–91, vol. ii, p. 2.

[2] This is from the well-known passage near the end of the first
book of *The Scholemaster*.

liked to think themselves related to the old British Kings. Not only were they pleased with the flattery of poets who connected them with those monarchs, but Henry VII showed interest in the ancient legends in naming his eldest son Arthur, a name borne by but very few English princes.[1]

Moreover, curious testimony may be found in Spain, in the last quarter of the sixteenth century, that some believers in the more remarkable events of the legends still remained. Ticknor says, in his *History of Spanish Literature:* [2] " Castillo, another chronicler, tells us gravely, in 1587, that Philip II, when he married Mary of England, only forty years earlier, promised that, if King Arthur should return to claim the throne, he would peaceably yield to that prince all his rights ; thus implying, at least in Castillo himself, and probably in many of his readers, a full faith in the stories of Arthur and his Round Table." The duration in Spain of this belief in a romantic Arthur seems the more extraordinary when we consider that the Picaresque novel, the most realistic, hard-headed fiction which exists, had developed in that country before the middle of the century.

Probably in other countries, as well, there were readers credulous enough to take for fact the most improbable achievements of the Round Table knights ; and, if not actually believers, most writers of the time, like Warner and Hughes, were still enough bound by earlier literature to stick closely to the old stories,

---

[1] One of the few to bear it is the present Duke of Connaught, whose father, as is well known, was a warm admirer of Tennyson's *Idylls.*

[2] Vol. i, ch. 12. Cf. also T. S. Perry, *English Literature in the Eighteenth Century,* New York, 1883, p. 299.

if they mentioned them at all. So, too, was Michael Drayton, who combined with poetic feeling strong antiquarian interests. More esteemed in his own time — and justly so — than Warner, he is but little better known now; and readers of our day, on hearing his name, are likely to exclaim, like Goldsmith's *Citizen of the World*, on seeing the poet's monument in Westminster Abbey, "Drayton! — I never heard of him before . . . "[1]

Michael Drayton, born about 1563, died in 1631. He is said to have come of a good Warwickshire family, and perhaps for a short time he held some government office.[2] Most of his poetry is historical or antiquarian. The best known bit of it now — barring his superb sonnet, "Since there's no help, come, let us kiss and part!" — is the ballad of *Agincourt*, in a spirited metre which scarcely any other poet has handled so well: —

> " Fair stood the wind for France,
>   When we our sails advance,
>   Nor now to prove our chance,
>   Longer will tarry ;
>   But putting to the main,
>   At Kaux, the mouth of Seine,
>   With all his martial train,
>   Landed King Harry.
>   .   .   .   ."

Both for length and for general excellence, Drayton's *Polyolbion* is usually regarded as his greatest work. It appeared in part in 1613, and was finished in 1622. An abridged transcript of the title-page sufficiently indicates the purpose of the poem: " A chorographi-

---

[1] *Citizen of the World*, Letter 13.   [2] Saintsbury, *op. cit.* p. 139.

call Description of all the Tracts, Rivers, Mountains,
Forests, and other Parts of this Renowned Isle of
Great Britain, with intermixture of the most Re-
markeable Stories, Antiquities, Wonders, Rarities,
Pleasures, and Commodities of the same. . . . Di-
gested into a Poem by Michael Drayton, Esq. With
a Table added, for Direction to those Occurrences
of the Story and Antiquitie, whereunto the Course of
the Volume easily leades not. London . . . 1622."

Drayton's Muse conducts the poet from the Channel
Islands to the extreme north of England, pointing out
in every part of the kingdom the objects set forth in
the title-page. Whenever the poet comes to a place
with Arthurian associations, he mentions them ; and
thus in the course of his excursion with the Muse, he
has a chance to work in a good deal of Arthurian
material. The River Camell,[1] for instance, in Corn-
wall, recalls " the last weird battle in the West," with
the mutual slaughter of Arthur and Mordred ; and
the hill above South Cadbury in Somerset recalls the
splendor of " Many-Towered Camelot." [2] In order to
give himself a chance to tell at some length a few of
the more romantic Arthurian incidents, Drayton in-
vents in his Fourth Song a dispute between the Eng-
lish nymphs and the Welsh, as to whether the Isle of
Lundy, at the entrance of Bristol Channel, belongs to
England or Wales. The question is to be decided by
a contest of song, in which the English nymphs take
for their subject the glory of the Saxons ; the Welsh
nymphs take for theirs the glory of Arthur.

[1] First Song, ll. 181 ff.
[2] Third Song, l. 395. For South Cadbury and Camelot, cf. ch. xi
of this book, p. 183.

" As first, t' affront the Foe, in th' ancient Britons' right,
With Arthur they begin, their most renownéd Knight ;
The richness of the arms their well-made Worthy wore,
The temper of his sword (the tried Escalaboure),
The bigness and the length of Rone, his noble spear ;
With Pridwin his great shield, and what the proof could
    bear ;
His baudric how adorn'd with stones of wondrous price,
  The Sacred Virgin's shape he bore for his device ;
These monuments of worth the ancient Britons song."

So even is the contest, and so unwilling is Drayton
to offend either England or Wales, that he makes the
River Severn, appointed arbiter, decide as follows : —

" My near and lovéd nymphs, good hap ye both betide :
  Well Britons have ye sung ; you English, well replied :

.   .   .   .

Then take my final doom pronouncéd lastly, this ;
That Lundy like allied to Wales and England is." [1]

These are fair samples of Drayton's Alexandrines.
His verse was facile, but it never rose to great poetry.
He had more poetical appreciation than power.

Though Drayton's Muse pretends to regard Arthur's
achievements as semi-historical, it is likely that Dray-
ton himself took merely a poetic and antiquarian
interest in them. Perhaps Thomas Heywood, the
dramatist, felt only similar interest in the old stories,
but the readers of a work of his entitled *The Life
of Merlin* seem to have had faith at least in the pro-
phecies of that sage. *The Life of Merlin* is a color-
less history of England carried down to the reign of
Charles I, in whose time Heywood wrote.[2] All the

---

[1] Fifth Song, ll. 39 ff.
[2] The first edition was in 1641.

previous events of English history are foretold by
Merlin, who, it is to be noted, generally foretells up
to, but never beyond, the time of the author who
reports his sayings. Whether from conviction or not,
Heywood wrote as if he had full belief in Merlin and
the marvels connected with him, a fact the more re-
markable since this was just before the Puritan Civil
Wars began, and after unromantic New England had
been founded twenty years.[1]

A little later was the interesting compilation of
verse, including about a dozen Arthurian pieces, known
as the *Percy Folio Manuscript*. This was probably
made between 1645 and 1650, for in the collection
are some Cavalier songs and one or two poems of
Lovelace and Waller. The manuscript shows both un-
derstanding of the archaic language of old Arthurian
ballads and short romances, and continued interest in
them. It does not necessarily show belief, however;
probably the compiler, like Drayton, had a purely
antiquarian interest in the old tales. No one knows
whose pen copied the manuscript, but from the con-
tents and from the fact that experts pronounce the
writing old-fashioned for the time, it seems safe to
conjecture it was that of rather a rough, elderly coun-
try gentleman. Probably he little thought, as he wrote
down old tales and songs which touched his imagi-
nation or his sense of humor, that his work would be

[1] An edition of Heywood's *Life of Merlin*, in 1812, is interesting on
account of a list of over three hundred subscribers, which gives a clue
as to what sort of people still had interest in Merlin. The majority
are Welsh, a fact which shows that Arthur's popularity lasted longest
in the land to which he belonged ; and many of them are tradespeople
of the lower classes : shoemakers, hairdressers, dressmakers, plaster-
ers, and the like.

famous in the annals of English literature. In its own age, to be sure, the manuscript had no literary influence, but through Bishop Percy it exerted considerable influence on the late eighteenth century.

And now we come to the next great English poet after Spenser to be influenced by the stories of Arthur, John Milton. He seems early to have been attracted to the Arthurian theme, no doubt by *The Faerie Queene*, a poem which he greatly admired, as well as by Malory's *Morte Darthur* and Geoffrey's *History*. When he was thirty — that is, in 1638, ten years after leaving Christ's College, Cambridge — Milton, in a Latin poem to his friend, Manso, mentions the possibility of some day recalling to song the native British kings, and "breaking the Saxon forces against the martial valor of the Britons." In another Latin poem he refers to the idea again. He would begin, he says, with the Trojan craft crossing the seas; that is, he would put into his verse the whole long history of Geoffrey of Monmouth. This Milton never did, though he did make a prose paraphrase of Geoffrey's chronicle. But though he never treated the old British theme in epic form, Milton, for all his Puritanism and common-sense republicanism, never ceased to feel its poetic charm. The stern fact of the Restoration, one would think, with its overthrow of Milton's moral and political ideals, would have crushed out of him his youthful joy in the exuberant fancy of old romance. But Milton himself was the best possible exemplification of that noble Puritan ideal that

> "The mind is its own place, and in itself
> Can make a Heaven of Hell, a Hell of Heaven."

Milton blind could see all the beauty of the enchanted
Arthurian lands.   In *Paradise Lost*, in recalling
famous warriors of the world, whose forces united
would still not have equalled Satan's, he refers to

> " . . . what resounds
> In fable or romance of Uther's son,
> Begirt with British and Armoric knights." [1]

And again, in *Paradise Regained*, he speaks

> " Of faery damsels met in forest wide
> By knights of Logres, or of Lyones,
> Lancelot, or Pelleas, or Pellenore." [2]

It would be hard to find two references more sen-
sitive to the beautiful poetry of Arthurian romance
than these.   No wonder Scott expressed his well-known
regret [3] that Milton did not write an Arthurian epic.
" What we have lost in his abandoning the theme can
only be estimated by the enthusiastic tone into which
he always swells when he touches upon the ' shores
of old romance.'   The sublime glow of his imagina-
tion, which delighted in painting what was beyond the
reach of human experience ; the dignity of his lan-
guage, formed to express the sentiments of heroes and
of immortals ; his powers of describing alike the beau-
tiful and terrible ; above all, the justice with which
he conceived and assigned to each supernatural agent
a character as decidedly peculiar as lesser poets have
given to their human actors, would have sent him
forth to encounter such a subject with gigantic might.
. . . What would he not have made of the adventure
of the Ruinous Chapel, the Perilous Manor, the For-

---

[1] Book i, l. 579.   [2] Book ii, l. 359.
[3] Scott's *Dryden*, Introduction to *King Arthur*.

bidden Seat, the Dolorous Wound, and many others susceptible of being described in the most sublime poetry ! "

Many critics have believed that Milton was wise in not writing an Arthurian epic as well as *Paradise Lost*. I cannot but regret with Scott, that Milton's genius did not produce such a poem. Whether or not the Milton of later days was too much of a Puritan to give his whole heart to it, the Milton of *Comus* would have treated the theme grandly.

XVII

THE AGE OF PROSE AND REASON

So far, no one had dared, or at all events cared, to follow Spenser in the great freedom with which he had treated Arthurian stories. Now conditions were more favorable than at any other time to a freedom of treatment equal to his, though unfortunately not accompanied by his poetical inspiration. There came about in the seventeenth century the most extraordinary change in English artistic taste in the whole history of our literature; one even more extraordinary than the counter change of the next century, for that was a return from gods in many ways false to gods indisputably true.

The change in the seventeenth century was a natural result of the Renaissance. As the years passed, classical antiquity, accurate knowledge of which, we have seen, was comparatively new, took on exaggerated importance; and with this went a blindness to all the poetic beauty of the Middle Ages. Meanwhile the transition was going on from mediæval social life to modern social life. Tourneys and pageants had had their day, theatres and ballrooms were growing in favor; feudal castles ceased more and more to be social centres; town society was becoming of ever greater importance; man in relation to his fellow men was a topic of ever-increasing consideration. Mediæval conditions of government, too, were either passing, as in

England, or trying, as in France, to work themselves
into conformity with modern society, but all in vain,
as the French Revolution was to show. In this effort
to make over mediæval Europe into modern Europe,
in this age of general change and reconstruction, men
naturally felt a desire for order and method; they
wished to have everything guided by rules of reason.
Even the fine arts had to be reformed and brought
into harmony with recognised rational principles; and
the nearer artists came to ideals of pure reason, which
they found more in the art of Greece and Rome than
anywhere else, the more they felt the need of pruning
mediæval and early Renaissance art of the beautiful
spontaneous shoots which give it, in our eyes, so much
beauty. Art was to be now like a bush formally
clipped; there was no chance for the unreasonable
poetic exuberance of a Spenser or a Malory, or of
those older Arthurian writers who did not attain to
the beauty of Malory's prose or Spenser's verse. If
the Arthurian stories were to be used at all in the
new Europe, they must be changed. Hence it came
about that in an age quite foreign to Spenser's in tem-
per we find, for the first time, a poet ready to go as
far as he in combining a little Arthurian material
here and a little more there with entirely extraneous
elements, in order to make up a new story.

The poet who first dared imitate Spenser in thus
boldly remaking Arthurian material was Dryden.
Born in 1631 and dying in 1700, and appointed in
1670 poet laureate to Charles II,[1] he lived just at the

[1] John Dryden, educated at Trinity College, Cambridge, of an aris-
tocratic family with royalist sympathies, grieved at the Common-
wealth, and rejoiced at the Restoration. It was for his loyalty and
recognised ability that he received the laureateship.

time when the transition in literary taste from the old
to the new was completed. This was unfortunate for
Dryden, for he could see the poetry to which his age
so stubbornly shut its eyes; had he been but a gen-
eration or two earlier, he would probably have given
us more of the genuine Arthurian material and of its
romantic charm than he has worked into his *King
Arthur*. And so, despite the unromantic temper of
the day, Dryden, like Milton, thought to write an
Arthurian epic. He was led, however, to give his time
to plays, not because of dramatic genius, but because
he thought there was more money in plays than in
epics, and Dryden needed money. Still, hé seems
never to have forgotten the theme which had attracted
him; and at last, in the year before Charles II's death,
he wrote, not an epic, to be sure, but *King Arthur,
or the British Worthy*, which he designated " a dra-
matic opera." The point of it was the glorification of
Charles II's political triumphs; but before the play
was performed Charles II died, and James II came to
the throne. The Revolution of 1688 drove James II
into exile, and still the play was not performed; nor
was it brought out until 1691, when William and Mary
had been sovereigns of England for nearly three years.
The point of *King Arthur* now was not so acceptable
to the court as it would have been seven years before;
the piece had to be much modified, and probably it
was not improved. As Scott says,[1] it was converted
from " an ingenious . . . political drama into a mere
fairy tale . . . divested . . . of any meaning beyond
extravagant adventure." Still, it met with considera-
ble success, to which, no doubt, Purcell's music helped

[1] Scott's edition of Dryden, introduction to *King Arthur*.

contribute. The musical portion of the play, however, was so small that we should call it nowadays a drama with musical interludes rather than a dramatic opera.

In *King Arthur*, as in the *Faerie Queene*, Guinevere is no longer the British monarch's consort. He marries, instead, a blind girl, Emmeline, who, like many other characters of the play, is Dryden's own creation. Nor are the characters mediæval, but only Dryden's contemporaries pretending to be so. Merlin, shorn of romantic mystery, is merely " a'famous enchanter." Still, *King Arthur* is not entirely unromantic. There is some martial romance in the conflict between the British and the Saxon armies; Emmeline is captured by the Saxons and rescued; her sight is given to her miraculously. But all this so far as possible, even the supernatural machinery which Dryden has used in his *King Arthur*, is romantic in a rational way. The wires are no longer pulled by fairies of the lake, but by two conflicting sets of spirits, who have some purpose in opposing one another. *King Arthur* to most readers will be only a curiosity, though Scott found it " a beautiful fairy tale, the story of which . . . might have been written by Madame D'Aulnoy." [1]

Similar freedom of treatment, combined, as in the *Faerie Queene*, with extensive allegory, appears in another author of the seventeenth century, Sir Richard Blackmore,[2] a doctor of note, physician to William III and afterwards to Queen Anne. Sir Richard, thinking himself a great scholar and poet as well as a great physician, decided to write an Arthurian epic. What both Milton and Dryden had wanted to do but

[1] M. W. MacCallum, *op. cit.* p. 159. Cf. Scott, *op. cit.*
[2] Blackmore died in 1729; the date of his birth is not known.

never found time for, Blackmore did. His *Prince
Arthur, an Heroick Poem in Ten Books*, was published
in 1695. Attempting to unite the *Æneid*, Arthurian
romance, and eighteenth-century prose and reason, it
tells how Arthur won for himself the crown of Britain,
after the Saxons had overrun that country.

Following Virgil closely as his model from his
very first line, " I sing the Briton and his righteous
arms," Blackmore proceeds to tell in heroic couplets,
with all the formality but without the finish of Pope's,
that Arthur, who for some time has been a refugee on
the Continent, is sailing back with an army to recon-
quer his own land. But he is the special enemy of
Lucifer and all the fiends of Hell ; for Blackmore,
like Dryden, rationalises his supernatural machinery,
and, taking a hint from *Paradise Lost*, he introduces
two hostile bodies of supernatural beings, the fallen
angels, who are Arthur's enemies, and the angels of
Heaven, who are Arthur's friends. Accordingly, when
Lucifer beholds Arthur's fleet on the sea, like Juno irri-
tated at sight of Æneas sailing towards Italy, he goes
to the God of the Winds, who in Blackmore's epic
is no other than the Scandinavian Thor. At Lucifer's
solicitation, Thor lets the winds loose, whereupon
ensues a storm compared with which the tempest that
afflicted Æneas was nothing : —

" The Dire Convulsions, for a certain Space
 Distorted Nature, wresting from its Place
 This Globe, set to the Sun's more oblique View,
 And wrenched the Poles some Leagues yet more askew."

Arthur's ship, nevertheless, came safe to land. The
angel Uriel flew down from Heaven and with his lyre

hushed the fury of the waves. The shipwrecked mar-
iners, at Arthur's bidding, made the best of their situ-
ation, and cheered themselves with what seems to have
been pretty good fare. To wash it down, —

> "Rich Wine of Burgundy, and choice Champaign,
> Relieve the Toil, they suffered on the Main."

But Arthur's talk cheered more than meat and wine.

Then the Angel Raphael came to tell Arthur that
all his ships, though separated from him, were safe;
and that he and his friends had been driven on the
coast of Armorica, whose prince, Hoel, was a heathen
and Arthur's enemy. But Hoel, who, hearing of Ar-
thur's arrival, set out to attack him, was changed from
his purpose and paganism both by a vision from
God. He therefore offered Arthur hospitality instead
of hostility. In due time Arthur was moved to relate
to his newly converted host the story of the Creation,
of the fall of Man, the plan of the Redemption, the
birth of Christ, His life and crucifixion, and finally of
the Day of Judgment. The last especially delighted
Hoel, who

> ". . . highly pleas'd, exprest
> The grateful Sense which fill'd his joyful Breast.
> 'Methinks,' he cry'd, 'I view th' Infernal Caves,
> And see the Damn'd float on the raging Waves
> In the dire Lake, where flaming Brimstone rolls,
> And hear the dismal Groans of tortur'd Souls!'"

With this agreeable picture before his eye, Hoel, who
hitherto had seemed a little doubtful, felt perfectly
satisfied with his new faith.

In due time followed sports, supper, and songs, after
which Arthur went to bed. Then Hoel begged Arthur's

general, Lucius, to tell of the state of Britain, and
Lucius began, like Æneas with his " Infandum, regina,
jubes renovare dolorem," —

> " How sad a Task do your Commands impose,
>   Which must renew unsufferable Woes."

The story which follows, though not close to the history
of Geoffrey, keeps to it in some particulars. Lucius
tells of Vortigern's reign in Britain, of the incursions
of the Scots and Picts, of the settlement of the pagan
Saxons, and of Uther's resistance and their defeat. But
Saxon gold could accomplish more than Saxon arms.
A Briton, bought by the Saxon general, opened the
British camp by night to the German invaders. The
result was a terrific slaughter of the Britons and the
death of King Uther. The royal councillors insisted
on Arthur's flight, though much against the prince's
will. Then Arthur, in his refuge in the Netherlands,
got together men and arms wherewith to undertake
the relief of Christian Britain groaning under Saxon
oppression. At last he sailed for his native land, with
the result which we have seen, of shipwreck on the
coast of Brittany. It turned out a benefit rather than
a misfortune, however, for Hoel was moved to aid the
British prince. Arthur's expedition was altogether
successful. He drove the Saxon oppressors out of
Britain, became himself monarch of the country, and
married a charming Saxon princess, Ethelina, a near
relative to the Saxon king.

The political allegory in all this could hardly be
plainer. Arthur is, of course, the Prince of Orange.
The heathen Saxon tyrant, who oppresses the Britons,
is the Catholic James II, oppressor of his Protestant

subjects. The princess whom Arthur marries, nearly related to the Saxon king, is Mary, James's daughter.

After *Prince Arthur*, Blackmore wrote another epic, likewise in heroic couplets, *King Arthur, an Heroick Poem in Twelve Books*. The political allegory here refers to what zealous English Whigs would have liked to see, rather than to anything which they ever did see. Arthur, waging war against the king of France, or Gallia, — that is, William III waging war against Louis XIV, — finally overcomes him, and conquers his whole realm.

Though Blackmore's epics never won the highest contemporary esteem (even Blackmore was a little too romantic for his time), they met with a fair amount of favor.[1] One appreciative reader has recorded his opinion between the lines of the preface in a copy of the first edition of *King Arthur*, published in 1697, now in the Harvard University Library. After Blackmore has complained of the attacks of the critics on *Prince Arthur*, there follows, apparently with all sincerity, the sentiment in faint, eighteenth-century handwriting: "Let them say what they please, damn them, this is a great epick poem." That many held similar opinions shows how little feeling there was for the genuine Arthur and his companions of the Round Table. In their old forms, none of these heroes could hope for serious or widespread recognition from the reading public, with one exception. This solitary one, who still enjoyed a kind of honor, was Merlin ; but his was a degraded honor, which he received from the more ignorant readers. Just when his degradation

---

[1] *Prince Arthur* got to its third edition in 1696, the year after the first edition.

began from the mystical seer to a vulgar enchanter and soothsayer, it is impossible to say; but by the first half of the seventeenth century it was well under way. At that time "general prophecies and almanac predictions . . . were fathered upon the national prophet. Merlin's name had long ceased to be a name to conjure with, but nothing was more natural than to take advantage of his celebrity in order to help the sale of the catch-penny pamphlets of a prophetical character."[1] In Charles I's reign a celebrated astrologer brought out *England's Propheticall Merline foretelling to all nations of Europe.* In 1642 appeared *A Prophesie* [of Merlin] *concerning Hull in Yorkshire.* And later there appeared *The Lord Merlin's Prophecy concerning the King of the Scots; foretelling the strange and wonderful Things that shall befall him in England.* . . . London, Aug. 22, 1651.

Merlin achieved even more vulgar notoriety in the reign of Charles II. The panic of the Plague in London and the consequent uncertainty of life, followed by the great fire, made ignorant people unusually anxious to know what was going to happen next. Accordingly, the town came to swarm with fortune-tellers, until it "became common to have signs and inscriptions set up at doors: 'Here lives a Fortune Teller,' 'Here lives an Astrologer,' 'Here you may have your Nativity calculated,' and the like; and Friar Bacon's brazen-head, which was the usual sign of these people's dwellings, was to be seen almost in every

[1] W. E. Mead, *Merlin*, London, 1899, i, Introduction, p. lxxviii. Professor Mead refers to several works on Merlin in the eighteenth century, which I have not space to mention.

street, or else the sign of Mother Shipton, or of Merlin's head . . ." [1]

Thanks to such notoriety, Merlin seemed a fit character to advertise a prophetic almanac which one Partridge brought out in 1680. In that year appeared "*Merlinus Liberatus*, by John Partridge, Student in Physick and Astrology, at the Blue Ball in Salisbury Street, in the Strand, London." Partridge being a rabid Protestant alarmist, got into so much trouble after Monmouth's Rebellion that he deemed it unwise to bring out another *Merlinus Liberatus* until 1689. Then the almanac appeared again, and in every succeeding year, always with the same name, till the end of 1707. It was such a blatant example of what we call nowadays Yellow Journalism, that finally the great Dean Swift decided to end it, and accordingly made Partridge the victim of one of the boldest and most famous of hoaxes. After *Merlinus Liberatus* for 1707 had appeared, Swift published his pamphlet entitled *Predictions for the Year* 1708. Among them was one that Partridge was to die " upon the 29th of March next, about eleven at night, of a raging fever." Shortly after the day set, there came another pamphlet from Swift's pen stating that his prophecy had been fulfilled ; that Partridge had died on the evening foretold, though about four hours earlier than was expected. Partridge was foolish enough to reply by the statement that he was " not only now alive, but was also alive " on the evening of the 29th of March. Steele and several other wits of the town, hugely entertained by this, joined Swift in trying to make out that the man was dead. Partridge was so dazed that for

[1] Defoe, *A Journal of the Plague Year.*

five years he stopped the publication of his *Merlinus Liberatus*. It appeared again in 1714 and in 1715, in which latter year the poor man really did die.

This incident is noteworthy in the history of Arthurian romance for two reasons. Partridge's title, *Merlinus Liberatus*, or " Merlin Freed," implies knowledge of the old story of the seer's enchantment by " Fay Vivien," [1] and intimates his return from his agreeable confinement to benefit the world once more with his prophecies. The incident shows, too, what class of people still gave credence to one of the old legends.

We are now at the time of very least interest in Arthur in the whole history of English literature. Other periods, like that between Drayton and Dryden, have been as barren of Arthurian production, but not from Geoffrey of Monmouth to the present was ever a period so contemptuous of the Arthurian legends as the first half of the eighteenth century. The reason is that, since our literature began, no age has been so intolerant in thought and expression. Full of new ideas, but not sufficiently master of them to see good in anything else, the early eighteenth century was like a self-conscious youth, whose principal claim to maturity seems to be disgust at everything he thinks young. Fearful, like Percival on his first visit to the Grail Castle, of saying or doing the wrong thing, he tries so hard to be right that in every act or word he is constrained. His expressed thoughts are not so much what he thinks as what he believes he ought to think. Towards the youthful follies of his

[1] The name " Merlin's Cave," applied to one of the London pleasure-gardens of the eighteenth century, testifies further to popular acquaintance with the Merlin legend.

fellows no one can be more uncharitable, for the best charity comes with maturity.

Two other periods in our literature since the Renaissance, like this early eighteenth century, are analogous to periods in the life of man. The Elizabethan, with its unbounded desire for knowledge, its ambitious hopes, its enthusiastic, spontaneous poetry, is the marvellously gifted childhood of our modern literature — even when artificial, so transparently so as to seem natural. The nineteenth century has appreciated the childhood beauties of that earlier time ; it has combined with the world-wide interest of the Elizabethan age, and with some of its spontaneous enthusiasm, a deeper, more serious understanding of life. It is the beginning of the full maturity of our literature, though lacking something, alas ! as does even young maturity, of the freshness of childhood, and especially of that Elizabethan childhood of stupendous genius. Between the two comes, self-satisfied and self-conscious, the age of prose and reason, the sophister or sophomoric period of our literature.

The peculiar spirit of this was strongest in the twelve years of Anne's reign, and in those immediately preceding and following. As critics have often said, the great poetic effort of the time was to express itself in rigid, heroic couplets like Pope's, with their interminable regularity of cæsura and end-stopped lines. We all know that Homer in this highly formal verse is unnatural enough ; we can imagine that Malory and the other romancers would have been still more so, had any writer seen fit to force them into it. But it was not likely that any one would do so, for if the pseudo-historical side of the old legends, which appealed chiefly to Blackmore, was too fantastic for the time, the purely romantic side would have been even more so. Addison no doubt expresses truly the attitude of his age toward romance, when in his *Account of the Greatest English Poets* he says of Spenser's *Faerie Queene*:

> "But now the mystic tale that pleas'd of yore
> Can charm an understanding age no more." [1]

Here we have the cardinal fault of the Queen Anne age: it was too understanding; it thought to live solely by common-sense fact. The humdrum imagination of Defoe, with its great capacity for all sorts of commercial and material details, which you may see in any of his stories, is typical of the time. Greater flights of fancy had to content themselves with the adventures, still matter-of-fact enough, of a Gulliver among the Laputians or Houyhnhnms. Such, if not probable, were at least possible on the other side of the yet imperfectly known world. Besides, Swift's satire and keen wit would have floated an even more remarkable island than that of the Laputian court. But while Laputians and Houyhnhnms were possible in some remote part of the South Sea, an irrational Celtic-French Britain, with confused geography, and enchantments, and knights ever ready to go at a moment's notice on the maddest quests, a country where you might find any day four queens strolling round hand in hand, — as in the real world you might come upon four peasant girls, — the whole radiant in the light "that never was, on sea or land " — all this to the

---

[1] Addison wrote this, to be sure, in 1694, when he himself was scarcely beyond the sophomoric age. Still, it would be hard to find a young man of literary feeling in the nineteenth century, twenty-two or twenty-three years old, of the same critical opinion as Addison.

early eighteenth century was impossible. No wonder that Arthur and his Round Table, Merlin and Vivien, Tristram and Iseult, and the others, were deemed beneath the contempt of serious people. It was enough for them now to figure in nursery tales, or in vulgar chap-books which the people bought who believed in the predictions of *Merlinus Liberatus*, or consulted fortune-tellers with heads of Merlin over their doors.

One of the odd things in the history of Arthur is his association in these chap-books with several heroes who to-day are known chiefly in the nursery. Early in the seventeenth century a popular ballad made the celebrated Tom Thumb a knight of Arthur's court. This was enlarged, until about 1700 it had grown to considerable length.[1] The hero met with various adventures — the most serious of them a tournament, in which his exertions made him fall sick and die ; an encounter with a cat that scratched him to death ; and finally a fall into the web of a spider that, taking him for a fly, —

> " . . . seized him without delay,
> Regarding not his cry,
> The blood out of his body drains,
> He yielded up his breath ;
> Thus he was freed from all his pains,
> By his unlook'd for death." [2]

The first two times that Tom died, he went to Fairy-Land, whence he was sent back to the land of mortal men by the Fairy Queen. What befell him after his third death, we are not told.

[1] J. Ashton : *Chap Books of the Eighteenth Century*, London, 1882, p. 206.

[2] J. Ashton, *op. cit.* pp. 220, 221.

Another nursery hero, who now became a great knight at Arthur's court, was the redoubtable Jack the Giant Killer. And it may have been about this same time that the feat of "stealing four pecks of barley meal to make a bag pudding" was given to Arthur, which probably of all his adventures is most widely known in the English world.

The happy result in literature of the association of Arthur with chap-books, and so in time with children's fiction, is Henry Fielding's play, *The Tragedy of Tragedies, or the Life and Death of Tom Thumb the Great*. Written for a burlesque on the ranting bombast of contemporary tragedy, it hit authors from Dryden, whose plays were still popular, to Fielding's contemporaries, Young and Thomson. The Elizabethan dramatists escaped ridicule, probably because they were not well enough known to audiences of Fielding's time, and partly, it may be, because Fielding had too much respect for them. *Tom Thumb*, offered as a one-act farce in 1730, had such success that it was enlarged to three acts, and so presented in 1731. The play, supposedly of the Elizabethan Age and now first called to the attention of Georgian England, was published with burlesque learned notes, or, as the title-page put it, "with the annotations of H. Scriblerus Secundus." The purpose of these was to cite parallel passages, which Fielding pretended had been copied from *Tom Thumb*, in order to show the better whom he was hitting. When one of the characters, for instance, an admirer of the princess who rejoices in the melodious name of Huncamunca, exclaims, "Oh! Huncamunca, Huncamunca oh!" Fielding subjoins a note to the effect that "This beautiful line, which ought to be written in gold . . . is imitated in the New Sophonisba: ' Oh! Sophonisba, Sopho- nisba oh!'" — the famous line which is said to have called out shouts for the author from the gallery, when the play was first performed, "Oh! Jemmy Thomson, Jemmy Thomson oh!"

It is not likely that Fielding in *Tom Thumb* aimed to ridicule Arthurian romance as well as contempo- rary tragedy. Had he done so, his audience would hardly have understood the point of his ridicule. Yet he himself must have been familiar with the main Arthurian story, for his grandfather's estate, Sharp- ham Park, where Fielding was born, is situated in the heart of Somerset, that county so rich in Arthurian traditions, and in plain sight of Glastonbury, less than three miles away, with its associations with Joseph of Arimathea and the Grail, Avalon, the abduction of Guinevere, and the tomb of Arthur. It may, there- fore, be more than coincidence that Tom Thumb, small as he is, — and he is the size which nursery tales have commonly ascribed to him, about as big as your thumb, — it may be more than coincidence that this diminu- tive knight is the Sir Lancelot of Fielding's Arthur. Like Lancelot of old, he is invincible in arms; at the time of the play he comes back a victorious general from a campaign against the giants. Like Sir Lance- lot, too, he is loved by Arthur's queen, here Dollalolla, a lady of Fielding's invention, described in the list of *dramatis personae* as " a woman intirely faultless, saving that she is a little given to drink, a little too much a virago towards her husband, and in love with Tom Thumb." Again, Tom Thumb is like Lancelot in that many other ladies love him, among them a

captive giantess queen — who, since her love is unre-
quited, may be said to play the part of Elaine — and
the daughter of Arthur and Dollalolla, Huncamunca,
whose love Tom Thumb returns. Huncamunca her-
self cannot make up her mind whether to marry him or
her other adorer, Lord Grizzle, but at length decides
in favor of Tom Thumb. Grizzle straightway raises
an insurrection, which Tom successfully quells. Then,
as the little knight returns triumphant to the court
to be rewarded with the hand of Huncamunca, great
is the rejoicing ; and when Arthur at the end of the
last act comes upon the stage, attended by his queen,
princess, and courtiers, he speaks as follows : —

" (*King.*) Open the prisons, set the wretched free,
And bid our treasurer disburse six pounds
To . . . pay their debts. — Let no one weep to-day.
             . . . This is the wedding-day
Of Princess Huncamunca and Tom Thumb;
Tom Thumb ! who wins two victories to-day,
And this way marches, bearing Grizzle's head."

Hereupon, just as a joyful dance begins, there enters
Noodle, a courtier, crying : —

"Oh ! monstrous, dreadful, terrible, oh ! oh !
Deaf be my ears, for ever blind my eyes !
Dumb be my tongue ! Feet lame ! All senses lost !
Howl wolves, grunt bears, hiss snakes, shriek all ye ghosts ! [1]
    (*King.*) What does the blockhead mean ?
    (*Nood.*)   I mean, my liege,
Only [2] to grace my tale with decent horror.
Whilst from my garret, twice two stories high,

---

[1] The note is as follows : " These beautiful phrases are all to be
found in one single speech of *King Arthur, or The British Worthy.*"

[2] "I was but teaching him to grace his tale
         With decent horror.
                                        Cleomenes."

I look'd abroad into the streets below,
I saw Tom Thumb attended by the mob ;
Twice twenty shoe-boys, twice two dozen links,
Chairmen and porters, hackney-coachmen, whores ;
Aloft he bore the grizzly head of Grizzle ;
When of a sudden through the streets there came
A cow, of larger than the usual size,
And in a moment — guess, oh! guess the rest! —
And in a moment swallow'd up Tom Thumb.

(*King.*) Shut up again the prisons, bid my treasurer
Not give three farthings out — hang all the culprits,
Guilty or not — no matter. — Ravish virgins :
Go bid the schoolmasters whip all their boys!
Let lawyers, parsons, and physicians loose,
To rob, impose on, and to kill the world.

(*Nood.*) Her majesty the queen is in a swoon.

(*Queen.*) Not so much in a swoon but I have still
Strength to reward the messenger of ill news. [*Kills* NOODLE.

(*Nood.*) O! I am slain.

(*Cleora.*) [1] My lover's killed, I will revenge him so.
[*Kills the* QUEEN.

(*Hunc.*) My mamma kill'd! Vile murderess, beware.
[*Kills* CLEORA.

(*Doodle.*) [2] This for an old grudge to thy heart.
[*Kills* HUNCAMUNCA.

(*Mustacha.*) [3]   And this
I drive to thine, O Doodle! for a new one. [*Kills* DOODLE.

(*King.*) Ha! murderess vile, take that.   [*Kills* MUST.
And take thou this.   [*Kills himself, and falls.*"

"I know of no tragedy," is the comment of H. Scriblerus
Secundus, "which comes nearer to this charming and bloody
catastrophe than Cleomenes, where the curtain covers five
principal characters dead on the stage. These lines too —

    ' I ask no questions then, of who killed who ?
    The bodies tell the story as they lie ' —

---

[1] Cleora is a maid of honor.   [2] Doodle is a courtier.
[3] Another maid of honor.

seem to have belonged more properly to this scene of our author; nor can I help imagining they were originally his. The Rival Ladies, too, seems beholden to this scene:

> ' We 're now a chain of lovers linked in death ;
> Julia goes first, Gonsalvo hangs on her,
> And Angelina hangs upon Gonsalvo,
> As I on Angelina.'

No scene, I believe, ever received greater honours than this. It was applauded by several encores, a word very unusual in tragedy. And it was very difficult for the actors to escape without a second slaughter. This I take to be a lively assurance of that fierce spirit of liberty which remains among us, and which Mr. Dryden, in his essay on Dramatick Poetry, hath observed : ' Whether custom,' says he, ' hath so insinuated itself into our countrymen, or nature hath so formed them to fierceness, I know not; but they will scarcely suffer combats and other objects of horror to be taken from them.' And indeed I am for having them encouraged in this martial disposition; nor do I believe our victories over the French have been owing to anything more than to those bloody spectacles daily exhibited in our tragedies, of which the French stage is so intirely clear."

In this capital burlesque of Fielding's, in Partridge's *Merlinus Liberatus*, and in Blackmore's epics, we see perfectly the attitude of this age of prose and reason towards the Arthurian stories. It could make them the subject of a satiric travesty, or it could treat them seriously with the dulness of Blackmore or the pretentiousness of Partridge. The former's clumsy, unpoetic narratives, with their scarcely recognisable Arthurian characters, show the only dignified treatment of the stories that was possible. When an Arthurian character still appeared true to his old self, he had to sink as low as Merlin in the company of vulgar almanac-makers and fortune-tellers.

XVIII

THE LATER EIGHTEENTH CENTURY

As the generation passed which had been in its prime when Anne was on the throne, the time came for Arthurian stories to receive more worthy treatment. Having steadily declined in favor for the last hundred years, they were now to grow in favor until in the nineteenth century they should hold as honorable a place as ever they held in the Middle Ages. This return of the legends to the high position which was their right came about with the growth of the romantic spirit in literature and the other fine arts.

Critics have found romanticism hard to define. We can form some idea of it only by saying that our literature in the first quarter of the nineteenth century was romantic as distinguished from that of the first quarter of the eighteenth century, which was classic, or rather pseudo-classic. A more exact definition is difficult because romanticism was made up of various elements, several of which especially deserve notice. In form, romanticism broke away from the precise verse and the artificial diction of Pope and his school. In mood, it substituted mystery, subjectivity, and individuality for reason, objectivity, and impersonality. And in matter, it extended its interest beyond contemporary society to nature and the society of former and rougher ages. Sometimes the various elements of romanticism are found together, but more often one of its elements is especially prominent in one man; as in Byron subjectivity, in Wordsworth love of nature, in Scott interest in the age of chivalry. This last phase of romanticism especially concerns us; for with the interest which the later eighteenth century felt in the age of chivalry went renewed interest in the art of that time, and so in the Arthurian legends, the best mediæval fiction.

No one man was the father of eighteenth-century romanticism in England. Romanticism there, as any one can see who reads Professor Phelps's *Beginnings of the English Romantic Movement*,[1] was a spontaneous, unconscious growth. Indeed, even at the height of the age of prose and reason, romanticism was not quite dead. Such a classicist as Addison devoted two *Spectators* to the good old ballad of *Chevy Chace*, though, to be sure, he found it worthy of commendation chiefly for its resemblance to Virgil's *Æneid*. Something of the romantic spirit crops out in Pope in his *Epistle of Eloisa to Abelard*, and in his *Elegy to the Memory of an Unfortunate Lady*, which begins with an almost conventional romantic picture: —

"What beckoning ghost along the moonlight shade
Invites my steps, and points to yonder glade?"

Even Matthew Prior, that Augustan of Augustans, was once moved to tell in his own words the old ballad of the Nut-Brown Maid, which, it is true, he put into stiff heroic couplets, under the name of *Henry and Emma*.

Then, too, there were minor poets in whom the romantic spirit was as strong as the classic, if not

[1] By W. L. Phelps, Boston, 1899.

stronger. One of these, Thomas Parnell, an Irish clergyman of the Established Church, makes what is perhaps the only sympathetic reference to Arthur in the whole Queen Anne Age. In telling an old Irish fairy tale, which, by the way, is not at all Arthurian, Parnell begins : —

> " In Britain's isle, and Arthur's days,
> When midnight fairies danced the maze,
> Lived Edwin of the Green ;
> Edwin, I wis, a gentle youth,
> Endowed with courage, sense and truth,
> Though badly shaped he been." [1]

The romantic spirit, moreover, was more or less stimulated all this time by collections of old songs and ballads, such as *Scots Poems*, published by John Watson at Edinburgh in 1706, and Allan Ramsay's *Tea Table Miscellany* of 1724, and *Evergreen* of the same year.[2] A similar collection by Ambrose Philips, *Old Ballads . . . with Introductions Historical, Critical or Humorous*, which came out in three volumes between 1723 and 1725, is worthy of mention because the second volume contained the old ballad, here entitled *King Arthur*,[3] which Falstaff was trying to sing,

---

[1] This beginning may have been suggested by the first lines of Chaucer's *Wife of Bath's Tale*.

[2] These were collections of ballads and songs, or, in the case of *The Evergreen*, of old poems interspersed with some contemporary songs.

[3] I have not attempted a careful investigation of these collections of ballads and songs. From what I have seen of them and read, I judge that nothing Arthurian may be found in them more important than Philips's *King Arthur*. The same ballad is found in Percy's *Reliques*, entitled *Sir Lancelot du Lake*. It begins : —

> " When Arthur first in court began,
> And was approved king,
> By force of armes great victorys wanne,
> And conquest home did bring."

"When Arthur first in court began," at the Boar's-head Tavern in Eastcheap.[1] These and other similar collections are referred to here because, through keeping alive the romantic spirit, they kept people ready to appreciate the Arthurian story when once more it should be offered to readers.

The Spenserian revival in the second quarter of the century deserves mention for the same reason. It led to study of the Elizabethan period and of Spenser himself, and then to some interest in the age of chivalry. The *Faerie Queene*, condemned, as we have seen, by Addison, commended itself to Pope and a few other Augustans in a curious way; they imitated its verse form for coarsely humorous purposes. By degrees there came to be more serious use of its beautiful stanza, and between 1730 and 1775, at least fifty poems in Spenserian stanzas were composed in England. Far and away the best of them, and more Spenserian than any other poem in the same stanzas except the original, was James Thomson's *Castle of Indolence* of 1748. These imitations of Spenser were one of the causes that led Thomas Warton in 1754 to publish his *Observations on the Faerie Queene*, which shows considerable knowledge of mediæval Arthurian romances.[2]

No doubt Horace Walpole's whim of turning his villa at Strawberry Hill into an imitation Gothic

---

[1] *Second Part of King Henry IV*, II, iv.

[2] The discussion of Spenser's indebtedness to Arthurian romances is found in vol. i of the *Observations*, beginning with the following passage in section ii, *Of Spenser's Imitations from Old Romances:* "Among others, there is one romance which Spenser seems more particularly to have made use of : . . . Morte Arthur . . . by one Sir Thomas Malory, Knight, . . . printed by W. Caxton."

castle still further set people towards the Middle Ages, for Walpole was a man of influence and fashion.[1] So, too, did his mediæval romance, *The Castle of Otranto*, written in 1764. And it was a sign of the times that Chatterton, in these years growing up in the shadow of the beautiful old Gothic church of St. Mary Redcliffe in Bristol, was drawing inspiration from the olden days in a way that made him an eighteenth-century forerunner of the Præ-Raphaelites. Had Chatterton lived, his interest in the Middle Ages might have given us a beautiful Arthurian poem with the mediæval picturesqueness and splendor of William Morris's *Defence of Guenevere*. But Chatterton, with his unreasonable pride, when still not quite eighteen, hungry and penniless, drank poison in his garret in London.

Yet another influence was preparing the way for an Arthurian revival. In 1757 appeared Gray's *Bard*, showing no inconsiderable knowledge of Welsh history and Welsh literature, which made the first worthy mention of Arthur in English verse, except Parnell's, since Milton. The Bard, foretelling to the "ruthless King," Edward I, the history of England, prophesies the reign of Elizabeth — to Gray an heroic age : —

> " ' Visions of glory, spare my aching sight,
> Ye unborn ages, crowd not on my soul !
> No more our long-lost Arthur we bewail.
> All hail, ye genuine kings, Britannia's issue, hail !

III. 2.

> " Girt with many a baron bold
> Sublime their starry fronts they rear ;

[1] As early as 1750, Walpole in his letters mentions his idea of a Gothic castle, but the structure was not completed for many years.

And gorgeous dames, and statesmen old
In bearded majesty, appear.
In the midst a form divine !
Her eye proclaims her of the Briton-Line ;
Her lion-port, her awe commanding face,
Attemper'd sweet to virgin-grace.
What strings symphonious tremble in the air,
What strains of vocal transport round her play !
Hear from the grave, great Taliessin, hear;
They breathe a soul to animate thy clay.' "

The Bard was the beginning of that Celtic cult
which within a few years has caused a member of
Parliament from the neighborhood of Dublin, where
nothing but English has been spoken for centuries, to
try to address the House of Commons in Irish, and
has put Gaelic inscriptions on the walls of one of the
principal hotels in Edinburgh, —from its founding, as
its name bears witness, an Angle city. This is the ab-
surdity of the cult ; its value to literature, however, has
been real. A few years after *The Bard*, between 1760
and 1763, James Macpherson published his so-called
poems of Ossian, which appealed at once to men with
romantic feeling like Gray. " I am so charmed," he
writes to Horace Walpole, probably in 1760, " with
the two specimens of Erse poetry that I cannot help
giving you the trouble to inquire a little farther about
them . . ." Impostures as they were, the subsequent
fame of the alleged poems of Ossian, in Macpherson's
beautiful, poetic English prose, is well known. " All
Europe felt the power of their melancholy ; " [1] and
men as different as Byron, Goethe, and Napoleon were
similarly under their spell.

---

[1] Matthew Arnold, *Celtic Literature*, p. 116.

Ossian had more Celtic spirit than substance. In 1764, however, there was published a book with genuinely Celtic substance, *Some Specimens of the Poetry of the Antient Welsh Bards*, by the Reverend Evan Evans. Translated into English prose, these *Specimens* greatly interested men of antiquarian taste, such as Gray, whom they led to further study of Welsh antiquities. Though they contained nothing Arthurian of note, they told the story of the discovery of Taliesin by Elphin, which in the next century the curious novelist, Peacock, was to combine with Welsh legends which did introduce Arthur. And so all this revival of interest in the Celtic peoples was preparing the English mind to receive with favor the stories of the most romantically famous champion of the Celtic race, when poets should be ready to call him back from Avalon.

Six such stories at last appeared in 1765 in Percy's *Reliques of Ancient English Poetry*,[1] the most important collection of poems and ballads in the whole eighteenth century — both a sign of the romantic feeling of the times and a stimulus to it. Yet the author, or rather editor, seems to have been fitted for anything but a romantic leader. Thomas Percy, born in Shropshire in 1729, was a smug, self-satisfied parson, who had the vulgarity to be ashamed of the fact that his father was a grocer. After graduating from Christ

---

[1] The Arthurian pieces in the first edition of the *Reliques* were as follows : —

Vol. i. *Sir Lancelot du Lake.*

Vol. iii. *The Boy and the Mantle. The Marriage of Sir Gawaine. King Ryence's Challenge* (not in the *Folio Manuscript*). *King Arthur's Death. A Fragment. The Legend of King Arthur.* This volume contained also *The Boy and the Mantle. Revised.*

Church, Oxford, he took orders, and was assigned to
a country living in Northamptonshire, where he mar-
ried Anne Gutteridge, of a family above his own.
Fanny Burney found Mrs. Percy [1] " very uncultivated,
and ordinary in manners and conversation; " but " a
good creature, and much delighted to talk over the
Royal Family, to one of whom she was formerly
nurse." [2] It was to his wife, whom he always admired,
that Percy wrote the ballad which both he and she
regarded so highly that when she had her portrait
painted, the ballad appeared on a scroll in her hand.
The first of the three stanzas was, —

> " O Nanny, will thou gang with me?
>   Nor sigh to leave the flaunting town ;
> Can silent glens have charms for thee,
>   The lowly cot, and russet gown ?
> No longer dressed in silken sheen,
>   No longer deck'd with jewels rare :
> Say, canst thou quit each courtly scene,
>   Where thou wert fairest of the fair ? "

Despite the conventionality and prosiness of his
verse, Percy had some taste for picturesque novelty in
literature, and also the commercial sense to under-
stand that his generation, tired of pseudo-classic mo-
notony, likewise cared for novelty. Accordingly, after
some experiments with Chinese subjects,[3] and then with
Old Norse,[4] Percy brought out his great work in 1765,

[1] Austin Dobson, *Diary and Letters of Madame D'Arblay*, London,
1905, v, 31 ; Hales and Furnivall, *Bishop Percy's Folio Manuscript*,
London, 1867-68, i, p. xxxii.

[2] This was the Duke of Kent, father of the late Queen Victoria.

[3] In 1761 Percy brought out a Chinese novel translated from the
Portuguese, and the next year, *Pieces Relating to the Chinese*.

[4] Perhaps it was the success of Macpherson with his *Ossian*, which
inspired Percy to make use of ancient European material, and to bring

Reliques of Ancient English Poetry, dedicated to
" Elizabeth, Countess of Northumberland : in her own
right Baroness Percy. . ." A second edition appeared
in 1767, a third in 1775, and a fourth in 1794. His
last important literary effort was the translation in
1770 of Mallet's *Northern Antiquities*. Though in
all these works Percy pretended to take only a dilet-
tante interest, without them his name to-day would
be forgotten, and in his own day they brought him
substantial rewards— recognition by the noble Percys
as one of their blood, of which it is doubtful that he
really came, and honors in the Church, culminating in
his appointment to the Irish bishopric of Dromore in
1782. He died in 1811.

The immediate impulse to the preparation of the
Reliques was the discovery of that old folio manu-
script collection of ballads and songs, which some
nameless country gentleman, probably of the north-
west, made towards the middle of the seventeenth cen-
tury. One day, when Percy was visiting a friend of
his, Humphrey Pitt, he found the manuscript " lying
dirty on the floor under a bureau in the parlour."
No one knew anything about it, except the house-
maid, who had torn away some of its pages to kindle
her fires ; and she could not tell where it came from.
Pitt, aware of Percy's interest in antiquities, gladly
gave him the manuscript. When Percy, for its better
preservation, had the folio bound, it was further dam-
aged by the binder's cutting off some of the top and
bottom lines on various pages.

out in 1763, *Five Pieces of Runic Poetry, translated from the Icelandic
Language*, which, as a matter of fact, he got through the Latin, for
he had no knowledge of Norse. See W. L. Phelps, *op. cit.* p. 143.

Meanwhile Percy's friends who knew his fondness for old ballads helped him with all they could find. In time Percy had enough to warrant the publication of the *Reliques*, which, he said, in the preface to the first edition, came chiefly, and without much change, from the manuscript found in Humphrey Pitt's parlor. Such was not the case. Of a hundred and seventy-six pieces in the *Reliques*, only forty-five came from the damaged manuscript. Nearly all the rest came from other ballad collections, either printed or in manuscript, and from songs which were popular at the time. Moreover, Percy often made over the old material to suit the taste of his age. In making these changes, Percy showed himself not only practical and wise, — without them he would probably have got but scant favor for his publication, — but also a man of poetic taste ; for among his additions to the manuscript poems were such beautiful lyrics as Marlowe's *Come live with me and be my Love*, and Lovelace's *To Lucasta on going to the Wars*. In the words of the late editors of the manuscript, Percy looked on the text as " a young woman from the country . . . whom he had to fit for fashionable society. . . . All fashionable requirements Percy supplied. . . . The desired result was produced ; his young woman was accepted by Polite Society, taken to the bosom of a Countess,[1] and rewarded her chaperon with a mitre." [2]

Of the forty-five pieces which Percy retained from his folio, but five[3] have to do with Arthur or his

---

[1] That is, Elizabeth, Countess of Northumberland, whose husband was subsequently created Duke of Northumberland.

[2] Hales and Furnivall, *Bishop Percy's Folio Manuscript*, i, p. xvi.

[3] A sixth Arthurian piece in the *Reliques*, *King Ryence's Challenge*, was not in the manuscript.

knights; and of these only two are of the better Arthurian pieces in the manuscript, namely, *The Boy and the Mantle* and *The Marriage of Sir Gawaine*. The former is the story of a chastity test, which is told in substantially the same form of several ladies of Arthur's court, but more often of the wife of Sir Cradock, the heroine of this ballad, than of any other. On the third day of May, when Arthur is at his meat, a small boy appears without apparent reason in the banqueting-hall at Carlisle, and displays a mantle that is destined to cause much trouble. " It will fit," says the boy, " no lady who has not always been chaste." Rashly incredulous, various ladies are unwise enough to try the mantle on, with disastrous results. Guinevere, whom the mantle does not begin to fit, is so irritated that she makes laughably unreasonable and exaggerated charges against Cradock's wife, who, nevertheless, putting on the mantle, finds that it crinkles only a little at her great toe. " Once," she says, " I did amiss; I kissed Cradock before he married me." Hereupon the mantle fits her perfectly. Then the troublesome little boy proposes similar tests with a knife and a drinking-horn, which redound equally to the credit of Cradock's wife.

The Marriage of Sir Gawaine tells the same tale as the short fifteenth-century romance entitled *The Weddynge of Sir Gawen and Dame Ragnell*. Arthur, hunting in Inglewood Forest, meets near Tarn Wadling a baron of gigantic proportions, armed with a club, who, since he has long been Arthur's enemy, will now have his life, unless the king can say at the end of a year what women most desire. Arthur sets to work directly to gather the necessary information,

and his nephew, Gawain, kindly helps him. As the
end of the year approaches, Arthur, riding towards
Tarn Wadling again, discouraged because he has no
confidence that he has found the right answer, meets
the most hideous lady he has ever seen. Much as he
loathes her, still, on her suggestion that she can help
him, he offers her Sir Gawain in marriage. Then she
tells Arthur the desired answer. Arthur, however,
hoping to save his nephew from such a repulsive spouse,
gives all the other answers to the baron before that of
the hideous lady. Since they are all wrong, Arthur
finally has to give hers: " Women desire most the
mastery of men." This is the right answer, and the
baron goes off dumfounded, cursing the lady who had
imparted the information and wishing her burned.

Gawain, always courteous, goes through the mar-
riage ceremony without complaint, though his ill-
favored wife, decked out in gorgeous wedding raiment,
is more repulsive than ever. The hardest time for
Gawain is the wedding night. Finally his courtesy tri-
umphs, and at the lady's solicitation, he says he will kiss
her, when straightway he finds her a beautiful young
woman. She then gives Gawain his choice, to have her
fair by night and foul by day, or foul by night and fair
by day. On his leaving the difficult matter for her to de-
cide, she says that she will be fair always ; and she adds
that she was bewitched by her stepmother. When
Gawain presents his transformed bride to Arthur, the
king and queen and all the courtiers are enraptured,
and offer general thanksgiving for Gawain's happiness.[1]

---

[1] Substantially the same story is told in Chaucer's *Wife of Bath's
Tale*, in Gower's story of *Florent* in the *Confessio Amantis*, and in the
Scotch ballad of *King Henry*. The origin of the story, analogues

Here is the place for a word on those pieces in the folio manuscript, which, though not included in the *Reliques*, are nevertheless of some importance in the history of Arthurian romance. Even now they exercised no direct influence on English literature, for they were known only to Percy and his favored friends; but indirectly through these, the old pieces did influence literary taste. Among them is *Sir Lambewell*,[1] the much amplified story of Thomas Chestre's *Sir Launfal*, which we have seen to be an adaptation of *Lanval*, of Marie de France. *Libius Disconius*[2] is here, too — the story of Gawain's son, who, by boldly kissing a frightful dragon, none other than the Lady of Synadowne, frees her from the disagreeable enchantment to which two wizards had subjected her. So, too, is that good story of *The Turke and Gowin*, in which Gawain, at the urging of the Turke, a curious little man, who came into Arthur's court,

> ("He was not hye, but he was broad,
> And like a Turke he was made
> Both legg and thye")

accomplished various adventures among giants in the Isle of Man,[3] which he could not possibly have got through without his companion's help. The adventures over, the Turke begged Gawain to gratify him by striking off his head. Much against his will Gawain did so, and up stood a stalwart knight, released from

of which appear elsewhere in English, in Gaelic, and apparently in French, German, Norse, and Welsh, seems to have been Irish. See G. H. Maynadier, *The Wife of Bath's Tale, Its Sources and Analogues*, London, 1901.

[1] Hales and Furnivall, *Folio Manuscript*, i, 142.

[2] *Ibid.* ii, 409.

[3] Man in this story seems to have been originally the other world.

the enchantment of which he had been the victim, who forthwith sang the " Te Deum."

And finally there is another good, rough old story, *The Carle of Carlile*. Gawain, Kay, and Bishop Bodwin, hunting in Inglewood Forest,[1] are misled by a mist, and seek refuge at the house of a hideous, gigantic man, with fingers like tether stakes, whom they find sitting before his fire, "his legg cast over the other knee." [2] Presently Kay goes out to the stable to look after his horse. Finding the Carle's foal feeding by his steed, Kay drives him out, whereupon the Carle suddenly appears and gives Kay a hard buffet. Soon the bishop goes out to look after his horse, with like result. Then Gawain goes. He, too, finds the foal in the stall with his horse, but instead of driving him out, he speaks kindly to the creature, and puts his own mantle over him because he is unblanketed. After supper, at which the Carle displays a monstrous appetite, drinking fifteen gallons of wine at one draught, there is further test of Gawain's courtesy, — in which the knight is bedded in a way most agreeable to himself, — and so, too, on the next day, when the Carle shows Gawain the bones of fifteen hundred men that he has slain in the last forty years. Finally the knight, at command of his host, strikes off the latter's head.[3] Then the Carle stands up a proper and a happy man, and explains that he has done his bloody work because he was under enchantment to kill every guest

[1] The knights seem to start from Wales, where Arthur is sojourning, but the Carle evidently lives near Carlisle, and therefore presumably in Inglewood Forest.

[2] *Percy Folio Manuscript, Carle of Carlile*, line 176.

[3] This incident is omitted in another form of the story preserved in the Porkington MS.

who failed to do as bidden. Because Gawain is the first who has courteously done all that was asked of him, the cruel spell which made the Carle so savage is ended ; he will henceforth forsake his horrid work ; his slaughter-house shall be a chantry, where priests shall sing till doomsday. Then the Carle marries his daughter to Gawain, and sends his guests on their way with presents, adding an invitation to Arthur, who heretofore has been his foe, to dine with him. This the king accepts, and makes the Carle Earl of Carlisle.

The service of the *Reliques* to the cause of Arthurian romance was twofold. Of chief importance was its work in familiarising readers with the old stories. Few as were the Arthurian pieces in the book, they constituted a greater amount of genuine Arthurian material than the English public had seen since the last edition of Malory, in 1634. For a hundred and thirty-one years, in which time Arthur had appeared as Dryden's hero and Blackmore's, and as Fielding's burlesque king, scarcely any Arthurian pieces had been published faithful to the old legends in substance and spirit. Only here and there in collections of ballads and old poems there had been a stray Arthurian piece that was genuine, as *King Arthur* in Ambrose Philips's collection. And so it meant something that now there should appear six Arthurian pieces, true for the most part to the old spirit and matter.

The less direct service of the *Reliques* to the cause of Arthurian romance was like that of so much of the romantic literature of the time. By stimulating interest in mediævalism, the *Reliques* made the way easier for the ultimate return to popularity of the tales of the Round Table. No publication in the eighteenth century had so much turned literary taste to mediæval stories. The influence of the *Reliques*, moreover, lasted long. It was a favorite book of Scott in his boyhood, and one of the causes that made him seek inspiration so often in the age of chivalry.

An unmistakable sign of the Arthurian awakening is seen in the poems of Thomas Warton, which were published in 1777. Warton, the son of a professor of poetry at Oxford, and the author of *Observations on the Faerie Queene* and the *History of English Poetry*, was not only a scholar but a facile versifier. In his last years he was poet-laureate. Of three Arthurian poems of his, the principal is an ode entitled *The Grave of King Arthur*, which recounts the dispute between two bards as to Arthur's death; one maintaining that Arthur was buried at Glastonbury, like any ordinary man, and the other that after his mortal wound he was carried by an elfin queen to Avalon. Warton's other two Arthurian poems were sonnets, one on the Round Table at Winchester, the other on Stonehenge. Parnell and Gray, we have seen, had referred to the Arthurian legends with evident appreciation of their poetry. Now, in these pieces of Thomas Warton, the legends for the first time since the Commonwealth inspire whole poems which treat them with reverence and fidelity. This means that the Arthurian stories, substantially unchanged from their mediæval forms, are again recognised as proper material for poets to work with.

But before notable production of Arthurian poetry could begin, it was necessary that various publications

should make people more familiar with the old roman-
tic themes. Among them were Ritson's *Collection of
English Songs* in 1783, M. G. Lewis's *Tales of
Wonder* in 1801, Scott's *Minstrelsy of the Scottish
Border* in 1802–03, Ritson's *Ancient Engleish Me-
trical Romancees* in 1802, and in 1805 Ellis's *Spe-
cimens of Early English Metrical Romances*. These
last two differed from the others in familiarising the
public with the longer Arthurian pieces;[1] previous
collections had included little or no Arthurian poetry
except ballads.

Joseph Ritson, the compiler of two of the collec-
tions just mentioned, rendered still further service to
Arthurian romance through his famous controversy
with Bishop Percy. It would be hard to imagine two
men more fitted to irritate each other, — Percy, con-
ventional and suavely tactful; Ritson, radical, inde-
pendent, and unamiable.[2] In person he is said to
have resembled a spider; and he seems to have been
what we should call a crank, and what is worse, a
crank who always had a chip on his shoulder. He was
a vegetarian, a spelling reformer, an atheist, a Jaco-
bite who kept with fasting and prayer the anniver-
sary of Charles I's death, and (after a visit to France
in 1791) a Jacobin who used the French republican
calendar and addressed his British fellow subjects as
"Citizen" or "Citizeness." When over thirty, Ritson
studied law; when thirty-six he was called to the bar.
Not a university man, he was nevertheless, deeply

[1] These were given generally in summaries, with many long quota-
tions.

[2] Born in 1752, Ritson was considerably younger than Percy,
though he died in 1803, eight years before the Bishop.

interested in literature, especially in the study of old ballads and romances, of which he had such knowledge that contemporary antiquarians feared him. In 1782 he made Thomas Warton squirm under an ill-tempered review of his *History of English Poetry*, and at the same time got in a hit at the editor of the *Reliques* by saying that Warton was inexact, like Bishop Percy. In 1783, in the preface to his *Select Collection of English Songs*, Ritson fell foul of the Bishop in earnest, whom he virtually accused of lying in the assertion that he had taken the greater part of his *Reliques* without change from his old manuscript. Though Ritson might have been more polite, he was saying what could not be denied; as we have seen, Percy not only made over his material, but of the pieces in the *Reliques* he took only about a fourth from his folio manuscript. Percy replied, nevertheless, to Ritson; and after that Ritson to Percy, going so far as to doubt the very existence of the manuscript.[1] Mrs. Gamp, on hearing the existence of Mrs. Harris doubted, was not more shocked than Percy at this. He had his portrait painted by Sir Joshua Reynolds with the manuscript in his hand, a portrait one likes to fancy hanging on the other side of the Percy chimney-piece from the portrait of Mrs. Percy with *Nanny* on a scroll in her hand. As a more convincing argument of authenticity, Percy allowed the manuscript to be exhibited for six months under a glass case in a shop in Pall Mall. Ritson was obliged, therefore, to acknowledge that the manuscript did exist, though still he did not cease his hits at the

[1] This was in an essay at the beginning of his *Ancient Songs from the Time of King Henry III to the Revolution*, 1790, p. xix.

Bishop. In his preface to *Ancient Engleish Metrical Romancëes*,[1] he wrote, using his particular brand of reformed spelling : —

"The existence and authenticity of this famous MS. in its present mutilateëd and miserable condition is no longer to be deny'd . . . at the same time, it is a certain and positive fact, that, in the elegant and refine'd work it gave occasion to, there is scarcely one single poem, song or ballad, fairly or honestly printed . . . from the beginning to the end ; many piecëes, allso, being inserted, as ancient and authentick, which, there is every reason to believe, never existed before its publication. To correct the obvious errours of an illiterate transcribeër, to supply irremediable defects, and to make sense of nonsense, are certainly essential dutys of an editour of ancient poetry ; provideëd he act with integrity and publicity ; but secretly to suppress the original text, and insert his own fabrications for the sake of provideing more refine'd entertainment for readers of taste and genius, is no proof of either judgement, candour, or integrity.

In what manner this ingenious editour conducted himself in this patch'd up publication will be evident from the following parallel, which may be useful to future manufacturers in this line."

Then followed, on opposite pages, versions of *The Marriage of Sir Gawaine*, one as printed in the *Reliques*, the other as the poem appeared in the mutilated manuscript found in Humphrey Pitt's parlor, which version Percy, stung by the taunts of Ritson, had felt obliged to add to the fourth edition of his *Reliques*. The difference between the two is so great that four fully printed pages of "the improvement," as Ritson sarcastically termed it, stand opposite four wholly blank

[1] London, 1802, vol. i, p. cix.

pages of the "original." The other pages vary in greater or less degree. Not one agrees with the page confronting it.

Though Ritson was a pedant who was exasperated at trifling inaccuracies and inexcusably harsh, nevertheless he did good work in awakening the antiquarian conscience which for so long had seemed dead. He was right in declaring that enjoyment of old romantic stories was possible with closer adherence to both text and spirit than Percy thought necessary ; and Percy, we can see, was the most conscientious of antiquarians compared with Dryden and Blackmore. The service of Ritson to Arthurian romance is that he thus stimulated antiquarian scholarship, which plenty of nineteenth-century writers were to show could be combined with human and poetic interest. From his time on, writers who have used Arthurian themes have been unsuccessful when they have ventured on anything like Spenser's freedom in treating them. Indeed, the most striking characteristic of nineteenth-century Arthurian poets, as distinguished from those between Spenser and Percy, has been fidelity to the incidents and the spirit of the old stories. Along with this tendency have gone others. More than ever before, poets of the nineteenth century have sought something deeper than a surface meaning in the old tales, — a meaning, furthermore, suited to the new times, — and they have made a greater effort than ever before to get at the motives of their characters.[1] Guine-

[1] Previously, poets here and there had tried to give more than superficial meaning to the Arthurian legends, and to get at the motives of the characters, but not before the nineteenth century had there been such a widespread effort to do so.

vere, whose fame no voice had sung worthily since Malory's, has taken her place on the throne again beside Arthur, beautiful and unfortunate still, but less imperious than of old; and once more she has received the homage of poets, who, unlike their predecessors, have chivalrously tried to whiten her character. With these tendencies ready to show themselves, the Arthurian stories entered on the century which was to see their return to the highest poetic honor.

XIX

THE EARLY NINETEENTH CENTURY

Arthurian poetry in the nineteenth century fittingly opens with Scott, the king of romancers, in whom the new fidelity to the incidents and spirit of the old stories is still combined with something of the earlier freedom in treating them. Scott's acquaintance with Arthurian romance began, no doubt, even before he became, at twelve,[1] a devoted reader of Percy's *Reliques*. Interest in the subject grew till, in the first year of the century, we find him in eager correspondence with George Ellis regarding the stories of the Round Table.[2] Later he had some thought, which he soon gave up, of editing Malory's *Morte Darthur*, "long a favourite" of his.[3] And in 1804 he proved himself a careful antiquarian in editing and concluding that *Sir Tristrem* of the end of the thirteenth century which had stopped at Tristram's receiving his mortal wound. Though Scott had not the linguistic knowledge which the nineteenth century has given scholars of to-day, yet on the whole he imitated well the language of the mediæval romance; it is not every student who can tell where Scott's work begins and the old ends. The stanzas which he added, more-

[1] See *Autobiography* in Lockhart's *Scott*.

[2] See Lockhart's *Scott*.

[3] See letters, November, 1807, and December 15, 1807, Lockhart's *Scott*.

over, give accurately, and in the mediæval temper, the incidents of the old legend.

Already Scott's friend, Dr. Leyden,[1] recalling a Scottish tradition which placed the Avalon where Arthur slept in the Eildon Hills, had urged Scott, "with summons strong and high," to

> " bid the charméd sleep of ages fly ;
> Roll the long sound through Eildon's caverns vast,
>
> .   .   .   .
>
> And peal proud Arthur's march from Fairyland."

With less fidelity to the old stories than he had previously shown, Scott tried to do so by introducing an Arthurian episode into *The Bridal of Triermain*, written in 1813. According to this, Arthur one day comes to a castle in the vale of St. John in Cumberland, where he yields to the fascination of the chatelaine, Gwendolyn — in nature something like the fays who beguiled Lanval and Guingamor, and other mortal young men, to palaces where years, or even centuries, passed like so many days. Charmed by her, Arthur remains three months at the castle, forgetful not only of his Queen, but of the invading heathen who have come over the seas. His

> " horn, that foemen wont to fear,
> Sounds but to wake the Cumbrian deer ;
> And Caliburn, the British pride,
> Hangs useless by a lover's side."

[1] Dr. John Leyden (1785–1811), who assisted Scott in preparing the *Minstrelsy of the Scottish Border*, makes two references of considerable length to Arthurian legend in his *Scenes of Infancy*, 1803, Part I and Part II. The lines quoted are from Part II. The poem is written in heroic couplets, pretty closely after the precise eighteenth-century model.

See M. W. MacCallum, pp. 179–181.

At length, roused by a sense of duty, he forces himself
to leave Gwendolyn ; but before he goes, he promises
that if the child to be born to them be a daughter, no
man may take her to wife, unless he prove himself the
best knight in a tournament, which may last, if need
be, a whole summer day.

Years passed, and Arthur was holding high feast,
when there appeared before him a beautiful girl, in
whose face shone the fairness of Gwendolyn with the
royal pride of the race of Pendragon. Arthur, recog-
nising her straightway as his daughter, kissed her
on the brow and proclaimed himself her father. The
girl, whose name was Gyneth, had come to Arthur for
protection on the death of her mother. And now the
King made proclamation, in accordance with his pro-
mise of long ago, that the best knights of his court
should strive a whole day, till one was proved worthiest
of the hand of his daughter. When the tournament
took place, the spirits of the knights were so high that
they got to fighting in grim earnest. One after an-
other fell dead, till Arthur was growing aghast at the
slaughter, but the proud girl refused to release her
father from his promise; nor did she, even when at
length she felt dismay herself, for she deemed that
respect for her mother demanded the continuance of
the fight. It would have lasted the whole day, had
not a youth, a kinsman near to Merlin and beloved
by him, been stricken dead at Gyneth's very foot-
stool. Then the great seer in anger raised his hand,
declaring that the conflict should stop, and that
Gyneth herself should lie in a magic sleep in the
Vale of St. John till — it might be centuries later —
a knight should wake her, as renowned in arms as any

warrior of Arthur's court. So Gyneth lay for years enchanted, and no man entered the castle where she slept, for to most knights it looked only like a castellated crag; and even when seen distinctly, it faded away before the venturesome knight who rode up to the gate.

At first, after Gyneth's enchantment, knights from all parts of Britain tried to rouse her from her sleep; but as none succeeded, those who attempted the adventure grew fewer and fewer. Therefore when Sir Roland de Vaux, Baron of Triermain, in the days of the Plantagenet kings, set forth from his castle in Cumberland to seek the girl in her magic slumber, his minstrels thought that he had set out on a mad quest. So did de Vaux himself for a time. Once by night, and again by day, he saw the enchanted castle in the vale of St. John, but each time, as he rode up to it, the castle faded, as it had faded before the eyes of other young knights who had attempted to enter. A third time when de Vaux saw the castle fade away, he threw his battle-axe in anger at a rock where, a few minutes before, had risen a turret. As the axe struck the rock, lo! it parted, revealing a staircase by which de Vaux mounted to the castle he had just seen. He entered the gate and passed through galleries and rooms full of terrifying marvels; but he went on undaunted till at last, asleep in her bower, he found Gyneth, her white robe still spotted with the blood of Merlin's young kinsman. De Vaux knelt and kissed the princess. At that, with peals of thunder and flashes of lightning, the castle and its attendants disappeared; but Gyneth remained, a breathing, beautiful woman, standing there hand in hand with de Vaux, who had proved himself the best knight in all the years since Merlin had put Gyneth to sleep.

Of course in this Scott has drawn on the common stock of European folklore; he has virtually told as an Arthurian story the tale of the Sleeping Beauty, or of the enchanted Brunhilda, told likewise of Guinevere as far back as Ulrich's *Lanzelet*. In thus working over old non-Arthurian material into a new Arthurian incident, Scott has kept consistently the proper romantic tone. His setting, too, is appropriate — Cumberland, that favorite locality of the Arthurian ballad-writers; and as in so many of the old poems, Arthur sets out, on the adventure which is to prove memorable, from merry Carlisle. Thus Scott in his new treatment of the Arthurian story is less free than Spenser or Dryden or Blackmore; but he is freer than most mediæval writers. Yet *The Bridal of Triermain* is as faithful to the old legends as Chrétien's *Cligès*, if not more so. Written in the twelfth century, it might conceivably have become one of the permanent stories in the great Arthurian cycle. After the Renaissance, however, it was too late for writers to fix new material in the old. But one change since Malory's *Morte Darthur* seems likely to be permanent — the account commonly accepted by English readers to-day of the meeting of Lancelot and Guinevere; and of this, as we have seen, the poetic charm was borrowed from the Tristram story. Such is its power, and so exquisitely has Tennyson made it felt, in bringing his Lancelot and Guinevere together amid the flowering spring, before Guinevere has met Arthur, that future poets and readers will probably remember this story of the meeting of the Queen and her true knight rather than the mediæval one which led Dante's Paolo and Francesca to declare their love.

The same year that Scott was writing *The Bridal of Triermain*, a friend of his, Reginald Heber, was likewise finding inspiration for original poetry in the old Arthurian legend. Heber we commonly think of as a zealous churchman, who wrote *Greenland's Icy Mountains* and other hymns; and yet had he possessed only a little more romantic inspiration, he might be remembered as the writer of an Arthurian poem. Interest in the Arthurian stories he always felt. At Oxford, not only the classic authors interested him, but also the older English writers, among them Spenser, from whom he seems first to have got his romantic taste, and Malory. In the faithful discharge of arduous parochial duties, whether in England or later in India, where he was sent as Bishop of Calcutta and where he died in 1826, Heber sought diversion by writing romantic pieces, which apparently he had little if any expectation of publishing. Thus he came to write his fragmentary *Morte d'Arthur*, in Spenserian stanzas, and his still more fragmentary *Masque of Gwendolen*, which tells virtually the story of *The Marriage of Sir Gawaine*.

Heber's *Morte d'Arthur*, which for the most part follows the old story of Malory, is noteworthy for its attempt thus early in the century to excuse Guinevere's sin. Ganora, as Heber chooses to call the great Queen, the daughter of the King of Carmelide (Malory's Cameliard), is sent away by her father to the Vale of Derwent to escape the ravages of Ryence of North Wales, quite as savage a king as Malory's. In the Vale of Derwent, with its beautiful lake and precipi-

tous mountain wall, Ganora, known only as a simple
village maiden, meets and loves a knight, who for
some reason does not reveal his name. Soon chance
separates them ; and since neither knows who the other
really is, try as they will, they see no prospect of
meeting again. Ganora resigns herself to a loveless
life ; and when courted by Arthur, the great King of
Britain, she is flattered enough to accept his hand.
But she is to know little calm happiness. Even at her
wedding feast Merlin prophesies woe. Still it does not
seem imminent, till one day the Queen by chance goes
into the Chapel of the Grail. There on the walls are
pictured the greatest heroes of the Table Round,
among them her old love of the Vale of Derwent ; and
to her amazement she sees under the picture the name,
Lancelot.

Though Heber broke off his story at this point,
there can be little doubt that, had he concluded it, he
would have brought it to a tragic end, like Malory,
to whom, in most details of the story, he is faith-
ful. At Arthur's marriage feast, for instance, a hind
enters the hall, and adventures follow, as in the older
Morte Darthur. In Balin's drawing the sword, too,
and in allusions to Tristram, Lancelot, and the Grail,
Heber is faithful to his original. But Mordred he
makes the son of Morgan le Fay and not of Morgause ;
nor is Arthur Mordred's father. Here again, as in the
effort to excuse Guinevere's guilt, is an attempt, like
that so conspicuous later in Tennyson's treatment of
the legend, to ennoble the principal characters.

It is a pity that Heber left his *Morte d'Arthur*
unfinished. We should like to know what he would
have done with the poem, for though at its worst in

extremely awkward Spenserian stanzas, still it is good enough on the whole to rouse our interest. Moreover, at its best it shows that the Spenserian verse is well suited to the subject, even when treated without the exuberant fancy of the *Faerie Queene*. Then, too, Heber's poem is interesting as a story ; it moves rapidly enough to hold our attention. The scenes of Balin's pulling out the sword from its scabbard and Guinevere's discovery in the Grail Chapel that her unknown lover is Lancelot are effectively dramatic.[1]

When Heber and Scott seek poetic inspiration in the Arthurian legends, it is evident that they are pretty well restored to favor. But for some time yet there was to be more appreciative allusion to Arthurian romance than new treatment of it. Perhaps the reason was that the Round Table stories were still not widely known at first-hand ; and poets may have hesitated to give their labor to themes whose popularity had not been proved. Heber had not written for publication ; Scott's *Sir Tristrem* had been only for the few; and his *Triermain*, but slenderly Arthurian, was deserv-

---

[1] In his other Arthurian poem, the *Masque of Gwendolen*, which is more in need of finishing touches than the *Morte d'Arthur*, Heber goes back to an old story, not an essential part of the Arthurian legend, but already long connected with it in the ballad, *The Marriage of Sir Gawaine*, and its close fifteenth-century analogue, *The Weddynge of Sir Gawen and Dame Ragnell*. These, I showed in the last chapter, tell substantially the same story as the *Wife of Bath's Tale*. Heber was doubtless familiar with the ballad and Chaucer's tale, both, if not also with *Dame Ragnell*.* He makes Gawain the hero, but puts in place of Arthur a young knight who, for some reason (we are not informed what), is to lose his head unless he or Gawain can tell what women most desire. For the rest of his dramatic fragment, Heber agrees virtually with the older stories.

---

* This was not printed, however, till Sir Frederick Madden included it in his *Syr Gawayne*, London, 1839.

edly less liked than *Marmion* or the *Lady of the Lake*. Whether such is the reason or not, the fact remains that Keats, who died in 1821, Shelley, who died a year later, Byron, who died in 1824, and Coleridge, who died in 1834, were not stirred to write Arthurian poems.

The ignorance of the public, however, in regard to Arthurian story was about at an end. The time was come for the resurrection of Malory, the last edition of whose work had appeared in 1634. Now in 1816 there came out two more editions of his *Morte Darthur*, and in 1817 a third. Much meaning there is in these facts; the various editions of Malory tell the whole story of the fall from favor of Arthurian romance, along with the romantic spirit, and its reinstatement. There were editions of the *Morte Darthur* at comparatively short intervals from the first in 1485 to 1634; then, for nearly two hundred years, there were none at all. From 1816 to our own time publishers have again found the book profitable to bring out.[1]

---

[1] Of the editions of 1816, one, in three volumes, was by F. Haselwood; another, in two volumes, was in Walker's British Classics. Both follow the edition of 1634, in which there was a division into chapters, but not into books. To the edition of 1817 Robert Southey gave his name, but in point of fact he did little more than write an introduction; the real editing was done by Upcott. This edition followed the division into books, as well as chapters, of Caxton's first edition. It seems to have been based, however, not only on that edition of 1485, but on Wynkyn de Worde's edition of 1498, and perhaps on other earlier ones. See Sommer's *Morte Darthur*, vol. ii, pp. 1–21; and Strachey's Introduction to the Globe edition of the *Morte Darthur*.

XX

THE HIGH TIDE OF MEDIÆVALISM

GROWING familiarity with the Arthurian stories and ever-growing antiquarian interest brought into existence the one Arthurian prose romance [1] of the nineteenth century, by Thomas Love Peacock, a novelist, in his peculiar humor, unlike any other who has written in our tongue. Irregular in his schooling, and not a university man, Peacock, nevertheless, being naturally studious, got a good education. Since business was not to his taste, he was at first inclined to live on his slender fortune, devoting himself to literature. When about thirty-four, however, he entered the employ of the East India Company, with which he was connected till his retirement from business late in life. He died in 1866, nearly eighty-one years old. In 1816 appeared his first satirical romance, *Headlong Hall*, which he followed with several others. The last came out in 1860, after almost thirty years of silence, of virtually the same nature as the first. Of all these, the only one which concerns us is *The Misfortunes of Elphin*, published in 1829.

His marriage to a Welsh lady no doubt stimulated Peacock's interest in the history and the literature of Wales, so evident throughout *The Misfortunes of*

[1] At least it is the only one now remembered.

Elphin. Thanks to this interest, the novel is more readable than any other of Peacock's, because he has got a fairly good plot from the old stories, weaving together two originally in no way connected; and good plots Peacock could not construct for himself. One story relates the submersion by the sea of Gwythno's kingdom, the subsequent poverty of Gwythno and his son Elphin, Elphin's discovery of the bard Taliesin as a babe floating in a coracle in Gwythno's fish-weir, and the marriage in due time of Taliesin and Elphin's daughter. With this Peacock connects the tale of Guinevere's abduction by Melvas to Glastonbury, and her restoration to Arthur, changing the stories but little as he unites them. In doing so, he makes no use of the French romances or the English ones founded on them; he relies entirely on Welsh material. What is more, with his extensive antiquarian knowledge, he tries to reproduce Welsh society of the sixth century, to give us not a romantic "Logres," [1] but the Britain in which the historical Arthur actually lived, — something which no writer of repute except Peacock has ever tried to do. On the whole, Peacock introduces his antiquarianism skilfully; the description of ancient Caerleon, for instance, comes appropriately in the account of Taliesin's arrival at that city. Peacock's Arthur, then, is not the splendid mediæval monarch whom we have come to know, but a rough Welshman of the sixth century with no knightly panoply. He is a king, nevertheless, as in Geoffrey's *History* and the romances, surrounded by the warriors of his court, and not simply the general, the Dux Bellorum, of Nennius. In thus changing

[1] The usual name for England in mediæval Arthurian romances.

slightly the historical Arthur, Peacock was but fol-
lowing mediæval Welsh tradition.[1]

As we might expect from Peacock's antiquarian
interest, there are many references in *Elphin* to
what we have already touched on in the history of
Arthurian romance. There is mention, for instance,
of Sir Cradock's wife, the chaste heroine of *The Boy
and the Mantle*. And Gwythno's marvellous hamper,
sent through the kindness of his neighbor kings after
his people have been driven from their homes· by the
sea, the very practical hamper, according to Peacock,
which has in it every morning a hundred hams and
a hundred flasks of wine, is no other than the "mar-
vellous vessel" or "mwys" of Gwythno, which, in the
Mabinogion, would always satisfy with food and drink
as many as came about it — the vessel which Professor
Rhys thinks to have had a share in the making of the
Holy Grail.[2]

Little as he changes the incidents of his stories, Pea-
cock does give his own interpretation to his characters.
By modernising them ironically, he gives his novel its
contemporary meaning, for he makes his characters
the vehicle of excellent satire, which is directed at
contemporary abuses almost as indiscriminately as Mr.
Bernard Shaw's. Apart from this, Peacock's charac-
ters have little to recommend them; they are almost
never alive. Only one is well drawn — Seithenyn,
one of the three great drunkards of Britain, through
whose carelessness the flood came which overwhelmed
the country of Gwythno. One of the best things in
the book is Seithenyn's account of his escape when the

[1] Compare ch. xi, *Kilhwch and Olwen*.
[2] *Arthurian Legend*, p. 316.

sea, breaking through the great dyke which it was his duty to keep sound, but which he had let decay, sapped the foundations of Seithenyn's castle till the whole structure fell into the water.

"It was well for me," says Seithenyn, "that I had been so provident as to empty so many barrels, and that somebody . . . had been so provident as to put the bungs into them, to keep them sweet; for the beauty of it was that, when there was so much water in the case, it kept them empty; and when I jumped into the sea, the sea was just making a great hole in the cellar, and they were floating out by dozens. I don't know how I managed it, but I got one arm over one, and the other arm over another : I nipped them pretty tight; and though my legs were under water, the good liquor I had in me kept me warm. I could not help thinking — as I had nothing else to think of just then that touched me so nearly — that if I had left them full, and myself empty, as a sober man would have done, we should all three — that is, I and the two barrels, have gone to the bottom together, that is to say, separately ; for we should never have come together, except at the bottom, perhaps, when no one of us could have done the other any good ; whereas they have done me much good, and I have requited it ; for, first, I did them the service of emptying them ; and then they did me the service of floating me with the tide . . . down to the coast of Dyfed, where I was picked up by fishermen ; and such was my sense of gratitude that, though I had always before detested an empty barrel, except as a trophy, I swore I would not budge from the water unless my two barrels went with me." [1]

The account of the Queen's return to Arthur's court gives another characteristic example of Peacock's humor. Seithenyn, who had been instrumental in bringing her back, assured Arthur in the name of her

[1] Chapter xi.

captor that the Queen returned as pure as on the day King Melvas had carried her off.

"'None here will doubt that,' said Gwenvach, the wife of Modred. Gwenyvar was not pleased with the compliment, and almost before she had saluted King Arthur, she turned suddenly round and slapped Gwenvach on the face, with a force that brought more crimson into one cheek than blushing had ever done into both. This slap is recorded in the Bardic Triads as one of the Three Fatal Slaps of the Island of Britain. A terrible effect is ascribed to this small cause; for it is said to have been the basis of that enmity between Arthur and Modred, which terminated in the battle of Camlan, wherein all the flower of Britain perished on both sides . . ." [1]

Taken all in all, *The Misfortunes of Elphin* is not read so much as it deserves. A mixture of veracious antiquarianism, old legends, humor, and satire, with a dash of poetry, — for there is good verse scattered through it, sometimes paraphrased from old Welsh, but more often original, — *Elphin* is unlike any other novel in the English language, unless one by the same author, *Maid Marian*, which tries to reproduce the England of the famous ballad heroine and her lover, Robin Hood.

The year after Peacock wrote his Arthurian novel, Wordsworth found inspiration in the old legends for his semi-lyrical story of *The Egyptian Maid*. His treatment of the old material, as he says in his introduction, is free. "For the names and persons in the following poem, see the *History of the Renowned Prince Arthur and his Knights of the Round Table*. For the rest the author is answerable."

Merlin, seeing the ship in which the Egyptian Maid,

[1] Chapter xvi.

who is a princess, is sailing to Britain, calls up a storm, apparently through mere wanton desire to show his magic, which dashes the ship to pieces. The Egyptian Maid alone of those on board is washed ashore. She is apparently dead, but it is ordained that she is to become the bride of one of Arthur's knights; and so she lies only in a trance, from which her destined husband may rouse her by the touch of his hand. The miracle ensues at Arthur's court. Various knights make trial, — Gawain, Tristram, Lancelot,

> " The royal Guinever looked passing glad
>   When his touch failed,"

and last Galahad, wearing the very mantle in which he appeared on that

> " day of glory,
> The day he achieved that matchless feat,
> The marvel of the Perilous Seat,
> Which whosoe'er approached of strength was shorn,
> Though King or Knight the most renowned in story."

As Galahad touched the girl, the color came back to her cheeks, her lips moved, and love stirred in Galahad's heart. And when the Egyptian Maid was quite restored to strength, Arthur bestowed her on the pure young knight as his bride.

That Wordsworth had the right feeling for Arthurian stories he proved as early as 1800 in lines of exquisite beauty, comparing a stately fern on the beach of Grasmere to the

> " Lady of the Mere,
> Sole-sitting by the shores of old romance." [1]

[1] These lines occur in the *Poems on the Naming of Places*, iv. For a fuller discussion of Wordsworth's interest in Arthurian story, see M. W. MacCallum, *op. cit.* pp. 208 ff.

His *Egyptian Maid*, which is not in his best manner, shows that thirty years later he still had the right feeling, but not the ability to express it. True, he belongs rather to the seventeenth century than to the nineteenth, in making up a new Arthurian story; but he has for the most part taken the characters for his new story from old romance faithfully, with their old characteristics and setting. And he is entirely of his own time in combining the old romantic spirit with new moral meaning. The poem, in fact, suffers from being clumsily moral. Because the Egyptian Maid personifies purity, she is the destined bride of only that one who is the purest knight of the Round Table, namely Galahad. In thus marrying off this ascetic mediæval celibate, Wordsworth is modern with a vengeance — so much so as to be again anachronistic. Such a fundamental change in an Arthurian character you would expect in the age of prose and reason rather than in Wordsworth's.

The next decade saw the work of various scholars who made the Arthurian stories still better known to readers. Sir Frederic Madden collected all the mediæval English poems, whether ballads or romances, which made Gawain their hero, and began the editing and translating into modern English of Layamon's *Brut*.[1] Various learned societies were formed about this time for the purpose of editing other ballads, romances, and chronicles. Above all, in 1838, Lady Charlotte Guest brought out her charming translation of the Welsh *Mabinogion*. Here the world had a chance to see at last how the race to which the actual Arthur belonged had treated in poetic story his achievements

[1] Madden's *Layamon* was published in 1847.

and those of other national champions. After such faithful scholarship and renewed interest in the spirit of the old romances, the work of Edward Bulwer Lytton, Lord Lytton, in the next decade, *King Arthur, An Epic Fable in Twelve Books*, is a surprising anachronism.

Though Bulwer belonged to a later generation than Wordsworth,[1] and even a later one than Peacock, he treated old legends as freely as Spenser, perhaps because of his love for that poet, to which the preface to *King Arthur* bears witness. Like Spenser, Bulwer associates Arthurian characters with non-Arthurian supernatural and mythological people ; and so in spite of some attempt to present the old Gawain and his friendship with Lancelot, Bulwer's poem is Arthurian in name and not in spirit.

Arthur, it seems, in order to defend his throne successfully, must achieve three labors. He must win

> " The Falchion, welded from a diamond gem,
>   Guarded by Genii in the sparry caves
>   Where springs a forest from a single stem,
>   Shadowing a temple built beneath the waves ;
>   Where bitter charms grant gifted eyes to mark
>   The Lake's weird Lady in her noiseless bark.

> " The silver Shield in which the infant sleep
>   Of Thor was cradled, — now the jealous care
>   Of the fierce Dwarf whose home is on the deep,
>   Where drifting icerocks clash in lifeless air ;
>   And War's pale Sisters smile to see the shock
>   Stir the still curtains round the couch of Lok.

---

[1] Bulwer was born in 1803, Peacock in 1785, and Wordsworth in 1770. *King Arthur* was published in 1848. Bulwer says in the preface that the work " for twenty years . . . has rested steadily on my mind."

" And last of all — before the Iron Gate
Which opes its entrance at the faintest breath,
But hath no egress; where remorseless Fate
Sits, weaving life, within the porch of Death;
There with meek, fearless eyes, and locks of gold,
Back to warm earth thy childlike guide behold." [1]

Having won these, " The sword, the shield, and that
young playmate guide," Arthur shall attain great fame
and live in song from age to age; but if he fail to
attain even one of them, for him shall be nothing but
woe. On his threefold quest, which is entirely suc-
cessful, Arthur visits places and people that no poet
had ever taken him to before, — among others the
North Pole, where he has a fight with walruses, and
the Esquimaux, in whose keeping he finds the shield
of Thor. When he returns at last to his own domin-
ions, Arthur does not succeed in expelling the Saxons
entirely. He learns, from the prophecies of Merlin,
that they are established in Britain forever, but that
in time one of his race, Henry Tudor, shall restore
the ancient line to the British throne. Here Bulwer is
borrowing directly from that prediction which Spenser
made Merlin utter to Britomart, the destined bride of
Arthur's half-brother. But the poem lacks the charm
of the *Faerie Queene*, which only could have made
such a singular treatment of the old stories acceptable.
Plenty of imagination it has, to be sure, but it is long
and uninteresting. It needs simplicity, both of pur-
pose and of diction. If Bulwer lives in the annals of
English literature, it will be for his novels and not for
his *King Arthur*.

Bulwer's anachronistic treatment of the Arthur

---

[1] Book i, stanzas 83–85.

story is the stranger because already for nearly twenty years the mediæval tendency of romanticism had been exceedingly strong in English thought and art. With it went the feeling that in retelling mediæval tales the incidents and characters should be altered as little as possible. The wonder is that mediævalism was not so strong sooner; that it should have been so long in becoming really popular. As far back as 1750, Horace Walpole had his plans formed to make over his villa at Strawberry Hill into a neo-Gothic castle; but until after Abbotsford became famous, in the second decade of the nineteenth century, the prevailing architecture remained Georgian. In America there was scarcely any Gothic until the thirties,[1] when Trinity Church in New York was built, one of the most skilful examples of Gothic in the United States. Then followed Gothic buildings of all sorts, some even of wood, still greater abominations than the wooden Greek temples of about the same period that commended themselves unfortunately to many American architects.

With the triumph of mediævalism in architecture went its triumph in religion. The Oxford Movement is one manifestation of romanticism, seeking as it did, among other things, the enrichment of church buildings and church service with mediæval beauty. It marked, therefore, a return, partial in some cases, in others entire, to the great mediæval church, the Church of Rome. The Reformation, as the leaders of the movement thought, "was a limb badly set which required to be broken again." Nominally confined to the Church of England, the movement has affected all

---

[1] Richard Upjohn's plans for the church were accepted in 1839. The building was not completed till 1846.

Protestant sects. There is not one of any note to-day which is not far more ritualistic than it was seventy-five years ago.

Of literature too, it may be said, despite Scott's romances and Keats's *Eve of St. Agnes*, that the mediæval tendency of romanticism was strongest after the first quarter of the nineteenth century. At any rate, it was not until then, after the tentative efforts of Warton, Scott, and Heber at original Arthurian composition, that interest in the old legends caused that great production of new Arthurian material which has continued to the present time. It began with Peacock's *Elphin* in 1829, which was followed the next year by Wordsworth's *Egyptian Maid*, when already the greatest Arthurian poet of the century was making his rough draft of *The Lady of Shalott* and planning his *Idylls*. Within ten years appeared Lady Charlotte Guest's *Mabinogion* and the new editions of romances and ballads already referred to. In 1842 Tennyson published his *Morte d'Arthur*; and in the fifties he wrote the four *Idylls* which, with this, have remained the most popular. In these same years, on the Continent, Wagner composed his *Lohengrin* and his *Tristan und Isolde*. Lowell in America had been inspired by the Grail legend to write his pretty sermon of *Sir Launfal*. And in the fifties began the Præ-Raphaelite treatment of Arthurian themes. The tide of mediævalism flowing in strongly so long was at last at the full. Since then, either the tide-gates have been shut, or another Joshua has made the moon stand still, for it bids fair to be long before the flats of unpoetic fact are laid bare again, as they were in the eighteenth century.

Præ-Raphaelitism was the manifestation of mediæ-valism in two of the fine arts, poetry and painting. It grew up in a coterie of four painters and sculptors, the so-called Præ-Raphaelite Brotherhood, who enlarged their number to seven, and then to eight, of whom the world has looked on Dante Gabriel Rossetti as the leader.[1] Their object in painting was not unlike that of the reformers of Oxford in religion. Like them, the Præ-Raphaelites sought the zealous sincerity of an earlier time, and its picturesque beauty. By 1851 they had attracted so much attention that Ruskin, who sympathised with them, and whose *Modern Painters*[2] had helped inspire them, wrote in explanation of the motives of the new painters : —

"They have opposed themselves . . . to the entire feeling of the Renaissance schools. . . . If they . . . paint nature as it is around them, with the help of modern science, with the earnestness of the men of the thirteenth and fourteenth centuries, they will . . . found a new and noble school in England. If their sympathies . . . lead them into mediævalism . . . , they will . . . come to nothing. But I believe there is no danger of this, at least for the strongest among them." [3]

Ruskin's hopes have not been entirely realised. The consensus of opinion is that the Præ-Raphaelites made a mistake in rejecting all the teaching of the

[1] See William M. Rossetti's preface to the *Collected Works of Dante Gabriel Rossetti*, 2 vols., London, 1886. Compare, however, William Holman Hunt, *Pre-Raphaelitism and the Pre-Raphaelite Brotherhood*, 1906. Mr. Hunt maintains that he and Millais were the original and true Præ-Raphaelites, and that Rossetti was only a mediævalist.

[2] Up to this time only two volumes of *Modern Painters* had been published.

[3] John Ruskin, *Pre-Raphaelitism*, New York, 1851, p. 23, note.

Renaissance; they did become too mediæval; they fell into mannerisms. A peculiar type of feminine beauty came to be recognised as their favorite: a woman always graceful, but always large-boned, long-limbed, long-necked, with long and more or less dishevelled hair. This figure they often placed before an ornate mediæval background. Nor did they stop with painting. The fact that Rossetti and two or three others of the Brotherhood were poets as well as painters led to the growth of a Præ-Raphaelite school of poets, who, like the Præ-Raphaelite painters, sought their inspiration in mediæval times. They tried to put into words such pictures as they had been painting on canvas, and so they have told us stories, chiefly mystical and mediæval, suited to such pictures, with the characters in the brilliant, picturesque garb of the Middle Ages, amid highly pictorial, brilliant surroundings.

One would naturally have expected Rossetti to write a notable Arthurian poem, for his illustrations for Moxon's quarto edition of the *Poems of Tennyson*, in 1857, show that he was appreciative of the pictorial beauties of Arthurian story.[1] So do the frescoes for the Oxford Union, which were partly his work. The fact remains, nevertheless, that he produced no such poem, but left the first Præ-Raphaelite treatment of Arthurian themes in verse to William Morris, born in 1834 and dead in 1896, who never felt truer poetic

---

[1] W. M. Rossetti, moreover, says that one of the books that influenced his brother's literary taste most was Malory's *Morte Darthur*. See preface to *Collected Works of Dante Gabriel Rossetti*.

Besides Rossetti, Millais and Holman Hunt contributed illustrations to Moxon's 1857 edition. See Elisabeth L. Cary, *Tennyson, His Homes, His Friends, and His Work*, New York, 1898, pp. 163-175.

inspiration than while under the influence of Malory and other mediæval romancers. True, the strongest mediæval influence he felt was the Scandinavian, as his translations and adaptations from the Norse show; and critics may regard *Sigurd, the Volsung,* published in 1877, as his principal work. Then, too, *The Life and Death of Jason,* various stories in *The Earthly Paradise,* and his translations of Homer and Virgil show that Morris was not blind to the beauty of classic poetry. But he sang most spontaneously as a lyric poet in that volume of verse which was his first, *The Defence of Guenevere and Other Poems,* published in 1858, when Morris was only twenty-four years old. Though but four poems in this volume are Arthurian, they are the poems which have the place of honor, standing first in the book, *The Defence of Guenevere,* which gives the volume its name; *King Arthur's Tomb; Sir Galahad, A Christmas Mystery;* and *The Chapel in Lyoness.*

In *The Defence of Guenevere,* the Queen seems to be pleading her cause before various judges, who have been chosen from Arthur's lords, waiting, as she talks, for Lancelot to come and fight in her behalf. The story is so faithful to the *Morte Darthur* that, to understand it, you need a knowledge of Malory. There is reference, for instance, to Mellyagraunce [1] and his abduction of Guinevere — the incident related first as we know it by Chrétien de Troies — which would be almost incomprehensible without knowledge of the old story. Yet in one respect Morris has made a change. According to Malory and the romancers before him, when the guilt of Lance-

[1] So Morris spells the name.

lot and Guinevere was discovered, Gawain was their
steadfast friend. He would hear nothing of the scan-
dal regarding them ; and when Sir Agravaine said
that he would disclose their guilt to the King, Gawain
replied, " Ye must remember how ofttimes Sir Laun-
celot hath rescued the king and the queen, and the best
of us all had been full cold at the heart-root, had not
Sir Launcelot been better than we ; and that hath he
proved himself full oft. And as for my part, said Sir
Gawaine, I will never be against Sir Launcelot, for
one day's deed, when he rescued me from king Cara-
dos of the dolorous tower, and slew him, and saved my
life. Also, brother Sir Agravaine, and Sir Mordred,
in likewise Sir Launcelot rescued you both, and three-
score and two, from Sir Turquin. Methinketh, brother,
such deeds and kindness should be remembered." [1]
Nor would Gawain's younger brothers, Gareth and
Gaheris, take any more part than he with Agravaine
and Mordred, but all three departed, unwilling to hear
another word against the Queen or Lancelot. For
some reason,[2] however, Morris saw fit to make Gawain
the Queen's chief accuser ; and she says to him three
times in the course of the poem : [3] —

" Nevertheless, you, O Sir Gauwaine, lie,
    Whatever may have happened through these years,
    God knows I speak truth, saying that you lie."

In making Guinevere answer the charge brought
against her, Morris shows something, though not so

[1] Malory, bk. xx, ch. 1.

[2] The reason could not be that the baser Gawain of Tennyson's
Elaine was known, because *Elaine* was not published till 1859. Is
Morris's Gawain partly responsible for Tennyson's ?

[3] There are a few changes in the words, as Guinevere speaks them
the second time and the third, but none of importance.

much as Heber and Tennyson, of the nineteenth-century inclination to excuse her conduct. Till she meets Lancelot, Guinevere has never found such love as she wishes; and that is why she falls. She says herself that she was bought by Arthur's great name and little love. Moreover, she struggles courageously against her growing affection for Lancelot. She meets him first at Christmas. The winter passes, and spring, summer, autumn, and winter again, and a second spring has come, before she grants the knight his first kiss. Whether she ever grants him much more, Morris does not say certainly in this poem. Were it not for *King Arthur's Tomb* which follows, and which may be taken as a sequel to *The Defence of Guenevere*, the Queen's guilt would not be indubitable.

In his characterisation of Guinevere, Morris has tried, no doubt, to present the great tragic, epic queen of Malory and the other old romancers. To my mind he has not succeeded. Morris's Guinevere is a woman at bay, with her nerves all unstrung, not an unreal woman by any means, but hardly the Guinevere whom Malory presents. She, like Tennyson's, could forget herself utterly in a storm of passion, and she does so at times in private, but not often, if ever, in public. Before the court she can assume queenly composure; and probably she would on such an occasion as this which Morris is describing. It seems to be a trial for which she has had some chance to prepare; she is not taken unawares. Under the circumstances, she would hardly charge the judges, in defending herself: —

> " say no rash word
> Against me, being so beautiful . . .

> " . . . see my breast rise,
> Like waves of purple sea, as here I stand ;
> And how my arms are moved in wonderful wise,
>
> " Yea also at my full heart's strong command,
> See through my long throat how the words go up
> In ripples to my mouth; how in my hand
>
> " The shadow lies like wine within a cup
> Of marvellously colour'd gold ; yea, now
> This little wind is rising, look you up,
>
> " And wonder how the light is falling so
> Within my moving tresses . . . "

With Guinevere talking like this, and with Morris leaving it uncertain whether he intended her to be guilty of adultery or not, you cannot help thinking that a dash of clear eighteenth-century reason would have made his poetry, as it would that of the other Præ-Raphaelites, a stronger thing than it is.

In *King Arthur's Tomb*, Morris tells the tale of Guinevere's last meeting with Lancelot, transferred for dramatic effect from the nunnery at Almesbury, where Malory puts it, to Arthur's tomb at Glastonbury. Otherwise there is little change, except that the quaint, conventional dignity of Malory's narrative has given place to a¹ peculiarly Præ-Raphaelite passion. There is reality in each, but not of the same kind. " Lady," says Malory's Lancelot, " I insure you faithfully I will ever take me to penance, and pray while my life lasteth." Here is Morris's : —

> " Guenevere !
> Do you not know me, are you gone mad ? fling
> Your arms and hair about me, lest I fear
>
> " You are not Guenevere, but some other thing."

And when the Queen refuses Lancelot even the
parting kiss which he asks for, he falls in a swoon,
according to Morris, and she cries out:—

> "Alas! Alas! I know not what to do;
> If I run fast it is perchance that I
> May fall and stun myself, much better so,
> Never, never again! not even when I die."

But Malory: "Nay, said the queen, that shall I never
do, but abstain you from such works. And they de-
parted." [1]

In his third Arthurian poem, *Sir Galahad*, Morris
is more inventive. He imagines Sir Galahad's mus-
ings on

> "the longest night in all the year,
> Near on the day when the Lord Christ was born,"

as the young knight ponders over the love which makes
joyous the men he knows. With a pang of regret he
remembers that for himself is, after all, only the quest
of the Grail. Then two angels enter in white, with
scarlet wings, and four ladies in red and green, who
are saints. When they have passed, Galahad's earthly
longings are stilled; he is at peace. And then there
enter Sir Bors, Sir Percival, and Percival's sister, who
tell that the knights who sought the Grail have either
met with death or come back wounded and sick, "foil'd
from the great quest." But we know that to Galahad
sight of the Grail is to be granted. On the whole, the
poem presents a Galahad who, with all the purity of
the mediæval knight, is more human.

Morris is more inventive yet in *The Chapel in Ly-
oness*, a fragmentary story of a knight, Sir Ozana

[1] Malory, bk. xxi, ch. 10; cf. ch. xiii of this book.

le Cure Hardy, whose name Malory gives us, but no-
thing else. Sir Ozana himself tell us, —

> " All day long and every day,
>   From Christmas-Eve to Whit-Sunday,
>   Within that Chapel-aisle I lay,
>   And no man came a-near."

There he lay with the truncheon of a spear in his
breast, no meat ever passing his lips, speechless,
trance-like, and yet not sleeping; and there Sir Gala-
had watched him day by day, till at last, by plucking
a faint wild rose and laying it across Ozana's mouth,
he brought the wounded knight out of the waking,
half-mad trance. Then Sir Ozana died in peace;
and Sir Bors, who stood by, looking at Sir Galahad's
great blue eyes which stared dreamily, as if they saw
what mortal man may not often behold, heard Sir
Galahad : —

> " Ozana, shall I pray for thee ?
>   Her cheek is laid to thine;
>   No long time hence, also I see
>   Thy wasted fingers twine

> " Within the tresses of her hair
>   That shineth gloriously,
>   Thinly outspread in the clear air
>   Against the jasper sea."

This is the sum of William Morris's Arthurian
poetry. In all of it, there is nothing modern except
the careful workmanship of his verse and his subjec-
tive, analytical method of portraying characters. Like
the other poems in his first volume, these four have a
singing fascination, and they are full of vivid, highly
colored mediæval pictures; they transport you, whether

their intangibility irritates or pleases you, into a remote, poetical Middle Age, which for the time being, unreal as it is, you accept as real. You may never be quite satisfied with these poems, because of their too little substance and their too much length and color and imagery; but their spontaneity must rouse your wonder. They seem to have come from Morris's pen as naturally as if this man of the nineteenth century, who deplored the sky-polluting smoke of its factories and the roar and clatter of its steam engines,[1] had lived in the earlier ages of which he wrote. No one has shown more clearly their power to inspire poets of later times — the power which Chatterton felt, and then Scott and Keats and Coleridge, but none so intensely and steadily as Morris and the other Præ-Raphaelites.

Robert Stephen Hawker is to be classed, on the whole, with the Præ-Raphaelite poets, for his inspiration, like Morris's, was drawn from the Middle Ages. But Hawker did not take the sensuous delight in their picturesque beauty which Morris took; he was inspired rather by their ascetic, religious zeal. Born near Plymouth, Devonshire, in 1803, he belonged to a generation older than Morris's. It was not, however, till five years after *The Defence of Guenevere* had appeared that Hawker produced his one important Arthurian poem, *The Quest of the Sangraal.*

This was written, according to the note of the editor at the end of the poem, "during the days of loneliness which followed Mrs. Hawker's death in February, 1863. Every one must regret that the suc-

[1] See ch. i, and *The Earthly Paradise, Argument.*

ceeding chants which were to have completed the plan of the poem were never composed." At that sad time, Hawker was at the vicarage of Morwenstowe in the extreme northeast of Cornwall, a parish whose vicar he was for forty years. His work, keeping him much in the Cornish country, with its traditions and legends, stimulated his natural interest in popular and romantic stories. Perhaps these had considerable part in turning him to mediæval literature; perhaps he was drawn to it by his ever growing fondness for mediæval mysticism and ritualism. He became steadily more of a mystic in religion, and only a few hours before his death, which occurred in 1875, he was received into the church of the Middle Ages, the Roman Catholic, in whose communion he died.

It is natural that the Grail story should have interested Hawker, and natural, too, that, substantially unchanged, it should have satisfied his imagination. What he would have made of the legend, had he given us more than the introductory chant to his poem, of course we cannot tell. So far as we may judge from what we have, Hawker intended to keep closely to the old story, except for limiting the number of questers to four, Lancelot, Percival, Tristram, and Galahad. These knights, who retain virtually their mediæval characteristics, ride in four different directions, determined by chance according to the courses taken by four arrows: Lancelot north, Percival south, Tristram west, and Galahad to the east. Each bears on his banner an appropriate cognisance: Lancelot's is a lily with a broken stem, the legend, " Stately once and ever fair ; " and Hawker adds, " It hath a meaning, seek it not, O King." Percival's motto is, " Whoso is strong with God shall conquer man." Tristram's motto under his device of a rainbow is, —

> " When toil and tears have worn the westering day,
> Behold the smile of fame ! So brief ; so bright."

An archangel is the device on Galahad's shield, and his motto, " I thirst ! O Jesu ! let me drink and die ! "

In a vision the night after the questers depart, Arthur sees that Galahad shall achieve the Grail. Beyond this the end is uncertain ; the fragmentary poem, especially indistinct and mystical at the last, does not indicate clearly what Galahad's adventures would have been. For this the more pity that Hawker did not complete his poem ; it would have been interesting to trace at length in the nineteenth century the course of such a thoroughly ascetic Grail hero as his. Moreover, Hawker's lines have generally a good ring and movement and dignity, as at the beginning : —

> " Ho ! For the Sangraal ! vanish'd Vase of Heaven !
> That held, like Christ's own heart, an hin of blood !
> Ho for the Sangraal ! . . .
>   " How the merry shout
> Of reckless riders on their rushing steeds,
> Smote the loose echo from the drowsy rock
> Of grim Dundagel, thron'd along the sea ! "

Only a few years later, in 1868, appeared another Grail poem, *The Quest of the Sancgreall*, by Thomas Westwood,[1] another poet whose fame has not proved

[1] Westwood was born in 1814, the son of a well-to-do tradesman, who retired to Enfield at the end of the eighteenth century, and set up there as a country gentleman. Through the friendship of his family with Charles Lamb, young Westwood had the run of Lamb's library, a circumstance, no doubt, which helped form a literary taste

lasting. From his boyhood fond of angling, at least as
taught by Izaak Walton, whose ardent disciple West-
wood became, and fond of writing poems, he beguiled
with these two diversions such leisure moments as
came to him in his busy life in Belgium, where he
went in 1844 to become Director and Secretary of the
Tournay Railway. He died in 1888.

Twice Westwood touched on an Arthurian theme.
His first attempt, *The Sword of Kingship*, in 1866,
was more successful in one respect than *The Quest
of the Sancgreall*; it was more distinct. The latter
shows the same besetting fault as Westwood's shorter
poems. With remarkable ability to write lines poet-
ical and musical in themselves, he was generally unable
to put them together to make a definite whole. In *The
Sword of Kingship* this difficulty is not apparent,
because Westwood, in telling of the birth, childhood,
and crowning of Arthur, follows the definite story of
the first book of Malory. As in that, Arthur gets
himself recognised as Uther's son by drawing from the
stone before the altar of the cathedral the sword which
no one else could move.

In the more charming but less organic *Quest of the
Sancgreall*, told in six chapters or books, we have the
old Quest-story of which Galahad is the hero, with
episodes added of Westwood's invention. The story
begins with the vow of the knights to seek the Grail,
and their departure. In the next book we learn that,
years before, Joseph of Arimathea brought to Britain

---

in the boy. His interest in Izaak Walton led him to collect such a
library of angling works, that he came to be recognised as the unri-
valled authority on angling in all England. His literary reputation
rests more on the works he collected than on his own achievement.

the shield of the converted heathen king, Evelake.
Foreordained to Galahad, it is hung round his neck
after misfortune overcomes the ribald knight, Sir Gal-
heron, for daring to bear this shield. Then comes the
Legend of the Syren Isles, all Westwood's own, in
which Sir Galahad and his father are both carnally
tempted. Galahad of course is not seduced, though
he is hardly saved through his own strength of char-
acter ; scarcely has the temptation begun, when in
the deep sky he sees an angel host, recalling the
vision which appeared when the Holy Grail hung over
Camelot and the knights vowed the Quest. The poem
ends with Galahad's achievement of the Grail in
the castle of Corbonek, and departure thence with
the sacred vessel to the holy city of Sarras, where he
dies.

> "Then suddenly he fell asleep in Christ,
> And a great multitude of angels bore
> His soul to Heaven. And out of Heaven there came
> The semblance of a Hand, that, reaching down,
> Caught up the Grail, and no man saw it more."

Almost as mediæval in temper as Morris and Haw-
ker, Westwood, unlike them, did not draw his inspira-
tion from mediæval material directly, but rather from
the mediævalism of his contemporaries. To Hawker
himself he owes something. The cry of Westwood's
Questers, "Ho! for the Sancgreall, blessed Blood of
God!" is a manifest echo of "Ho! for the Sangraal!
vanish'd Vase of Heaven!" of only five years before.
And to Tennyson he owes so much, that had Tennyson
not written, it is doubtful whether Westwood's Arthu-
rian poems had ever been. The influence and manner

of the greater poet appears often in *The Sword of Kingship*, though without full Tennysonian grace and dignity — as near the end of the story : —

> " So Arthur won King Uther's crown and throne !
>   And when his seat was sure, and not a knight —
>   Save caitiff Caradoc, the Cornish bear —
>   But had sworn fealty, wizard Merlin told
>   To him and to Igrayne his wondrous tale.
>   Great joy had Queen Igrayne ; her widowed heart
>   Waxed warm with household cheer ; but evermore
>   To good Sir Ector and his dame the King,
>   From old respect and fond familiar use,
>   Clung, with the love and duty of a son.
>   Sir Ector, his High Chancellor he made,
>   Sir Key, his Seneschal ; and when the dame
>   To Camelot in early summer came,
>   He saw, and ran to meet her from afar,
>   And kissed her mouth, and kissed her wrinkled cheeks,
>   And knelt before her, as had been his wont,
>   For daily blessing, in the years that were."

Two years later, Westwood had made the Tennysonian style much more his own. He is best in it in various descriptive passages, especially those which mark change of season, as when he writes of the passing of time after the Questers set out for the Grail : —

> " The snowdrop pierced the snow ; with belts of fire,
>   The crocus lit the borders ; Spring o'erran
>   The earth, fleet-footed, till the whitethorn bush
>   Broke into milky blossom of the May.
>   Queen Guenevere, with absent eyes, and cheeks
>   Love-pallid, paced her pleasance to and fro,
>   And twisted posies of red gilly-flowers,
>   Pansies and purple-globed anemones,
>   Then tossed them from her in a storm of sighs."

And so Tennysonian is the following, that were it submitted as something recently discovered of Tennyson's own, it would be a keen critic who should say it was not : —

> " So evermore the months drew to a close ;
>   The apple ripened to its ruddy prime ;
>   The pear dropped, golden, in the orchard grass ;
>   Athwart the gusty sky long flights of storks,
>   With whirl of wing and noisy clap of beak,
>   Passed southward . . . still no tidings, and the queen,
>   At midnight, kneeling in her oratory,
>   A *mea culpa !* quivering on her lip,
>   A *mea maxima culpa !* heard the bells
>   Roll forth their brazen clangour o'er the world,
>   Ring out the old year, welcome in the New."

Mr. Swinburne, scarcely less mediæval in his Arthurian poems than Morris and Hawker, wrote his *Tristram of Lyonesse* and his *Tale of Balen* at a time when the Præ-Raphaelite spirit had really waned. Unlike Morris, whose junior he was by only three years, Mr. Swinburne found his earlier inspiration in classical story or mediæval history rather than in romance. But later, when Morris had become less mediæval, Mr. Swinburne felt strongly the charm of Arthurian legend. And so, in 1882, he brought out his *Tristram*, and fourteen years later, his *Balen*.

In the former, Mr. Swinburne follows the mediæval *Tristram* stories with a good deal of fidelity. Though indebted most to Malory, he does not take his material entirely from any one romance, but seems to have been familiar with several, and with both versions of the *Tristram* legend. In his title, for instance, he follows the Béroul version, which makes Lyonesse

Tristram's native land; and this he is following, too, when he makes Tristram and Iseult guests of Lance-lot, at his castle of Joyous Gard. In giving the love potion lasting power, however, Mr. Swinburne follows the Thomas version, and so he does in making Tris-tram receive his mortal wound while rendering service to his namesake, a Tristram of Brittany. To either version Mr. Swinburne may be indebted for his con-clusion of the story, for both, we have seen, were substantially agreed as to that, till the later French romancers, and Malory after them, changed the more poetic account of Tristram's death — the sail reported black when it was white, and Tristram's consequent despair — to that which made him treacherously slain by Mark. Mr. MacCallum has suggested that Ten-nyson's choice of the less poetic conclusion, and his general debasing of the Tristram story in his *Last Tournament*, may be the reason why Mr. Swinburne, so late as 1882, was moved to write an Arthurian narrative of the length of *Tristram of Lyonesse*. By that time the success of the *Idylls* had made the treatment of Arthurian themes on a large scale so peculiarly Tennyson's own, that no contemporary could hope to equal him, except in telling a story which, for some reason, Tennyson had not chosen to tell, or to which he had not done justice. Perhaps for this rea-son, thinking that he could give to the great roman-tic love story the beauty which Tennyson had failed to give it, Mr. Swinburne decided to write his *Tris-tram*. Since he wished especially to emphasise the love in it, Mr. Swinburne omitted the early part of the story — the hero's birth, childhood, arrival in Cornwall, fight with the Irish champion, his tortur-

ing wound, and his final healing at the hands of the
Queen of Ireland and her daughter. Of all these we
have no circumstantial account, but only occasional
allusions to them.

The story begins on that fateful day when Tris-
tram and Iseult, sailing by the Cornish coast, drank
from the flask which Brangwain had carefully guarded.
Straightway —

> " Their heads neared, and their hands were drawn in one,
>   And they saw dark, though still the unsunken sun
>   Far through fine rain shot fire into the south ;
>   And their four lips became one burning mouth." [1]

Henceforth, through danger and disgrace, the two are
held in the chains of love till death.

In depicting this love, Mr. Swinburne is not essen-
tially different in spirit from Gottfried von Strassburg
and the other mediæval romancers. Each of his lovers,
like theirs, is ready for self-sacrifice, so the other be
helped, as Iseult shows in her prayer when she keeps
lonely vigil at Tintagel, not knowing that that very
night her lover has been married, almost unwittingly,
to another Iseult beyond the sea in Brittany.

> " Nay, Lord, I pray thee let him love not me,
>   Love me not any more, nor like me die,
>   And be no more than such a thing as I.
>   Turn his heart from me, lest my love too lose
>   Thee as I lose thee, and his fair soul refuse
>   For my sake thy fair heaven, and as I fell
>   Fall, and be mixed with my soul and with hell.
>   Let me die rather, and only ; let me be
>   Hated of him so he be loved of thee,

[1] *Tristram of Lyonesse and Other Poems*, sixth edition, London,
1899, p. 40.

Lord : for I would not have him with me there
Out of thy light and love in the unlit air,
Out of thy sight in the unseen hell where I
Go gladly, going alone, so thou on high
Lift up his soul and love him." [1]

But almost directly comes the passion, that in Mr.
Swinburne's presentation of the story is more empha-
sised than the unselfishness of the lovers. None of
his mediæval masters made it stronger.

" Yea, since I surely loved him, and he sinned
Surely, though not as my sin his be black,
God, give him to me — God, God, give him back !
For now how should we live in twain or die ?
I am he indeed, thou knowest, and he is I.
Not man and woman several as we were,
But one thing with one life and death to bear.
How should one love his own soul overmuch ?
And time is long since last I felt the touch,
The sweet touch of my lover, hand and breath,
In such delight as puts delight to death,
Burn my soul through, till spirit and soul and sense,
In the sharp grasp of the hour, with violence
Died, and again through pangs of violent birth
Lived, and laughed out with refluent might of mirth ;
Laughed each on other and shuddered into one,
As a cloud shuddering dies into the sun.
Ah, sense is that or spirit, soul or flesh,
That only love lulls or awakes afresh?
Ah, sweet is that or bitter, evil or good,
That very love allays not as he would ?
Nay, truth is this or vanity, that gives
No love assurance when love dies or lives?
This that my spirit is wrung withal, and yet
No surelier knows if haply thine forget,

[1] *Tristram of Lyonesse and Other Poems*, p. 89.

Thou that my spirit is wrung for, nor can say
Love is not in thee dead as yesterday?
Dost thou feel, thou, this heartbeat whence my heart
Would send thee word what life is mine apart,
And know by keen response what life is thine?
Dost thou not hear one cry of all of mine?
O Tristram's heart, have I no part in thee?"

Mediæval thus, Mr. Swinburne yet has his modern side, as we should expect of an author of the nineteenth century. Like Morris, he tries far more than mediæval writers to get at the motives of his characters; he is of his own time in laying bare the thoughts and emotions which their great love inspires. Indeed, he analyses this love too much. And he is of his own time, too, in his marvellous technique, in the easy, steady flow of his beautiful verse. This fluency and his fondness for analysis and mediæval pictures become faults. They give ground to Mr. Andrew Lang's criticism that "Mr. Swinburne's poem of 'Tristram of Lyonesse' merely showed that among Mr. Swinburne's many gifts the gift of narrative is not one. The story was clogged and covered out of sight by the heavy splendour of the style. Events and characters were lost in vast digressions of description." [1] This criticism, however, is over-severe. Mr. Swinburne's purpose, evidently, was not to give the adventures of Tristram and Iseult in consecutive narrative. It was rather to give the most significant scenes in their history; and the nine which Mr. Swinburne has chosen for the nine books of his poem are well chosen. Often, too, his pictures are appropriate ornaments to the narrative, as in the opening lines of the poem: —

[1] See Dr. Sommer's edition of the *Morte Darthur*, vol. iii, p. xxiv.

> "About the middle music of the spring
> Came from the castled shore of Ireland's king
> A fair ship stoutly sailing, eastward bound
> And south by Wales and all its wonders round
> To the loud rocks and ringing reaches home
> That take the wild wrath of the Cornish foam,
> Past Lyonesse unswallowed of the tides
> And high Carlion that now the steep sea hides
> To the wind-hollowed heights and gusty bays
> Of sheer Tintagel, fair with famous days."

At other times, however, you feel that Mr. Lang's criticism is justified. Mr. Swinburne's tendency to digression and to over-elaboration is too great; in his pictures you frequently do lose his story. In the eighth book, *The Last Pilgrimage*, there is an especially long digression. Tristram of Lyonesse, accompanying the other Tristram, has been camping over night by the sea; and as the summer day dawns, he feels the natural desire of a healthy young man for a swim in the shining water. But for a healthy young man, he moves slowly; it takes him two pages from waking to casting off his clothes. Once he touches the waves, their shock seems to accelerate his motions, but only slightly. The narrative has been held up in all for four pages before Tristram gets his clothes on again, and even then Mr. Swinburne stops us for another page to tell how refreshed his hero felt after the bath. Well, there are few goodlier sights than a graceful, strong-limbed young man, stripped for his plunge in lake or river or sea; but a few lines may suggest the picture as well as five pages, perhaps better. Though we feel at times that the divine afflatus came to no man in the nineteenth century more certainly than to Mr. Swinburne, such digressions as this, however beautiful, make us wish that he had had less fluency.

Yet he can be rapid when he wishes, as at the end of *Tristram of Lyonesse*, when things move quickly enough. In less than one page from Tristram's wondering on his bed of fever if Iseult of Ireland will come to him, his wife has given him the false information about the sail, and he and his Irish Iseult are dead.

" And high from heaven suddenly rang the lark,
Triumphant; and the far first refluent ray
Filled all the hollow darkness full with day.
And on the deep sky's verge a fluctuant light
Gleamed, grew, shone, strengthened into perfect sight,
As bowed and dipped and rose again the sail's clear white.
And swift and steadfast as a sea-mew's wing
It neared before the wind, as fain to bring
Comfort, and shorten yet its narrowing track.
And she that saw looked hardly toward him back,
Saying, 'Ay, the ship comes surely; but her sail is black.'
And fain he would have sprung upright, and seen,
And spoken: but strong death struck sheer between,
And darkness closed as iron round his head :
And smitten through the heart lay Tristram dead.
   And scarce the word had flown abroad, and wail
Risen, ere to shoreward came the snowbright sail,
And lightly forth leapt Ganhardine on land,
And led from ship with swift and reverent hand
Iseult : and round them up from all the crowd
Broke the great wail for Tristram out aloud.
And ere her ear might hear her heart had heard,
Nor sought she sign for witness of the word;
But came and stood above him newly dead,
And felt his death upon her: and her head
Bowed, as to reach the spring that slakes all drouth ;
And their four lips became one silent mouth."

The Tale of Balen is better narrative than *Tristram of Lyonesse*, because less digressive, though inferior in poetic imagery, and in itself a story less calculated to rouse human interest. Like all verse from Mr. Swinburne's pen, it is most musical. Of a manlier tone than *Tristram*, *The Tale of Balen* at the end attains almost equal power. From the fatal mistaken fight of the two brothers of Northumberland, it is genuinely moving. After both lay dying,—

> " Balan rose on hands and knees
> And crawled by childlike dim degrees
> Up toward his brother, as a breeze
> Creeps wingless over sluggard seas
> When all the wind's heart fails it : so
> Beneath their mother's eyes had he,
> A babe that laughed with joy to be,
> Made toward him standing by her knee
> For love's sake long ago."

Then came the explanation of Balen's bearing another shield than his own. And Balan and Balen died,—

> " And there with morning Merlin came,
> And on the tomb that told their fame
> He wrote by Balan's Balen's name,
> And gazed thereon, and wept."

This story of the two brothers and their mutual slaughter, neither recognising the other, is one of the best in Malory's *Morte Darthur*, and Mr. Swinburne has done wisely to modernise it but little. In consequence, his version is better than Tennyson's in the *Idylls*. Tennyson puts too much moral into the old tale; he makes Balin (as he spells the name) bring misfortune on himself almost entirely by his own

violent nature.   Now the quick anger of the knight
has something to do with his sad fate both in Malory's
story and in Mr. Swinburne's; in both he is called,
or rather, as Balan says, miscalled [1] the Wild.   But
there is greater tragedy in their version, which makes
Balen persistently the victim of fate, than in Tenny-
son's story with a moral.

[1] *The Tale of Balen*, London, 1896, p. 123.

XXI

THE NEWER SPIRIT

AFTER all, it must be said that the Præ-Raphaelites, despite the beauty of their mediævalism, have not produced the best Arthurian poetry of the nineteenth century. Opposed as the spirit of that century was to such violation of Arthurian traditions as Bulwer's introduction of romantic and mythological characters entirely foreign to the old stories, it sought nevertheless in its most characteristic manifestation to give them more of its own time than did the Præ-Raphaelites. Thus Peacock, whose antiquarian fidelity exceeded that of any other Arthurian writer, inasmuch as he tried to reproduce sixth-century Britain, was yet by his use of nineteenth-century satire more representative of his age than Morris, Hawker, Westwood, and Mr. Swinburne. They, apart from their elaborate technique, and sometimes extremely subjective method of portraying character, have been merely so many different manifestations of mediævalism. Other nineteenth-century writers, together with fidelity to the spirit and the incidents of the old stories, have sought still more than Peacock to bring them into conformity with contemporary feeling ; they have tried either to teach new lessons by the stories or to give new sentiments to the characters, or sometimes to do both. Thus Heber modernised his story by changing the natures

of his characters; with Wordsworth the modernisa-
tion took the form of a clumsy moral. In the best-
known Arthurian writers since his day may be seen
similar tendencies, to point contemporary morals and
to make their knights and ladies, so far as possible,
people of recent times. These tendencies are especially
conspicuous in the works of three poets who, judged
by the approval of the world, have been most success-
ful in treating the Arthurian legends: James Russell
Lowell, Matthew Arnold, and, above all, Tennyson.
It is now more than half a century since Lowell and
Arnold wrote their Arthurian poems, and about as
long since Tennyson wrote his best *Idylls*. There has
been time, therefore, to assign these works something
like their permanent place in our literature ; and it
seems likely that the popular judgment of the future
will agree, in regard to them, with the popular judg-
ment of to-day.

James Russell Lowell in *The Vision of Sir Laun-
fal* is of the three least successful in combining
the old with the new ; there is likely to be more differ-
ence of opinion between the critics and the people re-
garding him than Arnold, and more regarding Arnold
than Tennyson. Like Wordsworth in *The Egyptian
Maid*, Lowell has exaggerated the moral that he wished
to teach ; and as his own note on *Sir Launfal* ex-
plains, he has virtually rejected all the old material
and invented a new incident, which may be termed
Arthurian only so far as the Grail, that sacred quest
of Arthur's knights, is sought by the hero of Lowell's
poem : —

" The plot (if I may give that name to anything so slight)
of the . . . poem is my own, and, to serve its purpose, I

have enlarged the circle of competition in search of the miraculous cup in such a manner as to include, not only other persons than the heroes of the Round Table, but also a period of time subsequent to the date of King Arthur's reign." [1]

To his newly invented Grail-Quester, Lowell has given the name of Launfal — a name which comes indirectly from Marie's " Lanval." Thus it will be seen that, in his incidents, Lowell is almost as anachronistic as Bulwer. He has kept, however, to the best spirit of the Grail story, and so constructed a poem of which one sees the faults, it is true, more clearly as time passes, but of which the sweetness will never die.

Sir Launfal, a young knight of the north of England, in the pride of his youth, decides carelessly one June day to ride forth from his castle to seek that Holy Grail, to win which, in days of yore, knights of Arthur's court had given their lives. Fortunately, before he starts, Sir Launfal lies down to sleep, and a vision comes to him which materially changes his plans. He sees himself the next morning riding gayly from his castle gate, beside which crouches a wretched leper asking for alms. The young knight lightly tosses a piece of gold to the leper, and then rides on without one thought for the suffering of the man, who calls out that a coin thrown only from sense of duty is no true alms, and therefore not comparable to a crust given in sympathy or a poor man's hearty blessing. Launfal, unheeding, rides the world over; youth changes to middle age, and middle age to old age, but he never finds the Holy Grail. At last, worn out and old, he comes back one bleak December day to his castle.

---

[1] In later editions, the last words were changed to " the supposed date of King Arthur's reign."

Another earl sits there now, but nevertheless Launfal rides up to the gate to ask for admittance ; and as he does so, there is the leper, more loathsome than before, again asking for alms. This time Launfal, remembering with regret how haughtily, in the morning of his life, he had thrown his coin to the leper, felt

" The heart within him . . . ashes and dust ;
    He parted in twain his single crust,
    He broke the ice on the streamlet's brink,
    And gave the leper to eat and drink,
    'T was a mouldy crust of coarse brown bread,
    'T was water out of a wooden bowl, —
    Yet with fine wheaten bread was the leper fed,
    And 't was red wine he drank with his thirsty soul."

And the leper, transfigured in the image of the Christ, said to Launfal that the Holy Grail was there in that vessel which he had but just filled at the brook. Then Launfal woke from his vision, realising that if he would, he might find the Grail in his own castle; for to him only might the Grail appear who knew true charity, and no distinction of time and place in bestowing it.

The reproaches which critics have brought against this poem are not undeserved. The introductions do not really introduce; the castle in the north country of England is surrounded by a New England country; the famous day in June is all New England June; and the little December brook is a New England brook in winter. Moreover, the verse too frequently becomes either commonplace (as in the extract I have quoted) or conventionally academic. Still, the poem teaches a lesson which must always touch the hearts of men. Old as it is, it is yet ever sweet and ever needed; and Lowell makes the sweetness of it go far towards disarming unfavorable criticism.

Since Lowell in his essays speaks more than once of Wolfram von Eschenbach with admiration, we may say, almost without doubt, that the American poet was indebted for this lesson to the thirteenth-century Bavarian, in whose *Parzival* we have the Grail legend at its best. The fault of the ethical teaching in the romances of which Galahad was the hero was, we have seen, that no one profited so much by the achievement of the Grail as the successful quester. True, in many of them, the enchantments of Britain ceased when the holy vessel was won; the land immediately about the Grail Castle returned to a prosperity which it had long wanted; and the owner of the castle was released from suffering. But the primary object of Galahad himself seems to have been self-glorification. Now in Wolfram's *Parzival*, it is otherwise; the hero's wish to heal the King is his strongest motive in seeking the Grail Castle a second time; and when he gets there, he is declared worthy himself to be keeper of the Grail, because he knows the meaning of broad human charity. The similarity between this and the lesson in *Sir Launfal* could hardly be closer.

The Vision of Sir Launfal appeared in 1848. Only four years later came out Matthew Arnold's *Tristram and Iseult*, which was thus thirty years earlier than Mr. Swinburne's *Tristram of Lyonesse*, and five or six years earlier than Wagner's *Tristan*. Yet in spirit Arnold's poem is nearer to us than either of these. True, he keeps to the facts of the old story, except for a few changes, but two of these are radical.

He makes Iseult arrive at Tristram's sick-bed just before instead of just after his death — a change which it is not surprising that the deeper sympathy of the nineteenth century should bring about, for it seemed an unnecessarily cruel fate which forbade the lovers even one last word. The other important change is to give Iseult of Brittany two children. Furthermore, Arnold endows his characters with nineteenth-century feelings.

Nevertheless, in reading *Tristram and Iseult* we do not lose the charm of the Middle Ages. The castle in which Tristram dies is wholly mediæval, and so is the picture of Tristram as we first see him.

> " What Knight is this so weak and pale,
>   Though the locks are yet brown on his noble head,
>   Propt on pillows in his bed,
>   Gazing seaward for the light
>   Of some ship that fights the gale
>   On this wild December night ?
>   Over the sick man's feet is spread
>   A dark green forest-dress ;
>   A gold harp leans against the bed,
>   Ruddy in the fire's light.
>   I know him by his harp of gold,
>   Famous in Arthur's court of old ;
>   I know him by his forest-dress —
>   The peerless hunter, harper, knight,
>   Tristram of Lyoness."

Mediæval, also, are the pictures of the two Iseults. But when the characters speak and act, there are moments when you feel that they are no more mediæval than lords and ladies of our own day might be, if brought up in ancestral castles which have preserved as far as possible the aspect of feudal times.

The half-way mediævalism of Matthew Arnold is very different from the intenser mediævalism of William Morris.

Because of this merely half-way mediævalism, Tristram seems to have two characters which somehow Arnold has succeeded in blending. His hero is at once

> " The peerless hunter, harper, knight,
>   Tristram of Lyoness,"

and a nineteenth-century gentleman, who in his youth loved deeply though not wisely. Subsequently he has not neglected the wife that he has married. He is a conscientious husband and a conscientious father; but still his great passion is for his old love — Iseult of Ireland. And she is not only the beautiful Irish princess of mediæval imagination; she is also a great lady of our times, who suffers for her first love amid nineteenth-century surroundings in a nineteenth-century way. When, on her arrival at his castle, Tristram begs her to sit silently by him, fearing that if he hears her speak he shall find something altered in her tone, she replies sadly:—

> " Alter'd, Tristram ?   Not in courts, believe me,
>   Love like mine is alter'd in the breast;
>   Courtly life is light and cannot reach it —
>   Ah ! it lives, because so deep-suppress'd !

> " What, thou think'st men speak in courtly chambers
>   Words by which the wretched are consoled ?
>   What, thou think'st this aching brow was cooler,
>   Circled, Tristram, by a band of gold ?

> " Royal state with Marc, my deep-wrong'd husband —
>   That was bliss to make my sorrows flee !

Silken courtiers whispering honied nothings —
Those were friends to make me false to thee!

" Ah, on which, if both our lots were balanced,
Was indeed the heaviest burden thrown —
Thee, a pining exile in thy forest,
Me, a smiling queen upon my throne ?

" Vain and strange debate, where both have suffer'd,
Both have pass'd a youth repress'd and sad,
Both have brought their anxious day to evening,
And have now short space for being glad !

" Join'd we are henceforth ; nor will thy people,
Nor thy younger Iseult take it ill,
That a former rival shares her office,
When she sees her humbled, pale, and still.

" I, a faded watcher by thy pillow,
I, a statue on thy chapel-floor,
Pour'd in prayer before the Virgin-Mother,
Rouse no anger, make no rivals more.

" She will cry : ' Is this the foe I dreaded ?
This his idol ? this that royal bride ?
Ah, an hour of health would purge his eyesight !
Stay, pale queen ! for ever by my side.'

" Hush, no words ! that smile, I see, forgives me.
I am now thy nurse, I bid thee sleep.
Close thine eyes — this flooding moonlight blinds them ! —
Nay, all 's well again ! thou must not weep."

Iseult's tragedy — stifling from necessity the desires
nearest her heart, struggling on amid unsympathetic
surroundings with longings ever unsatisfied — this we
commonly fancy a form of suffering more acute now
than in the less introspective Middle Ages. With it

naturally goes more self-control than the Iseult of
old ever had. It was not often that her youth, any
more than Tristram's, however sad, could be called,
as Arnold has her call it, repressed. Such changes in
the nature of his characters, however, we should expect
a poet like Arnold to make ; and there is no reason
why he should not, for they bring his characters
closer to people of to-day. But he has made an unneces-
sary physical change in his heroine, which one familiar
with mediæval romance can hardly forgive. Iseult the
Blonde, she whose golden hair a swallow bore in its
beak to Mark, she than whom no lady of the Middle
Ages was more famous for the beautiful gold of her
locks, this same Iseult of Ireland becomes in Arnold's
poem a raven-haired beauty. And here, as in allow-
ing his lovers one last brief meeting before they die,
Arnold has been imitated by a greater poet than
himself. Wagner accorded a similar grace to his, and
Tennyson in *The Last Tournament* made Tristram
drawn away from his wife by the " black-blue Irish
hair and Irish eyes " of his first love.

Even more changed than Tristram or Iseult of Ire-
land is the other Iseult, she of Brittany, Iseult of the
White Hands. In the old stories this girl was petty
in spirit, if not mean, as in those versions of the tale
which made her wittingly misrepresent the color of
the sail which was bringing her rival to her husband's
bedside. Yet the poor girl was so deeply wronged, that
only a singular mediæval callousness could have been
indifferent to her sad state. It was but natural that
the more tender-hearted nineteenth century should ask
what became of her after Tristram's death ; and Ar-
nold, in answering this question, became so interested

in the injured Iseult that he made her the real heroine
of his poem — an almost impossibly patient, great-
souled woman, whose devotion to her husband won his
respect though it could not win his love.

After Tristram's death this Iseult of Arnold's crea-
tion seeks consolation in devoting herself to the chil-
dren whom in the old story she never had. In most
versions of the old legend, indeed, Tristram, faithful
to his first Iseult even after his mistaken marriage,
left the second a virgin. It is a question whether the
woman who later in jealous anger said that the sails
were black would have taken the virgin marriage, as
she did, more or less as a matter of course ; and so
perhaps Arnold was only following probability in giving
Iseult of Brittany children. However that may be,
their introduction was happy. There is nothing sweeter
and wholesomer in the entire poem than Iseult's ten-
der care of them after her husband's death ; but even
they are only a partial solace to her. After one of
their busy days with her on the moors in fine weather,
Iseult

> ". . . will go home, and softly lay
> Her laughing children in their beds, and play
> Awhile with them before they sleep ; and then"

when they are asleep,

> "in shelter'd rest,
> Like helpless birds in the warm nest,
> On the castle's southern side,"

will come the loneliness.

> "She 'll light her silver lamp, which fishermen
> Dragging their nets through the rough waves, afar,
> Along this iron coast, know like a star,
> And take her broidery-frame, and there she 'll sit

Hour after hour, her gold curls sweeping it;
Lifting her soft-bent head only to mind
Her children, or to listen to the wind.
And when the clock peals midnight, she will move
Her work away, and let her fingers rove
Across the shaggy brows of Tristram's hound
Who lies, guarding her feet, along the ground;
Or else she will fall musing, her blue eyes
Fix'd, her slight hands clasp'd on her lap; then rise,
And at her prie-dieu kneel, until she have told
Her rosary-beads of ebony tipp'd with gold;
Then to her soft sleep — and to-morrow 'll be
To-day's exact repeated effigy.
Yes, it is lonely for her in her hall.
The children, and the grey-hair'd seneschal,
Her women, and Sir Tristram's aged hound,
Are there the sole companions to be found.
But these she loves; and noisier life than this
She would find ill to bear, weak as she is.
She has her children, too, and night and day
Is with them; and the wide heaths where they play,
The hollies, and the cliff, and the sea-shore,
The sand, the sea-birds, and the distant sails,
These are to her dear as to them; the tales
With which this day the children she beguiled
She gleaned from Breton grandames, when a child,
In every hut along this sea-coast wild;
She herself loves them still, and, when they are told,
Can forget all to hear them, as of old."

The introduction of the children and the modernising
of his characters make Arnold himself apparently for-
get the age of his story. His Iseult tells her children the
tale of Merlin and Vivian as one which she " gleaned
from Breton grandames, when a child." [1] It is seem-

---

[1] Mr. MacCallum points out this anachronism in his *Tennyson's
Idylls and Arthurian Story.*

ingly as remote to her as it is to us; and yet Merlin's enchantment by Fay Vivian under the blossoming hawthorn could not have occurred very long, if at all, before Iseult's day. Moreover, Arnold appears to turn attention from his main story, by concluding his poem with this tale of Vivian. But was he unwise in doing so? The mediæval effect of his *Tristram and Iseult* owes much to the prominence given to the legend of Merlin.

Arnold's verse is less mediæval and less spontaneously melodious than Morris's and Mr. Swinburne's; at times it is a bit academic; but in his poem is that which is not in theirs. Some modernising of the old characters was necessary, if they were to rouse wide sympathy among Arnold's readers; and it is through his new conception of the characters that Arnold has given his *Tristram and Iseult* something of the meaning which, in one form or another, the highest poetry never lacks.

As we come now to the latter part of the nineteenth century, we may note still another tendency in the treatment of Arthurian themes, besides those which we have already marked as characteristic of it. From the publication of the best *Idylls of the King*, fifty years ago, there has been no doubt of Tennyson's primacy among English Arthurian poets since the Renaissance. His contemporaries appear to have recognised this no less than we who live in an age that, even in the few years since his death, shows marked differences from his. It may be only coincidence, but more likely it is this recognition, conscious or unconscious, which has kept both his contemporaries and the newer poets from treating at length any Arthurian story which he treated in his best manner. Mr. Swinburne, to be sure, had reason to be dissatisfied with the way Tennyson told the stories of Balin and Tristram; but unless there was some such cause for dissatisfaction, poets of the last half century have generally fought shy of attempting again what Tennyson had already done. They might try Arthurian incidents which he had not attempted, as Hawker and Westwood, who wrote their poems in the sixties, before Tennyson's *Coming of Arthur* and *Holy Grail* had been published. Or they might treat themes in some different fashion, — as dramatically or lyrically, or in short semi-lyrical narrative poems, like Lowell's and Arnold's, — which Tennyson had already made use of in the *Idylls*. Thus Mr. Comyns Carr, soon after Tennyson's death, retold in his play of *King Arthur* the story of Guinevere's jealousy of Elaine. Since then Mr. Davidson has written of the love of Lancelot and the Queen in a " ballad." But poets have not tried, and in view of the signal popularity of the *Idylls*, it is unlikely that one will try for a long time, to retell the Round Table stories comprehensively as simple narrative.

Richard Wagner, a German whose works, since music is a universal language in our western civilisation, are more familiar to the English world than those of many a native poet, would naturally not show this last tendency so much as a poet born to the same language as the great Laureate. Moreover, there was no reason why he should not have treated the same stories as Tennyson, because he joined poetry with the kindred art of music. It is a fact, nevertheless, that of the three Arthurian legends which Wagner has treated, The Swan-Knight, Tristram, and The Grail, Tennyson has not touched on the first at all; his version of the second Wagner completed before Tennyson made public his conception of it in *The Last Tournament;* and the third, *Parsifal*, treats the Grail legend in such a different way from Tennyson's *Holy Grail* that it might almost deal with another subject. Nothing in the nineteenth century has roused such wide interest in Arthurian subjects as these three mediæval stories interpreted through Wagner's music.

Lohengrin, Wagner's earliest Arthurian opera, or to use the term which he himself preferred, music-drama, was produced in 1850. It shows that mediævalism was for Wagner one of the strongest influences of his century; and it shows substantially the method that he was to follow in every subsequent treatment of a mediæval theme. In spirit he kept so close to the old story as to be virtually a Præ-Raphaelite;[1] in the wonderful elaboration of his music, by which he suggested the mediæval spirit, he was even more characteristically of his own time. The exigencies of the drama, however, made him sometimes alter the old incidents considerably.

Thus in *Lohengrin* Wagner chose, and then still further simplified, the least complicated of the several mediæval forms[2] of the Swan-Knight story accessi-

[1] And yet Wagner himself called his *Lohengrin* "the type . . . of the tragic element of modern life." Any biography of him will show that he intended to have allegorical significance read into his operas, which not one in a hundred hearers of these will understand, or for enjoyment need understand.

[2] Those mediæval stories to which he was most indebted were Wolfram's brief narrative of the Duchess of Brabant and the *Lohengrin* of the fourteenth century. See ch. ix.

ble to such a scholar as himself. He made the distressed Duchess not a matron with a marriageable daughter, but a maid who married her champion herself; and instead of postponing the conflict between Lohengrin and Telramund to another day and place, Wagner made it occur on the very spot where the Swan-Knight landed, and within an hour of his doing so. For the same reason Lohengrin's forced departure was not after some years, but the day after the wedding. Naturally Elsa could not be left with the child or children to console her whom most mediæval forms of the story gave her. The logical conclusion, then, was for her to die,[1] as she does, even though Wagner gave her a brother Gottfried, who might have protected and comforted her after her husband went away. This brother, it seems, had been transformed into a swan—the very same that guided Lohengrin to Elsa—by Ortrud, wife of Elsa's cousin and next heir to the Duchy of Brabant, Friedrich von Telramund. Ortrud herself had some claim to Brabant, being descended from its ancient kings. By transforming the young duke, Gottfried, Ortrud and Telramund thought to get rid of the sister as well; for when the youth disappeared, they accused Elsa of murdering him in order to win the throne for herself. In making the Swan an enchanted brother of the Duchess instead of a brother of her champion, Wagner gave him even more reason to be anxious to lead Lohengrin to the lady's aid. It is entirely in the mediæval spirit for the knight sent from the

---

[1] As the opera is usually presented, one is likely to think that Elsa is merely fainting, but Wagner's stage direction says that she falls to the ground dead — *entseelt.*

Grail to disenchant Gottfried, and once he has done so, what guide more likely to lead him back to Monsalvat (Wolfram's Munsalvaesch) than the sacred dove of the Grail? A reference which Wagner makes to a chain on Gottfried's neck was probably a recollection of the silver chains about the necks of the swan children in the mediæval stories of Helias.

Tristan und Isolde was first produced in 1865, though it was mostly composed between 1857 and 1859, that is about ten years after *Lohengrin*. The changes from the old Tristram legend, which Wagner knew through Gottfried and other mediæval German poets, are of the same nature as those which Wagner made in treating the Lohengrin legend. From dramatic necessity he has selected for his three acts three incidents which he thought most significant in the adventures of his lovers. Two of these could be nothing else than the drinking of the potion and the death of the lovers. It was less easy to choose a third, for we know that the mediæval writers gave Tristram and Iseult many sweet meetings, when they narrowly escaped detection, and many adventurous partings, which each feared might be final. Wagner, with sure dramatic instinct, chose a meeting which was typical of all, and yet marked a crisis : that one when Mark surprised his queen and his nephew together, having given out that he was gone far to hunt, but in reality was spying by his palace.

Two considerable changes Wagner has made in the incidents of the legend. He states clearly what the mediæval writers only hint at, that the potion is after all but symbolical of the love which, against their will, has sprung up between Tristram and Iseult. The knight on shipboard keeps away from the princess, behaving almost discourteously in the hope of checking his love. She, feeling that she ought to hate him as the slayer of Morolt, her country's champion, decides at length, affianced bride of Mark though she is, to give Tristram due punishment. She will make him drink poison, and the punishment will be sweet to her, for she will drink the poison with him and die by his side. But Brangaene, when ordered to fetch the poison, horror-stricken, decides to bring instead the love potion entrusted to her keeping, which causes Tristram and Iseult instantly to declare their mutual love.

Wagner's other essential change, which occurs in the last act, was probably suggested by Matthew Arnold's *Tristram and Iseult*. Composing his drama in 1857, Wagner would naturally have made himself acquainted with any recent treatment of the story that was notable. Perhaps he already felt, as doubtless many poets and readers had previously felt, that Iseult might just as well have reached Tristram a few minutes before he died instead of a few minutes after. Accordingly, Wagner, like Arnold, is more merciful to the lovers than were mediæval writers. His Tristram, still unmarried, for Wagner saw no place for Iseult of the White Hands in a three-act tragedy, lies dying in his castle in Brittany, which here has become his native country. The faithful Kurwenal attends him. Iseult, called over the seas by Tristram's message, hurries up from the ship to the castle, and into the sunny courtyard where her knight lies, and he, in a delirium of joy tearing the bandages from his wounds, dies in her arms.

In *Parsifal*, too, based on Wolfram's poem, the

exigencies of stage production have caused Wagner's principal departures from the old legends. It was manifestly impossible to give anything like the comprehensive story of Perceval's growth in wisdom and charity between his first visit to the Grail Castle and the second. Accordingly, Wagner, who wished to show us Perceval as the raw, thoughtless youth and his return to the castle as the appointed Grail-Keeper, unselfish and chastened, has condensed Perceval's intervening adventures into one, which is of the nature of the temptation of St. Anthony. This takes up nearly the whole second act, by far the most dramatically effective and the most pleasing musically in all this over-praised opera. Wagner's temptress borrows her name, Kundrie, from the Grail Messenger of old; and as that Kundrie [1] apparently could change her shape from ugliness to beauty, so this Kundrie certainly appears at one time of wild and fearful aspect, and at another most seductively fair. A very different personage from that older Kundrie, however, she is Wagner's principal Arthurian creation. She is a winsome woman of old Jerusalem, condemned to a punishment everlasting as the Wandering Jew's, because she laughed at Christ carrying the Cross; and since then it has been her fate to live young outwardly, however world-weary within, tempting men to sin. She shall find relief from her hated work only when at last she meets a youth who can resist her fascinations. That youth is Perceval; and not only does he resist her, but he wins from Klingsor, arch-enemy of the Grail Knights, and an enchanter in whose garden the temptation occurs, — he wins from Klingsor the spear that pierced Christ's

[1] The name in editions of Wolfram is generally spelled Cundrie.

side. This only, according to Wagner, preserved sacredly beside the Grail till Amfortas used it for an unholy cause, can bring relief to the wounds of that suffering Grail-King. Parsifal wins it back because in Klingsor's hand it has no power against a pure knight. When Klingsor hurls it, the spear stands harmless over Parsifal's head, who then makes the sign of the Cross with it; and the whole fabric of Klingsor's castle, with its lovely garden of enchantments, crumbles to ruin. Here is manifestly a reminiscence of Balin's Dolorous Stroke when, in the castle of King Pelles, he caught up and hurled for defence the same spear of Longinus, and Pelles lay for days as if dead, and all the country round was blighted until the true knight inquired concerning the Grail.

In these three Arthurian operas there is no essential departure from the mediæval spirit. Even in *Parsifal*, which has been greatly praised for its beautiful lesson, there is nothing new spiritually. The teaching of broad Christian charity is taken, like Lowell's, from Wolfram; only Wagner makes his Christianity more ascetic and less practical and worldly than that sane knightly poet made his. Wagner's Parsifal is really a Galahad, except in name.

And for all the beauty and poetry in these operas, — at best, supreme beauty and poetry, — it is but a commonplace now to say what fifteen years ago would have been deemed heresy. The verse, fairly dignified and impressive in *Lohengrin*, is harsh and affected in the others, and they would all profit by excision. In each there is grandeur of conception which is colossal, but they are unevenly worked out. In one act Wagner keeps to the greatest dramatic heights : in the next he may fall to the depths of tediousness, and sometimes even of cheapness. Like children, and like many writers of the Middle Ages, he seems to think that what has won applause once will win it a second and even a third time. Thus, after the exquisite prelude of *Lohengrin* and a superb first act that moves rapidly and artistically to its climax, there follows a second act in which Ortrud and Telramund bewail and berate each other interminably; and then the wedding party, marshalled always in much the same order, make no less than three attempts to get into the church. In *Tristan*, the hero, like Charles II, might well apologise for being such an unconscionable time dying. And in the last act of *Parsifal*, despite the grandeur of the music, one cannot but feel that feet-washing is not suited for dramatic presentation, and that it is a mistake to repeat religious ceremonies almost identical with those of the first act. A mighty genius, Wagner was not an unerring artist.

Whatever reason Mr. Swinburne might have had for dissatisfaction with Tennyson's treatment of the stories of Tristram and Balin, whatever justification any other poet might have had in telling any of the *Idylls* dramatically or lyrically, there was not similar justification for the attempt of an American poet to retell virtually the whole of them to a generation which had reached maturity before Tennyson died. The poet who sought to do so was Richard Hovey, born a little more than forty years ago. A graduate of Dartmouth College, he wrote what critics will probably regard as his best work in poems for Dartmouth dinners and other college reunions. He was a friend of Mr. Bliss Carman, with whom he collaborated in two volumes of poems. Towards the end of his life he was a Professor of English Literature at Barnard College in New York. He died in that city in the spring of 1900.

Despite Hovey's plan, as announced on his title-pages, to write an Arthurian " poem in dramas," his work may rather be regarded as a long narrative poem made up, like the *Idylls*, of various significant incidents ; for each play that he completed is more a "closet drama" than one suited for stage presentation.[1] How many dramas he would have required to tell his whole tragic story is not recorded. Only four have been published, — two masques, *The Quest of Merlin* and *Taliesin*, and two five-act plays, *The Marriage of Guenevere* and *The Birth of Galahad*. These are enough to show Hovey's method, faults, and ability. Part of the last is his remarkable command of verse forms ; in the two masques, the ease with which he passes from one metre to another is marvellous. There is poetry in his verse, too, but unfortunately of uneven distribution. At worst, his verse is little better than doggerel, as in four lines from a song of the fauns in his first piece, *The Quest of Merlin :* —

> " Foxes in the poultry-yard,
>   Making free with chickens !
>   Crows in the corn field,
>   Pecking like the dickens ! "

Nor at its best is Hovey's verse sure. One moment near the highest poetic refinement, it may drop at the next to vulgarity. Moreover, when Hovey is best, he

---

[1] Two of Hovey's dramas are five-act plays that might be presented on the regular stage, though it is doubtful if they would meet with much success. The others are masques which could not be performed except as curiosities.

is least individual. There is now and then a suggestion
of Tennyson — the Queen's addressing her lover as
" My Launcelot," for instance — and there is often
palpable imitation of Shakspere. The love-making of
Lancelot and Guinevere in the five-act *Marriage of
Guenevere* is reminiscent of that of Romeo and
Juliet, and the watchmen in the same play are a long
way after Dogberry and his crew. Some of their
"derangements of epitaphs " — such as " The King
. . . is not to be supposed," meaning "deposed," " The
King is the head in things temporary, and the Pope in
things spirituous "— would be good enough if Dog-
berry's three hundred years earlier, and Mrs. Slip-
slop's and Mrs. Malaprop's in the eighteenth century,
had not been better.

Then, too, Hovey is not always a good story-teller.
The two dramas, to be sure, are sufficiently organic ;
but not so the masques. In them Hovey suffers from
his own facility, as Mr. Swinburne has suffered from his.
Like him, Hovey drags in unnecessary incidents. In
The Quest of Merlin, for example, there is a scene of
the sage's getting drunk, which is not only disagree-
able, — for Merlin does not get drunk pleasantly, —
but, so far as we can see at present, purposeless. True,
Hovey did not complete his dramatic series. Had he
done so, perhaps a reason would have been apparent
for this incident and for others. But as the poems
stand, much in them seems superfluous.

In the use of his romantic material Hovey is some-
times as anachronistic as Bulwer in his *King Arthur*.
He is before and not of the nineteenth century in
introducing into his two masques all sorts of super-
natural and mythological characters, Norse, Greek,

and Christian, who never in mediæval days so much as heard of Arthur. A glance at the *dramatis personae* of *The Quest of Merlin* is enough to make this peculiarity apparent.

PERSONS

MERLIN.

Beneath Hecla

URD
VERDANDE } *The Norns.*
SKULD

In Avalon

ARGENTE.	MAB.
NIMUE.	PUCK.
Eight Other Maidens.	OBERON.
	TITANIA.
Sylphs.	ARIEL.
Gnomes.	*Fairies.*
Naiads.	*Elves.*
Dryads.	*Goblins.*
PAN.	APHRODITE.
BACCHUS.	*The Loves.*
Fauns.	*The Valkyrs.*
Satyrs.	*The Angels.*
Mœnads and Bassarids.	

In being so anachronistic, Hovey is bearing out one of Professor Barrett Wendell's theories in regard to English literature in America.[1] Cut off from close and easy communication with Europe, America has often presented in its literature and thought a case of arrested development. And so we have, according to Professor Wendell, at the time of the American Revo-

[1] Barrett Wendell, *A Literary History of America*, New York, 1900.

lution, an American temper in regard to public affairs like that which existed in England at the time of the Civil Wars or even earlier : and one in regard to artistic affairs, only a little nearer contemporary. Washington Irving, writing in the early nineteenth century, is a belated Addison or Goldsmith. Now at the end of that century we find Hovey doing what, since the Romantic Revival, no English writer except Bulwer has dared in treating Arthurian themes. Lowell, we have seen, in his *Vision of Sir Launfal*, to be almost as free. And it may be added, in further support of Professor Wendell's theory, that whereas the only notable English burlesque to deal with Arthurian characters was Fielding's *Tom Thumb* in 1730, the much less notable American burlesques — Mark Twain's unintelligent and disagreeable *Connecticut Yankee in King Arthur's Court* and Eugene Field's pleasanter and cleverer *Proper Trewe Idyll of Camelot* — were not written till the last quarter of the century just passed.

However free with the old story he was in his masques, in his two five-act dramas Hovey was on the whole faithful enough to suit the literary conscience of his time. He does, it is true, introduce more or less American nature, which seems odd in connection with Camelot; the lakes are still ice-bound in April — a condition of affairs truer of Hovey's New Hampshire than of Arthur's Britain ; and he gives us information about the members of Guinevere's family which we have never had before ; she has a brother, Peredur, for example, who is in love with Arthur's guileful half-sister, Morgause, the Queen of Orkney. Then, too, Hovey makes Guinevere follow Arthur to Rome ;

but so she might naturally have done after his success-
ful campaign. After all, such departures from the old
legend, which did not essentially change its spirit, were
in accord with the tendencies of the nineteenth cen-
tury in treating it; they are not more radical than
the changes of Morris, Hawker, Westwood, Arnold,
Wagner, and some, which we shall see, of Tennyson.
Likewise in modernising the natures of his characters,
and in giving the old incidents so far as possible a
new meaning for the new time, Hovey was again in
the spirit of his age. Moreover, Hovey shows that
the centre of interest of the old stories for him, as for
Heber and Morris, was in the two guilty lovers rather
than in Arthur; and so the name of his completed
poem was to be *Launcelot and Guenevere*. Here at
last is acknowledgment, franker yet than in Morris's
title, *The Defence of Guenevere*, of what even some
mediæval writers insensibly felt: that there is more
abiding interest in the love of the Queen and her
knight than in the achievements of the King.

In thus taking Lancelot and Guinevere for his cen-
tre of interest, Hovey's object seems to have been to
ennoble their love; and so, like Tennyson and Heber,
and Morris to a less degree, he tries to excuse their
conduct. Borrowing a page from Heber, he makes out
that they met in a wild, remote country before Gui-
nevere had ever seen Arthur. Lancelot loved her at
once, but she did not realise her love for him till they
met again at Camelot. She yielded to him the more
readily because war had called Arthur to Cornwall so
soon after the marriage ceremony that, save for the
marriage vows, he left Guinevere a maid. And so
Hovey would have us think the Queen really Lance-

lot's bride rather than Arthur's; and that their love should be deemed pure, he introduces a momentous change in the story. He makes Galahad not the son of Lancelot and Elaine, daughter of King Pelles, but the son of Lancelot and Guinevere. However commendable Hovey's purpose may have been, judged by its results this change is a signal failure. His Guinevere has unfortunately retained the faults of the Guinevere of the prose romances, who, when Lancelot was too shy, and perhaps too honorable, to kiss her, at last caught him by the chin and kissed him. Nor was it necessary or wise to change the meaning of the old love-story. We have seen that the relation of the Queen and the greatest knight of her husband's court has come down from the age of a conventional, fashionable system of love, when the great ladies of England and France hoped to receive from other knights the pure, devoted affection which probably few of them ever received from their rough, crusading husbands. As this old love-story was told then, invented perhaps by Chrétien de Troies, it is unmoral rather than immoral. We had better accept it virtually as it stands; we should not try to infuse modern morals into it, more than into the story of Helen of Troy. Tennyson, who changes the old story very little, changes it as much as is wise. He makes us sympathise with Lancelot and the Queen; he makes the beginning of their love excusable; but he makes their love still a crime. With Hovey, apparently, it is not; or at least, so the end of his second masque, *Taliesin*, gives us to understand. One of the angels who guard the Holy Grail instructs Percival as follows:[1] —

[1] *Taliesin*, p. 51.

"Better the rose of love out of the dung-hill of the world's
    adulteries
Than the maid icicle that keeps itself from stain of earth
    where no life is
In the aloof of splendors boreal."

And then again the angel says that when Galahad shall
come

"and sit in the Siege Perilous, and live,"

in him we

"shall behold how light can look on darkness and for-
    give,
How love can walk in the mire and take no stain there-
    from."

This seems to be the lesson that Hovey would teach
in his *Launcelot and Guenevere*. Unfortunately, in
the presentation of his characters, Hovey has coars-
ened them so much that we are disinclined to accept
his lesson. Any way, though love *can* walk in the
mire without stain, if it does so often, it is likely to
get smirched.

Mr. J. Comyns Carr had more reason for his drama
of *King Arthur*, an attempt to retell not the greater
Round Table cycle, but one of its lesser stories. Then,
too, the play was written primarily for stage presen-
tation, and was produced at the Lyceum Theatre in
London in January, 1895, with Henry Irving as
Arthur, Miss Terry as Guinevere, and Mr. Forbes
Robertson as Lancelot. The story is told in a pro-
logue, in which Arthur receives Excalibur, and four
acts, which introduce the tragic story of Elaine of
Astolat, Mordred's treachery, and the passing of
Arthur. Mr. Carr has followed Tennyson in ennobling

his principal personages. Arthur is not the incestu-
ous king of the old romances, but the stainless king
of the *Idylls*; Guinevere and Lancelot love against
their will, first overcome by the magic of the flower-
ing spring as he, the King's ambassador, fetched her
from Cameliard to Camelot. The principal change in
the old story is that Lancelot meets Elaine before
he has met the Queen, and apparently might have
loved her, had not the greater charm of Guinevere
won him. Before he and the Queen have declared
their love, Elaine comes to the court, love-sick, begging
the Queen to intercede for her with Lancelot; and
so, in a scene of considerable dramatic power, Guine-
vere, at Elaine's request, bids him not go in quest of
the Grail, though for her own peace, she would have
him far from court. Soon the two are forced to de-
clare their mutual love. Their detection by Mordred
and his plotting mother — here Morgan le Fay —
speedily follows, and then Mordred's treachery and
civil war. On the whole, Mr. Carr's play, noteworthy
because so few dramatists have attempted Arthurian
themes, suggests that they have neglected such sub-
jects unwisely.

At least one act, the second, of Mr. Carr's later
play, *Tristram and Iseult*,[1] produces the same im-
pression. It shows that there is effective dramatic
material in Tristram's adventures at the Irish court,
which poets since Malory have generally thought not
worth treating. Mr. Carr's attempt, however, to intro-
duce Iseult of the White Hands, who is not a real
woman, but is seen only in dramatically unnecessary

[1] A play in four acts, presented at the Adelphi Theatre, London,
September 4, 1906; published by Duckworth & Co.

visions, confirms our belief that Wagner was wise in
not finding room within the narrow limits of a play
for both her and the other Iseult. Nor has Mr. Carr
happily altered the old story in his one important
change from it—that is, making Andred, a treacherous
Cornish baron, kill Tristram by a sword-thrust in the
back when Mark, Andred, and the dwarf surprise
Tristram and Iseult by a moonlit pool in the forest —
a scene evidently suggested by the mediæval garden
scene, in which the moonlight reveals to the lovers,
just in time for them to escape surprise, the shadows
of the spying Mark and his dwarf.

After all, poetic drama in blank verse nowadays,
even at its best, as perhaps in Mr. Stephen Phillips's
plays, is likely to seem artificial ; the prose plays of
Mr. Jones, Mr. Pinero, Mr. Shaw, and Mr. Barrie, in
their different ways, are more of our time. Probably,
therefore, the lyrical poet, Mr. John Davidson, rather
than Mr. Carr, points the way to the treatment of
Arthurian stories which in the immediate future will
appeal to the greatest number of authors and will
meet with most success. A Scotchman and a teacher
in various academies of his native land, Mr. Davidson
was encouraged by the recognition which some of his
poems won to take up the life of a journalist in Lon-
don about 1890. Since then he has allowed volumes
of his poems to appear at comparatively frequent in-
tervals. A bitterly irreligious tone, the natural reac-
tion from a Presbyterianism which, in its harshest
form, is said to have oppressed Mr. Davidson's child-
hood, occasionally mars his poetry. Otherwise, its
faults, as well as its excellences, are fairly stated in
two recent criticisms of Mr. Davidson in the *Academy*

and the *Fortnightly Review:* " Were he less a child of nature, Mr. Davidson might sing less ; upon a broader intellectual basis he might sing more wisely." [1] Again : " His metaphor is sometimes strained and unnatural, his imagery brought from too far." Nevertheless, from him " we hear that strain of lyric ecstasy with which English song has thrilled and trembled from the days of the Elizabethans down to the days of Shelley, Keats, and Tennyson . . ." [2]

The Last Ballad is the title of a volume of Mr. Davidson's poems that appeared in 1899, of which the first, that which gives its name to the volume, deals with an episode of Malory. It represents Lancelot keeping away from the court to escape his infatuation for Guinevere. He is not banished, as Malory makes him out, and then mad after his unwitting infidelity to the Queen through the machinations of Dame Brisen, attendant of Elaine, the daughter of Pelles ; according to Mr. Davidson, Lancelot has gone away from a stern sense of duty, and in distant parts of Arthur's realm he fulfils conscientiously the King's commands. But wherever he goes, he sees visions of the Queen.

> . . . " On high,
> When midnight set the spaces free,
> And brimming stars hung from the sky
> Low down, and spilt their jewellery,
>
> " Behind the nightly squandered fire,
> Through a dark lattice only seen
> By love, a look of rapt desire
> Fell from a vision of the Queen.

[1] *Academy*, vol. lii, p. 489.
[2] *Fortnightly Review*, vol. lxiii, p. 393.

" From heaven she bent when twilight knit
  The dusky air and earth in one;
  He saw her like a goddess sit
  Enthroned upon the noonday sun.

" In passages of gulfs and sounds,
  When wild winds dug the sailor's grave,
  When clouds and billows merged their bounds,
  And the keel climbed the slippery wave,

" A sweet sigh laced the tempest; nay,
  Low at his ear he heard her speak;
  Among the hurtling sheaves of spray
  Her loosened tresses swept his cheek.

" And in the revelry of death,
  If human greed of slaughter cast
  Remorse aside, a violet breath,
  The incense of her being passed

" Across his soul, and deeply swayed
  The fount of pity; o'er the strife
  He curbed the lightning of his blade,
  And gave the foe his forfeit life.

" Low on the heath, or on the deck,
  In bloody mail or wet with brine,
  Asleep he saw about her neck
  The wreath of gold and rubies shine;

" He saw her brows, her lovelit face,
  And on her cheeks one passionate tear ;
  He felt in dreams the rich embrace,
  The beating heart of Guinevere."

And so, once more before he dies, Lancelot decides
to return to his love. But on his way to Caerlon-on-
Usk, where Arthur holds his Easter court, Lancelot

is oppressed by the thought of his broken faith to his lord and his weakness in yielding to his love; and in despair he wanders into the wilderness, driven mad by the thought, not, as in Malory, of infidelity to the Queen, but of infidelity to the King. So he lives a whole year, till the next Easter comes round, and Lancelot, meeting his son Galahad, is by his comforting words restored to sanity. With Galahad, Lancelot sets out to seek the Holy Grail. But in vain he looks for a vision of the blessed cup; the thought of Guinevere prevents him from seeing it. She is as much before him on his quest as she was when, in the remote parts of Arthur's empire, he was fulfilling the King's commands. Now, however, his thoughts of the Queen have become spiritualised; they are no longer carnal, but the permanent consolation of his life.

In this poem it is easy to see that Mr. Davidson's purpose was to make the love of Lancelot more spiritual than it generally appears — as much so as it becomes at the very conclusion of Malory's *Morte Darthur*, when the knight and the Queen take their last farewell of each other. And so Mr. Davidson, borrowing Lancelot's madness from Malory, has attributed it to a new cause. With Malory the madness arose, according to the rules of courtly love, from Guinevere's unreasonable harshness. Now the madness arises from Lancelot's own realisation of his baseness. When it passes, therefore, Lancelot is in a condition to make his love one that through self-sacrifice shall no longer debase but rather uplift.

XXII

TENNYSON

NEARLY seventy years before Mr. Davidson wrote his *Last Ballad*, he who, more grandly than any since Malory, has pealed "proud Arthur's march from Fairyland," had written what still remains the most exquisite of Arthurian lyrics. Alfred Tennyson was born in 1809 at his father's rectory at Somersby, a place between Horncastle and Spilsby, "in a land of quiet villages, large fields, gray hillsides and noble, tall-towered churches, on the lower slope of a Lincolnshire wold."[1] The principal facts of his life are so well known that only the briefest mention of them is necessary. A poet by his own choice, even before he won the Chancellor's Prize for verse at Cambridge; severely criticised after his first two publications, but after the third appreciated and extolled throughout the English world; Laureate in 1850 and Baron in 1884; happily married; a conscientious, conservatively broad-minded gentleman — that is the whole story. Death came to him at his house at Aldworth on the 6th of October, 1892; an appropriate death for a great romantic poet, for he died just after midnight, with no light in the room but that of the full moon streaming through the oriel window, and in

[1] Hallam Lord Tennyson, *Alfred Lord Tennyson, A Memoir*, London, 1897, vol. i, p. 2.

his hand a volume of Shakspere which he had asked
for in the afternoon.

Whether or not the world will deem the *Idylls of
the King* Tennyson's most important work, they are
his life work. He had them in mind from the early
thirties to the publication of *Balin and Balan*, the
last, in 1885 ; and before any *Idyll*, came three Ar-
thurian lyrics. *The Lady of Shalott* in 1832 [1] was
the first published, though Hallam Lord Tennyson
says that *Sir Launcelot and Queen Guinevere* had
been partly, if not wholly, written in 1830. It is the
more interesting, therefore, as showing that Tennyson,
in his first conception of the Arthurian story, ima-
gined a different meeting of Lancelot and the Queen
from that related by mediæval poets, who put the
meeting at Arthur's court after his marriage. Neither
Sir Launcelot and Queen Guinevere nor *Sir Gala-
had*, however early they were composed, came out till
1842. All three lyrics, written twenty years before
the Præ-Raphaelite school of poets was heard of,
have much in common with that school. They have
the lavish color of the Præ-Raphaelites, and they are
full of the spirit of the Middle Ages. In fact, *Sir
Launcelot and Queen Guinevere* and *Sir Galahad*
have little else, and yet they throw you into your
far-away, mediæval mood without any of the Præ-
Raphaelite oddity.

Even more picturesquely mediæval is *The Lady
of Shalott*, a mystical and more fanciful version of
Malory's beautiful story of Elaine of Astolat.[2] You

---

[1] The volume in which it appeared came out late in 1832, though
dated 1833.

[2] The home of Elaine was variously written by the old romancers

may see in the poem, if you will, merely a highly picto-
rial fantasy; or again, if you choose to seek it, the
deeper meaning which Tennyson's age asked for in art.

> " ' I am half sick of shadows,' said
> The Lady of Shalott.' "

This, according to Hallam Tennyson, is the key of the
poem.[1] The Lady of Shalott sees everything — the
river flowing to Camelot, the barges trailing by, the
gay shallops floating downstream, the men and women
riding along the river-road — these she sees, never as
they are, but only reflected in her mirror. And so
she lives in a shadow-world, thinking that a curse is
on her if ever she looks out into the real world down
to many-towered Camelot. But at last the mirrored
Sir Lancelot, riding by in full armor, wakens her
from her dream. She looks down to Camelot, and the
curse comes upon her. Her mirror cracks, the web
that she is weaving flies out of her hand, and, singing
a mournful carol, she gets into a boat; then floating
down to Camelot, she dies, and dead is borne to the
royal palace, where the lords come and cross them-
selves as they look upon her.

> " But Lancelot mused a little space ;
> He said, ' She has a lovely face ;
> God in his mercy lend her grace,
> The Lady of Shalott."

Here is manifestly a parable of a dream-life — one
so remote from the vital reality of the great world that

Astolat, Ascolot, or Escalot, from which last Shalott comes indirectly.
Tennyson got the name from an Italian novelette, *Donna di Scalotta.*
Memoir, vol. i, p. 91.

[1] *Ibid.* vol. i, p. 117.

if the dreamer goes out into it, he finds himself unable
to cope with its perplexities and hopelessly gives up
the struggle. Whether or not you choose to see this
allegory in *The Lady of Shalott*, — and if you do not
like allegory, you are not obliged to see it, — you can-
not help finding the poem most fancifully mediæval
and full of Tennyson's best melody, with the subtly
witching music of the words supplementing the poetry
of the thought. It is full, too, of the exquisite little
pictures which Tennyson could paint so well, as in the
description of the stream that washes The Lady of
Shalott's island : —

> " Willows whiten, aspens quiver,
> Little breezes dusk and shiver
> Thro' the wave that runs forever
> By the island in the river
> Flowing down to Camelot."

A charming river to drift down in a canoe on a
summer afternoon, like the Thames above Eton, or
the Concord or the Charles in New England ! [1]

In his late years, Tennyson wrote *Merlin and the
Gleam*, a poem much esteemed by some people. The
present Lord Tennyson says that it was largely auto-
biographic. The Gleam is the poetic ideal which
Merlin, personifying the poet, ever seeks : and when
Merlin himself is no longer able to keep up the quest,
he gives it over to the poet who is to succeed him.

---

[1] Tennyson may have had a larger river in mind. When he was
travelling in Germany with his friend Arthur Hallam, the latter wrote
to Tennyson's sister, Emily, to whom he was engaged, that an island
in the Rhine just above Bonn is " rather larger, according to Alfred,
than that of the ' Lady of Shalott,' and the stream is rather more
rapid than our old acquaintance that runs down to Camelot." *Memoir*,
vol. i, p. 88.

Nobly conceived, and not lacking in vigor, the poem is yet rough in form, compared with Tennyson's earlier lyrics. The harsh rhythm most lovers of Tennyson will be unwilling to accept as a substitute for his usual melody.

Just how early Tennyson conceived the plan of a long Arthurian poem, it is difficult to say. "The vision of Arthur as I have drawn him," he said to his son, " had come upon me when, little more than a boy, I first lighted upon Malory." [1] "From his earliest years," Hallam Tennyson tells us also,[2] "he had written out in prose various histories of Arthur." Though Malory [3] was Tennyson's direct source, he seems nevertheless to have regarded Arthur always as the peerless king of the first chroniclers, " flos regum, gloria regni." [4]

It took Tennyson years to decide what form he should give to his Arthurian story. The lyrics were only experimental; they were never to have been the final form of the poem. From the first, some sort of an epic seems to have been in the poet's mind; and about 1833 he made out a fragmentary sketch for the beginning, which his son quotes.[5]

[1] *Memoir*, vol. ii, p. 128.

[2] *Ibid*. vol. ii, p. 121.

[3] It is not recorded what edition of Malory Tennyson first became acquainted with. An edition which he used when he was at work on his *Morte D'Arthur*, is that published in 1816 by Walker and Edwards. Leigh Hunt writes in 1835 that "the *Prince Arthur* which I should have brought with me, I will send to-morrow . . . by a messenger." And Hallam Tennyson says in a note to this: " This copy of Malory I have still in my possession, a small book for the pocket . . . much used by my father." *Ibid*, vol. i, p. 156.

[4] *Ibid*. vol. ii, p. 129.

[5] *Ibid*. vol. ii, p. 122.

KING ARTHUR

On the latest limit of the West in the land of Lyonesse, where, save the rocky isles of Scilly, all is now wild sea, rose the sacred Mount of Camelot. It rose from the deeps with gardens and bowers and palaces, and at the top of the Mount was King Arthur's hall, and the holy Minster with the Cross of gold. Here dwelt the King in glory apart, while the Saxons whom he had overthrown in twelve battles ravaged the land, and ever came nearer and nearer.

The Mount was the most beautiful in the world, sometimes green and fresh in the beam of morning, sometimes all one splendour, folded in the golden mists of the West. But all underneath it was hollow, and the mountain trembled, when the seas rushed bellowing through the porphyry caves; and there ran a prophecy that the mountain and the city on some wild morning would topple into the abyss and be no more.

It was night. The King sat in his Hall. Beside him sat the sumptuous Guinevere and about him were all his lords and knights of the Table Round. There they feasted, and when the feast was over the bards sang to the King's glory.

In the later thirties Tennyson made another sketch, this time for a five-act musical masque, thinking that he might cast his Arthurian story in that form. Among his papers was preserved the first rough draft of the scenario : [1] —

First Act

Sir Mordred and his party. Mordred inveighs against the King and the Round Table. The knights, and the quest. Mordred scoffs at the Ladies of the Lake, doubts whether they are supernatural beings, etc. Mordred's cringing interview with Guinevere. Mordred and the Lady of the Lake. Arthur lands in Albyn.

[1] *Memoir*, vol. ii, p. 124.

Second Act

Lancelot's embassy and Guinevere. The Lady of the Lake meets Arthur and endeavours to persuade him not to fight with Sir Mordred. Arthur will not be moved from his purpose. Lamentation of the Lady of the Lake. Elaine. Marriage of Arthur.

Third Act

Oak tomb of Merlin. The song of Nimue. Sir Mordred comes to consult Merlin. Coming away meets Arthur. Their fierce dialogue. Arthur consults Sir L. and Sir Bedivere. Arthur weeps over Merlin and is reproved by Nimue, who inveighs against Merlin. Arthur asks Merlin the issue of the battle. Merlin will not enlighten him. Nimue requests Arthur to question Merlin again. Merlin tells him he shall bear rule again, but that the Ladies of the Lake can return no more. Guinevere throws away the diamonds into the river. The Court and the dead Elaine.

Fourth Act

Discovery by Mordred and Nimue of Lancelot and Guinevere. Arthur and Guinevere's meeting and parting.

Fifth Act

The battle. Chorus of the Ladies of the Lake. The throwing away of Excalibur and departure of Arthur.

It is interesting to see that in this sketch several incidents are like those subsequently worked out in the *Idylls*, even to some of the poet's own invention, such as the last meeting between Arthur and the Queen, and Guinevere's throwing the diamonds into the river.

That his great work was to be Arthurian, Tennyson was now sure. " I felt certain of one point . . . ." he said. " If I meant to make any mark at all, it must be by shortness, for most of the big things except

King Arthur had been done." That he still thought of treating his Arthurian story dramatically is all the stranger, because he had already discovered its final form. As early as 1835, Edward Fitzgerald saw in manuscript the *Morte d'Arthur*, the first *Idyll* written, subsequently enlarged to *The Passing of Arthur;* and various letters from Tennyson and his friends show that he was at work on the poem more than a year before.[1] It was still, when Fitzgerald saw it, without the introduction and the epilogue, which were added before it was published in 1842. The introduction speaks of twelve books of an epic, all burned but this one. Though it was probably fiction that there had ever been eleven other books, the statement is interesting, as showing that even then Tennyson had in mind what was to be the ultimate number of his *Idylls* — twelve.

From now on, what Tennyson " called ' the greatest of all poetic subjects ' perpetually haunted him ;" [2] but it was not until 1855 that he realised that he had already hit upon the proper form for his poem, an epic in several distinct parts. Then he set to work to compose four more of these, in his zeal visiting Wales and studying Welsh. By 1857 he had virtually completed *Enid*, *Vivien*, *Elaine*, and *Guinevere*, which were all published in 1859 under the title, *Idylls of the King*. Nothing from Tennyson's pen had been so enthusiastically received. Arthur Hugh Clough, the Duke of Argyll, Macaulay, and Thackeray all joined in the great chorus of praise — the

---

[1] See letters written in the years 1833, 1834, and 1835, quoted in chs. v and vi of the *Memoir*.

[2] *Memoir*, vol. ii, p. 125.

last, according to his nature, a little too gushingly, as a letter from him will show : [1] —

My dear Old Alfred, — I owe you a letter of happiness and thanks. Sir, about three weeks ago, when I was ill in bed, I read the " Idylls of the King," and I thought, " Oh I must write to him now, for this pleasure, this delight, this splendour of happiness which I have been enjoying." But I should have blotted the sheets, 'tis ill writing on one's back. The letter full of gratitude never went as far as the postoffice and how comes it now ?

D'abord, a bottle of claret. (The landlord of the hotel asked me down to the cellar and treated me.) Then afterwards sitting here, an old magazine, *Fraser's Magazine*, 1850, and I come on a poem out of " The Princess " which says, " I hear the horns of Elfland blowing blowing," no, it's " the horns of Elfland faintly blowing " (I have been into my bedroom to fetch my pen and it has made that blot), and, reading the lines, which only one man in the world could write, I thought about the other horns of Elfland blowing in full strength, and Arthur in gold armour, and Guinevere in gold hair, and all those knights and heroes and beauties and purple landscapes and misty gray lakes in which you have made me live. They seem like facts to me, since about three weeks (three weeks or a month was it ?) when I read the book. It is on the table yonder, and I don't like, somehow, to disturb it, but the delight and gratitude! You have made me as happy as I was as a child with the *Arabian Nights*, every step I have walked in Elfland has been a sort of paradise to me. (The landlord gave me *two* bottles of his claret and I think I drank the most) and here I have been lying back in the chair and thinking of those delightful " Idylls," my thoughts being turned to you : what could I do but be grateful to that surprising genius which has made me so happy. Do you understand that what I mean is all true and that I should break out were you sitting opposite

[1] *Memoir*, vol. i, p. 444.

with a pipe in your mouth? Gold and purple and diamonds,
I say, gentlemen and glory and love and honour, and if
you have n't given me all these why should I be in such an
ardour of gratitude? But I have had out of that dear book
the greatest delight that has ever come to me since I was
a young man; to write and think about it makes me almost
young, and this I suppose is what I 'm doing, like an after-
dinner speech.

There were five *Idylls* now, though the *Morte d'Ar-
thur* was not yet associated with the others; but still
Tennyson hesitated to go on with his work. One rea-
son he mentioned for pausing was that he "could
hardly light upon a finer close than that ghost-like
passing away of the King" in *Guinevere*, although the
Morte d'Arthur "was the natural close." [1] A second
was "that he was not sure he could keep up to the
same high level throughout the remaining 'Idylls.'
'I have thought about it,' he writes in 1862, 'and
arranged for all the intervening "Idylls," but I dare
not set to work for fear of a failure and time lost.'
The third was, to give it in his own words, 'I doubt
whether such a subject as the San Graal could be
handled in these days without incurring a charge of
irreverence. It would be too much like playing with
sacred things.'" [2] Later on, however, *The Holy
Grail* "seemed to come suddenly, as if by. . . in-
spiration; and that volume was given to the world in
1869" which contained *The Coming of Arthur*, *The
Holy Grail*, *Pelleas and Ettarre*, and *The Passing
of Arthur*." [3]

Previously, in 1862, shortly after the death of the

---

[1] *Memoir*, vol. i, p. 482, and vol. ii, p. 126.
[2] *Memoir*, vol. ii, p. 126.   [3] *Ibid*.

Prince Consort, Tennyson had written the dedication to his memory. In 1871 he added to the eight *Idylls* now written — for *The Passing of Arthur* was not a new *Idyll*, but the *Morte d'Arthur* of 1842 with additions — *The Last Tournament*. The next year came the epilogue *To the Queen* and *Gareth and Lynette*, which made ten *Idylls* in all. In 1884, Tennyson divided *Enid*,[1] which was much longer than any other one *Idyll*, into two, — *The Marriage of Geraint* and *Geraint and Enid*. In 1885 he added to the eleven already composed the last which he was to write, *Balin and Balan*.[2] Still his interest would not allow Tennyson to cease tinkering lines here and there in the now completed *Idylls*. Only the year before his death, he made his last addition to the poem, one line in the epilogue, to make clearer what he wished to be understood as the meaning of the whole series.

This was a remarkable way of composing a poem, the last part first, and the others in no certain order ; nevertheless, there was always some design in the *Idylls*, though Tennyson himself may not have been aware of it. The wonder is, not that the *Idylls* are not a unit, but that they are so near being a unit. Together they tell a plain story, though, to be sure, one not already familiar with it surmises rather than is sure of it. Still, there are connecting threads of narrative running through the *Idylls* — the high endeavor of the King and that which brings it to naught, the sin of the two highest in the land after him. From these two, sin works relentlessly down till all the court are corrupt. Though the three chief characters, whose

---

[1] Tennyson had previously changed the title to *Geraint and Enid*.
[2] A large part of this had been written soon after *Gareth*.

fortunes are the links between the twelve *Idylls*, are the central figures in only four, — *The Coming of Arthur*, *Lancelot and Elaine*, *Guinevere*, and *The Passing of Arthur*, — the other *Idylls* reflect their changing fortunes. So in *Gareth and Lynette*, a poem of youth and innocence, there is no hint of the doom impending over the order of the Table Round. In the third *Idyll*, *The Marriage of Geraint*, there is the first faint whisper of sin. From this, the evil talk grows steadily till it culminates in the open shamelessness of *The Last Tournament*.

Then there is in the *Idylls* the further unity which comes from the poet's peculiar charm and power. In every one we hear, like Thackeray, the horns of Tennyson's mediæval Elfland blowing; not always so loudly as Thackeray, but never silent. And in expression the poems are almost unfailingly noble. If one be tempted at moments to call some lines cheap, it is largely because they have become hackneyed from too much quotation, like those about Lancelot's honor rooted in dishonor and faith unfaithful. Furthermore, to strengthen the unity of the *Idylls*, Tennyson made symbolical use of the seasons, as he himself pointed out. *The Coming of Arthur* is at the New Year. When Lancelot fetches Guinevere to be Arthur's bride, it is earliest May. Gareth and Lynette ride to the aid of Lady Lyonors in very early summer. In *Geraint and Enid* we have the mowing season. In *Balin and Balan*, *Vivien*, and *Elaine* we have full summer. On a summer night the vision of the Grail appears. *Pelleas and Etarre* brings us into the late summer. The sad day of *The Last Tournament* is in yellow October. It is early November when Arthur in *Guinevere* takes his last leave of the Queen. And the last great battle in the West is fought on the shortest day of the year.

Finally, there is allegorical unity in the *Idylls*, and as in the *Faerie Queene*, both in the poem as a whole and in its various parts. But Tennyson's allegory is by no means to be insisted on so strongly as Spenser's; indeed, it would be a mistake to place much insistence upon it. Some allegory, nevertheless, the poet intended, as he says explicitly himself in the Epilogue *To the Queen :* —

> " . . . But thou, my Queen,
> Not for itself, but thro' thy living love
> For one to whom I made it o'er his grave
> Sacred, accept this old imperfect tale,
> New-old, and shadowing Sense at war with Soul,
> Ideal manhood closed in real man,
> Rather than that gray king whose name, a ghost,
> Streams like a cloud, man-shaped, from mountain peak,
> And cleaves to cairn and cromlech still; or him
> Of Geoffrey's book, or him of Malleor's, one
> Touch'd by the adulterous finger of a time
> That hover'd between war and wantonness,
> And crownings and dethronements : . . . "

According to this, Arthur is the Soul, the spiritual ideal which is always warring with Sense. Arthur, in slaying beasts, driving out the heathen, and suppressing robbers, is not only the just king of the romantic chroniclers, but man's spiritual ideal overcoming base passions. Then why, one may ask, if this is what Arthur represents, should there be the final crash of the Round Table institutions? This, it seems to me, Tennyson introduced for two reasons. He was primarily a poet and not a philosopher, and so with

poetic instinct he kept to the old poetic tragedy. He
was, furthermore, too much a representative of the
nineteenth century to be false to the faithful veracity
of that century in dealing with the incidents of the
old romances. Besides, as a philosopher, Tennyson
must have felt that the ideal is never a sure victor.
The warfare between Soul and Sense is unending. All
that men may hope is that the victories of the ideal
shall never cease, that the soul shall never be discour-
aged, that though one idealist pass, another shall take
his place. And such is the final message of hope in
the *Idylls* in the words that Arthur slowly speaks to
Bedivere from the black barge, moving stately from
the shore: —

> " The old order changeth, yielding place to new,
> And God fulfils himself in many ways."

But the new shall be as good as the old. The best
that is in man, wounded and cast down, goes only for
a while to the island-valley of Avilion, there to be
healed of grievous wounds, to take new courage, and
in all good time to come again.

Even more meaning than this, Tennyson intended
readers should find in his *Idylls*. He gave his sanction
to articles in the *Contemporary Review* for January,
1870, and May, 1873, in which he admitted that
Merlin typified intellect, and the Lady of the Lake
religion. And he said that the end of *The Holy
Grail*, " when the king speaks of his work and of his
visions, is intended to be the summing up of all in the
highest note by the highest of human men." [1] So it
is ; nothing could be at once more common-sense and

[1] *Memoir*, vol. ii, p. 90.

more idealistic than Arthur's explanation of his rea-
sons for not going himself in quest of the sacred cup:

> " And some among you held that if the King
> Had seen the sight he would have sworn the vow:
> Not easily, seeing that the King must guard
> That which he rules, and is but as the hind
> To whom a space of land is given to plow,
> Who may not wander from the allotted field
> Before his work be done, but, being done,
> Let visions of the night or of the day
> Come as they will; and many a time they come,
> Until this earth he walks on seems not earth,
> This light that strikes his eyeball is not light,
> This air that smites his forehead is not air
> But vision — yea, his very hand and foot —
> In moments when he feels he cannot die,
> And knows himself no vision to himself,
> Nor the high God a vision, nor that One
> Who rose again ; ye have seen what ye have seen."

This teaching — that the soul sees its best visions,
gets its glimpses of the Grail, not in unpractical ascetic
quests, but by working among men — is, like Lowell's
moral in *Sir Launfal*, precisely that of Wolfram von
Eschenbach.

Critics of Tennyson have seen more symbolism,
some very much more, in the various characters and
incidents of the *Idylls*. They would have us think
that Gareth represents happy, courageous youth, as
perhaps he does. In the boy masquerading as the
Knight of Death whom Gareth so easily overcomes,
we may see how little Death is to be feared. Balin
stands for wild passion ; Enid for true patient woman-
hood ; and Vivien for falsity and sensuality. Elaine
typifies sweet girlish innocence ; hers is not such a

narrow, shadowy existence as that of her sister, the Lady of Shalott, but still she is little better fitted to cope suddenly with the problems of the great world. And Mr. MacCallum feels pretty sure [1] that Guinevere stands for sense, and surmises that Lancelot may stand for the imagination. When commentators get as far as this, they had better remember that, according to Tennyson himself, all his allegory, even that to which he gave a certain sanction, is to be taken with a grain of salt. Towards the end of his life, he often said of the allegory in the *Idylls*, that critics

"have taken my hobby, and ridden it too hard, and have explained some things too allegorically, although there is an allegorical or perhaps rather a parabolic drift in the poem. . . . Camelot, . . . a city of shadowy palaces, is everywhere symbolic of the gradual growth of human beliefs and institutions, and of the spiritual development of man. Yet there is no single fact or incident in the 'Idylls,' however seemingly mystical, which cannot be explained as without any mystery or allegory whatever." [2]

Again Tennyson would affirm in regard to the various meanings of his work : —

"'Poetry is like shot-silk with many glancing colours. Every reader must find his own interpretation according to his ability, and according to his sympathy with the poet.' The general drift of the 'Idylls' is clear enough. 'The whole . . . is the dream of man coming into practical life and ruined by one sin. Birth is a mystery and death is a mystery, and in the midst lies the tableland of life . . .'" [3]

To this the present Lord Tennyson adds his testimony, that the general impression he got from his

---

[1] *Tennyson's Idylls and Arthurian Story*, pp. 327 ff.
[2] *Memoir*, vol. ii, p. 127.   [3] *Ibid.*

father regarding Arthur was that the King should be
taken as " a man who spent himself in the cause of
honour, duty and self-sacrifice, who felt and aspired
with his nobler knights, though with a stronger . . .
conscience than any of them," [1] a man who might only
possibly be taken to typify conscience. And in regard
to the exaggeration of the allegory in the *Idylls* he
says, " Lancelot, . . . Tristram, . . . Galahad, . . .
Bors, . . . Bedivere, . . . all have been to me from
boyhood living personalities, natural human charac-
ters, each with some dominant trait; and the allegori-
cal (if alone accepted) would be to me the death-war-
rant of many an old friend." [2]

For all such disclaimers, as the composition of the
Idylls progressed, the use of allegory tended to com-
mend itself to Tennyson rather more than less. Thus
the *Idylls* of 1869 and afterwards are more allegori-
cal than the earlier.[3] Some readers will think this an
advantage ; they will prefer to see in Arthur, Guine-
vere, and their knights and ladies, less flesh and blood
and more symbolism. The more strongly, though,
readers allegorise the characters of the *Idylls*, the
more likely they are to destroy the vital interest of
the poem. Tennyson himself made a mistake in em-
phasising the allegory of the later *Idylls* so much as
he did. It is the earlier ones which year after year
the best critics have pronounced best —the *Morte*

---

[1] *Memoir*, vol. i, p. 194.   [2] *Ibid.* vol. ii, p. 128.

[3] At the very first, though, Tennyson intended to put considerable
allegorical meaning into his work. A memorandum referring to it
which Tennyson drew up in the early thirties, makes King Arthur
represent religious faith, Mordred sceptical understanding, Merlin
science, Excalibur war, and the Round Table liberal institutions.
Ibid. vol. ii, p. 123.

d' Arthur, made over into *The Passing of Arthur*, with its mystery of death, which lends itself to successful allegorical treatment, and the four next earliest, which appeared in 1859, with either no allegory at all, or next to none. Of these the two favorites have been *Guinevere* and *Lancelot and Elaine*. In the latter, there is probably no allegorical meaning, and no *Idyll* is more touching in its human interest. After all, if there is true human interest in a work of art, will it not teach its lesson sufficiently well?

To any reader of this book, it must be plain now that Tennyson has followed the example of all his predecessors who have worked to best advantage the rich poetic mine of Arthurian story. They have not dug out the ore for themselves, but taking what others have given, they have moulded and polished it with their own individuality. Geoffrey of Monmouth may have invented much, but much too he must have got from the tales of his native land, and perhaps from the book, if such there ever were, which Walter of Oxford brought out of Britain. Chrétien, likewise, got his stories in the main from current romantic tales, though he probably changed the spirit of some of them considerably, as in the *Lancelot*. So, too, did other romancers and chroniclers, some more inventive than others, who followed their originals with more or less fidelity, till Malory, drawing material from his "French book" and one or two English romances, wrote what has become an English classic. From him in turn Tennyson borrowed; Malory's *Morte Darthur* became the principal source of the *Idylls of the King*. It seems to have been the only long mediæval romance which Tennyson ever liked. "I could not read 'Palmerin of England' nor 'Amadis,' nor any other of those Romances through," he said to his son. "The 'Morte d'Arthur' is much the best: there are very fine things in it, but all strung together without Art." [1]

Malory, however, was not Tennyson's sole source. For the two Idylls of *Geraint*, he was indebted to the *Mabinogion*. To a lesser extent he was indebted to Geoffrey, Nennius, and Gildas, and possibly to the octosyllabic *Morte Arthur*, to which Malory himself was indebted. The list of Arthur's battles in *Lancelot and Elaine* is close to the lists given by Nennius and Geoffrey.[2] And the picture of Britain in the first *Idyll*, when King Leodogran

> "Groan'd for the Roman legions here again
> And Cæsar's eagle,"

and sent to Arthur imploring his help,

> "For here between the man and beast we die,"

is copied unmistakably from that sad picture which Gildas painted in strong colors, when he wished to rouse his countrymen from their slothful degeneracy. But the material taken from these old sources Tennyson makes entirely his own by his imagination, which vivifies what he borrows and sometimes adds new incidents to it. The stories of the ruby necklace in *The Last Tournament* and the diamond joust in *Elaine* are Tennyson's invention. His invention appears, also, in his rearrangement of Malory's incidents in order to make them show in consecutive narrative the steady, pitiless growth of corruption at Arthur's court. The tale of Gareth, a sweet idyll of youth, is suitable to

---

[1] *Memoir*, vol. i, p. 194.
[2] Geoffrey names fewer battles than Nennius.

show court life still in its purity; accordingly, though it is in the seventh book of Malory, Tennyson makes it precede the more gloomy story of Balin in Malory's second book. Again, in *Elaine*, Lancelot becomes sincerely contrite after the death of the Maid of Astolat: repentance for sin is one reason for his seeking the Grail. Tennyson therefore puts the story of Elaine, which is found in the eighteenth book of Malory, before the Quest of the Holy Grail, which is found in the thirteenth book. The two concluding *Idylls*, *Guinevere* and *The Passing of Arthur*, are in their proper places relative to Malory's arrangement, for, representing the sad end of the Round Table institutions, they could come only at the last.

Tennyson's invention perhaps had freest play in remodelling the old characters, who become more modern and more complex. Vivien, a shadowy personage in Malory, is a woman in the *Idylls*, sensual, unscrupulous, and yet not altogether uncharming. Pelleas, before a conventional romantic hero, becomes a bashful, muscular young man. Sometimes in thus vitalising the old characters, Tennyson changes their natures, and not always for the better. Gawain, for instance, is not unattractive in Malory : in fact, he is an interesting psychological study — false to Pelleas, it is true, when he promises to plead that young knight's cause with the fickle Ettard, as Malory calls the lady, but reverencing his king and his queen, and staunchly true to Lancelot, till the death of his brothers forces him to draw the sword against that old friend. In Tennyson, on the contrary, Gawain is almost wholly bad. What we best remember of him is that when sent to give the prize of the diamond joust to Lancelot himself and to no other, he wearies of his search, and, forgetful of his king's command, entrusts the gem to Elaine, and then, lightly kissing her hand, rides away carolling a ballad. A very different Gawain this, from him of courtesy and truth and honor who is the hero of *Gawain and the Green Knight!* Nor is Gawain the only one who suffers at the hands of Tennyson. I have already spoken of the degeneration, among later story-tellers, of Tristram and Iseult. They appear no-where so petty and selfish in their love as in *The Last Tournament*, and nowhere do they die more ignobly.

Fortunately, Tennyson has not been similarly un-kind to his three principal characters. To Guinevere he is as chivalrous as could have been the most loyal of her courtiers. He makes the gallant nineteenth-cen-tury attempt to excuse the conduct of the great Queen; like Heber before him, he imagines that Guinevere saw Lancelot and loved him before her eyes had ever rested on Arthur to know him. We have seen that as far back as 1830 Tennyson had hit on this excuse for Guinevere's fault in his lovely spring lyric of *Sir Launcelot and Queen Guinevere.* And he referred in his first *Idyll*, and more than once afterwards, to Lancelot's riding, Arthur's ambassador, in late April to fetch Guinevere from her father's court; and in the soft air of green, blossoming May they set out together towards Camelot, with throstle whistling and linnet piping.

> " Then, in the boyhood of the year,
> Sir Launcelot and Queen Guinevere
> Rode thro' the coverts of the deer,
> With blissful treble ringing clear.
> She seem'd a part of joyous Spring:

A gown of grass-green silk she wore,
Buckled with golden clasps before;
A light-green tuft of plumes she bore
    Closed in a golden ring

.   .   .   .

"As fast she fled thro' sun and shade,
The happy winds upon her play'd,
Blowing the ringlet from the braid:
She look'd so lovely, as she sway'd
    The rein with dainty finger-tips,
A man had given all other bliss,
And all his worldly worth for this,
To waste his whole heart in one kiss
    Upon her perfect lips."

It is not so in Malory and in the French romances. The Queen's adultery there we have found to be without good excuse.[1]

If the mediæval Guinevere was more wanton in her marriage than Tennyson's, she showed herself more noble in her sin because more constant. Once she loved Lancelot, she loved him to the death. Tennyson's apparently did not; after Arthur has left her at Almesbury, she decides that she really loves him the more. He is "the highest and most human, too," she cries in repentant anguish, "Not Lancelot, nor another." And again,—

    ". . . Is there none
Will tell the King I love him tho' so late!"

Had Lancelot come a few months after, full of love and pity, to fetch her over-seas from her convent to

[1] As I have suggested, ch. x, the part the witchery of the spring plays here reminds one of the witchery of the sea in the love of Tristram and Iseult.

Joyous Gard to be his wife, there would not have been that finely penitent leave-taking which Malory relates, not so "high," it may be, as Arthur's and Guinevere's in the *Idylls*, but more "human." On the whole, Tennyson's Guinevere loses as much as she gains by this change in her character.

Except in this one respect, Tennyson's Guinevere is pretty true to Malory's, who was a sort of summing-up of various mediæval Guineveres, a stately, often sweetly gracious queen, who could inspire in her courtiers unselfish devotion, and yet might at any moment rage in jealous passion. So is Tennyson's. In the first six *Idylls* she is almost always a sweet, gracious, queenly woman. Then in *Elaine* comes that undignified storm of jealous passion. The diamonds are flung out of the window; the charges are hurled at Lancelot that leave him half in disdain at love, life, everything. Could this Guinevere have married this Lancelot in the beginning, perhaps the storm had never come. As it is, the tumult in her can cease only in the quiet convent life at Almesbury, in the peaceful Avon valley.

It is a fair question which Arthur — Tennyson's or Malory's — would be the better for Guinevere, had she no Lancelot to console her. Would it be the rougher mediæval Arthur, by no means the blameless king of the *Idylls*, or Tennyson's ideal monarch? Despite Tennyson's desire to make his Arthur "the highest of human men," the king fails to be so. He lacks that subtle thing called magnetism; and talk as he will about staying at home rather than going in search of the Grail, about works of practical service to his fellow creatures, he is so interested in his Round Table and the institutions which he establishes, that his wife suffers, the fellow creature whom he should first consider. Too often he is almost selfish; at any rate, a cold, distant husband. No wonder Guinevere thought she "could not breathe in that fine air;" no wonder she "yearn'd for warmth and color" which she found in Lancelot. Quite unintentionally, Tennyson has made his Arthur not so very different from Malory's when the latter cries out: [1] "Wit you well my heart was never so heavy as it is now, and much more I am sorrier for my good knights' loss, than for the loss of my fair queen, for queens I might have enow, but such a fellowship of good knights shall never be together in no company." Tennyson's Arthur comes nearest to this when in the parting scene at Almesbury he preaches to his wife, as Mr. George Meredith says, "like a curate," but hardly like a normal husband talking to an erring woman. The trouble comes from the allegory. Slight as that was in the earlier *Idylls*, Tennyson nevertheless, always having it a little in mind, here allowed it to become prominent enough to mar reality. Arthur, in thus talking to Guinevere, is really Soul explaining its failure in the war with Sense. Much more human is Arthur in his next speech, though, to be sure, it begins, "Yet think not that I come to urge thy crimes" — a good time to say so when Arthur has been urging them for over a hundred lines. But as he goes on, wondering how to take last leave of all he loved, of Guinevere's golden hair with which he used to play, of her "imperial-moulded form," and "beauty such as never woman wore" — in all this, Arthur is a real husband for whom we feel sympathy. Were he so always, we

[1] Book xx, ch. 9.

should always like him better. Nor is he less noble in
this last farewell, or again when he bids good-bye to
Bedivere, in *The Passing of Arthur*, than elsewhere
in the *Idylls;* he is only more humanly noble, because
more than usual he is aware of normal human frailty
in himself.

As for Tennyson's Lancelot, he is not essentially
different from Malory's, though more interesting be-
cause more lifelike. Despite Tennyson's desire to pre-
sent the ideal man in Arthur, Lancelot is often the
real hero of the *Idylls*. In this one character, better
than in the whole series, you may see the war between
Soul and Sense. It was only in his one sin — his
loving the Queen, the wife of his best friend — that
Sense triumphed. The victories of the Soul were many.
The most dearly and sadly bought was his showing
his one discourtesy to the Lily Maid of Astolat at the
request of her father, hoping to cure her love. Lancelot
rode from the castle without any good-bye to the girl
who had tended him so carefully in his sickness ; and
the maid, —

> " when she heard his horse upon the stones,
> Unclasping flung the casement back, and look'd
> Down on his helm, from which her sleeve had gone.
> And Lancelot knew the little clinking sound ;
> And she by tact of love was well aware
> That Lancelot knew that she was looking at him.
> And yet he glanced not up, nor waved his hand,
> Nor bade farewell, but sadly rode away.
> This was the one discourtesy that he used."

In these three chief characters of Tennyson's, and
in the minor ones too, we see, as in Matthew Arnold's,
mediæval and modern traits combined. A similar

blending of old and new we see, likewise, in the setting
of the *Idylls*, — a pleasant English country, both mod-
ern and mediæval. Indeed, the whole poem is a happy
blending of contemporary sentiment with old manners
and customs, picturesqueness, gallantry, and chivalry.
And be it emphasised that the blend is happy. Less
modernism would make the *Idylls* too aloof from us,
would rob them of much of their meaning and senti-
ment ; less mediævalism would take away from their
romantic picturesqueness.

The over prominence of allegory here and there in
the *Idylls*, and occasional unkindness to some of the
characters, are not their only faults. One might ob-
ject that at times the style is cold, especially in the later
Idylls ; that the verse is elegant with an academic
polish rather than with the poetical inspiration of the
Morte d'Arthur. There is sometimes coldness in feel-
ing, too, as in that interview between Arthur and the
Queen at Almesbury, which might to advantage have
been fired by a little of the superabundant passion of
Mr. Swinburne's *Tristram of Lyonesse.* But art is
seldom perfect ; Homer has been known to nod. After
all possible faults are found with the *Idylls of the
King*, they remain a work of the highest nobleness.
It was not easy to make the Arthurian stories over into
a poem which, modern in spirit, should keep the old
incidents and the picturesqueness of the mediæval
romances. But Tennyson has succeeded in writing
his score so that the horns of his Arthurian Elfland,
always distinct whether faintly or loudly blowing, are
in harmony with all the new instruments in the
mighty symphony of Victorian England.

Critics have called the *Idylls* the noblest English

blank verse since Milton. It is not too much to say
that for their melody, dignity, beauty, meaning, and
human interest, they present the huge conglomerate
mass of the Arthurian stories in their noblest form.
Tennyson has adapted the legends to modern times
with such genius that we may well believe many a day
will pass before any poet attempts again to tell in
English the whole long story.

Only familiarity with the art of letters leads us to
accept wonderful results as matter of course. Consider
what George Eliot says rather self-consciously at the
beginning of *Adam Bede:* " With this drop of ink at
the end of my pen-I will show you the roomy work-
shop of Mr. Jonathan Burge, carpenter and builder,
in the village of Hayslope, as it appeared on the
eighteenth of June, in the year of our Lord 1799."
Then she presents a picture such as she could see with
her own eyes in many a carpenter's shop of her own
England. It is marvellous thus to create in words even
a commonplace scene; it is far more marvellous to
make real for age after age, mountains, lakes, rivers,
and seas not of this world, the Castle of Wonders of
the Grail, and the enchanted wood of Broceliande.
Yet so long as our literature endures, these bid fair
to endure too.

True, none but Tennyson, of our greater English
poets, has treated the Arthurian legends adequately.
Nevertheless, they have become — to quote Lowell's
expression again, and again to disagree with his re-
striction of it — one of the "abiding consolations of
the mind," of which imaginative people in our genera-
tion are fortunate enough to possess many. We may

feast our eyes on beautiful prospects of field, wood, mountain, and ocean that modern travel makes accessible; and on pictures, statues, and fair stately buildings which the artists of the past have given us. We have ever more frequent opportunities to delight our ears with glorious music. And more and more we have books, in which to wander from the cares of actuality into that braver world which poets have always loved to reveal.

We walk in the fields at eventide with Isaac, and look up and see the camels coming and Rebecca lighting down to greet the man she is to comfort for the death of Sarah, his mother. With the Wise Men of the East, following the star, we come to the manger at Bethlehem. The tragedies of Thebes and Pelops' line enact themselves again, and the chieftains of Agamemnon and Priam fight in the Xanthian plain. Virgil shows us his Trojan hero striving undaunted to lay the foundations of the "walls of lofty Rome." Dante, with this same poet for his guide, gives us awful visions of the Inferno, or led by Beatrice shows us the divine splendor of Paradise. Among wilder peoples, meantime, Siegfried has won Brunhilda to be Gunther's bride. Roland dying has defended the pass of Roncesvalles; Charlemain and all his chivalry have perished at Fontarabia. Then kindly mad Don Quixote makes us see Dulcineas in peasant wenches and giants in windmills. We laugh with Rabelais and we smile with Molière. We are weary with the world-wearied Faust. For us, all sorts and conditions of men and women throng the Elizabethan stage, or pass, a long line, through the pages of the English novel.

And always for us, too, when we will, the horns of Elfland shall blow again. Then rude British Arthur shall change into the great king of romance. At Christmas, Easter, or Whitsuntide, he and Guinevere shall hold high feast. They shall speed Perceval to seek again the Castle of the Grail, where he may ask the healing question; and welcome Iseult, fled from loveless state at Tintagel by the Cornish sea: and gay pied heralds shall call the knights to tourneys at Caerleon and Camelot.

INDEX

INDEX